FRONTLINE FEMINISMS

GENDER, CULTURE, AND GLOBAL POLITICS
CHANDRA TALPADE MOHANTY, *Series Editor*

FRONTLINE FEMINISMS
WOMEN, WAR, AND RESISTANCE

EDITED BY
MARGUERITE R. WALLER
JENNIFER RYCENGA

Routledge
NEW YORK / LONDON

To activist women . . . everywhere

Published in 2001 by
Routledge
29 West 35th Street
New York, NY 10001

Published in Great Britain by
Routledge
11 New Fetter Lane
London EC4P 4EE

Routledge is an imprint of the Taylor & Francis Group.

First hardback edition published in 2000 by Garland Publishing, Inc.
First paperback edition published by Routledge, 2001.
Copyright © 2000 by Marguerite R. Waller and Jennifer Rycenga

10 9 8 7 6 5 4 3 2 1

The Library of Congress has cataloged the Garland edition as follows:

Frontline feminisms : women, war, and resistance / edited by Marguerite R.
  Waller, Jennifer Rycenga.
      p.   cm.   —   (Gender, culture, and global politics ; v. 5)
  (Garland reference library of social science ; v. 1436)
    Includes bibliographical references and index.
    ISBN 0-8153-3442-7 (alk. paper) ISBN 0-415-93239-4 (pbk.)
    1. Women and war. 2. Women and the military. I. Waller, Marguerite
  R., 1948– . II. Rycenga, Jennifer, 1958– . III. Series. IV. Series ;
  Garland reference library of social science ; v. 1436.
  HQ1236.F78 2000
  305.42—dc21   99-38045
                                                                 CIP

Contents

v

Series Editor's Foreword

Five years after the United Nations Fourth International Conference on Women in Beijing (September 1995), I reflect on what feminists have achieved after more than four decades of organizing around issues of social and economic justice for women. I realize that civil rights are not the same as economic justice. While issues such as health, nutrition, reproductive rights, violence, misogyny, and women's poverty and labor struggles have achieved widespread global recognition, women still constitute the world's poor and the majority of the world's refugees. The so-called structural adjustment policies of the International Monetary Fund and the World Bank continue to have a devastating impact on Third World women. Militarization, environmental degradation, the WTO, heterosexist state practices, religious fundamentalism, and the exploitation of poor women's labor by multinationals all pose profound challenges for feminists as we embark upon the twenty-first century.

While feminists across the globe have been variously successful, we inherit a number of challenges our mothers and grandmothers faced. But there are also new challenges as we attempt to make sense of a world indelibly marked by the failure of postcolonial capitalist and communist nation-states to provide for the social, economic, spiritual, and psychic needs of the majority of the world's population. At the beginning of the Christian millennium (year 2000, also 5760 according to the Hebrew, 4697 according to the Chinese, and 1420 according to the Arabic calendar—"just another day" according to Oren Lyons, Faithkeeper of the Onandaga Nation), globalization has come to represent the interests of corporations and the free market rather than self-determination and freedom from political, cultural, and economic domination for all the world's peoples.

These are some of the challenges addressed by the series Gender, Culture, and Global Politics. It takes as its fundamental premises (1) the need for feminist engagement with global as well as local ideological, economic, and political processes, and (2) the urgency of transnational dialogue in building an ethical culture capable of withstanding and transforming the commodified and exploitative practices of global culture and economics. The series foregrounds the need for comparative feminist analysis and scholarship and seeks to forge direct links between analysis, (self)-reflection, and organizing. Individual volumes in the series provide systematic and challenging interventions into the (still) largely Eurocentric and Western Women's Studies knowledge base, while simultaneously highlighting the work that can and needs to be done to envision and enact cross-cultural multiracial feminist solidarity.

Frontline Feminisms: Women, War, and Resistance, the fifth volume in the series, is an important embodiment of the links between analysis, (self)-reflection, and organizing and the enactment of feminist solidarity encouraged by this series. Drawing on work presented at the historic 1997 "Frontline Feminisms" Conference in Riverside, California, Waller and Rycenga have assembled a wide-ranging, eloquent, original critique of global masculinist militarism, foregrounding women's resistance to it. This volume is also a testament to the creativity, resilience, and deeply thoughtful feminist activism engendered by women on the various "frontlines" created by wars around the world.

Palestinian Laila al-Saith says in "Intimations of Anxiety":

> *You do not know how hard it is*
> *transfiguring blood into ink—*
> *emerging from one's secret dream*
> *to voicing that dream. . . .*
> *These are the things we must share,*
> *and how the word takes shape within me.*
> *Pulled between a world that created me*
> *and a vaporous world I wish to create,*
> *I begin again. . . . ("Roots that Do Not Depart," 1984)*

In these pages, women transfigure blood into ink, and pain and despair into the courage, creativity, and joy of struggle. In the midst of war, "the frontline"—as a concept, as a span of time, as a place to grow, change, and transform—is known as a gritty, multifaceted reality" (Introduction).

In the context of this very multifaceted reality, women voice the dream and enact the vision of resistance, agency, and justice.

The writings in this collection cover a range of genres from memoir, historical accounts, and critical essays, to an exercise on "art as a healing tool" for adult survivors of domestic violence. What holds the writings together is an urgency to reflect on and analyze women's activism on the frontlines—from Palestine, Sudan, Iran, Kosova, and rural India to Serbia, Croatia, Okinawa, Israel, U.S. prisons, and the racialized American South. The essays introduce and elaborate upon concepts fundamental to a transnational feminist politic: (1) the "frontlines" of feminist struggle, (2) the masculinist nationalism of the rhetoric and practice of "national security," (3) the profound links between domestic and public/state violence against women, (4) the role of nonviolent and not-nonviolent action against patriarchy and militarism, and (5) women's labor militancy as a form of struggle against a racialized, capitalist patriarchy.

This is an important collection, encapsulating transnational feminist thought in the context of war in sharp, finely drawn, intellectually provocative terms. It is a book that illustrates the spirit (and heart) of comparative feminist praxis that the series Gender, Culture, and Global Politics is committed to.

Chandra Talpade Mohanty
Ithaca, New York
March 2000

Introduction

Memory says: Want to do it right? Don't count
on me.
I'm a canal in Europe where bodies are floating
I'm a mass grave I'm the life that returns . . .
I'm a corpse dredged from a canal in Berlin
a river in Mississippi   I'm a woman standing
with other women dressed in black
on the streets of Haifa, Tel Aviv, Jerusalem
there is spit on my sleeve there are phonecalls in
the night
I am a woman standing in line for gas masks . . .
  —ADRIENNE RICH, "EASTERN WAR TIME"

MANY FRONTS

The levels of explicit militarism in the world have escalated since the
contributors to this volume finished writing their chapters. In Kosova,
where one-quarter of the population had already been forced out of their
homes by Serbian forces as of October 1998, the majority of the inhabitants have now been expelled, including those who were living in the
capital, Pristina. The United States is actively fighting on two fronts: the
little-reported bombing of Iraq and NATO's bombing of Serbia and
Kosova. India and Pakistan, now nuclear powers, are engaging in a fierce
conflict in Kashmir, and clashes related to state violence continue in Indonesia. In California more prisons are being built, despite a dramatic
decrease in the crime rate, and, within weeks of each other, two African
American women, Tyisha Miller and Margaret Laverne Mitchell, were
shot dead by the police officers summoned to help them, the former
while she was unconscious in her car and the latter, a mentally ill homeless woman, as she tried to protect her few belongings from confiscation.
The genocidal wars in Rwanda, Bosnia, and Kosova have put civilian security much more squarely on the front page, and the war—together with
its long prelude—between NATO and Serbia has rekindled and recast
questions of violent and nonviolent resistance.

xiii

The dramatic rise of women's activism around the world has not been as well documented, despite the unprecedented numbers of women who participated in the 1995 United Nations Conference on Women in Beijing, China, and its parallel NGO (Nongovernmental Organization) Forum in Huairou. In June 1998, a reporter asked editor Marguerite Waller whether she agreed with *Time* and other organs of the mainstream U.S. press that "feminism is dead." The occasion of the reporter's interest was the 150th anniversary of the Seneca Falls Convention of 1848, at which U.S. women had first publicly and effectively declared their rights as full citizens. Forty-five minutes into the ensuing telephone conversation, the reporter's question had changed: now she wanted to know why she and other educated, news-literate women and men in the United States know so little about the effects on women of the policies of the International Monetary Fund (she had never heard of the IMF), about the women's tribunals backed by the Asian Women's Human Rights Council in Japan, the Philippines, and North Africa, about the Women in Black in the Middle East and Central Europe, about coalitions between Kosovar and Tibetan women, about the energy that has moved from Beijing into connecting women's activism everywhere. This book manifests the energies of the Beijing conference and Huairou Forum as they have moved during the ensuing years into connecting the thousands of groups of women around the world who are redefining the front lines of response to escalating militarizations and their attendant social, economic, political, and cultural dynamics.

Ironically, the *Time* article betrayed its own cause by describing the U.S. end of a particularly effective international collaboration as an example of the simply "mindless sex talk" into which once high-minded feminism had fallen (Bellafante 56). Referring to a benefit performance of Eve Ensler's theater piece "The Vagina Monologues," the *Time* article failed to mention either Ensler's long-standing involvement with Bosnian refugee women, the Women in Black, and the Center for Women War Victims in Zagreb, or the fact that money raised by the benefit performance was earmarked for these groups. And it completely missed the relevance of Ensler's reconfiguration of how we think about the female body to questions of militarism. *Time* could not or would not connect Ensler's work with the "mindless sex talk" of the military and paramilitary rapists and torturers in former Yugoslavia, Guatemala, and elsewhere, and/or the generals and heads of state who have collaborated on the construction of prostitution camps around U.S. military bases in countries around the world.

It should not be news that media representation works poorly as a source of information about women's and/or feminist activism. Profoundly implicated in the issues of ideology, policy, and procedure raised by these movements, the mass media are owned by (ever fewer) corporate entities. The so-called "media monopoly" (Bagdikian 1983) means that newspapers, magazines, television networks, radio stations, and publishing houses protect the interests of the handful of financial institutions that own them.

But the conceptual lens or "media frame" through which U.S. news gets filtered exercises a second, more subtle (and related) censorship. It became apparent in the coverage of the U.N. Conference on Women in Beijing that the U.S. press structures news in terms of conflict, problems, crises, and manifestations of state power. This was how the epochal Non-Governmental Organization (NGO) Forum in Huairou passed entirely beneath the radar of U.S. journalists. They had no means of appreciating what the galvanization of thirty thousand grass-roots activists into a "world wide web" of activists might signify. Not representing nation-states, the organizations participating in Huairou, one could argue, better represent the interests of a majority of the world's population than do the world's legislative bodies. Yet, as participants in the NGO Forum learned from the plenary speaker on media, they were being dismissed by mainstream U.S. editors as "wildlife"—a designation that neatly combines disdain for the environment with disdain for anyone outside the managerial classes of the corporate state. Women and "nature" are regarded as jokes, nonstories, by the unaptly named "mass media." Symptomatically, even the ostensibly progressive National Public Radio (NPR) strongly "Othered" the women activists who participated in the Frontline Feminisms Conference; when the Santa Monica NPR affiliate was contacted about publicizing the conference, the call was routed to the station's food editor!

Ironically, the media frame of the tightly controlled, heavily censored Chinese press lent itself far better to reporting the events and the significance of those two weeks. Chinese journalists, allowed to say only positive things and more inclined to focus on "people" than on the state apparatus, were free to go into great detail concerning what was said (virtually none of which was reported in the *New York Times* or the *L.A. Times*). Paradoxically, that is, although there was literally no overlap between the media frame of the purportedly "free" U.S. press and what was said and done at the Forum, the Chinese frame and the Forum were an excellent fit. The Chinese reportage corresponded closely, in fact, with that of the Forum participants' own newspaper, the *Independent Daily*.

Without privileging one media frame over another, we can see in the discrepancy itself a simple example of the kinds of unlikeness, some subtle, some not so subtle, that have made communication among feminist and women activists problematic. Especially across boundaries of ideology, wealth, and power, both the flow of information and the ways that information has been assimilated have been inadequate to the task of opening and sustaining supple, heteroglossic dialogues. As in the media, so in the academy. As Jacqueline Siapno has formulated the problematics of writing about female agency in the kingdom of Aceh on the island of Sumatra, "I face a serious problem in the conceptualization of a feminist analytic of power: the major privileging of secularized rationalism in the production of theories about power in Euro-American academic circles" (7). Angela Davis, in this volume, points out that within the United States structural racism and nineteenth-century historical categories have kept separate the domestic violence and the women's prison movements, camouflaging their historical and philosophical relationship. Currently in the U.S. academy, not only are there remarkably few English-language texts available in the areas of non-Western and Central European feminist discourses, but there are fewer still that open themselves to the logics, strategies, and actual and potential coalitions evolving outside the hegemony of Western industrial ideology (Penezic). The political and epistemological effects of these different histories, economies, and knowledges, these different modalities of religious belief, of constructions of gender, sexuality, race, and ethnicity, to name just a few of the most obvious differences among us, are ultimately incalculable and unpredictable. They are also, the conference organizers and editors maintain, one of the greatest resources currently available to feminist scholars and activists.

The conference "Frontline Feminisms: Women, War, and Resistance," from which the following essays, reports, interventions, images, and testimonies have been drawn, ambitiously aimed to address the complex communication gaps in U.S. feminisms from several directions at once. Organized around the perception that innovative new feminist praxes were rapidly evolving in the context of militarized situations around the world, the conference brought together activists and academics from over twenty-five countries and from different regions and communities in the United States. Our three primary objectives were (1) to bring new feminisms from elsewhere to the attention of U.S. feminists; (2) to address the strains in U.S. feminism, including the alienation of academic from activist projects, and racial, ethnic, and class-related conflicts; and (3) to take the achievement of the Beijing conference to the next level of integration, actively encouraging the creation of new collaborations—scholarly, activist, and both—that would further challenge the sociopolitical and the conceptual status quo. The deepest wish of the conference organizers was to create a space and time for the fruitful encounter of heterogeneous feminist discourses, a context in which difference could become a source not of strain but of creativity—a reason to exchange ideas, and a precondition to forging new alliances and identifying new points of departure.

As one participant phrased this principle, "It is so good to be at a meeting like this one that is *not* organized by the U.N." As editors, we felt it was crucial to maintain this kind of space. Thus, the present volume is not shaped by any single overarching centrist structure, whether institutional or ideological. The greatest challenge facing us has been finding ways to represent the textures, rhythms, and intensities of the conference interactions. Much as we would have liked to, we could not publish all the presentations, some of which, in any case, were delivered as brilliant orations, without the aid of written texts, and some of which featured other media: painting, sculpture, music, film, video, or photojournalism. We offer a glimpse of the diversity of modes of participation in the volume's "Inter-Missions," short breaks that map specific interactive spaces "between" cultures, between individuals, between refugees and relief workers (some of whom are both), between survivors of domestic violence and art instructors (some of whom are both). These are spaces in which the self-expressive possibilities of women contending with the physical and epistemic violences of battering, immigration/emigration, or war can regenerate and metamorphose. The essentials are a medium of expression—film, words, colored chalk—and an interlocutionary community—spectators, readers, relief workers, group leaders, and other participants in a group.

The same paradigm realized on a more abstract plane informs the overall organization of the book. Presentations have been selected and sequenced in montages that form communities of expression where texts can "talk" to one another about a common issue. These montage sequences make no pretense to being all-inclusive or definitive. They are designed to evoke the richness of cultural and other kinds of incommensurability, while tracing certain patterns of likeness and interaction across these differences. For us and, we hope, for readers too, the analogues, complementarities, and contrasts that emerge from this configuration of fields of thought and action make strikingly visible the potential for transformative *inter*relationships.

These interrelationships may be literal ones among individuals, groups, or causes; or they may be the sudden connection a reader makes between two widely separated situations or between one writer's theory and another's experience. It becomes not impossible, for example, to envision a conversation among Acehnese (Siapno), Sudanese (Ibrahim), and Croatian women (Kesic) about how to abrogate state-imposed family roles. Could women in Gaza (el Sarraj) and Aceh (Siapno) sue for reparations for the multiple burdens of violence they have sustained at the hands of occupying forces and their own patriarchal communities? Why not recognize the Iranian (Rajavi), Sudanese (Ibrahim), and Acehnese (Siapno) women described in these pages as highly significant figures in late twentieth-century Islam? What is to prevent rural women (Chatterjee, Eli), from organizing internationally?

One important result of cross-referencing feminist analyses and discourses is a deconstruction of the concept of "national security." Julie Mertus and Jasmina Tesanovic have called attention elsewhere to the startling fact that in contemporary warfare, 95 percent of the casualties are civilians, the majority of them women and children (Mertus and Tesanovic 1997, 4). The lingering impression that the actors in militarized situations are male has meant, however, that military violence against women in a number of struggles has remained relatively invisible (el Sarraj, Mrsevic, Kesic, Siapno, and Rhodes). Not only that, but if only about 5 percent of the dead and wounded in war are combatants, then it would appear that unarmed civilians have become the *preferred* military target. As feminists in the former Yugoslavia have put it, it is far cheaper to kill unarmed civilians than armed military personnel. Margo Okazawa-Rey and Gwyn Kirk point out, additionally, that the presence of armed forces, which is generally portrayed as essential for "national security," is, in practice, anything but a means whereby the safety of the nonmilitary citizens of a particular geographical locale is protected. The 90 percent ethnic Albanian population of Kosova remained committed for ten years to nonviolent resistance to Serbian occupation for precisely this reason. In these instances, it is militarization itself that presents a clear and present danger to civilian life, regardless of which side of the conflict (if either) one is on. Fatima Ibrahim reminds us that, not coincidentally, modern warfare, like global capitalism, serves to consolidate wealth in the hands of the powerful. Thus, contemporary militarization emerges, perhaps counterintuitively, as more dangerous to civilian women than to armed men, a lesson that makes the decision of the feminist-oriented Iranian Resistance to put women in command in its National Liberation Army seem less paradoxical than it might first appear.

WHAT IS A "FRONTLINE"?

The insight that feminism—born amidst urgency, movement, and contradiction—is always on the "frontline," forms a starting point for this collection. From the women's liberation movements of nineteenth- and twentieth-century America, which emerged from Abolitionism and the Civil Rights movements (Rycenga, Green), to the Eritrean and Iranian rethinking of gender relations in the context of national liberation struggles (Hale, Rajavi, Shahri), women's claiming their own self-determination arises in relation to—and as a catalyst for—other movements. Women's self-defense, as self-development—whether confronting domestic violence (Mrsevic, el Sarraj) or protesting police brutality (Rhodes, Williams),—is not a stratagem born of leisure.

The concept of the "frontline" itself comes from military parlance but expands through the thought of the contributors to this volume. The frontline is the place where combat and the brunt of the fighting actually occur, and is therefore the location of the greatest carnage. Furthermore, the lived realities of the frontline are usually (and increasingly) distant from the generals, heads of state, and policymakers: the privileged don't live on the frontlines, nor do they dirty their hands in an era of televised, computerized "precision" bombing sorties.

The forms of feminism chronicled in this book arose on a variety of frontlines, but always they were self-assertive, rather than self-abnegating. Whether pacifist or not, the strategies, activities, and thoughts developed here are not passive or self-sacrificing. These women do not tell sob stories—though there are many horrifying crimes recorded herein—nor do they spin theories of an abstract relationship between women and war. Instead, the frontline—as a place, as a concept, as a span of time, and as a place to grow, change, and transform—is known as a gritty, multifaceted reality.

The frontline is not restricted to military locations: the frontline can be standing in a welfare line or a police line-up, stitching a hemline, or writing a byline. The frontline becomes wherever women know that their lives—"the rich plenty of our existence" (Wolf 85)—is at risk, and wherever women intervene to "make our lives and the lives of our children richer and more possible" (Lorde 55). The frontlines keep moving and proliferating, ubiquitous whether in war, work, or love.

A distinguishing characteristic of these frontline feminisms, though, is how they are more than chronicles of life-and-death struggles. Even while these women are engaging in battle (Hale, Rajavi) or applying triage (Eli, Salser), they insist on thought, theory, philosophy. However diverse the situations, the analyses, and the strategies put forward in these articles, their authors recognize that the frontline is not only a physical location, but a battlefield for control of the mind. The exploitative "plantation mentality" in the American South (Leachman, Green) or Bengal tea fields (Chatterjee) illustrates one such example.

This "battle for the mind" (Green) reveals the faultlines along the frontlines: how women's voices challenge and enrich simultaneous struggles. One common theme emerges in how these feminists, unlike soldiers on a frontline, refuse to take orders from any imaginary "above." This reflects a further refusal to wait until "after" the war, or "after" the revolution to address gender relations and women's lives. The full vitality of women's lives cannot be a deferred promise pushed into an indefinite future. Acting and thinking on the frontlines are a way to actualize the struggle, or, to quote from Rosa Luxemburg's letter from prison in 1916 (a prison to which she was condemned for opposing the senseless slaughter of World War I): "Being human means joyfully throwing your whole life on 'the scales of destiny' when need be, but all the while rejoicing in every sunny day and every beautiful cloud" (quoted in Dunayevskaya 199, 260).

Vigorous discussions of violence and nonviolence are not unique to feminists, and the authors in this collection can be located along the continuum of those age-old debates. But there is this difference: there is no lusty embrace of violence for its own sake, or concession to its inevitability, or paeans to the power of death-dealing. This is why we have subtitled the third section "Nonviolent and Not-Nonviolent Responses to Patriarchy"—in recognition of the fact that feminist positions that support or enact violence are articulated in relation to nonviolence. That is, they take nonviolence as their point of departure, and presume it as a foundation of sustainable intra- and intercommunity relations.

The Beijing Conference of 1995, wonderfully evoked in Julie Mertus's account of "The Restaurant" in Huairou, supplied much of the energy, context, and direction for the writers in this volume. Beijing fueled the need to share stories, to compare organizational forms, to exchange thoughts. The role of religion in women's oppression and women's liberation, as it threads through this volume, provides one such illuminating nexus of comparison. Religious rhetoric has been enlisted to support narrow nationalism (Siapno), to justify structural sexism (Hughes and Mladjenovic, Kesic), and morally to browbeat women into childbearing (Metikos). But religion has also been a source of strength for many women on the frontlines, giving their actions an authority which transcends that of the state or the given social structure (Green, Rycenga, Siapno, Rajavi). Even the institutional forms of religion are seen to carry these contradictions within them, as the experiences of Tibetan nuns (Gould) or the role of the radical clergy within Guatemala (Matthews) reveal.

REPRESENTATIONS AND TRANSLATIONS

It is a sign of the robustness of women's and feminist activism worldwide that no book could hope to be inclusive. Nor, we might add, should we take each other to task for not being universal intelligences, a subject position long since discredited as a denial of difference and a cover for political and cultural imperialism. This volume's editors encourage readers to notice what is absent, the better to activate the dialogic possibilities of the spaces created by the texts we have included, and we take the opportunity here to set the ball rolling. The conference itself, for example, included several panels of indigenous North and Central American speakers, voicing their resistance to forms of state violence ranging from nuclear testing and dumping to military brutality and human rights abuses. Carrie Dann of the Western Shoshone Defense Project participated in the plenary panel with speakers from the Sudan, India, Israel, Chile, Kosova, and the state of Tennessee. Maria Patricia Jimenez Ramirez from the Fray Bartolome de las Casas Human Rights Center in Chiapas, Mexico, participated in a panel discussion with representatives of indigenous resistance movements in Guatemala and Baja California. Also represented at the conference were South American feminist initiatives; the cross-cultural work of the Asian Women's Human Rights Council, now active in North Africa as well as in India, Japan, the Philippines, and elsewhere; the worldwide Gabriela and LILA Pilipina networks based in the Philippines; the Association of Women of the Mediterranean Region, the Creative Women's Workshop of Belfast, Northern Ireland; Lideras Campesinas based in Pomona, California; representatives of the resurgent union movement in Los Angeles; and many other initiatives and organizations. Under- or unrepresented, either at the conference or in this volume, are West European feminisms and women's movements in sub-Saharan Africa, China, the countries of the former Soviet Union, and Australia.

"Representation," we would also point out, is itself a hotly contested concept with a problematic history. Mulling over the slipperiness of Marx's terms *vertretung* and *darstellung*, Gayatri Spivak, explains that the terms can refer to a range of relationships, including having authority over, standing in for, and appropriating, that neither the conference nor these proceedings would support (Spivak 1985). Even to represent "oneself" is by no means a straightforward proposition, as Shashwati Talukdar's brilliant film *My Life as a Poster* and her essay "You Have a Voice Now: Resistance Is Futile" cannily demonstrate. French feminists have persuasively argued that representation is irretrievably implicated in the patriarchal regime of Western metaphysics known as "phallocentrism," which is predicated upon the privileging of a transcendental signified (the "phallus") to which all signifiers sooner or later refer. It is this logic, for example, that underwrites the otherwise illogical and materially unsupported notion that female citizenship has the same sense that male citizenship does in, say, the United States, when the wealth, power, and gendering of the state are, symbolically and empirically, conspicuously male.

A more useful metaphor for this volume than representation, then, might be "translation." This term, too, has many senses. For the antifascist German Jewish theorist Walter Benjamin, the task of the translator is to manifest the process of moving between incommensurate languages, revealing the limits and possibilities of each (Benjamin 1969). Trinh T. Minh-ha, in her film *Surname Viet Given Name Nam*, takes this principle one step further. She chose to have ordinary Vietnamese women living in the United States speak the lines of Vietnamese women in Vietnam whose monologues had already been translated, first into French and then into English (Trinh 1992). The "actresses" themselves have difficulty speaking English, and the labor they put into giving life to the voices from Vietnam is palpable. What results from this relay of interviews, translations, and performances, though, is an extraordinary community—not an "imagined" community of citizens, unknown to each other, who identify with a hegemonic nation-state (Anderson 1983, 37–46), but a diasporic community of women dedicated to being each other's links across the heterogeneous spaces and times of (at least) three "nations," two wars, and myriad histories. Similarly, here, the essays might best be seen as linking to and for one another—readers, in turn, empowered to include the work of these communities in their own relays of translation.

Conversations and Interrelations

Frontline Feminisms is divided into four thematic sections: "Domestic and Public Violence"; "Gender, Militarism, and Sexuality"; "Nonviolent and Not-Nonviolent Action Against Patriarchy"; and "Where are the Frontlines?"

In the first section on "Domestic and Public Violence," Angela Davis singles out the gender assumptions behind the growth in imprisonment of women in the United States. She points out that women's punishment includes a heavy dose of female socialization, meant to tame and control women who challenge the status quo. She sees this as a socially mandated violence that is hidden away from view. Shadia el Sarraj similarly traces the ripple effects of public violence in Palestine. Noting that almost two-thirds of adult Palestinians report being publicly humiliated and harassed by Israeli forces, she shows how this leads to an increase in domestic violence and stress within families. Vesna Kesic, offering a crucial perspective from Croatia, points out another dynamic in domestic and public violence: how "ethnic and national exclusivity" often leads to a simultaneous rehabilitation of "the traditional patriarchal stereotypes embodying the traditional roles of woman as mother, wife, nurturer." But once women (and ethnic "Others") have been dehumanized, these same valorized stereotypes easily slip into the degradation of women. In the short report she wrote with Lepa Mladjenovic of Serbia, they discuss the myriad ways in which women in former Yugoslavia tried to short-circuit this propaganda machinery through open dialogue with each other. Zorica Mrsevic's piece, also from Serbia, provides additional theorizing and personal narratives about the relation between the public violence of war and domestic violence, while she provocatively includes burnt-out frontline feminists themselves among the casualties. Lucinda Joy Peach examines structural connections between gender and violence, specifically in U.S. law, which, she contends "itself understands violence as male" and so is ineffective in dealing with either women who are victims of domestic violence, or women who kill their batterers.

Opening the next section, "Gender, Militarism, and Sexuality," Irene Matthews' powerful presentation of the feminist dimensions of *I, Rigoberta Menchu* analyzes why the Guatemalan military uses rape and torture, and how the specific violence directed against women calls forth the need to reconstitute community and memory. Her analysis devastatingly critiques the recent attempts to discredit Rigoberta Menchú's writings. The different ways in which Israeli militarization seeps into every crevice of the lives of two friends, one a Jewish Israeli and the other a Palestinian from Israel, are explored in Isis Nusair's factional/fictional, academic/personal dialogue, which holds many surprises, including Isis's realization that rape is an appropriate metaphor for the psychological and epistemological violence suffered by her Israeli friend Hilla. Fatima Ahmed Ibrahim's history of the women's movements in Sudan, spanning as it does almost forty years, touches on many of the issues facing women internationally today: economic policies, cultural diversity, and what she sees as the misuse of religious rhetoric. Noting the history of repression of feminists in Sudan, she calls for unity against the current Islamist regime. Two articles deal with militarism's need to exploit, sexualize, and degrade women: treatment that is patent in the GI towns that grow up around U.S. military bases overseas. Saundra Sturdevant describes, in photographs as well as words, the lives of the women who are prostituted to service the military, while Gwyn Kirk and Margo Okazawa-Rey summarize women's organized resistance to this exploitation in Okinawa (Japan), Korea, the Philippines, and the United States. Kathryn McMahon traces how women's organizations in two countries—Cambodia and Vietnam— are responding to the ravages of warfare and how they show different profiles concerning government control and/or support for women's organizations. Sorayya Shahri's detailing of women's successful military leadership upsets any essentialist notion of women as nonviolent by nature. In detailing this most literal frontline, Shahri acknowledges that for women to fight in the National Liberation Army of the National Council of Resistance of Iran, both men and women had to change their preconceived attitudes; but, far from seeing this as an impossible task, she claims it has been successfully accomplished.

Setting the stage for "Nonviolent and Not-Nonviolent Action Against Patriarchy" Julie Mertus's "Kitchen Cabinet" takes us to Huairou, where women activists, including Palestinian, Tibetan, and Kosovar veterans of occupation, compared notes and exchanged views. Not just about talk, the meetings of women dining at "The Restaurant" included the fuller communicative registers of laughter, song, conflict, tears, and dreams. Next, Benina Berger Gould makes an impassioned argument for understanding the positive role of religion in the Tibetan struggle. While she shows how the history of Tibetan women's resistance to the Chinese occupation has not been uniformly nonviolent, she says that the living practice of Tibetan women can aid in the development of a feminist theory of nonviolence. Gila Svirsky's reflections on the history of Women in Black in Israel raise questions without foreclosing on them. The silent witness of Women in Black can change some minds, but not all, and the ways in which the ideas of Women in Black were adopted by allied groups around the world, and also the attempts at appropriation by opposing groups, provide much food for thought about how international communication among feminists operates. Lepa Mladjenovic and Donna Hughes' piece on feminist opposition in Serbia to ethnic cleansing and militarism has only gained in importance in the light of the resurgence of both in Kosova and the war between NATO and Serbia. The complexities of women's agency, when the category of woman is seen to include differences in culture, language, religion, and class, is examined in an Indonesian context by Jacqueline Siapno. The women in Aceh and East Timor involved in struggles against the Indonesian government utilize a wide variety of strategies, eliminating neither violence nor nonviolence. Jennifer Rycenga gives this stance historical and international resonance in her study of Maria Stewart, nineteenth-century African American antislavery activist, whose profoundly original thought about violence also reopens the question of what freedom is. Maryam Rajavi's greeting from the Iranian Resistance stresses that women refused to capitulate to the levels of misogyny and violence unleashed against them by the Khomeini regime, and instead joined the Resistance in order to fight back. Rajavi, who argues that gradual change in gender relations does not lead to lasting results, urges that a decisive and affirmative change be made, and describes the successful outcome of the "Equality movement" in the political and military sections of the Resistance movement she heads.

Concluding by reopening the question "Where are the Frontlines?," Eli writes movingly of the empowerment of women in rural Kosova, who already faced many obstacles in a situation where an ethnically based apartheid system had been in effect long before the war with NATO began. (Kosova is where Slobodan Milosevic first launched his narrow nationalist program.) The dislocation of almost the entire population, the wholesale destruction of towns and villages, and the many rapes, deaths, and disappearances—already on the horizon when this piece was updated in the fall of 1998—now make this contribution almost unbearably poignant. The work of Eli and others goes on, however, in the refugee camps of Macedonia and Albania, while her account stands as an important historical record of how the Kosovar activists operated during pre-NATO bombing period. Another frontline is traced by Sondra Hale, who raises a key question about women who have joined combat in liberatory and resistance struggles: what happens after a revolution has been successful? When the women who fought in the Eritrean revolution return to civilian life, what happens to the new gender relations forged in the field? Nancy Keefe Rhodes points to the police violence in American communities directed against families and children, when home searches turn into home-trashings, recalling Shadia el Sarraj's depiction of family life in Gaza. Women's agitation on these issues is further examined in the contribution from Georgiana Williams, the cofounder of the LA4+ Defense Committee. Ida Leachman and Laurie Beth Green consider the frontline in the American South, where Black working-class women are displaying a labor militancy that grows out of the Civil Rights struggle. The totality of women's struggles can be seen here, when they include race, class, gender, and the legacy of slavery. Piya Chatterjee discusses a similar structure in Bengal, where women are silenced in multiple ways, through government, union, and party mechanisms, and yet retain their own sense of solidarity with each other and knowledge of their shared struggle.

Jennifer Rycenga and Marguerite R. Waller
Santa Monica, California, May 1999

REFERENCES

Anderson, Benedict. 1983. *Imagined Communities: Reflections on the Origin and Spread of Nationalism*. London, New York: Verso.

Bagdikian, Ben H. 1983. *The Media Monopoly*. Boston: Beacon Press.

Bellafante, Ginia. 1998. "Feminism: It's All about Me!" *Time*, 29 June, 54–62.

Benjamin, Walter. 1969. "The Task of the Translator." In *Illuminations*, edited by Hannah Arendt, 69–82. New York: Schocken Books.

Dunayevskaya, Raya. 1996. *Women's Liberation and the Dialectics of Revolution: Reaching for the Future*. Detroit: Wayne State University Press.

Lorde, Audre. 1984. *Sister Outsider*. Freedom, CA: Crossing Press.

Mertus, Julie and Jasmina Tesanovic. 1997. "Introduction." In *The Suitcase: Refugee Voices from Bosnia and Croatia*. Berkeley and Los Angeles: The University of California Press.

Penezic, Vida. 1995. "Women in Yugoslavia." In *Post-communism and the Body Politic*, edited by Ellen E. Barry, 57–77. New York and London: New York University Press.

Siapno, Jacqueline. 1997. *The Politics of Gender, Islam and Nation-State in Aceh, Indonesia: A Historical Analysis of Power, Co-optation and Resistance*, Ph.D. Dissertation, University of California, Berkeley. Ann Arbor: University Microfilms International.

Spivak, Gayatri. 1985. "Can the Subaltern Speak? Speculations on Widow Sacrifice," Wedge 7.8 (Winter/Spring).

Trinh T. Minh-ha. 1992. "Surname Viet Given Name Nam." In *Framer Framed*, 49–91. New York and London: Routledge.

Wolf, Christa. *Cassandra: A Novel and Four Essays*. Trans. Jan van Heurck. New York: Farrar Straus Giroux.

Acknowledgments

This book grew out of an extraordinary conference, held at the University of California, Riverside, in January 1997, entitled "Frontline Feminisms: Women, War and Resistance," co-organized by Piya Chatterjee and Marguerite Waller of the Center for Women in Coalition Research Center. Bringing together, from across the world, the live voices and perspectives of women who were engaged in forging new feminisms in the context of militarized situations was both a logistical challenge and an exhilarating experience. So many people contributed to the success of that initial event that we cannot begin to name them all. They include colleagues of the College of Humanities, Arts, and Social Sciences, a dedicated group of staff, and a legion of graduate and undergraduate students who volunteered countless hours of their time and energy. Institutional support for the conference and for participants was provided by UC Riverside's Center for Ideas and Society, the Global Fund for Women, Mamacash, the American Friends Service Committee, the Open Society Institutes of Macedonia and Croatia, the Central European University in Budapest, UCMEXUS, The University of California Office of the President, Dean Carlos Vélez-Ibáñez of the College of Humanities, Arts, and Social Sciences, and over two dozen departments, programs, and individuals.

Preparing this volume for publication entailed (virtually) recreating this web of participants, through correspondence, e-mail, and telephone. Among the people who have facilitated this process, we want to mention Gila Svirsky, Judy Tanzawa, Scott Long, Julie Mertus, Sondra Hale, and Laurie Green, all of whom helped us to trace peripatetic contributors. Editing sessions have benefited from the generosity of friends who provided hospitality, child care, and moral support, including Ruth Charloff, Christine and Sarah Gailey, Susan Cope, Meredith Masters, Judy Branf- man, Rosie Arvizu, Julia Buchanan, Ross Parke, and Emily Culpepper. Technical support and computer trouble-shooting were supplied by Bren- dan Howard and Jaime Hammond, and Sharon Snyder gave the right ad- vice when the dangerous last-minute virus threatened to eat the project.

Our editors at Garland manifested the grace to be both enthusiastic and patient. We want to thank Chandra Mohanty for including this vol- ume in her series, "Gender, Culture, and Global Politics." Kristi Long guided the beginning of the process, and Mia Zamora has seen us through the rigors of preparing the manuscript.

Various colleagues at both San José State University and the Univer- sity of California at Riverside and on other campuses have been sources of support and founts of ideas. In particular, Jennifer would like to thank Lois Helmbold, Mira Zussman, Selma Burkom, Chris Jochim, Richard Keady, and Ken Kramer. Marguerite would like to thank Alicia Arrizón, Parama Roy, John Ganim, Piya Chatterjee, Christine Gailey, Jennifer Brody, Deborah Wong, Ethan Nasreddin-Longo, Emory Elliott, Sandra Harding, Beatriz Manz, Shirley Lim, Michele Weber, and Devra Weber. The life of this project is also deeply indebted to activists and friends who introduced the editors at crucial moments to new universes of thought and action. For Marguerite these include Emily Hicks, Biljana Kasic, Jill Small, Xiaoquong Shi, Judit Hatfaludi, Beverly Allen, Donna Culpepper, Bea Nemlaha, Amanda MacIntosh, Soona Samsami, Kate Hartford, and the women of the art-making collective Las Comadres. Jennifer would acknowledge the sparking energies of Karen Barad, Ruthie Wilson Gilmore, Sue Houchins, Sallie Roesch Wagner, Emily Culpepper, Louis Mazza, Michelle Gubbay, Laurie Green, Lou Turner, Lois Helmbold, and the fabulous activists of Queer Revolution. We join in warmly thanking Erla Martiensdottir, Jeanne Cancel Sikoff, and Bar- bara Roos for their care and efficiency in bringing the project through the final stages of production.

Dolores Rycenga early instilled a sense of justice in her daughter, and continues to be an examplar of how one can stay cheery while also recognizing and fighting the evils in this world.

Lea Waller has been the delight of her mother's life during the preparation of this volume, and uncannily understanding, for a two-year- old, of the importance of the work for both of us, while Mac and Martha Waller and their other offspring, Susan, Liz, Don, and Richard, have been, as always, steady sources of wisdom and support.

Illustrations

PHOTOGRAPHS

MAPS

FRONTLINE FEMINISMS

PART I

Domestic and Public Violence

CHAPTER 1

Public Imprisonment and Private Violence
Reflections on the Hidden Punishment of Women

ANGELA Y. DAVIS

Over the last twenty-five years, feminist research and activism on sexual assault and domestic violence have generated campaigns and services on local, national, and international levels and an increasingly popular culture of resistance, which has helped to unveil the global pandemic of violence against women. At the same time, research and activism have developed, on a much smaller scale, around women in prison. The work in these two areas has intersected in a number of important ways, including the amnesty campaign for women convicted of killing abusive spouses or partners. Moreover, one of the salient themes in the current literature on women in prison is the centrality of physical abuse in the lives of women subject to state punishment. Even so, the domestic violence and women's prison movements remain largely separate.

Considering the enormous increase in the numbers of imprisoned women during this contemporary era of the prison industrial complex, we need to examine the potential for establishing deeper and more extensive alliances between the antiviolence movement and the larger women's prison movement. Therefore, this article explores preliminarily some of the historical and philosophical connections between domestic violence and imprisonment as two modes of gendered punishment—one located in the private realm, the other in the public realm. This analysis

Reprinted from: Angela Y. Davis. "Public Imprisonment and Private Violence: Reflections on the Hidden Punishment of Women." *New England Journal on Criminal and Civic Confinement* 24:2 (Summer 1998): 339–351.

3

suggests that the women's antiviolence movement is far more integrally related to the women's prison movement than is generally recognized.

The history of prison reform reveals multiple ironies. While imprisonment is now the dominant mode of public punishment and is associated with egregious human rights abuses, it was once regarded as a promise of enlightened moral restoration and thus, as a significant improvement over forms of punishment that relied on the infliction of corporal pain. In the era of flogging, pillories, and stocks, reformers called for the penitentiary as a more humane alternative to the cruelty of corporal punishment. During the nineteenth century, however, even as (mostly white) men in Europe and the United States convicted of violating the law were increasingly sentenced to prison, as opposed to being subjected to torture and mutilation, (white) women's punishment remained emphatically linked to corporal violence inflicted upon them within domestic spaces. These patriarchal structures of violence affected black women in different ways, primarily through the system of slavery. Today, it is easy to see how gender and race limitations of the nineteenth century discourse on punishment reform ruled out the possibility of linking domestic torture with public torture, and thus of a related campaign against the gendered violence visited on women's bodies.

Sometimes, however, the boundaries between private and public punishment were blurred. Long before the emergence of the reform movement, which succeeded in establishing imprisonment as generalized punishment, there was a prison for women. The first documented prison for women was, in fact, in the Netherlands (Zedner 1998). Amsterdam's Spinhuis, which opened in 1645, contained cells for women who could not "be kept to their duties by parents or husbands" (Zedner 1998, 292, 295). In seventeenth-century Britain, use of the branks—sometimes known as the scold's or gossip's bridle—to punish women who did not respect patriarchal authority also indicates the permeability of borders between public and private. According to Russell Dobash et al.,

> The branks was an iron cage placed over the head, and most examples incorporated a spike or pointed wheel that was inserted into the offender's mouth in order to 'pin the tongue and silence the noisiest brawler.' This spiked cage was intended to punish women adjudged quarrelsome or not under the proper control of their husbands. The common form of administering this punishment was to fasten the branks to a woman and parade her through the village, sometime [sic] chaining her to a pillar for a period of time after the procession. . . . Al-

> though these were public chastisements they were integrally linked to household domination. In some towns arrangements were made for employing the branks within the home. . . . [M]en often used the threat of the branks to attempt to silence their wives, "If you don't rest with your tongue, I'll send for the town jailor . . . to hook you up." In this example, we see how patriarchal domination and state domination were intricately intertwined (Dobash et al. 1986, 19–20).

When early reformers like John Howard and Jeremy Bentham called for systems of punishment that would putatively minimize violence against the human body, prevailing ideas about the exclusion of women from public space did not allow for the emergence of a reform movement that also contested the ubiquitous violence against women. Such movements did not develop until the late twentieth century. Ironically, as "private" sexual and physical assaults against women are increasingly constructed as "crimes" and, therefore, subject to "public" sanctions, the "public" imprisonment of women remains as hidden as ever. At the same time, greater numbers of women, especially women of color, are subjected to the public punishment of prison as they simultaneously experience violence in their intimate and family relationships. The two modes of punishment remain as disarticulated in both popular and scholarly discourse as they were over a century ago.

Today, as structural racism becomes more entrenched and simultaneously more hidden, these two forms of punishment together camouflage the impact of racism on poor women of color. Domestic violence as a form of punishment is rarely perceived as integrally connected to the modes of punishment implemented by the State. Many recent studies recognize that large numbers of imprisoned women are survivors of family violence. Joanne Belknap's, *The Invisible Woman: Gender, Crime, and Justice*, which looks at the impact of the criminal justice system on women, insightfully examines both imprisonment and battering. As a criminologist, however, Belknap necessarily frames her study with the categories—rarely problematized in criminological and legal discourses—of "female offender" and "female victim" (Belknap 1996). Her examination of women's imprisonment constructs women prisoners as "female offenders," while her analysis of male violence against women constructs women as "victims" of crime (Belknap 1996). In the first instance, women are perpetrators and in the second, they are victims. Belknap develops a range of important feminist critiques of traditional criminological theories and sheds light on the ways women tend to suffer more from imprisonment practices than do their male counterparts. She also makes valuable observations on the continued invisibility of male violence, even in an era of expanding campaigns, services, and feminist theorizing around these issues. This article suggests, however, that her work can also encourage us to think more deeply about the patriarchal power circuits from the state to the home, which are disconnected by the ideological division of the "public" and the "private," thus rendering the underlying complexities of women's punishment invisible.

Pat Carlen's 1983 study, *Women's Imprisonment: A Study in Social Control,* highlights the co-constitutive character of women's public and private punishment. This case study on the Scottish women's prison, Cornton Vale, argues that both violent and nonviolent informal disciplining in the home are as important to the construction of domestic life as the parallel, often similar, and indeed symbiotically related discipline that is the foundation of prison practices (Carlen 1983).

> In general, the motto of those charged with the penal regulation of deviant women has been 'discipline, medicalise, and feminise'! Women's imprisonment, both in Great Britain and in the United States, has traditionally been characterized by its invisibility, its domesticity, and its infantalisation (Carlen 1983, 18).

In Scotland, the inhabitants of Cornton Vale are largely working-class white women and, as Carlen points out, the intersection of public and private axes of domination is very much class-determined. While Carlen's study does not put into the foreground the influence of race—which is no less important to an understanding of white women's imprisonment than of the imprisonment of women of color—it should be pointed out that throughout the urban areas of Europe and the United States, a vastly disproportionate number of women prisoners come from racially marginalized communities. What Carlen refers to as a "fusion of the private and public realms of family discipline with the penological regulation of deviant women [which] has, in fact, received nominal recognition" (Carlen 1983, 86), then becomes even more complex when race is taken into consideration.

Sociologist Beth Richie, who has also attempted to link the private and public punishment of women, has studied what she calls the "gender entrapment" of black women, who are, in many instances, "compelled to crime" and subsequently, imprisoned by the same conditions that inform their subjection to violence within their personal relationships (Richie 1996). She writes about

> African American women from low-income communities who are
> physically battered, sexually assaulted, emotionally abused, and in-
> volved in illegal activity. Their stories vividly contradict the popular
> impression—perpetuated by mainstream social scientists, human ser-
> vice providers, public policy analysts, and legislators—that the esca-
> lating rates of violence against women, poverty, addiction, and
> women's participation in crime is because of women's psychological,
> moral, or social inadequacies (Richie 1996, 2).

Richie chose to translate the legal category "entrapment" into the theoretical paradigm "gender entrapment" because it allows her to examine
the intersections of gender, race, and violence. This paradigm also facil-
itates an understanding of the ways in which women who experience
poverty and violence in their personal lives end up being punished for a
web of social conditions over which they have no control.[1] While Richie
presents a provocative analysis of the means by which women can be led
to engage in illegal activities, either as a direct result of the violence in
their intimate relationships, or the threat of it, it is not within the purview
of her sociological study to examine the historical continuum between
domestic and state-inflicted punishment of women.

In much of the historical literature on women's imprisonment, the
emergence of a "domestic model" of imprisonment for women toward
the end of the nineteenth century is represented as the advent of a specifically female approach to public punishment. This relocation of domestic
punishment regimes to the public sphere did not result in any less punishment in the home. The continued social sanctioning of private violence against women historically has minimized the numbers of women
subject to public punishment. Because of the ironclad ideological connection between "crime" and "punishment," women's punishment is seldom disarticulated from the unlawful activities that lead them to prison,
which makes it all the more difficult to articulate "private" and "public"
punishment. The assumption that women constitute a relatively small
portion of the imprisoned population simply because they commit fewer
crimes continues to reign over common sense and over criminological
discourse. Therefore, the fact that women are punished in venues other
than prison and in accordance with authority not directly assumed by the
State might begin to explain the relatively small numbers of imprisoned
women.

State-sanctioned punishment is informed by patriarchal structures
and ideologies that have tended to produce historical assumptions of female criminality linked to ideas about the violation of social norms

defining a "woman's place." Feminist historians have uncovered evidence of severe corporal punishment inflicted on women accused of adultery, for example, while the behavior of male adulterers has been normalized. At the same time, violence against women inflicted within domestic spaces has only recently begun to be "criminalized." Considering the fact that as many as half of all women are assaulted by their husbands or partners (Belknap 1996, 172), combined with dramatically rising numbers of women sentenced to prison, it may be argued that women in general are subjected to a far greater magnitude of punishment than men. At the same time, because patriarchal structures are contested in so many arenas, including transnational campaigns challenging domestic violence, women are now subjected to public punishment in greater numbers than ever before. Even though women are still represented as negligible targets of the prison system, the continued pandemic of private punishment, connected with the soaring numbers of women being sent to prison, combine to create a picture of the lives of poor, working-class, and racially marginalized women as overdetermined by punishment. This is not to dismiss the extent to which middle-class women are also victims of violence in their families and intimate relationships. They are not, however, "entrapped"—to use Richie's term—in the same web of social conditions that places many poor women of color on the track that leads to prison and thus, causes them to experience surplus punishment.

Paradoxically, prison reform movements in general have tended to bolster, rather than diminish, the stronghold of prisons on the lives of the individuals whom they hold captive. Michel Foucault has pointed out that from the beginning, reform has always been linked to the evolution of the prison, which, in turn, has become more entrenched due in part precisely to the effectiveness of reforms (Foucault 1979).

> [T]he movement for reforming the prisons, for controlling their functioning is not a recent phenomenon. It does not even seem to have originated in a recognition of failure. Prison 'reform' is virtually contemporary with the prison itself: it constitutes, as it were, its programme. From the outset, the prison was caught up in a series of accompanying mechanisms, whose purpose was apparently to correct it, but which seem to form part of its very functioning, so closely have they been bound up with its existence throughout its long history (Foucault 1979, 234).

In other words, prison reform campaigns, focusing on men's as well as women's institutions, generally have called for the improvement of prisons, but rarely have problematized the role of prisons as the dominant mode of punishment. Thus, as reforms have been instituted, prison systems have become more entrenched both structurally and ideologically. Today, when punishment in the United States has become a veritable industry consolidating the linkages between government and transnational corporations in ways that mirror and strengthen the military industrial complex, it is as difficult to question the need for prisons on such a large scale as it is to question the need for such a vast military machine.

When the reform movement calling for separate prisons for women emerged in England and the United States during the nineteenth century, Elizabeth Fry, Josephine Shaw, and other advocates argued against the prevailing conception that criminal women were beyond the reach of moral rehabilitation. Like male convicts, who presumably could be "corrected" by rigorous prison regimes, female convicts, they suggested, could also be molded into moral beings by differently-gendered imprisonment regimes. Architectural changes, domestic regimes, and an all-female custodial staff were implemented in the reformatory program proposed by reformers (Freedman 1991, chs. 3–4), and eventually, women's prisons became as strongly anchored to the social landscape as men's prisons. Their relative invisibility was as much a reflection of the domestic space reinscribed on women's public punishment, as it was of the relatively small numbers of women incarcerated in these new institutions.

This feminization of public punishment in England and the United States was explicitly designed to reform white women. Twenty-one years after the first reformatory in England was established in London in 1853, the first U.S. reformatory for women was opened in Indiana.

> [The] aim was to train the prisoners in the "important" female role of domesticity. Thus, an important part of the reform movement in women's prisons was to encourage and ingrain "appropriate" gender roles, such as vocational training in cooking, sewing, and cleaning. To accommodate these goals, the reformatory cottages were usually designed with kitchens, living rooms, and even some nurseries for prisoners with infants (Belknap 1996, 95).

This feminized public punishment, however, did not affect all women in the same way. When black women were imprisoned in reformatories, they often were segregated from white women. Moreover, they tended to be disproportionately sentenced to serve time in men's prisons. In the southern states in the aftermath of the Civil War, black women endured the cruelties of the convict lease system unmitigated by the feminization of punishment; neither their sentences, nor the labor they were compelled to do, were lessened by virtue of their gender. As the U.S. prison system evolved during the twentieth century, feminized modes of punishment—the cottage system, domestic training, etc.—were designed, ideologically, to reform white women, relegating women of color, in large part, to realms of public punishment that made no pretense of offering them femininity.

Moreover, as Lucia Zedner has pointed out, sentencing practices for women within the reformatory system often required women to do more time than men for similar offenses. "This differential was justified on the basis that women were sent to reformatories not to be punished in proportion to the seriousness of their offense but to be reformed and retrained, a process that, it was argued, required time" (Zedner 1998, 318). At the same time, Zedner points out, this tendency to send women to prison for longer terms than men was accelerated by the eugenics movement, "which sought to have 'genetically inferior' women removed from social circulation for as many of their childbearing years as possible" (Zedner 1998, 318). Although Nicole Rafter points out that racism may not be the primary explanatory factor underlying late nineteenth-century eugenic criminology (Rafter 1998, 30), the eugenic discourses that presumed to define white normalcy against white deviancy—intellectual impairment, criminality, physical disability, etc.—relied on the same logic of exclusion as racism itself, and therefore, could be easily retooled for racist uses.

In the latter twentieth century, women's prisons have begun to look more like their male counterparts, particularly those that have been constructed in the era of the prison industrial complex. As corporate involvement in punishment begins to mirror corporate involvement in military production, rehabilitation is becoming displaced by penal aims of incapacitation. Now that the population of prisons and jails is approaching two million, the rate of increase in the numbers of women prisoners has surpassed that of men. As criminologist Elliot Currie has pointed out,

> [f]or most of the period after World War II, the female incarceration rate hovered at around 8 per 100,000; it did not reach double digits until 1977. Today it is 51 per 100,000. . . . At current rates of increase, there will be more women in American prisons in the year 2010 than there were inmates of both sexes in 1970. When we combine the effects of race and gender, the nature of these shifts in the prison population is even clearer. The prison incarceration rate for black women today exceeds that for white men as recently as 1980 (Currie 1998, 14).

A quarter-century ago, in the era of the Attica uprising and the murder of George Jackson at San Quentin, radical movements developed against the prison system as a principal site of state violence and repression. In part as a reaction to the invisibility of women prisoners in this movement, and in part as a consequence of the rising women's liberation movement, specific campaigns developed in defense of the rights of women prisoners. While many of these campaigns put forth, and continue to advance, radical critiques of state repression and violence, those taken up within the correctional community have been influenced largely by liberal constructions of gender equality.

In contrast to the nineteenth-century reform movement, which was grounded in an ideology of gender difference, late twentieth-century "reforms" have relied on a "separate but equal" model. This "separate but equal" approach often has been applied uncritically, ironically resulting in demands for more repressive conditions in order to render women's facilities "equal" to men's. For example, Tekla Dennison Miller, former warden of Huron Valley Women's Prison in Michigan, identifies her crusade for equality during the 1980s as strongly feminist. The problematic character of such an approach is revealed in her discussion of security.

> Staffing was far leaner at Huron Valley Women's than at men's prisons. When it opened . . . [t]here were no yard officers at Women's, let alone a yard sergeant to watch prisoner movement and yard activities. The yards are the favorite areas for prisoner on prisoner assaults. There was also only one Assistant Deputy Warden. Men's prisons were allowed two ADWs, one for security and one for housing, but male central office administration claimed, 'Women prisoners pose no security threat. They're just basic pains in the ass and are mostly interested in painting their nails and harassing us for more personal property. They need a housing deputy, not a security deputy' (Miller 1996, 97).

In her campaign for gender equality, Miller also criticized security practices for the unequal allocation of weapons:

> Arsenals in mens' [sic] prisons are large rooms with shelves of shotguns, rifles, hand guns, ammunition, gas canisters, and riot equipment. . . . Huron Valley Women's arsenal was a small, five feet by two feet closet that held two rifles, eight shotguns, two bull horns, five hand guns, four gas canisters, and twenty sets of restraints (Miller 1996, 97–98).

After a prisoner, intent on escaping, successfully climbed over the razor ribbon and was captured after jumping to the ground on the other side, a local news reporter, whom Miller described as "an unexpected ally in the ongoing fight for parity," questioned the policy of not firing warning shots for women escapees. As a result, Miller observed,

> escaping women prisoners in medium or higher [security] prisons are treated the same way as men. A warning shot is fired. If the prisoner fails to halt and is over the fence, an officer is allowed to shoot to injure. If the officer's life is in danger, the officer can shoot to kill (Miller 1996, 100).

Paradoxically, demands for parity with men's prisons, instead of creating greater educational, vocational, and health opportunities for women prisoners, often have led to more repressive conditions for women. This is not only a consequence of deploying liberal, that is, formalistic, notions of equality, but more dangerously, allowing male prisons to function as the punishment norm. Miller points out that she attempted to prevent a prisoner, whom she characterizes as a "murderer" serving a long term, from participating in graduation ceremonies at the University of Michigan (Miller 1996, 121). (Of course, she does not indicate the nature of the woman's murder charges—whether, for instance, she was convicted of killing an abusive partner, as is the case for a substantial number of women convicted of such charges.) Although Miller did not succeed in preventing the inmate from participating in the commencement ceremony, the prisoner was made to wear leg chains and handcuffs with her cap and gown (Miller 1996, 121).

A more widely publicized example of the use of repressive paraphernalia, historically associated with the treatment of male prisoners to create "equality" for female prisoners, was the 1996 decision by Alabama's prison commissioner to establish women's chain gangs.[2] After Alabama became the first state to reinstitute chain gangs in 1995, then State Corrections Commissioner Ron Jones announced the following year that women would be shackled while they cut grass, picked up trash, and worked a vegetable garden at Julia Tutwiler State Prison for Women. This attempt to institute chain gangs for women was in part a response to lawsuits by male prisoners, who charged that male chain gains discriminated against men by virtue of their gender. Immediately after Jones' announcement, however, he was fired by Governor Fob James, who obviously was pressured to prevent Alabama from acquiring the dubious distinction of being the only U.S. state to have equal opportunity chain gangs.

Four months after Alabama's embarrassing flirtation with the possibility of chain gangs for women, Sheriff Joe Arpaio of Maricopa County, Arizona—represented in the media as "the toughest sheriff in America"—held a press conference to announce that because he was "an equal opportunity incarcerator," he was establishing the country's first female chain gang (*48 Hours* 1996). When the plan was implemented, newspapers throughout the country carried a photograph of chained women cleaning Phoenix's streets. While Sheriff Arpaio's policy regarding women prisoners has been criticized as little more than a publicity stunt, the fact that this women's chain gang emerges against the backdrop of a generalized increase in the repression inflicted on women prisoners—including the proliferation of security housing units, which parallel the development of super maximum security prisons—is cause for alarm. Since the population of women in prison is now comprised of a majority of women of color, the historical resonances of slavery, colonization, and genocide should not be missed in these images of women in chains and shackles.

As the level of repression in women's prisons increases, and, paradoxically, as the influence of domestic prison regimes recedes, sexual abuse—which, like domestic violence, is yet another dimension of the privatized punishment of women—has become an institutionalized component of punishment behind prison walls. Although guard-on-prisoner sexual abuse is not sanctioned as such, the widespread leniency with which offending officers are treated, suggests that for women, prison is a space in which the threat of sexualized violence that looms in the larger society is effectively sanctioned as a routine aspect of the landscape of punishment behind prison walls.

According to a recent Human Rights Watch report on the sexual abuse of women in U.S. prisons:

> Our findings indicate that being a woman prisoner in U.S. state prisons can be a terrifying experience. If you are sexually abused, you cannot escape from your abuser. Grievance or investigatory procedures, where they exist, are often ineffectual, and correctional employees continue to engage in abuse because they believe they will rarely be held accountable, administratively or criminally. Few people outside the prison walls know what is going on or care if they do know. Fewer still do anything to address the problem.[3]

The following excerpt from the summary of this report, *All Too Familiar: Sexual Abuse of Women in U.S. State Prisons*, reveals the extent to which women's prison environments are violently sexualized, thus recapitulating the familiar violence that characterizes many women's private lives:

> We found that male correctional employees have vaginally, anally, and orally raped female prisoners and sexually assaulted and abused them. We found that in the course of committing such gross misconduct, male officers have not only used actual or threatened physical force, but have also used their near total authority to provide or deny goods and privileges to female prisoners to compel them to have sex or, in other cases, to reward them for having done so. In other cases, male officers have violated their most basic professional duty and engaged in sexual contact with female prisoners absent the use or threat of force or any material exchange. In addition to engaging in sexual relations with prisoners, male officers have used mandatory pat-frisks or room searches to grope women's breasts, buttocks, and vaginal areas and to view them inappropriately while in a state of undress in the housing or bathroom areas. Male correctional officers and staff have also engaged in regular verbal degradation and harassment of female prisoners, thus contributing to a custodial environment in the state prisons for women which is often highly sexualized and excessively hostile (Human Rights Watch 1996, 2).

This report argues that the prevalence of sexual abuse in women's prisons is in violation of the U.S. Constitution as well as of international human rights laws. The visit in summer, 1998, to a number of U.S. women's prisons by the United Nations Special Rapporteur on Violence Against Women further highlights the importance of framing the conditions of imprisoned women within the context of the anti-violence movement and within a larger human rights context. As Linda Burnham has pointed out.

> [t]he intent of the human rights paradigm is to position women's issues central to human rights discourse; negate the tendency to view women's issues as private matters; provide teeth and a structure of accountability for women's oppression that includes but is not limited to the state; and provide an overarching political framework capable of connecting the full range of women's issues and the full diversity of their social identities and circumstances (Burnham 1996, 16).

The sexual abuse of women in prison is one of the most heinous state-sanctioned human rights violations within the United States today. Women prisoners represent one of the most disenfranchised and invisible adult populations in our society. The absolute power and control the state exercises over their lives both stems from and perpetuates the patriarchal and racist structures that, for centuries, have resulted in the social domination of women. As the prison industrial complex threatens to transform entire communities into targets of state punishment, the relatively small but rapidly increasing percentage of imprisoned women should not be used as a pretext for ignoring the complicated web of women's punishment. The moment may very well be ripe for forging alliances and for establishing links with international movements for human rights.

NOTES

1. See Richie 1996, 4.

> When applied to African American battered women who commit crimes, I used gender entrapment to describe the socially constructed process whereby African American women who are vulnerable to men's violence in their intimate relationships are penalized for behaviors they engage in, even when the behaviors are logical extensions of their racialized gender identities, their culturally expected gender roles, and the violence in their intimate relationship. The model illustrates how gender, race/ethnicity, and violence can intersect to create a subtle, yet profoundly effective system of organizing women's behavior into patterns that leave women vulnerable to private and public subordination, to violence in their intimate relationships, and, in turn, to participation in illegal activities. As such, the gender-entrapment theory helps to explain how some women who participate in illegal activities do so in response to violence, the threat of violence, or coercion by their male partners.

2. See Wilkie, Curtis. 18 May 1996. "Weak Links Threaten Chain Gangs: Revised Prison Work Program Facing Voter Disapproval," in *Boston Globe*: at 1, 1.

3. See Human Rights Watch. 1996. *All Too Familiar: Sexual Abuse of Women in U.S. State Prisons.* Web page address: <http://www.hrw.org/ hrw/summaries/s.us96d.html>.

REFERENCES

Belknap, Joanne. 1996. *The Invisible Woman: Gender, Crime, and Justice.* Belmont: Wadsworth.

Burnham, Linda. 1996. "Beijing and Beyond," in *Crossroads*. March.

Carlen, Pat. 1983. *Women's Imprisonment: A Study in Social Control.* Boston: Routledge & Kegan Paul.

Currie, Elliot. 1998. *Crime and Punishment in America*. New York: Metropolitan Books.

Dobash, Russell P. et al. 1986. *The Imprisonment of Women*. New York: B. Blackwell.

48 Hours (CBS Television Broadcast). 19 September 1996. "Arizona Sheriff Initiates Equal Opportunity by Starting First Chain Gang for Women."

Foucault, Michel. 1979. *Discipline and Punish: The Birth of the Prison*. Trans. Alan Sheridan. New York: Vintage Books.

Freedman, Estelle B. 1991. *Their Sister's Keepers: Women's Prison Reform in America, 1830–1930*. Ann Arbor: University of Michigan Press.

Human Rights Watch. 1996. *All Too Familiar: Sexual Abuse of Women in U.S. State Prisons*. <http://www.hrw.org/hrw/summaries/s.us96d.html>

Miller, Tekla Dennison. 1996. *The Warden Wore Pink*. Brunswick, Maine: Biddle Publishing Company.

Rafter, Nicola Hahn. 1998. *Creating Born Criminals*. Urbana: University of Illinois Press.

Richie, Beth E. 1996. *Compelled to Crime: The Gender Entrapment of Battered Black Women*. New York: Routledge.

Zedner, Lucia. 1998. "Wayward Sisters: The Prisons for Women." In *The Oxford History of the Prison*, edited by Norval Morris & David J. Rothman. New York: Oxford University Press.

CHAPTER 2

Screaming in Silence

SHADIA EL SARRAJ

On the 23rd of December 1996, on my way back from Jerusalem to Gaza, I was stopped by Israelis at the Eretz checkpoint. With me were about two hundred women and children travelling back to Gaza after having visited their brothers, sons, mothers, and fathers, still inside Israeli prisons. It was a very cold night. We were ordered to sit on the ground and were not allowed to ask why. The children, who had started their visit at three o' clock in the morning, were crying. Tired and hungry, they were being punished because they had visited their loved ones inside the Israeli prisons. (It is a basic human right to return home at any time.) Here are some other facts about the "peace" we are living through these days as Palestinians:

- Palestinians are not allowed normal access through the Israeli checkpoint. Instead they are forced to go through passageways, the way cattle are driven through sale yards. This is humiliating for Palestinians and also causes distress for women and children.
- Between February and June, eight Palestinians died as a result of being delayed at the Eretz checkpoint.
- Because of the closure, the rate of unemployment is 68 percent.
- 40 percent of Palestinian children are working in the streets and inside small factories, leaving school to earn whatever they can to help their families survive.
- Since 1993 around four hundred Palestinians have been killed, including seventy in the recent uprising.

I am a Palestinian from a refugee family. My parents were forced to leave their home and properties in 1948 like the rest of the Palestinians. Physical force, psychological intimidation, terror, and death threats accompanied the expulsion or exodus of Palestinian refugees from their own homeland in 1948. As though they were denying the fact of their exile, Palestinian refugees guarded the keys of their old houses and the deeds of their lands, keeping all the documents that attested to their connection with lost homes. They held onto these documents as if they might need them at any moment. Such documents proved, at least, that the owners were not merely derelict nomads, but people with status and rights, the owners of houses and property. When my grandmother died in 1969, she still had the key to her house in Beir El Sabaa, which is now known as Beir Sheva. Now, my father keeps this key with other documents of family properties, still dreaming of the day he will return.

The 1948 catastrophe has been a central locus of fear and insecurity, deeply affecting the innermost layers of the Palestinian psyche. The shocks of being uprooted and living in exile have resulted in widespread feelings of helplessness and dependency. In 1967, when I was only twelve years old, the Israelis occupied Gaza. During the raids we spent days and days inside a shelter, tens of people unable to move. I remember the fear on men's faces, frightened that the Israelis would act as they had in 1956, when they tried to occupy Gaza before. They had killed thousands of innocent people, especially from the Kan Younis area. Men were ordered to stand up facing the walls, and they were all shot.

The lightning speed of Arab defeat in 1967 and the resulting occupation of the West Bank and Gaza shocked the Arab masses, but particularly the Palestinians. Their dreams of liberation, Arab unity, and victory were suddenly shattered, while their underlying feelings of helplessness, victimization, and paranoia were deepened. Unprepared and unprotected, the Palestinians found themselves face-to-face with an old enemy, who was now armed with a sophisticated, modern arsenal.

Clinically, the forty years during which the Palestinian community has been terrorized and increasingly haunted with a sense of helplessness and frustration have translated into various psychopathologies, particularly depression and anxiety. Drug addiction has spread rapidly among the young. Throughout the general population, various forms of physical and verbal violence and antisocial behavior have increased. Families, clans, and political factions have been plagued by infighting, while men have abused women and children, the most helpless and vulnerable members of society. I read these phenomena as indications that Palestinians have directed aggression inward, in reactive self-destruction.

Initially, the Intifada transformed this psychological pattern; it restored a positive self-image, high self-esteem, and national pride. Helplessness was replaced overnight by a positive assertiveness. Individuals felt responsible and identified strongly with the national struggle. The Intifada was an outlet for the simmering, bottled-up anger. The individual and the communal psychic tension found a legitimate target: the Israeli soldiers.

Four years after the Intifada started, the picture changed. The stagnant political process and the aggressive Israeli response have both contributed to the re-emergence of feelings of frustration and of calls for radical and violent tactics. This is particularly the case in the Gaza Strip, which in many ways fits the model of a prison. It has become a huge detention center. More than 6,000 Palestinians are still in Israeli prisons. Palestinians in exile are not allowed to return home. Families of ex-political prisoners often become targets of those ex-prisoners' anger and frustration. The unstable political situation, the Israeli practices of closure of the Gaza Strip, and restrictions preventing Gazans from moving freely and finding work to support their families result in a deteriorating economic situation.

In this environment, everyone is affected by the overwhelming stress, which is bound to reactivate various forms of violence. According to a study of adult Palestinians, 64 percent of the participants had been subjected to humiliation, harassment, and beating. The resulting anxiety is then transmitted to children. Children themselves have experienced a variety of traumatic events, such as being beaten or injured or witnessing their parents being beaten or killed. Some have been terrified by night raids by soldiers, and not a few have been forcibly separated from their parents. The youth are now prepared to sacrifice everything, even their lives, for the cause of liberation of the Holy Land. Glorification of the life hereafter makes death acceptable.

In 1990, I started to work at the Gaza Community Mental Health Programme. This programme was founded to help Gazan people overcome their traumas. It was through this work that I began to understand more about the problems and feelings of my people. I was shocked when I visited the El Shati refugee camp for the first time to study the situation of the displaced wives of Palestinian prisoners. Their shacks or cinderblock houses have no electricity or running water. There are open drains in the streets, and everywhere one is confronted by swamps of rubbish. In the absence of their husbands, uneducated, desperate young women and their young children live with their families-in-law and describe themselves as failures in their roles as mothers and wives. Palestinian women, I realized, are faced with two burdens: the violent environment and a seemingly eternal victimization by our own authoritarian and patriarchal society. They are victims of all kinds of violence: political, social, domestic.

The human rights of Palestinian women are violated daily in a variety of ways. They are not free to choose when or whom to marry or how many children to have and when to have them. There are innumerable inequalities and injustices in opportunity in education, employment, and health care. As everywhere else in the world, child care and domestic labor have little or no value. Concerning education, the percentage of women being educated at the elementary level is 44 percent that of the men. At the preparatory stage it is 38 percent, and at the secondary stage, 34 percent. Between 33 and 56 percent of Palestinian women from fourteen to forty-four years of age are illiterate (*Al Quds*, Sept. 4. 1995).[1] Furthermore, Palestinian women suffer from the general deterioration of educational standards.

During and after the Intifada, the number of women leaving school before graduating was particularly high, despite the fact that education had been seen as a major resource in Palestinian society after the 1948 catastrophe with its resulting loss of land and properties. The lower female enrollment in educational institutions was partly due to the closure, curfews, and strikes. Also, families with limited resources have, in general, invested their resources in the education of males rather than that of females. A third significant factor has been the increase of arranged marriages at very young ages. Research has shown that in 46 percent of divorce cases, the age of the husbands was between fifteen and twenty years (*Al Quds*, Sept. 1995).

Palestinian women and work present another important issue. The Israelis deliberately used economic measures to impoverish the Palestinians. The Israeli confiscation of Palestinian lands and water resources, for example, made the Palestinians consumers of Israeli products and prevented them from building an infrastructure of their own. The Palestinian territories thus became a slave market where the Israelis could get cheap labor. Many young Palestinians had to leave the area to find work in Israel. This, in turn, hurt families and especially women. Furthermore, Palestinian women were forced to confront the economic and social fallout of the increase in divorce and early marriage, not to mention the problems presented simply by being wives and mothers. Out of the total 1990 work-force, 15 percent were women. In 1992, unemployment among women reached 88 percent. Whether employed or unemployed, women were, and still are, constantly exploited.

These circumstances already translate into multiple hardships for women. Add to them the ways the politically turbulent recent history of Palestinian society has put the Palestinian woman in a number of contradictory positions. First, she has had to confront displacement due to the massive Jewish refugee settlement movement that led to the creation of the State of Israel. This uprooting affected the economic base that sustained basic cultural values, including gender roles and the division of labor. Without the benefit of a normal process of adjustment allowing the development of new roles within society, Palestinian women, from all sectors of the society, have found themselves forced to step out of their domestic cocoon into the unfamiliar terrain of social and political activism, sometimes even into participation in military operations. I would emphasize, though, that their activism is an aspect of the general national movement. Though Palestinian society needs women's active participation, its various institutions have not gone through the stages of development necessary to facilitate more effective and continuous participation of the female sector. Palestinian women's participation has been thought of in terms of traditional values, not redefined by the intensity of political conditions and the severity of the economic reality.

To conclude, I will offer two stories that exemplify the compounding of military violence by social victimization. Fatma got married at the age of sixteen. Her husband was wanted by the IDF (Israeli Defense Force) and was later killed. She was then pregnant with their second child and, therefore, forced to move back to her family, returning to their control. Fatma decided to take revenge for her husband's death. She joined the faction her husband used to belong to, the PFLP (Popular Front for the Liberation of Palestine), and, because of her political activities, she was imprisoned for a few months. Her imprisonment was a severe shock to her family, and they were very angry with her. As a result, they regularly beat Fatma and her children. Fatma, however, decided to continue the struggle despite the pressure and cruelties from her family towards her and her children. She was imprisoned a second time for more than five years. Fatma had to leave her two children behind with her mother. They kept visiting her in prison. "I felt guilty. Every time they visited me, I felt how sad they were. Their eyes full of tears and sadness. They kept asking me: 'Why did you leave us on our own?'" When Fatma was released, she started to question many things: she no longer covered her head, she wanted freedom to move and to join meetings and political activities. These ideas were not accepted by her family. She was, and still is, beaten and humiliated by her brothers. Fatma's daughter was forced to marry at the age of fourteen, against her will. Fatma has tried to commit suicide many times.

Sometimes, women suffer abuses such as political repression in ways that are similar to those inflicted on men. But since the dominant image of the political actor in our world is male, the problem for women is visibility.

Samiha, twenty years old, was beyond tears; dry eyes, a tense little face, and a child's body. She couldn't make herself tell me what had happened. I had to coax the words out of her, one by one. "I was married at the age of sixteen. It was an arranged marriage like most marriages. I moved to join his family in their home. One week later I was in despair. He used to beat me with plastic pipes. I was locked in the toilet, unable to move, night after night. I kept knocking on the door the whole night calling for help. His mother also joined him in beating me sometimes. When they started they did not stop until I was bleeding. I lost weight, teeth, and hair. Once I was locked in the pigeons' cage for the whole night. My husband was imprisoned before we got married. Everything he experienced in prison, he used against me. He pulled out my nails. He banged my head on the wall. I decided to run away. The moment I entered my family home, my sister fainted. I had changed so much. Was this really the beautiful bride from six months ago?"

Asserting their position, following many years of sacrifice and struggle, women have realized that they have not made many social and political gains and are doubly burdened, both by new political and economic responsibilities and by the traditional view that they should be subservient to men. Thus the Intifada has brought about basic changes in the way women themselves view their role in the political movement.

Dear sisters, what we need and are calling for is a just peace, respect as human beings, and freedom.

NOTE

1. *Al Quds* is a daily Palestinian newspaper, published in Jerusalem and distributed in Gaza and the West Bank.

CHAPTER 3

From Reverence to Rape
An Anthropology of Ethnic and Genderized Violence

VESNA KESIC

Ethnic nationalisms have historically been present in the region of former Yugoslavia, either in latent form or as open conflict. But so has the coexistence of multifaith, multilingual, and multiethnic societies of the region, which was reinforced as a practice and as a political structure in multiethnic, socialist Yugoslavia. "The fall of the Berlin Wall," the discrediting (internally and externally) of the historical socialist project(s), the exhaustion of its utopian energies, and weak, "noncompetitive" socialist economies—all that, and specifically Yugoslav conditions—created the context in which the "partition of Yugoslavia" and the war happened. In brief, as to the main causes of the breakup of Yugoslavia, Susan Woodward points to the disintegration of governmental authority and the breakdown of civil and political order.[1] Woodward is right when she states that under the circumstances: "There is no need for any history of ethnic animosity or civil war to predict growing uncertainty, social chaos, and potential violence."[2] But neither can mere political analyses explain how these political conditions were transformed into violence— that is, how the "potential violence" became real.

Many aspects of the wars that appeared in sequence from 1991 to 1999 bear the characteristics of "dirty wars." The term originates in Latin America and implies the emergence of physical and psychological terrorism unleashed against the civilian population. A "culture of terror" is

An early version of this chapter was published in Croatia as "Od stovanja do silovanja." Kruh i ruze Zenska Infoteka, Zagreb 1994, and was translated for Warreport, Institute for War and Peace Reporting, London 1995.

created, which can be traced to political formations, groups, and the state. Although the wars in Yugoslavia eventually came to be known as wars between states—due to international recognition of the sovereignty of Yugoslav successor states—they did not begin as such. The cultures of terror and fear were actually created some time before the outbreak of the "proper" war. Unexplained "flows of refugees," occasional extrajudicial killings, threats to civilian populations, disappearances, the appearance of paramilitary groups and armed civilians—all that, combined with the heated nationalistic rhetoric of the state-controlled media and the graphic, detailed presentation of alleged "massacres," without clear information about "who massacred whom"—became a part of daily reality in the contested Yugoslav republics. No clear line between regular armies and paramilitary groups was established for a long time. Civilians and so-called ordinary people participated at large, as victims and as perpetrators. War conventions and customs of war were not respected.

However, in the case of Yugoslavia, most analysts agree, ethnonationalisms, induced and invoked by ethnically based nation-building, political projects, created the space for incredibly brutal and violent war (Denitch 1994).

The fact of the massive rape of women and other forms of the "sexualization of war" (men have been raped and sexually humiliated, too) as a part of that terror has been acknowledged and described by several sources and authors.[3] Most of them choose to attribute sexual military violence against women to the ethnically centered notion of the genocidal aims of Serbian war "rationale." Rape is seen as part of a deliberate, carefully planned tactical military operation within the strategy of ethnic cleansing. In the words of Catherine MacKinnon, "This is ethnic rape as an official policy of war . . . rape under orders; not out of control, under control" (MacKinnon 1993). I want to argue that such a restricted approach obscures the understanding of gender-specific forms of war violence. It again positions women only within the nation, the ethnic group, and patriarchy without questioning the potentials for violence within those positions.[4] It does not offer a nuanced explanation of gender-specific forms of military violence, nor can it explain how and why sexual violence against women gets implicated in wars and/or ethnic conflicts.

While discussing problems of meaning in the violent events of the Partition of India, Veena Das articulates the question as follows: "How is it that the imagining of the project of nationalism in India came to include the appropriation of bodies of women as objects on which the desire for nationalism could be brutally inscribed and a memory for the future made (Das 1997)?" The question can be formulated in a similar way for former Yugoslavia—with all due differences—especially because violence against women was inflicted by all the warring sides (ethnic groups) and factions, although not at the same rate.[5] How did the space for the most brutal violence against women and against different ethnicities get created, and how were Others—"women" and "Muslims/Croats/Serbs"—constructed such that the "desire for nationalism . . . became metamorphosed into sexual violence (Das 1997, 69)?"

I will analyze discourses about woman, her appearance in the public and cultural realm as a symbol and metaphor, and the changes in that (symbolic) status of woman within growing ethnic nationalisms. The symbolic status of woman, her use and presentation in metaphoric language, will be compared with her social position as revealed in the legal and economic systems of two different moments: under socialist rule and during the changes that were enacted with the upsurge of nationalisms. I will also look at how the rhetoric and narratives of nationalistic political projects pertained to the symbolization, creation, and re-creation of gender stereotypes, and how it might have contributed to genderized violence at the hand of armed combatants. In particular, the Croatian media, political campaigns, and nationalistic rhetoric will be analyzed. Similar studies should be conducted in other parts of former Yugoslavia (FR Yugoslavia, Bosnia and Herzegovina, Slovenia). To get the full picture, those studies should be compared and contrasted.

Feminist authors (and not only they) have researched and demonstrated structural and cultural congruity between nationalism and patriarchy (Brownmiller 1986; Yuval-Davis & Anthias 1989; Reardon 1996). Both structures appear "natural" and imply domination, fixed hierarchy, superiority, exclusivity and exclusion, actual divisiveness and isolation, silencing of Others, territorialization, and conquering of bodies and territories. Stanley Tambiah, in his article, "Obliterating 'Other' in Former Yugoslavia," analyzing the mass rape of women, states: "The entrenched tradition of patrilineage-affirming feuding and waging vendettas strengthens the use of women merely as pawns in the politics of identity, and merely as possessors of a procreative sexuality appropriated by the nationalist imperative" (Tambiah 1997). The forms of violence inflicted against women in wars vary in form, scale, and intensity from killing, rape, torture, forced impregnation, body searches at checkpoints, imprisonment, settlement in concentration camps and refuges, and forced prostitution to verbal insults and degradation, psychological suffering for losses, and the burden of responsibility that women carry as survivors. It is important to note that women's groups from different parts of former Yugoslavia also reported increases and changes in modes of domestic violence during the war. Women were attacked by their partners with guns and knives and even killed in the streets with hand grenades (Autonomous Women's House, Zagreb, Autonomous Women's Center, Belgrade, Medica Zenica).

German historian Mechthild Rumpf, building upon Hannah Arendt's political analyses of the nation-state's sovereignty and violence, argues that the state's monopoly on violence, as formulated by Weber and other classical state theorists, was, from the beginning, a myth as far as its bearing on patriarchy in family and gender relations. Through patriarchal marriage and family, which, from the Enlightenment on, are seen as civilizing—as instances of social-order—violence remained structurally anchored in society: "In monopolized violence, the everyday violence of patriarchy went on" states Rumpf (Rumpf 1992).[6] Carole Pateman similarly argues that the sexual contract, which precedes even the patriarchal contract as described by Hobbes, Locke, and Rousseau, gives to the "fraternity" of men the right to women and sex (Pateman 1988). Thus, not all the violence comes from the state, although, especially in this century, we have witnessed how much nationalism, militarism, and the military industry can contribute to the mobilization of violence. But state-enacted violence in wars, combined with social-patriarchal violence, should be held responsible for gender-specific forms of war violence.

In former Yugoslavia, on the level of state formations and institutions, patriarchy was obscured within the ideology of equality and equity being enacted by socialism. At the same time, within families and in everyday gender relations, patriarchal structures and norms remained strong (Sklevicky 1997). As soon as nationalistic political projects came to power after the first multiparty elections (1990), even before they were able to change social structures and institutions, nationalists started to implement changes in all levels of the symbolic order. For instance, the Yugoslav Academy of Science and Arts, founded in Zagreb over a century ago by Catholic Bishop J. J. Strossmayer, who was known for his support of the idea of the unification of all Southern Slavs in one state, was renamed the Croation Academy of Science and Arts. The old pro-Yugoslav ideology was dissolved—its historical origins erased and silenced. Ethnic nationalists and their political proponents called for the reinterpretation of historical events, reopened hardly healed old wounds, and emphasized and absolutized cultural and religious differences that had been repressed under the former regime. Collective identities were appealed to and contested at the same time.

Language itself, which gives the names and shapes to memories, was to undergo radical changes. "Renewal" and "cleansing" of the language meant restoring archaic forms that were presented as "pure Croatian," our original "mother tongue," uncontaminated by socialism, "Yugoslavism," or the linguistic characteristics of other ethnicities. The performative force of language was utilized in a very literal way. One could even argue that language was used like a magical power for performing changes.

Before the outbreak of the war and during the war, the dynamic of military activities and terror was entwined with the struggle for interpretation and meaning, projected or derived from the past, the present, and the future. The most apparent examples of this "war for meanings" are the different names/identifications that different people and agencies, local and international, use to name these wars: "civil war," "wars for independence," "separatist wars," "homeland (heimat) war(s)," "ethnic wars in former Yugoslavia," etc. The war in Croatia (1991–1992) was, from the Croatian side, officially defined as a defensive war, but simultaneously it was presented and symbolized as a "holy war" of Croats for "the realization of the thousand years' long dream" of national sovereignty and as a war for the establishment of "our own" state, one that will be politically and culturally different from that of the neighboring nations. The notion that ethnic character ultimately embodies the state was subsumed and reinforced through a nationalistic interpretation of history.

Among the first public images that were to be re-conceptualized was the image of woman. Or, to be more precise, the new national identity of woman had to be created and reinstalled. The question that poses itself first concerns the general image or identity of a "Yugoslav Woman." How was she represented in the media and popular culture, or by official education, which was under state control? It is rather difficult to answer that question. During the first years of Yugoslav socialism (1945–1948), the Soviet social realist representation of woman as a "comrade worker" or a *kolhoz* woman dominated public space (posters, children's texts and coloring books, political propaganda and popular culture alike).[7] But such imagery was abandoned already in the early fifties and, since then, "a Yugoslav woman" has become more and more a void, or at least a very eclectically filled space in Yugoslav ideology and adjoining symbolic imagery. The official slogans of the Yugoslav social and economic experiment were "brotherhood and unity," and "socialist self-management." Political rituals and imagery, constructed to maintain the social "glue" of an officially multicultural and egalitarian society, were maintained long after they lost any actual meaning and real content in people's everyday lives.

The economic position of women in the Yugoslav mixed economy was ambiguous. Women composed about 40 percent of the labor force, which means that overall employment of women was higher than average in Western European countries. The principle of equal wages was proclaimed by law, and the social infrastructure to assist working mothers was developed (kindergartens, pre-school, and after school care). At the same time, women made up almost 90 percent of the employees in low-profit industries (textile and chemical manufacturing) and services like tourism, where wages were considerably lower than in, for example, the heavy metal or mining industries that employed almost exclusively men. National legislation concerning the equal status of women was pretty progressive by the 1980s and favorable to women, although there were some differences among individual republics. Abortion was decriminalized and accessible as of 1978, single mothers were guaranteed many rights and benefits, the rights of children born out of wedlock were fully recognized, and nonmarital relationships were basically equalized in status with marriage, though only for heterosexuals.

In contrast to the public realm, the private sphere, such as the household division of labor and responsibilities, or women's rights within it, was not a concern of the state or legislation. Domestic violence was not addressed legislatively. There were no restraining orders or similar provisions for women and children victims of domestic violence, and there were no specialized family courts. Domestic violence was not an issue in public debates until the late '80s. Overall violence against women and daily sexism were even less so. Although traditional patriarchy was seemingly destroyed through quick modernization in socialist Yugoslavia, patriarchal structures and gender relations were at work—somewhat undercover in public and completely unquestioned in the private sphere. Unproblematized gender relations remained a source of silenced violence in the private sphere, although women did maintain some kind of "private power," or power of resistance within the family. One of the proverbial sayings in many regions of Croatia goes: a woman holds three corners of the house, meaning that women are "in power" at home. (During the election campaigns after 1990, feminists reformulated this saying, "We want to exchange one corner of the house for a seat in Parliament.") Yugoslav ideological egalitarianism as the official norm wiped away many differences and hindered many conflicts, gender among them. The so-called "women's question" was simply lost within the proclaimed ideology of egalitarianism.

Yugoslavia was, as is well known, a mixed economy. Some kind of market system was established within the country through the system of self-management, but it never fully entered the world market, as a consequence of both external and internal limitations.[8] As a consequence, the Yugoslav market was a very confused phenomenon, limited to the national economy, but with the abundant penetration of consumer goods from the West.

All this affected the way in which women were represented, especially in the world of mass media and popular culture that actually shapes contemporary stereotypes and prevailing images. From the 1970s on, Western commercial principles and consumerism penetrated fully into the everyday life of Yugoslav society. We had it all—beauty contests, soft porn, the import and advertising of cosmetics and other beauty industry merchandise. Women's popular magazines were a mixture of beauty-youth-fashion-cooking recipes—"liberated" female images of sexuality. At the same time, no significant women's movement or feminist questioning of gender relations within our societies existed. Consumerism of limited power (limited because of the limited power of the national economy) was the prevailing ideology of everyday life. It was well supported and tolerated by state policy.[9]

At any rate, the notion of woman was "liberalized" and "Westernized." In a way, such a notion did pertain to some classes and social groups, especially to the middle-class urban women, but it was very distant from the experience of a vast majority of men and women who still lived under conditions between traditional and modernized industrial society. The huge gap between rural and urban cultures and life-styles completely disappeared from sight and critical research. Yugoslav society was represented merely by its urban and middle-class version. Although it is difficult to infer any direct connection between this insight and the appearance of wartime violence against women, a correspondence should be noticed. The majority of abuses of women happened in rural areas, and perpetrators were recognized as paramilitaries recruited from patriarchal rural or poor suburban areas.

As the political and cultural accents shifted toward ethnic and national exclusivity, the traditional patriarchal stereotypes embodying the traditional roles of woman as mother, wife, nurturer (and somehow also a virgin, which, as we shall see, easily metamorphoses into a whore and a sinner) surfaced in public discourse. Concepts such as "Mother homeland," "Mother nurturer," "Mother earth," "Croatia, a proud woman," and similar terms that equate woman with her biological, procreative function and with a mythical territoriality, imbued not only Croatian lyric and poetic language, but also the political and legal language of the new nation-state building forces. At the beginning of the war, the image of beautiful young women in military uniform also appeared in the mass media as a part of propaganda for warmongering and national homogenization. The "inclusion" of women started through contradictory representations. And, as I shall demonstrate, the potential for violence was written into these contradictory constructions, whether they were "our women," or "their women."

The Catholic Church became very active and visible, promulgating its own doctrine of women. At the same time, the state promoted its "Program of Demographic and Spiritual Renewal," which formulated a precise pro-natalist, pro-life, ethnic-oriented population growth.[10] The program was announced by the president of the state as "nonpartisan" and "nonpolitical," but of a national scope and importance: "a range of symbols and ways of thinking of the highest importance for the Croat State." Women's role was termed "Mother-Nurturer"; men's role was termed "guarantor of family's and national well-being" (Agency for Renewal 1997). The ban on abortion was one of the first publicly led campaigns by government and church in concert. Everything happened at an unprecedented rate.

Let me demonstrate with one particular case how easily the religiously and nationalistically exalted symbolic image of woman and its corresponding stereotype can change from that of virgin/mother/virtue to one that signifies sin or weakness (from a "Holy Virgin" to "Magdalena"). A year after euphoric celebrations on the occasion of declaring independence (June 1991) and less than six months after the international recognition of Croatian sovereignty (January 1992), in the summer of 1992, people in Croatia were confronted with the painful results of war. At that time, Croatia was "losing the war," more than a third of the territory was "occupied"[11] by local Serbs, and the international community was not yet willing to support and legitimize Croatian military intervention (that happened only in '94 and '95).

The status of "no peace-no war" that appeared in early 1992, after an internationally imposed cease-fire, led to disappointment and frustration. The public figure of a nationalistic poet/warrior—whose voice was strong from the beginning of nationalist insurgence—suddenly changed his heroic, victorious language into an angry, victimized loser's lament. The mode of involving women's image in nationalistic rhetoric changed simultaneously. The columnist of a widely-circulated national weekly proclaimed Croatia to be a "Fallen Woman" (Ivkosic 1992). In his whining article, the motherland abruptly turned into a dubious immoral and disgraced woman. "Croatia experienced," said the columnist, "a moral collapse, something that only a woman can experience because there are no loose men. Only a loose woman surrenders without a fight and takes this as inevitable destiny, as fate. Men, however, put up a fight." He goes on and on describing, with exalted passion, the moral and constitutional nothingness of women. I would say that in such discourse not only was the implied symbol of woman quickly changed—from that of the virgin/mother/nurturer to that of a fallen, cheap woman/whore—but also the responsibility (for losing the war) was shifted from men to women. Through such transformation of symbols, the potential for violence described earlier becomes ever nearer to empirical violence.

To clarify, the women of "Others," that is, Serbian and Muslim women, were already stereotyped, attacked, and sexually insulted, as were Croat women if they were perceived as political adversaries.[12] And there had always been differences in the depiction of male and female adversaries. Men, attacked for their ethnic background, had their political or ideological standpoint always kept in focus. Their "masculinity," sexual histories, or sheer bodily constitution were never questioned, even when they had allegedly or really committed a sexual crime. Women's sexuality, on the other hand, was always targeted, even when their ethnicity or political standpoint was the aim of the campaign. But now at stake was the symbolic representation of women in general, that is, their use as reproducers of ethnic-ideological constructs (Anthias and Yuval-Davis 1989). In short, all women became endangered—"our women" because they have been invested with a collective desire whose magnitude they prove unable properly to reflect and "their women," because they have been constructed as equally magnified counter-images, which resist or threaten our images. This is how women's bodies become, first symbolic, then real battlefields, where all kinds of violence can be inflicted on them.

When the world and local media started to spread the news about mass rapes in Bosnia (summer 1992), popular writing immediately sublimated the terrible experience and suffering of concrete women and turned it into ethnic metaphors. Although the majority of the victims of Serb rapes in Bosnia were Muslim women, and there were no registered mass rapes during the war in Croatia, Croatian nationalist rhetoric was mostly concerned with Croatian victims, implying that "the rape of a Croat woman stood for the rape of Croatia." On rare occasions the alliance in victimhood was established: "I would not permit anyone to talk about a raped Croat or Muslim woman while failing to mention the raped Croatia or raped Bosnia" (Corak 1993). Through the mystic unity of woman, land, and nation, the land and the nation were as much violated as the body of a particular woman. A unique human being with a unique experience of suffering disappeared and was turned into a powerful national symbol.

The incorrect assertion that these crimes were unique and unprecedented in history was repeatedly made. This reinforced the exclusion, outcast status, and dehumanization of the Other. This differentiation implicated not only individual perpetrators and those who caused the war— politicians, generals, and possible strategists of systematic campaigns of rape and ethnic cleansing, but, in effect, the entire nation, the population as a whole, including women. This construction of Otherness and of nonresolvable differences created the symbolic space that preceded real exclusion and expulsion. As Veena Das states: "Such acts of totalisation seem to be normal characteristics of times of collective violence; they are also apparent in the processes of ethnic and religious mobilization in the service of violence" (Das 1998). The following example (one of many among dominating rhetorics) illustrates the process. Sometime in mid-1993, the Croatian state commission "Documenta Croatica,"[13] researching and documenting war crimes (exclusively against Croats in Bosnia and Croatia), published a series of articles by Croat writers and intellectuals. Here we can read: "The Serbian people are outside the context of civilization, which is founded on Judeo-Christian morality. They have remained in the darkness of the godless world, it is definitely second-rate, and different" (Coruk 1993). Here we can see that it was not enough to see Serbs as demonized enemies of a specific nation. If ethnic cleansing was to be performed, Serbs had to be constructed as ultimately different, the Other that cannot be integrated under any condition, that must be excluded from the entire "civilized world." The paradox of this statement is so extreme as to make it absurd. First, since only Judeo-Christianity is recognized as a context of civilization, the statement implies a global cultural racism. Second, it wittingly and voluntarily excludes the dominant Serbian religion, Orthodox Christianity, from Christianity. A third, and major, paradox is that such statements started to appear when the conflict between Croats and Bosniacs took place, involving mutual violence and atrocities against civilians on both sides.[14] The political and military background of the armed conflict was the Croatian conquest of Bosnian territories. Until mid-1993, everyone was fighting everyone else in Bosnia-Herzegovina. Armed conflicts between different nationalities emerged, but sometimes so did conflicts among members of the same ethnic groups who had different political interests. Rapes took place along similar lines.

Veena Das concludes her article on the social production of hate by stating that it can give birth to discourses and practices of genocide, but there are special conditions through which such transformations become possible: "My *fear of the other* is transformed into the notion *that the other is fearsome*" (Das 1998). And what could we fear more than those who are outcasts of our most universal values and from the whole of civilization.[15]

Das also demonstrates how such transformation is bound to the perception of important past events as "unfinished" and capable of molding the present in new and unpredictable ways. Recalling and (re)interpreting an "unfinished past," not integrated into a stable understanding, was a permanent, maybe even dominant, means of producing hate, fear, and mistrust among peoples of former Yugoslavia. Some Bosnian women who were raped or tortured by Serb militants reported that perpetrators often called them "bule" or "balije," which are the traditional names for women who, during the Ottoman invasion, converted to Islam. According to the popular Serbian mythology, converted Christians, "janjicarke," were even more cruel persecutors than Turks were. Thus we see an example of the historical memory of five-hundred-year-old "unfinished businesses," disengaged from the troublesome past and now entangled in ethnicized and genderized military violence.

What I am trying to demonstrate is that two master meta-narratives appeared in the Yugoslav wars simultaneously—one about the victimization of women, another about ethnicity. They both performed stereotyping and totalization, denying people subjectivities and human faces (dehumanization). In this context, the two meta-narratives tend to become entangled and to merge. National identity—whether a victorious or victimized one—was, on a grand scale, constructed over woman's body. The raped woman is also a fallen woman; her symbol calls for revenge, incites the willingness to fight, but also victimizes women and inspires violence against women. Reducing women to extreme patriarchal stereotypes (of virgin or whore) and comparing a raped woman to the disgraced country are a part of the process of creating utterly different Others, whether from the "second sex" or from different ethnicities. Both Others have to be segregated, excluded, exorcised, and expelled from the healthy body of the nation-state, which is conceived as the organic unity of the people of a certain ethnicity, religion, territory, and nationalistic leadership *(ein Fuhrer, ein Volk und ein wahrer Glaube)*. In the situation of war, symbolically only one species can enjoy full sovereignty, citizenship, and rights within such a unity. This is the national male warrior who uses rape as a war weapon.

NOTES

1. Woodward, Susan L. 1995, *Balkan Tragedy: Chaos and Dissolution after the Cold War*, Brooking Institution Press, Washington, D.C.

2. See Susan Woodward's article, "Violence-Prone Area or International Transition? Adding the Role of Outsiders in Balkan Violence," which accurately explains the political processes preceding the war and the collapse of Yugoslavia (unpublished, conference paper).

3. Main documents: EC Investigative Commission's Report "Rape and Sexual Abuse of Women in Bosnia-Herzegovina," Bruxelles, February 1993; Tadeusz Mazowiecki's Report to secretary general, February 1993; U.N. Human Rights Commission: "Rape and Abuse of Women in the Territory of Former Yugoslavia," February 1993. Authors: Stiglmayer 1994, Gutman 1993, Vranic 1996, Allen 1996.

4. See Anthias and Yuval-Davis (1989) for the process of legitimizing and institutionalizing gender hierarchies in the nation-state in five categories.

5. The differences in numbers are important in a legal and political analysis (war crimes, etc), but the process of creating violence is the same.

6. On that issue, see also Carole Pateman's criticism of Hobbes's, Locke's, and Rousseau's "contractualism." Pateman sees the patriarchal contract between man and woman as preceding any social contract (1988).

7. The well-known sculpture "Kolhoznik and Working Woman" by the Soviet sculptor Vera Muchina, which appeared on Mosfilm features, is a typical example of such monumental and representative state-sponsored art.

8. As external limits I see the economic barriers imposed by the EC on socialist economies; the internal limit was the domestic economy itself, still in various modes controlled by the state.

9. Some explanations say that the high level of social security provided by the state (through "artificial" employment, health, and retirement schemes) combined with consumerism and citizen's liberties, which were greater than in other socialist countries, secured social and political peace. At the same time, proper freedoms and any questioning of the power relations, including patriarchy, were forbidden and swept under the carpet.

10. The Ministry for the Renewal of the Republic of Croatia was established in May 1992. The public campaign for its agenda was launched at least a year before that.

11. I am putting this word in quotation marks because I found the state-promoted official term, "occupied," to be a dubious one. A Serbian ethnic population has inhabited these territories for a century. The breakup of Yugoslavia has resulted in a change in their constitutional status and turned them into a minority in

Croatia. The state, at that time, was unwilling even to recognize their political and cultural rights, which was a primary motive for their rebellion and occupation of territories.

12. The case of the "Witches from Rio" became internationally known when five women writers and journalists were accused of "national treachery" because of their antinationalistic writing. They were accused of a variety of crimes, but the reason for their political standpoint was represented by the state as their ugly, sexually-frustrated feminism. (See: Meredith Tax, 1993, "Five Women Who Won't Be Silenced," *The Nation*.)

13. Even the use of the Latin name is significant in the function of underlining the differences from Serbian language.

14. "Bosniac" is the ethnic-religious denomination that Bosnian Muslims chose after Bosnia-Herzegovina achieved sovereignty.

15. In 1997 the Serbian Academy of Science (SANU) issued a well-known, although somewhat phantom, document, "Memorandum." It outlined the origins and present conditions of alleged cultural, political, and national threats and the oppression of the Serbian nation within Yugoslavia. The notion of a widespread "international conspiracy" against Serbs, embodied in the alliance of the Vatican, Islam, and socialism, imposed on Serbs by late President Tito, who was a Croat, was also implied. The "Memorandum" unfortunately gained popularity and influenced numerous Serbs, becoming an underpinning program of Milosevic's politics.

REFERENCES

Allen, Beverly. 1996. *Rape Warfare: The Hidden Genocide in Bosnia-Herzegovina and Croatia*. Minneapolis: University of Minnesota Press.

Brownmiller, Susan. 1986. *Against Our Will: Men, Women, and Rape*. New York: Penguin Books.

Corak, Zeljka. 1993. "Children of Paradise." In *Mass Rapes as War Crimes*. Zagreb: Documenta Croatica.

Croatian Government's Agency for Renewal. 1992. "Spiritual Renewal of Croatia." Zagreb.

Das, Veena. 1997. "Language and Body: Transactions in the Construction of Pain." In *Social Suffering*, edited by A. Kleineman, V. Das, and M. Lock. Berkeley and Los Angeles: University of California Press.

———. 1 November 1998. "Specificities: Official Narratives, Rumor, and the Social Production of Hate," *Social Identities* 4.

Denitch, Bogdan. 1994. *Ethnic Nationalism: The Tragic Death of Yugoslavia*. Minneapolis: University of Minnesota Press.

Gutman, Roy. 1993. *A Witness to Genocide*. New York: Macmillan.

Ivkosic, Milan. 1992. *Hrvatksa, posrnula zena*. Globus.

MacKinnon, Catherine. 1993. "Turning Rape into Pornography: Postmodern Genocide," *Ms. Magazine* July/August: 24–27.

————. 1994. "On Human Rights: The Oxford Amnesty Lectures," *Hastings Woman's Law Journal* 5.

Pateman, Carole. 1988. *The Sexual Contract*. Stanford: Stanford University Press.

Reardon, Betty. 1996. *Sexism and the War System*. New York: Syracuse University Press.

Rumpf, Mechthild. 1992. "Staatliches Gewaltmonopol, Nationale Souverenanitat und Krieg," *L'Home. Zeitschrift fur Feministische Geschihtswissenschaft*, "Krieg" 3. Jg.Heft 1. Bohlau Verlag.

Sklevicky, Lydia. 1997. "Zene, Konji, ratnici." Zagreb: Zenska Infoteka.

Stiglmayer, Alexandra. 1994. *Mass Rape: War Against Women in Bosnia-Herzegovina*. Lincoln: University of Nebraska Press.

Tambiah, Stanley. 1997. "Obliterating 'Other' in Former Yugoslavia," *Nethra* 1:2 (Jan–March): 7–36.

Tax, Meredith. 1993. "Five Women Who Won't Be Silenced." *The Nation*.

Vranic, Seada. 1996. "Pred zidom sutnje," Antibarbarus. Zagreb.

Woodward, Susan L. 1995. *Balkan Tragedy: Chaos and Dissolution after the Cold War*. Washington, D.C.: Brooking Institution Press.

————. "Violence-Prone Area or International Transition? Adding the Role of Outsiders in Balkan Violence." Unpublished conference paper.

Yuval-Davis, Nira and Floya Anthias, eds. 1989. *Woman-Nation-State*. New York: St. Martin's Press.

CHAPTER 4

Laughter, Tears, and Politics—Dialogue
How Women Do It

VESNA KESIC AND LEPA MLADJENOVIC

Seventeen women from Belgrade and Zagreb met from March 17–20, 1995 in Medulin, Istria. The aim was for feminists and activists to exchange experiences, to free frozen feelings toward one another, and to restore women's political dialogue. All participants were members of women's groups with a long tradition of cooperation who, in the course of this war, have been oriented toward the politics of peace, nonviolence, and opposition to war, militarism, and nationalist sowing of hate.

The process of dialogue began with practice in active listening: how to listen without intervening and advancing one's thoughts before the other finished her story, how to disentangle ourselves from subject matter, interpretation, and a priori judgment and enable a woman's story to emerge before us. We tried to show that lives in different surroundings create different experiences and different perceptions of events.

We started well and so we proceeded. We created a discourse on differences. The good will of women to listen to one another and the desire to be heard remained present. We started with questions. Women from Belgrade wanted their sisters from Zagreb to hear and know why some of them were already crying on the bus to Zagreb. Some women from Zagreb wanted their sisters from Belgrade to know why they had decided "never again in Belgrade." We asked one another what we wanted to know and what our mutual expectations were.

The majority of women who took part in the Istrian dialogue had met over these last years at various international meetings and conferences. For all our desire for sisterly cooperation and solidarity, these meetings did not always take place without pain or encumbrance. It was

necessary to answer some questions. Could we participate there as individuals or as representatives of our groups? The answer: both, depending
on how and when. Could we be representatives of our nations? Naturally,
no! Are we guilty for what our governments' politics perpetrated? Not in
the least! But we were conscious of the responsibility for our own political work in our environment.

What if incidents and disagreements sprang up between us? If we
hurt one another, that was not our intention. Maybe because of the international "throng" we weren't able to honestly hear and listen. In intensive and concentrated conversation by the sea, it wasn't hard to arrive at
consensus: it's useful to constantly validate our own statements and test
our impressions. Every disagreement or incident increases distrust and
fear, which can easily build up to the level of conflict.

There was discussion about many other things. We heard the stories
of women from mixed marriages and their problems with male children
who yielded to military call-ups. We listened to stories of families divided by borders, nations, ideologies, of close ones who lost their lives in
this war or the previous one, and of the graveyards of friendship. We told
one another the stories of our hopes, illusions, delusions, mistakes, fears,
and successes.

What was important to us? Women's dialogue starts from personal
stories and arrives at the political level. Women's dialogue starts from
tears and laughter, from five hours of singing in an Istrian tavern, from
the level of "mother/father/I," from childhood and our grandmother's
story. Women's dialogue begins and returns to our own experience of
war, genocide, home, land, nation, and then develops into an exchange of
our political ideas and positions on the questions of Krajina, Kosovo,
Jasenovac, Bleiburg, mass rape of women. Then, together, we ask how
much do our personal stories determine who we are and how much do we
want them to prevail over us? We wonder how to balance between the
continuity of the personal history of our ancestors and discontinuity of
the political decisions that we alone have to make.

Yes, then we ask ourselves the same question together, and we
laugh, cry, and sing together and think up new projects: when and how
will we include other women in this dialogue, which is as necessary to us
as bread (and roses)?

In this feminist dialogue of women from Croatia and Serbia and Is-
tria, women participated from the following groups: Antiwar campaign
Croatia, Arkadija, Autonomous Women's House, Autonomous Women's
Center Against Sexual Violence, B.a.B.e., Belgrade Women's Lobby,

Center for Girls, Center for Women War Victims, Homo, SOS Telephone, Zagreb Women's Lobby, Women's Studies Belgrade, Women's Studies Zagreb, and Women in Black. Sisterly support and organization of the gathering was provided by human rights activists from Istria. For organizational and financial help and moral support, we thank women from the Delphi/STAR project.

CHAPTER 5

The Opposite of War Is Not Peace—It Is Creativity

ZORICA MRSEVIC

AN INTERESTING QUESTION

An interesting question was raised recently: Did the civil war in the former Yugoslavia cause an increase in domestic violence, or did domestic violence cause the war? The usual position of feminists in Belgrade is that the war, along with the economic, political, and social crises, produced an increase in domestic violence (Mrsevic 1994). Some representative facts support this view:

1. Unemployed husbands "lost" their dominant position, "lost face" as breadwinners. Some began to drink and to beat family members.
2. Waves of domestic violence characterize so-called "post-television news syndrome" (violent behavior following the broadcast of inflammatory war propaganda).[1]
3. Young men returning from the battlefield started to assault members of their families.
4. Men behaved violently after visiting certain restaurants for war veterans.[2]
5. More and more previously decent people became involved in criminal activities. Hooked by vague expectations of earning a lot of money in a short time, they became caught up in increasingly violent criminal activities.
6. Many unemployed people survived by smuggling everyday staple items or by selling smuggled goods. Because smuggling was

dominated by Mafia-style organizations, these people were
drawn unintentionally into violent criminal activity (Hughes and
Mrsevic 1997, 101, 128).

But I would propose that each of these examples points to secondary
sources of violence (Mrsevic 1996, 220, 327). The primary, or structural,
source is built into the very foundation of patriarchal Serbian society
(and many others) (Mrsevic 1994, 99). In a patriarchal society, a model
of aggressive masculinity is not only tolerated but encouraged
(Schechter 1982, 27). This aggressiveness expresses itself in a wide
range of violent deeds, including morally justified domestic violence.
Patriarchal societies are often characterized by a lack of institutional response and an absence of legal provisions concerning domestic violence.
Such a context is ripe for the proliferation of all types of violence. Thus,
violence is both a symptom of patriarchy and its cause, both a typical
consequence of patriarchy and one of the most effective means to maintain a patriarchal system, both a consequence of war and one of its
causes. Domestic violence is therefore caught in a vicious circle of mutual consequence and causation, along with patriarchy and war.

So the query, "did the war cause domestic violence or did domestic
violence cause the war?" looks similar to the famous chicken and egg
question. The most likely answer is that both were caused by a third
phenomenon: patriarchal society with all its supporting structures. Not
only did the war contribute to the increase of domestic violence in Serbia, but also domestic violence against Serbian women contributed significantly to the expansion of violent behavior on the battlefield. It is not
the case that domestic violence alone caused the war in former Yugoslavia. Other reasons were behind the war—political, historical, ethnic,
etc. But what is obvious to Belgrade feminists is that tolerated domestic
violence contributed significantly to the "ease" with which young men
suddenly changed from apparently decent boys to brutal perpetrators of
violent acts.[3]

It has been said that one Lakota Indian in the nineteenth century remarked to another, "Look what they (white men) do to their women and
children! What can we expect them to do to us—the enemy?" The same
question can be posed in former Yugoslavia. It is plausible to imagine
Serbian people asking themselves: "Look what Croat (Muslim) men do
to their wives and children—what can they do to us?" and to imagine
Croat (Muslim) people asking the same question concerning men from
other nations.

Societies with a lack of specific laws dealing with domestic violence and those who tolerate and "legitimate" violent behavior from men experience a high level of street violence or other public manifestations of aggression (*The Special Rapporteur on Violence Against Women* 1995, U.N. Document E/CN. 4/1995/42). The spread of domestic violence into the public domain, a situation which is to be expected if a society does not react appropriately, could even cause a war, as I have proposed in the case of Serbia. This war serves as a warning that if societies do not make clear to violent perpetrators of domestic violence that they cannot continue freely to beat and torture members of their families, violent behavior will increase, within and beyond the home.

Domestic violence therefore comes within the purview of international human rights. Before World War II, there was an egregious infringement of human rights in Germany. At that time, this infringement was considered by the international community to be the internal affair of an independent sovereign country, which was entitled to deal with its citizens according to its internal laws and procedures. After World War II, the international community recognized that the so-called internal affairs that included violations of basic human rights and freedoms had ramifications beyond the borders of their nation of origin, that is, destabilizing the political situation of the whole region and creating a war that was dangerous to the entire industrialized world. The concept of human rights arose from this postwar recognition. An assertion was made that no state has the right to deny human rights and basic freedoms to its citizens and that the international community is entitled to intervene when violations occur. This so-called narrow concept of sovereignty was established together with the concept of human rights. By creating this concept of human rights, the international community expressed a clear and strong desire to end not only future world wars, but also local and regional conflicts.[4]

Domestic violence, it is now being asserted, is a violation and a denial of all human rights, including the most profound right of survival, to particular categories of human beings, namely women, children, the disabled, and the elderly. Like all violations of human rights, domestic violence has a tendency to expand beyond the borders of private houses, creating a publicly visible presence of violence in the society and posing the danger of more and more frequent public acts of violence (*Special Rapporteur* 1995, par. 52; Mrsevic 1997, 84). Domestic violence "teaches" male children to be future perpetrators, providing them role models of violent men (*Special Rapporteur* 1995, par. 64). Domestic violence also "teaches" female children to be future victims, providing them role models of adult women permanently suffering violence at home. Violent men, whose acts of violence in domestic situations are not called to account, feel free to commit violence elsewhere, are encouraged to express their masculinity in violent ways, and feel entitled to solve all kinds of problems by "quick and efficient" violent means. As more and more people become involved in perpetuating the cycle of violence, the society, as a whole, becomes more and more accustomed to violence and brutalized by its ubiquitous presence.

The crux of the problem of reducing domestic violence is its categorization as a "private matter," in which all participants are equally responsible (*Special Rapporteur* 1995, par. 70; Mrsevic 1997, 88). But just as the infringement of human rights in a given country cannot be treated as an "internal affair," neither can domestic violence be treated as "a private family matter." Outside intervention in both cases is not only legitimate but necessary in order to end the violation of human rights. Human rights are not only the rights of abstractly defined citizens, but the rights of women and children as well. As states are responsible for securing the human rights of their citizens, so they are also responsible for securing safe, violence-free homes. Governmental inaction with regard to crimes of violence against women is one of the principle factors in violence against women and children.

BREAKING THE SOUND BARRIER: THE FIRST TASK OF WOMEN'S GROUPS

> *A struggle against power is the struggle of*
> *memory against forgetting.*
> —MOTTO OF BELGRADE FEMINISTS

Belgrade's women's groups are the places where the women and children victims of violence of all kinds can come and give accounts of their experiences. The stories that follow were recorded by Zorica Mrsevic, either in person or via telephone or E-mail communication, during a three-year period of volunteering at the SOS Hotline and at the Autonomous Women's Center Against Sexual Violence. The stories have many similarities: there was no justice for any of the victims, no intervention or protection from any side, and no readiness on anyone's part to listen and believe. The stories reflect the lives of thousands of women of all ages, nationalities, ethnic origins, and educational backgrounds. Like their problems, the women had become invisible (Mrsevic 1995a, 2).

The purpose of storytelling or narrative is twofold: we create a record of experiences with violence and we perform a political action, defying the invisibility of women. Men have created history through writing, noting, registering, and archiving all that has been in their interest. Women's absence from their history ends at the moment when and where we start to write and read our own stories. The stories that deserve to be noticed first are the stories about the most invisible violence, the most invisible sufferings of invisible women.

In the following cases, both the storytellers and the story keepers felt a need to be identified, to be recognized, to be named (Mrsevic 1995b, 94). This was the point of departure in a feminist strategy of resisting hate, prejudice, violence, and discrimination against women, and of exorcising the interiorization of such treatment. It was also a first step in revealing the realities of women's experiences to ourselves and to others—realities that had previously been unknown and ignored (Mrsevic 1995c, 43, 49).

BECOMING VISIBLE CAN MEAN BECOMING VULNERABLE, AS WELL

There were and are moments when we feel so psychically and physically menaced by the patriarchal society that we simply have no choice but to become feminists.[5] Our society found itself in the historical circumstance that men had become lethally dangerous to women, children, and men themselves, endangering nature, the environment, the air, the history, and the future of humankind. That is why we have had to become feminists. Men have become advocates of the status quo, "family value" and "tradition," while minimizing the problems of incest and domestic violence. Silence develops out of their domination of women. Women continue to fight violence against women and the silence it creates by establishing women's groups, creating places and hotlines for counseling, and personally supporting victims and survivors. Feminist-organized groups of women in all the former socialist countries, fighting against both violence and silence, are giving birth to a new civil society.[6]

The struggle against domestic violence must be twofold. The fight must consist of both governmental actions and the initiatives of autonomous women's groups. The latter are responsible for explaining their work so that they are heard by the system without being swallowed by its gender insensitive language and procedures.[7] Our governments must condemn violence against women and use all available instruments of public authority to punish such acts.

ELEVEN STORIES[8]

1. A man intentionally killed his ex-wife with a knife, stabbing her in the breasts and back several times. Although divorced, they shared the same yard. After the divorce, the ex-husband asked the woman to cook and wash and iron his clothes. He also considered it his right to continue to control her private life. Murder was the consequence when he asked her to whom she happened to be taking a cup of coffee. She responded briskly: "It is my business to whom I'll bring coffee." The ex-husband was sentenced to a prison term of ten years.

2. A woman lived with her partner (to whom she was not married) and her mother. The partner had been drinking for several years. During the war he had been in battle and upon returning home, he went completely mad, refusing to deal respectfully with anyone. He had an illegal gun and a large knife. He created chaos in the household, threatening to kill both the woman and her mother. "You won't live till tomorrow morning; first I'll kill your mother before your eyes and then you. . . . " The woman was completely panicked. She did not trust the police: "They will come when everything is over, and that will be too late if he decides to finish us." The story has a fatal ending. One night when he started with a knife toward her mother, the woman killed him with his gun.

3. A: "The sexual abuse began when I was five and when my family moved into a new house, one part of which was already occupied by my uncle and his family. My uncle was, at the time, an active army officer, but he was later dismissed from the army for misbehavior and various serious incidents. I remember, he always had a loaded gun with him. He raped me immediately after we arrived, in a still empty room. We had not even unpacked. From that moment on, he did that frequently, using his loaded gun pointed at my forehead, putting it into my nose, my mouth, my vagina and anus, threatening to shoot me, and that I didn't doubt at all. Once he took me and his daughter to the barracks

where he worked, bought us ice creams, ordered us to sit calmly on the bench in front of the entrance and to watch him 'shoot somebody.' There was a group of soldiers passing by, and he really did shoot, wounding one of them. He later argued that the gun shot accidentally, by mistake, and he was believed mostly because of our presence. I spent all my childhood in permanent fear of him, praying to God that one of us would die, he or I, it didn't matter."[9]

4. E: "I have a common story about my father, similar to many other girls all over the world. Maybe you guessed what it was: incest, of course. The story began when I was six and continued till thirteen without any interruption. As I remember, because I forced myself to forget everything, he always wanted 'it' two to three times a day. I told everything to Mom when I was aware what he did to me. They were unbearable days for me, because I was sent to a clinic 'to recover.' My mother has never thought about getting a divorce. Her only thought was how to protect my father from being accused as a criminal. She was very proud he was never prosecuted, thanks to her."

5. N: "My parents divorced when I was 12, and shortly thereafter I broke off all contact with my father. I hated him, but over the years the pain would fade, and he would suddenly be thrust back into my life, trying to be reconciled with me and denying that anything ever went on. But even my younger brother has started to recall things, and where once before he and father were close, upon remembering things when on his last visit to father's, he witnessed father hitting his stepson, my brother left, unable to stop the flooding of memories so long repressed. Anyway, father was bad at poker and when he lost big, he paid his buddies by letting them have turns at me and my little brother. And this is only the surface. I know there's more, but I'm not ready to face it yet. So, my mom calls me and tells me that her and father are friends again and (she doesn't know the extent of the abuse) I should forgive him because he's getting old and wants forgiveness. I don't want to forgive and don't feel I should have to forgive!"

6. L:[10] Wrote a love letter to her teacher when she was a teenager. A teacher (female) gave the letter to her parents, warning them to take better care of L because something was going "wrong with L." L was sent to a mental hospital by her family where she was

exposed to electroshock therapy intended to cure her of what
was diagnosed as "a lesbian perversion." By the way, from the
earliest age, she had been subjected to permanent sexual mo-
lestation from her older brother. When she returned home from
the hospital, her father started to "teach her to be a real woman"
by having sexual intercourse with L against her will. At the age
of twenty, L gave birth to a baby girl, her sister and at the same
time a daughter of her father. The baby was taken from her instantly and given up for adoption. L remembers only the image
of herself screaming while her just born baby was taken forever
from her. L was sent to the mental hospital again and doctors
were generously bribed by her father not to pay attention to her
stories about allegedly giving birth to a daughter of her father.[11]
L was heavily treated with medications for the next few years.
Although visibly distracted because of her two treatments in the
mental hospital and the incest experience, L obtained a university degree. L has never been employed. She is now about fifty
years old, strange in appearance, and permanently taking "relaxing" pills. She was severely punished for something that has
never been a crime. Her father and brother, criminals and incest
perpetrators, are still respected as decent citizens and members
of the community.

7. D: "This is all related to childhood, when I was constantly told I
   was 'stupid' either for no apparent reason or when I lost my voice
   through fear because of abuse. Yet oddly I am in many ways a
   capable and competent women (this I recognize only when my
   self-esteem is OK). I was a good scholar and achieved distinctions in many subjects when studying. None of that seems to
   help when one carries such legacies from childhood. Maybe one
   day I will believe in myself enough not to worry if someone
   laughs at the way I slice bread, even if my self-confidence is low.
   One day I will look in the mirror and see not a helpless, frightened child, but a self-confident woman who may smile back at
   me and say, 'Wow, look at all you have done.' May we all be
   proud of our reflections in the mirror and see the strength and
   beauty we surely have."

8. When her husband died, she continued to live in his apartment.
   A new man came into her life. They married. The new husband
   convinced her (more or less without her real permission) to sell
   her apartment and with the money build a new, bigger house. To

this new house he invited all his family. Together they threw her out and took her pension. She now sleeps in the fields, on the streets, and once came hungry and dirty to Women's Center. Now she is in a shelter and court procedures are in process. By the way, she is over seventy.

9. G: "The physical violence was not the worst. It was the ever-present humiliation and sarcasm. At times I would have to stand in front of him and stare into his eyes. If I looked away, then I was shifty, dishonest, hiding something. Because I was a girl, he frequently told me that I would get married and have children—and that was all. He used to ask me who/where were the famous or productive women. Women were second-class citizens, he often told me. My mother was emotionally unavailable and un-able to protect me. I had to 'keep quiet' and not 'antagonize' him, because he would start with me and end up with her. I can remember the sounds of him raping her and her cries of pain, her begging him to stop. I was often in trouble if I did well in school, ignored when I learned not to do well."

10. P: "About my abusive past: my father enjoyed beating the hell out of my mother, dragging her around by her hair in front of their children, and then when he got tired of her, he came after us. My mother often took my sister with her, leaving one person behind with him, me, the youngest, to take all his rages."

11. M: "I had a big, secret smile when my grandfather died. I will have one hell of a smile the day my son-of-a-bitch father dies. My grandmother is harder to hate, though she was extremely cruel to me as a child, constantly putting me down and humiliat-ing me. She's now so sick and so old, but still a bitch. She even asked me one day when I was about sixteen if my father had used a condom when he had molested us. I have no memory of him molesting us. I have few memories before the age of four-teen anyway. It just pissed me off that she asked me that. Not only did it hurt me that she put that seed into my mind, looming over me, but if he was and she knew, why didn't she help us? How come that 'condom advice' was the best she could offer me? I've always been angry with my grandparents. They knew how abusive my father was. They saw my mom's face all cut and bruised and swollen. They saw the bruises on my legs with cuts down the middle from the special belt buckle my father had made to beat us with. She also told me that she saw him beating

on me as early as just a few months. And yet I had to live through fourteen years of it. I'm still so angry that no one helped us even when they all knew and didn't live that far away."

WAR FEMINISM MAKES US BURNT-OUT

The civil war, widespread domestic violence, and the entire war culture have significantly changed us women, members of feminist groups, and left us exhausted. We were not prepared for what feminism and activism in a time of civil war and economic crisis could actually mean. Although Belgrade was not in the battlefield, and we have not directly experienced the horrors of war atrocities, we became overburdened with feminist activities.[12] We feel destroyed, tired, confused, and sometimes disappointed. As part of war culture we have experienced internal conflicts, betrayal of sisterhood, the end of friendships, cynicism, discrepancies between proclaimed aims and everyday practice. We have experienced distrust and disloyalty. Sometimes we feel like expendable persons, to be used, abused, and forgotten in the shadows of main-stage politics conducted by men. We have also learned that anger is a necessary reminder that something hoped for and greatly valued has been lost.

But perhaps we have merely worked and loved each other too much. The effects of burnout was one of the workshop topics during the Women for Peace Conference held in August of 1997 in Novi Sad (a town in northern Serbia). Thirty women from various parts of the former Yugoslavia, including Croatia, Macedonia, Bosnia, Serbia, and Kosovo took part in the workshop. They said:

> *We are tired, aggressive toward anybody coming closer than five meters, don't want to answer any telephone calls, hate the telephone as a device, as well as the computer, hate women clients, make nasty jokes about women-victims of violence who are our clients, dare not to say openly that we hate them, sometimes feel like the loneliest people in the world, get frequent illnesses like diarrhea, flu, bronchitis, headaches, stomach aches, etc., get irregular periods, disturbing dreams, disturbed hormonal situations, previously had the impression that we needed two weeks of holiday per one working year to recover, and now have the impression that we need one year of holiday to recover from two weeks of work. We split into smaller and smaller groups to repeat in them again the same conflicts and wishes to separate, become disappointed in feminism, become lesbians, stop being lesbians, neglect our*

*private lives, neglect our children, neglect our own appearance, ne-
glect our studies, neglect old friends, lose good characteristics, which
we had already forgotten we once had, expel others from our groups,
are expelled by others from their groups, isolate from other groups, get
angry more easily, cry and shout at others without reason, ignore each
other, drop dead of tiredness, stop raising our heads out of tiredness. In
the morning we are not able to get out of bed, we gain new pounds, lose
pounds drastically, cannot bear those older than we are, cannot bear
youngsters, are especially nervous with our own generation of women,
ask ourselves what is the purpose of everything while giving a negative
answer at the same time, read only the last pages in a book, do not read
anything, do not go to theaters or cinemas anymore, have theater in
our own groups everyday, do not meet anybody except women from
feminist groups whom we'd rather not meet, truly enjoy intrigues, recognize the need for balance between negative and positive stresses but
do not find the balance, attend seminars and training all the time. We
continue to fight against each other, feel fed-up with foreigners visiting
us as if we were a zoo, dream of living just a normal life, working from
8 A.M. to 5 P.M. Daily in an office or a factory, dream of a life without
stresses, dream about going to the market and other daily routines of a
majority of normal women, do not have any dreams of tiredness, because as soon as we put our heads on the pillow, an alarm clock rings,
as if we had gone to bed a few minutes before. We smoke more and
more, drink more and more, recognize friendship as a consumable
good with a limited shelf life, become skeptical, biting, waspish, cynical, inconvenient, not responsible, revengeful. But still, we are feminists, pacifists, and fighters for women's human rights.*

*We are perpetually late, cry without reason, cry only when it will
impress somebody, or when it is ideologically and politically appropriate, like only our cats (parrots), sometimes have the impression that we
are not normal and the worst is that others have the same impression.
We hear buzzing in our ears and heads, frequently perspire without
reason, feel that our methods of work are becoming obsolete, not to
mention our goals. We feel overcome by our struggle, rusty, are dropping dead of tiredness, are most tired when there is nobody to notice
how much we work, work on everything except the things we have
learned to do, have nightmares in which we endlessly run from mon-
sters through dark tunnels, have dreams with us in heroic roles.*

*All of the above, we in Belgrade would not dream to say openly
because we would immediately be expelled as negative individuals, but*

in fact, it is all pure truth. We have the impression that it is going better with everybody than with us, that everybody knows better than we do how to structure a group, that everyone works against us, that everyone benefits from our hard work except us. We secretly watch sports on TV and enjoy them very much, knowing that we could be condemned by our feminist friends because of this. We do not believe in anybody, lose criteria for what is morally justified and what is not, ask ourselves what to expect from patriarchal society when our friends have done such bad things to us, know that these are the childhood diseases of all new social movements, without this knowledge making our lives any easier. And in spite of everything, we change the world, we are strong women, we can and dare everything.

And all that was said during the workshop in Novi Sad was just the tip of a volcano. Beneath this tip lies lava, lava mixed with love, passion, sex, lust, jealousy, happiness, sorrow, depression, love-vows, unfaithfulness, cheating, promises, commitments, triangles, quadrangles, polygons, seduction, rivalry, animosity, friendship, devotion, care, solidarity, confession, tears, smiles, gifts, meetings, visits, newborn feelings, fading feelings, emotion, crying, laughter, flirting, fantasizing, daydreaming, night-dreaming, questions, doubts, curiosity, politeness, rudeness, disappointment, joy, ambivalence, loneliness, humor, bitterness, revenge, affection, pride, fear, hesitation, guiltiness, hope, expectations, likes, dislikes, understanding, secrets, break-ups, romance, poems, strength, weakness, memories.

NOTES

1. The term "post-TV-news syndrome" was spontaneously coined by Belgrade's feminists during 1990 when media propaganda, especially on the first TV Channel (official) News, spread hatred among people of various nationalities and ethnic origins. These broadcasts were frequently followed by an increase in acts of domestic violence. During the civil war, the situation grew worse because television news broadcast increasingly brutal war scenes that provoked more anger and violence, which men directed toward the nearest targets—women, children, parents, and neighbors (Hughes and Mrsevic 1995; 509, 532).

2. The general atmosphere in such gathering places was one of violent exasperation. The collective feeling among the current and former soldiers, current and former private militiamen, and others who had returned from the battlefield was a sense of having been "betrayed" by commanding officers, supreme com-

manders, politicians, and powerful civilians who allegedly did not provide them enough opportunity to "win." Their anger also stemmed from the fact that they were not rewarded for what they considered "heroic deeds" on the battlefield. This aggressive, mutually shared bitterness often led to various kinds of violence, from public acts to acts of domestic violence (Mrsevic 1995d; 28, 34).

3. A characteristic of stories by various war veterans (with some of whom the author has personally talked) is the "easiness" with which young men, who, until yesterday, were "boys from the neighborhood," began fighting, shooting, killing, and burning. Conversely, single violent acts, whether done by individuals or in groups, became "easy" following battles.

4. The broad concept of state sovereignty means that each government rules its citizens as it considers most appropriate, without outside interference in so-called "internal affairs." Full sovereignty was primarily a nineteenth-century phenomenon and was increasingly criticized during the first part of the twenti-eth-century as a pretext used mostly by nondemocratic, despotic, unlegitimated rulers who terrorized their own citizens. After World War II, it was replaced by the so-called narrow concept of state sovereignty, limited by the basic standards of human rights and freedoms established by the international community.

5. A discussion of the question, Why did we become feminists? was led during the summer of 1996 on the women's E-mail list called ZAMIR/WOMEN. ZAMIR (meaning FOR PEACE), the BBS E-mail system for the territory of the whole ex-Yugoslavia, enable women from Zagreb and Belgrade to communicate even in times when there were no telephone lines between the two countries, when open battles were being fought, and during the armed conflicts between the two nations. Feminism was described as a practice, a woman's personal experience, and a theory. Starting from the doctrine of equality among men and women, feminism creates an ideology of social change with the aim of annulling economic, social, and political discrimination of women and other oppressed social groups.

6. In all post-communist and post-fascist states, citizens still have fresh memories of the first seeds of resistance in formerly underground, illegal, forbidden groups. These groups exist lawfully today, though accepted by the official structures of their states mostly because they have outside funding.

7. The level of communication with the government depends on the aims of each particular group. When the focus is domestic violence, a minimum amount of information should be disclosed—not too much to threaten the autonomy of the groups, not too little to leave them invisible and unknown. The minimum requests such groups make of a government are partial financing, recognition of women's human rights, and recognition of the profound impact that violence against women has on those rights.

8. Whenever possible, the stories are verbatim reports. Many women, though, were not able to narrate the horror of their lives; their stories are told in third person.

9. The man in this story was released from the army before the war, but, as the victim indicates, he later probably joined a paramilitary force or private militia.

10. She has never been able to tell her story completely, interrupted by crying, entering into deep silence, taking sleeping pills. Here and there she remembers, speaks, but only in fragments, and always to the same two people. We together created her story from those pieces.

11. The father, throughout his life, had been a never-detected criminal who, with his son, made all his money through unlawful activities.

12. "To have war experiences it is not necessary to experience them personally on the battlefield," said Emir Kusturica, the well-known film director (*Underground, The Time of the Gypsies*) from Serbia who has won multiple awards at the Cannes Film Festival and been nominated for the Oscar (Kusterica 1997).

REFERENCES

Hughes, Donna, and Zorica Mrsevic. 1995. "Feminist Resistance in Serbia." *The European Journal of Womens Studies*.

———. 1997. "Violence Against Women in Belgrade, Serbia, SOS Hotline 1991–1993," *Violence Against Women*.

Kusturica, Emir. 1997. Interview. *NIN* (Belgrade weekly magazine) 27 April.

Mrsevic, Zorica. 1994. "The Serbian Custom Is When a Husband Beats his Wife," *Pacifik* 6:2. (In Serbian: Srpski je obicaj da muz tuce zenu.)

———. 1994. *Women's Rights Are Human Rights*. (In Serbian: Zenska prava su ljudska prava.)

———. 1995a. "Incest," *Review for Clinical Psychology and Social Pathology* 13:52. (In Serbian: Incest, Revija za klinicku psihologiju i socijalnu patologiju.)

———. 1995b. "Grievance and Mourning: the Process," *Psychology of Crime* 78:94. (In Serbian: Proces zaljenja, Psihologija kriminala.)

———. 1995c. "Incomprehension of Women Victims of Violence," *What We Can Do For Ourselves* 4:49.

———. 1995d. "Ten Steps Through War Sexual Violence," *Women In Black* 3–4.

———. 1996. "Women's Rights are Human Rights," *Women for Living Without Violence: A Handbook for SOS Volunteers*. (In Serbian: Zenska prava su ljudska prava - zene za zivot bez nasilja - prirucnik za volontorke SOS telefona).

———. 1997. *Supplementary Materials for the Comparative Legal Feminist Theory.*

Schechter, Susan. 1982. *Women and Male Violence: the Visions and Struggles of the Battered Women's Movement.* London: Pluto Press.

United Nations. 1995. *The Special Rapporteur on Violence Against Women.* Document E/CN. 4/1995/42.

CHAPTER 6

Is Violence Male? The Law, Gender, and Violence[1]

LUCINDA JOY PEACH

INTRODUCTION: THE GENDERED LAW OF VIOLENCE

American law embodies a curious gender bias: it treats women and men differently in relation to violence, typically in ways that disadvantage women. Despite feminist recognition in recent decades that "the central condition of many women's lives [is] that they are ruled by male violence" (Cohen 1994, 350), the law has been unresponsive and ineffective in several respects. This bias is evident in the striking consistency with which the law regulates and responds to the use of violence by men and women in military and civilian society. Whereas the law generally recognizes the military as a social institution vested with legitimate authority to engage in the use of violence, it excludes women from most roles involving violence while at the same time ignoring much of the violence unleashed by military men against women.

Similarly, although law has traditionally interpreted domestic life as one of affective bonds within which violence has no legitimate place, it overlooks much of the violence by men against women while denying women the right to use violence in self-defense. In both military and civilian contexts, then, when the law recognizes women at all in relation to violence, it is primarily as victims. Women who do or would act as agents of violence are ignored as nonexistent, excluded as illegitimate, or punished as transgressive.[2] How can we explain this gendered disparity in the law; a law which purports to operate on the basis of constitutional principles of "equal protection"?

The leading scholarly theories addressing the law and violence provide only partial and incomplete explanations of this paradox. As I will discuss below, feminist legal scholars have pointed to the "maleness" of law to explain its gender bias more generally, but are unable to account for the peculiar contours of the law in relation to violence. Socio-legal scholars, especially Austin Sarat and Thomas Kearns, argue that the law itself is violent (Sarat and Kearns 1992; Sarat and Kearns 1991), yet do not explain how or why this violence is gendered. As neither of these theories provides a full account of how the law's regulation of violence is gendered, I will propose an alternative theory, premised on the notion that the law understands violence as a form of male power and thus genders violence male. In this account, the law reflects essentialist understandings of violence as gendered in a way that makes only male use of violence legitimate. This alternative approach to understanding the law and violence, I will argue, offers a better basis for developing strategies designed to empower women by deconstructing the law's gender-biased treatment of violence.

THE LAW, GENDER, AND VIOLENCE

The law's failure to recognize or acknowledge women in relation to violence is evident in civil law. The common law doctrine of coverture originally operated to deprive women of their legal status by declaring their interests merged into those of their husband upon marriage. Coverture legitimated marital rape and husbands' "chastisement" of their wives (see, e.g., Crowell and Burgess 1996; Siegel 1996; Whatley 1993). Until recent years, the law considered it impossible for a husband to rape his wife, and thus did not allow prosecutions for marital rape. Marital rape has only been recognized as a crime in all fifty states since the 1990s (see Whatley 1993, 32). Mark Whatley describes the marital rape exception as "protecting male rights and power, while implying that powerlessness and helplessness belong solely to women" (Whatley 1993, 31).

Once formal laws recognized violence against women, the legal system often continues to turn a blind eye. Acts of violence committed against women—ranging from domestic violence to stranger and date rape to childhood sexual abuse—traditionally have been prosecuted in ways which accrue primarily to benefit men. Using the cloak of "privacy rights," until the 1970s, courts and legislatures permitted rampant abuses of women and children to continue without formal legal protection or remedy, even though the vast majority of incidents of domestic violence were perpetrated by men against women and "domestic violence is the leading cause of injury to women in the United States"[3] (Boumil and Hicks 1992, 554). Studies of the law in relation to domestic violence conducted during the mid-eighties, "confirmed the pandemic extent of victim-blaming, identification with the aggressor, and brute unresponsiveness by police and the judiciary" (Cohen 1994, 353).

In more recent years, as legislatures have amended their domestic relations and criminal law codes to outlaw domestic violence, mostly male police and prosecutors and judges have continued to engage in gender bias by failing to arrest and/or prosecute and/or to convict male perpetrators of domestic violence (Jones 1994, 76). Lesbian victims are even more invisible, since homophobia adds an additional layer of prejudice to injustices based on gender. Ann Jones suggests that "the law has never been able to address battering effectively because of its own peculiar structure. Written by men for men, the law is designed to protect men from the power of the state and to adjudicate conflicts between men, to preserve order in a society of men" (Jones 1994, 24).

At least part of the reason for the law's inadequate response to domestic violence is its failure to acknowledge women's status as persons who have a legal right to be protected from male violence. When the law has recognized women's rights, it has frequently done so on the basis of stereotypes of women as victims "too helpless or dysfunctional to pursue a reasonable course of action" (Mahoney 1991, 4). Such images carry "cultural notions of deservedness" (Ferraro, 89).

Even more deeply rooted than its failure to treat women as legitimate victims of violence is the law's refusal to recognize women as agents of the use of violence.

Until just the last couple of decades, women have been excluded from participating in police forces. Although formal legal barriers have been removed, significant opposition to women working in policing and other "violent" professions remains. For example, in 1977, the Supreme Court upheld Georgia's law prohibiting female prison guards from working at a maximum security male prison. The court's rationale included the protectionist rationale that female prison guards would be less able to protect themselves from violence by the male inmates (*Dothard v. Rawlinson*, 433 U.S. 321 (1977)). While this decision may have been made with the best of intentions, its effect has been to perpetuate the view of women as victims of male violence rather than as agents of violence themselves.

The law's gender bias is starkly evidenced by its treatment of battered women who kill their abusers. Donald Downs argues that the

battered women syndrome (BWS) defense constructs battered women
who kill their abusers as solely victims, and portrays them as "incapable
of exercising reason and responsibility" (Downs 1996, 7). He argues that
BWS also "presumes that most or all battered women react in similar
fashion to their victimization; they lack the *will* that characterizes distinctive individuals." To succeed with BWS as a defense, a survivor
of domestic violence is forced to "convince a jury that she is a 'normal'
woman—weak, passive, and fearful." Even where BWS is successful as
a defense to criminal homicide, it reinforces stereotypes that women who
use violence against their husbands are mentally unstable, and perhaps
even murderous (see Stell 1991, 251), certainly not legitimate agents of
the use of violence.

In addition, women who *do* exercise violence by, for example, causing serious bodily harm or death to their abusers, are frequently treated
more harshly than men are for similar offenses (Schneider 1994, 44).
Legal personnel, ranging from prosecutors to judges to juries, have tended
to treat men who killed their wives' lovers more leniently than women
who kill their batterers (Stell 1991, 241). This double bind prevents
women from being fully recognized as either victims or agents of
violence.

The same pattern is evident with respect to the law's gendered treatment of violence in relation to the military. Whereas women in the military frequently have been the victims of violence, especially of sexual
violence by their comrades, they seldom have been permitted to be
agents of state-sanctioned violence through participation in combat roles
in all the armed services. Historically, women were banned from all
combat roles in the Navy and Air Force by congressional statute and
from the Army and Marine Corps by policy. Although many combat
roles on aircraft and ships have been opened to women since the early
1990s,[4] women are still barred from almost all assignments that involve
operating offensive, line-of-sight weapons, and from all positions involving ground fighting. This includes armor, infantry, and field artillery, the
three specialties considered to be the core of combat.

These prohibited specialties constitute the majority of combat positions in the military, the very aspect of the armed services in which the
use of violence is concentrated. The law's refusal to recognize military
women as legitimate agents of violent force is not separate from its view
of women as (only) victims of violence. Indeed, one of the most frequently raised arguments in opposition to military women serving in

combat duty is that they need to be protected from the kinds of physical
and sexual violence that would be inflicted upon them if they were captured by enemy troops and became prisoners of war (POWS).

Based on the exclusion of women from most combat positions, the
Supreme Court upheld Congress's exemption of women from the military draft (*Rostker v. Goldberg*, 453 U.S. 57 (1981)). This has resulted in
treating women as unqualified to contribute to national defense, one of
the traditional—and still important—ways of satisfying the obligations
of citizenship. The law's gender-biased treatment of military personnel
reinforces the perception—both within and outside the military—that
women are weak and, consequently, ineffective agents in the use of
violence.

The law's response to sexual abuse scandals within the military in
recent years reinforces the image that military women are essentially
victims of violence. In recent years, both the Navy's Tailhook "incident"
involving the drunken hazing of several female personnel by their fellow
officers at a conference hotel, and the Army's confrontation with dozens
of allegations of sexual harassment and abuse against drill sergeants and
fellow recruits at Aberdeen Proving Ground, were met with slow, lax,
and inefficient legal responses. The law's treatment of incidents of sexual
and physical abuse against female cadets at military training academies
in recent years has been similar. Thus, in both civilian and military contexts, the law continues to treat women (essentially) as victims, rather
than (also) as responsible agents of violence, thereby reinforcing the perception that if women are to be acknowledged in relation to violence at
all, it is only as victims (Howes and Stevenson 1993, 211). Since judges
have discretion whether or not to instruct juries to consider self-defense
when BWS has been raised, especially since the BWS defense cuts
against the grain of traditional self-defense arguments, this enables the
male biases of judges and juries to operate without constraints.

The consequence of the law's gender-biased treatment of violence is
to place women in a double bind: On one side, the lack of adequate legal
protections accorded to women for the "private" violence they endure at
the hands of men serves to reinforce and foster social attitudes that
women are helpless victims who are not valued enough or who do not
deserve effective protection from violence. On the other side, legal restrictions on women's use of state-sanctioned violence reinforces social
attitudes that women lack the agency to defend themselves or others
from violence. This double bind insures that women remain essentially

the victims of violence. In order to be able to offer possible effective solutions to the law's intolerable positioning of women in relation to violence, it is first necessary to better understand its cause.

THEORETICAL EXPLANATIONS

Two legal theories offer potential explanations of the law's gender-
biased treatment of violence. The first is that the law is gendered male.
The second is that the law is itself violent. As we will see, although both
of these theories have some value, neither is able to offer a full explanation of the specific contours of the law's gendered treatment of violence.

A. The Law as "Male"

Some scholars argue that the gender-biases in the law's response to violence are due to the "maleness" of the law. Feminist legal scholars have
long argued that the law is gendered "male." By this, they explain that the
law has been designed and written by men for men's purposes, with little
regard for women's needs and interests (Baer 1992; Hoff 1991). Although women have gained many legal rights they were not granted in
earlier decades of American history, the male bias of the law still exists.

One key aspect of the maleness of law is its traditional segregation
of men and women into "separate spheres," with men in control of the
"public" spaces of government, lawmaking, and employment, including
military service, and women relegated to the "privacy" of the "domestic
sphere," responsible primarily for childbearing, rearing, and homemak-
ing. The selective application of law in the so-called "private sphere"
uses "privacy" as a rationale to protect male domination (Schneider
1994, 37–38). The legal doctrine of privacy has been used to justify the
law's nonintervention into male violence in *both* the military as well as
the domestic spheres. To compensate husbands for their responsibility
for their wives' actions, the law governing the "private" sphere of domestic relations traditionally permitted men to "chastise" their wives, under
the guise that such actions were "private" and domestic, and thus beyond
the reach of the law (Jones 1994, 20; Crowell and Burgess 1996, 65).
Paramour statutes excused men who killed their wives' lovers, but provided no comparable excuse for women.

As Elizabeth Schneider argues, "the concept of privacy encourages,
reinforces, and supports violence against women. Privacy says that violence against women is immune from sanction, that it is permitted, ac-

ceptable, and part of the basic fabric of American life. . . . Privacy operates as a mask for inequality, protecting male violence against women" (Schneider 1994, 43). The law of privacy further legitimates male violence by prosecuting battered women for homicide when they protect themselves, and by prosecuting women more harshly than men accused of similar crimes (Schneider 1994, 44).

American law is premised on liberal assumptions about citizens as autonomous, individual male agents, not as interdependent, relational female subjects. This bias is evident in domestic violence cases. Feminists have recognized for almost two decades that the law of self-defense is not gender-neutral, but is premised on male experiences of violence (Stell 1991, 241).[5] A typical reaction of male-dominated judges and juries to reports of ongoing physical and emotional abuse of women in domestic violence cases is Why didn't she leave? Martha Mahoney observes that "social and legal emphasis on exit [in domestic violence cases] reflects a concept of agency as the functioning of an atomistic, mobile individual, and this concept of agency also reflects a binary opposition between agency and victimization" (Mahoney 1994, 74).

Women's use of deadly force in self-defense cases is often appraised by jurors on the basis of what they would do in the same circumstances. Traditionally, male-dominated juries *would* do what the battered women did *not* do, for example, leave long before the abuse reached the stage where the use of deadly force was necessary to repel it. This male bias in the law ignores the reality that it is the very act of leaving which often provokes the most serious violence against battered women by their abusers, and which frequently exposes battered women to the risk of other types of violence. In addition, the requirement that the force used be proportionate is biased against smaller, weaker persons, whose only realistic hope of self-protection is to use deadly force to repel their attackers (Stell 1991, 248).

When the law *has* recognized women as victims of violence, it has generally done so on the basis of sexist assumptions of women as lacking in full agency, and as dependent upon men for their very survival. This places women victimized by domestic violence in a double bind: if they fail to exercise agency and leave their abusers, they are criticized, viewed as crazy or masochistic, yet if they do leave, they are criticized for failing to adhere to the characteristics deemed appropriate to the female gender. Cynthia Gillespie has observed that "testimony that focuses on the helplessness and passivity of battered women tends to reinforce some of the very stereotypes about women that expert testimony about the battered woman syndrome was originally intended to counter" (Gillespie 1994, 559).

Similarly, laws governing the military perpetuate male-biased assumptions about the "natures" and capabilities of both men and women (see Baer 1992, 18). Here the prevailing gender ideology is that war is a theater in which men can prove their masculinity, and in which masculinity is deemed a necessary prerequisite to success. As Jean Bethke Elshtain explains, the reigning ideology locates "women in an auxiliary and pacific role in relation to war, . . . leaving the war fighting and dying to the men. Though women may be war's victims, they are, in this reigning narrative, neither its initiators nor its perpetrators" (Elshtain 1987, 164). Ideological identifications of the military—and the armed violence that is the state-authorized province of the military to wage—as masculine makes males the standard by which females are assessed—and found wanting. Laws legitimating a male-only draft and the exclusion of women from most combat roles reveal the continuing male bias of the law.

Although persuasive as far as it goes, the "maleness of law" interpretation is inadequate to fully explain the law's gendered treatment of violence. Even if the law *is* male in the ways feminist scholars have alleged, there is no logical or necessary reason why it would treat violence against women at all (as long as that violence did not harm the "property" interests of other men in specific females). Even the assumption that the law *permits* male violence against women by failing to restrain it implies that the law has (at least potential) control over the mechanisms of violence. Isabel Marcus's question: "What are we to make of a situation in which specific formal structures of subordination and control articulated in legal doctrine are eliminated by legislative enactment and/or judicial construction, but the coercive practices of violence, or the threat of it, which support and maintain such subordination and control, are tacitly endorsed?" (Marcus 1994, 18) is better answered by the second theory to be considered here, that law is itself violent.

B. The Violence of Law

According to socio-legal scholars Austin Sarat and Thomas Kearns, the law does not merely regulate violence that exists "out there," outside of the rule of law. Rather, the law is itself a source of violence. In this view, since law's violence "is inflicted wherever legal will is imposed on the world, wherever a legal edict, a judicial decision, or a legislative act cuts, wrenches, or excises life from its social context," the "law's violence is hardly separable from the rule of law itself" (Sarat and Kearns 1991, 210). In accordance with the conventional account of law—what Sarat and Kearns call "the official story"—violence against women in the military and the home is the result of either a failure or an inability of law to control violence against women. But according to a jurisprudence of violence, these same instances are the indirect consequence of the law's monopoly over violence, and of how lawmakers, adjudicators, and administrators shape the law.

The violence of the law is largely invisible, however. In part, this is because the law portrays itself as an alternative to violence. It is the professed alternative to the "war of all against all," the Hobbesian state of nature which dominates outside of—and in the absence of—the rule of law (Sarat and Kearns 1991, 222).[6] The rule of law also disguises the law's violence because of its ostensible reliance on reason rather than the use of force or coercion. As Sarat and Kearns suggest,

> the attention lavished on rules does more than just make impersonal the doing of legal violence; it also diverts attention from the pain law inflicts, focusing instead on matters of meaning and interpretation. The effect is to induce a vague but indelible impression that law is impersonal and temperate, rather than terrifying and painful (Sarat and Kearns 1991, 217).

Law's violence is also invisible because those who are responsible for unleashing the violence of the law (i.e., those who make and interpret the law) are far removed from its actual implementation. Thus, although "the law's rules may require that blood be spilled, . . . those who interpret the rules are spared that unseemly sight" (Sarat and Kearns 1991, 235). In the context of violence against women, the law's violence—in failing to protect the female victim—is deflected onto the individual male perpetrators who carry out the acts. With respect to the military, the rules restricting women from combat positions and the atmosphere that allows sexual harassment and the assault of women to flourish—is deflected onto the military officers rather than the law itself.

The law's violence is visible, however, in legal interpretations of what counts as illegitimate violence. As Martha Mahoney says, "law especially emphasizes acts of physical violence, and this emphasis in turn hides broader patterns of social power, patterns of power within a given relationship, and complexity in the woman's life, needs, and struggles" (Mahoney 1991, 60). Sexual harassment, for example, has only been recognized as legally actionable in recent years, in part because this type of abuse typically does not include physical violence. Similarly, coercive sex without overt physical violence typically is not considered to be rape, even though statutory definitions do not require violence as a necessary requirement of the crime.

Some feminist scholars have found explanatory appeal in this understanding of the law as itself violent. For example, Isabel Marcus recognizes that "a legal system which 'naturalizes' violence against women in the home, by allowing perpetrators to act without fear of punishment by the state, is a legal system devoted to maintaining control over women" (Marcus 1994, 18). Ann Jones discovers the law's violence in its failure to adequately protect women against battering: "Instead of safeguarding woman's right to be free from bodily harm, the law itself does her harm, . . . by declining to treat as a crime what is in fact a crime on the books of every state, and by cruelly punishing women who injure or kill men while defending themselves and their children" (Jones 1994, 35). And Martha Minow recognizes that "the social failure to intervene in male battering of women on grounds of privacy should not be seen as separate from the violence, but as part of the violence" (Schneider 1994, 43). These views suggest that there is a certain explanatory power in the "law is violent" thesis that is missing from the "law is male" explanation.

Yet, like the "maleness of law" theory, the "violence of law" thesis does not provide a complete explanation of the gender-based peculiarities of the law. It cannot, for example, fully explain why law is gender-biased in recognizing women only as victims of violence and not also as themselves legitimate wielders of violence. It fails to explain why the law frequently accords agency to men over the use of violence, and also condones male violence against women, but denies the same privilege to women. Rather, the way the "violence of law" thesis has been framed suggests that the law should be gender neutral in its response to violence, regardless of the gender inequalities in society that make women more vulnerable to the law's violence than men may be.

The inadequacies with both the maleness of law and violence of law theories for a full understanding of the law's treatment of women in relation to violence suggest the need for another explanation—one that is sensitive to both the gender biases in the law itself as well as the law's violence. Such an explanation is provided by the thesis that the law genders violence as male.

C. The Gender of Violence in the Law

According to this third approach, the law is not only male-biased and it-self violent, but the law also operates on the basis of an understanding that violence is male.

In some respects, the law's gendering of violence as male accurately mirrors larger social realities. Certainly, violence in our society can be characterized as male gendered when one focuses on the fact that ap-proximately 89 percent of violent crimes are committed by males, and that wars have always been initiated and carried out by men.[7] But in ad-dition, it is better able to elucidate the anomalies in the law's gendered treatment of violence in both military and civilian contexts. As noted above, through the gendering of the combat exclusions and draft exemp-tions, the law assumes that the state-sanctioned violence of the military is male. Such assumptions help to perpetuate the view that women are out of place in the military, particularly in combat roles, where the use of violence is most likely and most visceral. The law's assumption that the virtues of "manliness" are necessary for effective combat soldiering, and that women are incapable or ill-suited to the development of these virtues, reflects a view of violence as a male province in which women have no legitimate business.

It follows logically from this view that the law can only permit women to be viewed as victims of violence, not as its agents. If violence is male, of course military women will be excluded from combat and from access to other means of violent force. And if violence is male, and the law is male, then, of course, sexual harassment, assault, and domestic violence against women will not be prohibited with the same vigor as crimes of violence waged against men, such as those committed under the influence of BWS. If the law genders violence as male, then it is not surprising to find remedies for male violence against women ineffective nor a lack of increased resources to facilitate women's ability in "suc-cessfully making a life outside of an abusive relationship" (Ferraro 1996, 88). In these respects, the thesis that the law itself understands violence as male provides a more complete understanding of the gender-biases in the law's treatment of violence than either the "violence of law " or "maleness of law" theories.

SUMMARY AND CONCLUSIONS

Understanding the law's treatment of violence as itself based on a gender-bias suggests that empowering women will require deconstructing the law's linkage of violence with maleness. This deconstruction entails a recognition that gender and violence are both cultural constructions—and consequently mutable—rather than inherent characteristics, which are fixed and permanent. Until this can be done, women will be unable to obtain legal justice, as either victims or agents in the use of violence.

Deconstructing the gender ideology embedded in the law that men are the perpetrators and women are the victims of violence would result in significant changes in both the civilian and military spheres. If the law viewed battered women as *both* victims and agents, often possessing "more capacity for judgment than a defense based on learned helplessness acknowledges" (Downs 1996, 8–9), it would facilitate the use of the BWS defense by victims of domestic violence who exercise violence in self-defense. If the law recognized that women, as well as men, are capable of using state-sanctioned forms of violence in effective and responsible ways, the military would be required to accord greater respect to women, both as potential combatants as well as in terms of being the unjustified victims of sexual and physical abuse.

This development would likely have several beneficial consequences, including creating opportunities for more women to occupy more positions of authority and leadership, both within and outside of the military. Given the gendered dichotomy of victimhood and agency in the law's grammar of violence, the deconstruction proposed here would both enhance the legitimacy of women's use of violence in defense of self and others, and delegitimate the use of violence against women.

NOTES

1. The author kindly acknowledges the organizers of the Frontline Feminisms Conference, at which portions of this paper were presented, as well as John Douglas Nazelrod, a former sergeant in the Army Special Forces, who provided insights into gender relations in the military.

2. Feminists themselves often have failed to recognize that women can be *both* agents and victims. Liberal feminists tend to view women primarily as individual, autonomous agents, especially with respect to matters such as reproductive rights (see, e.g., Williams 1982). By contrast, radical feminists tend to view

women essentially as helpless, dependent victims, especially in the context of pornography and sex work (see, e.g. MacKinnon 1985; Dworkin 1987; Mahoney 1991). In addition, with a few exceptions, most feminist theorists ignore women's capacity for and use of violence.

3. "According to FBI statistics, one woman in the United States is beaten every eighteen seconds" (Schneider 1994, 41).

4. In 1991, Congress lifted the ban on women flying combat aircraft, and in 1993, on women's service on combat ships. The Navy opened aircraft carriers to women in 1994, but still excludes women from positions in SEAL Commando units, on nuclear submarines, and mine sweepers (the latter ostensibly because of their cramped quarters).

5. The requirements of traditional self-defense doctrine "developed in the common law from a self-defense scenario based upon archetypically male persons of roughly equal strength" (Gillespie 1994, 559).

6. Sarat and Kearns suggest that "in large measure, then, law authorizes itself and its bloodletting as a lesser or necessary evil and as a response to our inability to live a truly free life, a life without external discipline and constraint" (Sarat and Kearns 1991, 222).

7. In addition, the association of women with peace and peace movements, rather than war and violence, is a long-standing one, extending back as far as the classical Greeks and Romans (Peach 1996, 179–80).

REFERENCES

Baer, Judith. 1992. "How is Law Male?" In *Feminist Jurisprudence; the Difference Debate*, edited by Leslie Friedman Goldstein, 147–72. Lanham, MD: Rowman & Littlefield Publishers, Inc.

Boumil, Marcia Mobilia and Stephen C. Hicks. 1992. *Women and the Law*. Littleton, CO: Fred B. Rothman & Co.

Bowman, Tom. 1997. "APG Case Takes Twist," *Baltimore Sun* (Feb. 23), 1A, 7A.

Cohen, Jane Maslow. 1994. "Private Violence and Public Obligation: The Fulcrum of Reason." In *The Public Nature of Private Violence: the Discovery of Domestic Violence*, edited by Martha Fineman and Roxanne Mykituik, 349–81. New York: Routledge.

Crowell, Nancy and Ann Burgess, eds. 1996. *Understanding Violence Against Women*. Washington, D.C.: National Academic Press.

Downs, Donald. 1996. *More Than Victims: Battered Women, The Syndrome Society, and the Law*. Chicago: University of Chicago Press.

Dworkin, Andrea. 1987. *Intercourse*. New York: Free Press.

Elshtain, Jean Bethke. 1987. *Women and War*. New York: Basic Books.

Ferraro, Kathleen. 1996. "The Dance of Dependency: A Genealogy of Domestic Violence Discourse." *Hypatia: Special Issue on Women and Violence* 11:4, 77–91.

Gillespie, Cynthia. 1994. "Justifiable Homicide: Battered Women, Self-Defense, and the Law." In *Cases and Materials on Feminist Jurisprudence: Taking Women Seriously*, edited by Mary Becker, Cynthia Grant Bowman, and Morrison Torrey, 557–59. St. Paul: West Publishing Co.

Hoff, Joan. 1991. *Law, Gender, and Injustice*. New York: New York University Press.

Howes, Ruth and Michael Stevenson. 1993. "The Impact of Women's Use of Military Force." In *Women and the Use of Military Force*, edited by Howes and Stevenson, 207–18. Boulder: Lynne Rienner Publishers.

Jones, Ann. 1994. *Next Time, She'll Be Dead: Battering and How to Stop It*. Boston: Beacon Press.

MacKinnon, Catherine. 1985. "Pornography, Civil Rights, and Speech," *Harvard Civil Rights—Civil Liberties Law Review*, 20:1, 1–70.

Mahoney, Martha. 1994. "Victimization or Oppression? Women's Lives, Violence, and Agency." In *The Public Nature of Private Violence: the Discovery of Domestic Violence*, edited by Martha Fineman and Roxanne Mykituik, 59–92. New York: Routledge.

———. 1991. "Legal Images of Battered Women: Redefining the Issue of Separation," *Michigan Law Review* 90: 1, 1–94.

Marcus, Isabel. 1994. "Reframing 'Domestic Violence': Terrorism in the Home." In *The Public Nature of Private Violence: the Discovery of Domestic Violence*, edited by Martha Fineman and Roxanne Mykituik, 11–35. New York: Routledge.

Peach, Lucinda. 1996. "Gender Ideology in the Ethics of Women in Combat." In *Its Our Military Too! Women and the U.S. Military*, edited by Judith Stiehm, 156–94. Philadelphia: Temple University Press.

Sarat, Austin, and Thomas Kearns, eds. 1992. *Law's Violence*. Ann Arbor: University of Michigan Press.

———. 1991. "A Journey Through Forgetting: Toward a Jurisprudence of Violence." In *The Fate of Law*, edited by Sarat and Kearns, 209–74. Ann Arbor: University of Michigan Press.

Schneider, Elizabeth. 1994. "The Violence of Privacy." In *The Public Nature of Private Violence: the Discovery of Domestic Violence*, edited by Martha Fineman and Roxanne Mykituik, 36–58. New York: Routledge.

Siegel, Reva. 1996. "'The Rule of Love': Wife Beating as Prerogative and Privacy," *Yale Law Journal* 105, 2117–2207.

Stell, Lance. 1991. "The Legitimation of Female Violence." In *Justice, Law, and Violence*, edited by James Brady and Newton Garver, 241–60. Philadelphia: Temple University Press.

Whatley, Mark. 1993. "For Better or Worse: The Case of Marital Rape," *Violence and Victims* 8:1, 29–39.

Williams, Wendy. 1982. "The Equality Crisis: Some Reflections on Culture, Courts, and Feminism," *Women's Rights Law Reporter* 7:3, 175–200.

CHAPTER 7

Art as a Healing Tool from "A Window Between Worlds"

CATHY SALSER

A Window Between Worlds (AWBW) is a nonprofit organization based in the United States. Since 1991, AWBW has supported the recovery of thousands of battered women and children by offering them the healing and empowering tool of the creative arts. Women who leave their batterers and seek refuge in a shelter have taken a courageous first step. Yet in order to fully reclaim their lives and make healthy decisions for their future and that of their children, these women need a way to reexamine their feelings and develop a stronger sense of self and personal vision.

Unfortunately, due to the challenges of the crisis environment in shelters, and the pressing needs for legal, medical, and employment assistance, an art program often falls to the back burner. Although art workshops often provide some of the most significant and meaningful experiences for the shelter residents, shelters are often unable to make an art program a priority. This is where A Window Between Worlds offers a hand, assisting the shelters to offer weekly art workshops. For many women and children in the shelters, art offers "a window between worlds," helping them to transition out of a painful past into a more hopeful future, recovering their sense of safety, power, possibility, and identity.

Through our Children's and Women's Windows Programs, AWBW has developed over sixty different art workshops. New workshops are constantly being developed and shared among the network of AWBW leaders. The following is a description of one basic workshop, "Pastel Windows," designed by AWBW Founder, Cathy Salser, for use with adult survivors of domestic violence. Cathy, and Dolores Sanico,

AWBW executive director, invite all who wish to become involved to contact us at: AWBW, 710 4th Ave. #4, Venice, CA 90291. In the words of one survivor, "We are learning that creating heals the pain."

PASTEL WINDOWS ART WORKSHOP

Overview

This is the simplest and clearest, expressively focused exercise of "A Window Between Worlds." It is basically the title exercise, during which we literally practice creating with the chalk a window into the world of our feelings and needs. We create a window into our present world of feelings, and then another window into our future world: our visions and hopes for the future. It is an exercise during which we literally practice putting our hopes and dreams into a tangible form, and the piece of paper literally becomes a window between worlds.

Variations

This exercise can be used to explore many areas other than present and future worlds. It can be wonderful to use the pastel windows to explore a negative feeling and a positive feeling. (This can be great with younger children—a feeling you don't like, and a feeling you love.) This exercise can follow a writing session during which each woman writes about herself. She can circle the most positive thing and the most negative thing in her writing, and use the drawing as an arena to explore those poles in depth.

This exercise can also be adapted to a variety of materials and techniques. Even if you only have pencils and paper, you can still do the warm-up, expressing various feelings in textures and motions of the pencil. The windows into the present and the future can be done with lines and textures.

You can adapt the structure of emotional sharing and exploring to any materials you have on hand. The important thing is to create that "window of time" to practice respecting the feelings and thoughts that arise.

Introduction

"This workshop is a special time for *you*, for you to feel, relax, and take time out from everything else. This is a window of time for you to practice respecting your feelings, your needs, and your visions and your hopes. Respect whatever you feel, even if you feel like putting your head down and resting. This is a time for *you*. None of this is required. It is all offered to you as a window of time for you to respect your own needs."

"Nonartists" Are Welcome

"You don't need to be an artist. All you need to do is relax and respect what you make. If you are an artist, I hope you will let yourself be completely free today: free to make a mess, free to respect whatever comes out of you, even if it looks like nothing you'll ever make again."

Opening Circle

An opening circle can be the first step in creating a sense of safety for the session, so that it can truly become "a window of time during which to practice respecting ourselves." Although circles can vary each time you lead the workshop, it is very useful to begin with these three introductory areas:

1. Your name
2. How you are feeling at the moment
3. How you feel about art (encourage the sharing of any negative feelings about art)

This gives each woman the opportunity to identify her current state of mind, a first step in transforming it. It also gives the entire group the opportunity to air any tough feelings about art, rather than feeling isolated or insecure. This is an opportunity for each woman to share any nervousness she may have about her creative abilities.

Just Listening and Welcoming the Feelings

When you encourage the women to share their feelings, some women may be surprised by their emotions. If a woman cries during her sharing, just encourage her to let the tears come. Explain to her that her tears are welcome, and each tear is a part of her healing.

Technical Demonstration

"What we will be doing today is making two windows with the pastels—one window into how you are feeling in the present moment, and one window into how you want to feel in the future. The point of this is not to worry about how it *looks*, but rather to concentrate on really giving yourself freedom of expression. If anger is what you are expressing,

there is no need to make it 'look nice' . . . So this is a demonstration of
how to make an absolute mess (and enjoy it)! It is not a demonstration of
what you 'have to' do." (Begin taping the paper down with masking tape,
forming a frame line on all four sides, and ask why they think you're taping it . . . then demonstrate vigorous strokes and smearing and how much
fun it is to be free with it . . . then remove the tape and show the crisp
edge.) "The wonderful thing about this material is that the crisp edge
seems to pay respect to the depth of the emotion expressed. Angry scrib-
bles, done in this technique, end up looking as important as they truly are
(which somehow doesn't seem to happen if it's done in crayons)."

Pass out materials (if they aren't already passed out). Have each
woman choose a color of paper to represent the future and tape it down.
Choose a color of paper to represent the present, and tape it directly over
the other piece, and then a third sheet of paper for practice, and tape that
directly over the two previous sheets. Once everyone has her three papers
taped, begin the technical demonstration. (It's good to get all the taping
done first, so that this activity doesn't interrupt the flow of creative expression once it starts.)

Warm-up

"We are all fairly used to putting our feelings into words, but we
rarely practice putting them into shapes and colors. To get used to the
process of putting emotions into shapes and colors, we are going to try a
very loose, quick warm-up. We're going to move quickly, so that no one
has time to think too carefully, and you can practice grabbing your first,
fresh thoughts, without having time to criticize them."

"Ready? OK, first look at the pastels in front of you. Go ahead and
grab whatever color you're instantly drawn to . . . Go ahead and cover
the page with that color . . . Cover it however you feel like—in big scrib-
bles, in smooth strokes, however you want . . . Then see what it's like to
smear it in with your hands . . . Now think of anger—what color, what
shape comes to mind for *anger?* . . . Go ahead and grab your first thought
for anger and put it onto the page . . . If there's any anger in your body,
feel it and let it come through your body onto the page . . . And now think
about *peace* . . . What color and what shape come to mind? . . . Go ahead
and grab your first thought and make a mark on the page for peace . . .
And now think of *sadness* . . . What color and what shape come to mind
for sadness? . . . Go ahead and put your first thought on the page . . . And
now think of *joy* . . . What color and what shape come to mind for joy? . . .

Go ahead and make a mark for joy on the page . . . And now think of *masculine* . . . What color and what shape are masculine to you? . . . When you're ready, go ahead and make a mark for masculine . . . And now think of *feminine* . . . What color and what shape are feminine to you?—first thought—grab it, and put it on the page . . . And now think of your *father*—make a mark for your father—first color and shape that come to mind . . . and now think of your *mother*—make a mark for your mother—first color and shape that come to mind . . . And now think of your self . . . What color and shape comes to mind for your self? . . . Make a mark for your *self* on the page . . . When you're ready, remove the tape."

"How did that feel? Was it difficult? Was it strange to put feelings into shapes and colors? Is it something you've ever done before?"

Relaxation

"Now we are ready to begin the windows. I'd like to begin with a relaxation, to help each of us really notice that this is time for us, time apart from the rest of the day. Like everything we are doing today, this is optional. For some people, a relaxation is the most unnerving thing they could do—it's not relaxing at all. If you are one of these people, respect that and don't feel odd about it. There is no need for you to feel obligated to do it."

"Ready?" (Begin to play relaxing music) "Go ahead and get comfortable—let your eyes close and take a deep breath . . . " Then at the end of it, add the following in order to guide the women into the drawing process. ". . . Notice that this is time for you, time for you to notice how you are feeling . . . Take a moment to notice the world on the inside of you. What does it feel like? Notice if any colors come to mind, or any shapes . . . Would the world on the inside of you be many colors? Or just one? Would it be dark? Would it be light? Would it have sharp lines? Or curves? Would it be foggy? Or clear? And take some time to notice what the world around you feels like: Do any colors or shapes come to mind? Would the world around you be dark? Or light? Would it be foggy or clear? Would it have many colors or just one? Whenever you are ready, go ahead and begin to draw a window into your present world . . . "

Pastel Window into the Present

(Relaxing music continues, the women begin to draw as they become ready.) As they begin to draw, it can be helpful to throw out some re-

minders: "If you notice yourself worrying about what your drawing
looks like, see if you can remember that this is free time. See if you can
send the critical thoughts out of the window—see if you can let yourself
be as free and bold as you were during the warm-up . . . " (As the first
women look like they are finishing:) "When you are ready, go ahead and
remove the tape from your drawing . . . Notice if there are any words in
your mind that go with this image, and take a few minutes to write the
words on the back of your drawing . . ." (This gives the women who
aren't yet finished a signal that we are wrapping up that drawing, while
giving the ones who are already done a way to continue their expression
while waiting for the others to catch up.)

Transition
(Stop the music. It can be important, before going on to the drawing
of the future, to share what was felt and discovered in the process of this
drawing. If there is a small group, and time allows, it is wonderful to give
each woman an opportunity to share whatever she wants to share of what
she made and how it felt to make it. If the group is large and time is too
tight for such in-depth sharing at this point, it is helpful to have each person think of *one word* to describe how it felt to do this drawing, and have
each share their one word. Then ask if everyone is ready for the future.)

It can be helpful to share a note about the future: "It can be quite difficult to ask ourselves what we *really* want in our future—as important as
that question is, we don't spend a lot of time with it, and it can be discon-
certing to discover that we really aren't sure what we want. Be patient
with yourself during this exercise. This is a window of time for you to
consider this question and to practice respecting your true feelings about
it. If you are uncertain, respect your uncertainty. Don't feel like you have
to 'make something up.' It is most important to honor what you really
feel, and it is wonderful if, even at the end of ten minutes, you have only
clouds of uncertainty on your page. That is valuable, and important. That
is what this time is for. So see if you can take the risk of being as honest
as possible with yourself during this time."

Relaxation
(Begin music again.) "Go ahead and get yourself very comfortable
again—let your eyes close and take a deep breath. Notice if there is any
part of your body that has become tense in doing the drawing you
just completed. Take another deep breath, and imagine any tension flow-
ing out of your body with the air. Now picture the drawing of your

present world. Picture in your mind's eye the colors and shapes you just created. Notice if there is anything in that world that you are ready to leave behind as you move ahead into your future. Are there any shapes and colors that you would like to leave behind? Imagine breathing those colors out with your breath. Imagine exchanging the old air with fresh, new air."

"Now, with your eyes still closed, take some time to ask yourself 'what do I want in my future?' . . . As you ask yourself this question, notice if any shapes or colors come to mind. Imagine how you want to feel on the inside. What colors would you imagine for your inner world? Would it be dark or light? Clear or foggy? Curving or straight? . . . And take time to notice how you want the world around you to feel in your future. Would it be dark or light? Foggy or clear? Curving or straight? Take as long as you want, just to imagine your future. Whenever you are ready, go ahead and open your eyes, and begin to draw your window into your future . . ."

Pastel Window into the Future

(Music continues, the women begin to draw at their own pace, you may want to remind the women to send their critical voices away . . . As the first women wrap up their work, let everyone know that they can remove the tape whenever they feel complete, and they can take time to write any words that go with their image on the back.)

CLOSING

(If you asked for one word about how the Present Window felt, it is good to ask for one word about how the Future Window felt. Remark if the words are different from the previous round of words. It is important to give each woman time at the end of the drawing session to express anything she wants to share about her drawings, and about how it felt to create. It can be wonderful to hold up each woman's drawing, if she is willing, so that everyone, including her, can see it from a distance as she talks about it.

Giving the women frames for their images can be a wonderful conclusion to this project. The content of the drawings is so valuable. They deserve to be honored in this way. The framed images can serve as tangible reminders for the women of where they are and where they are aiming to go in their lives.)

PASTEL WINDOWS MATERIALS LIST

ALPHA-COLOR PASTELS—a wide assortment, including fluorescent colors if affordable;

COLORED CONSTRUCTION PAPER—pre-cut to frame size (colored pastel paper can be nicer, if affordable);

MASKING TAPE—a roll for each woman, otherwise, too much time is spent passing tape around and waiting for each woman to get set up for the exercise. Drafting tape, magic removable tape, or blue painter's tape are all easier to remove without ripping the paper, but are more expensive;

FRAMES—Simple 8 × 10 frames can sometimes be purchased for a dollar;

TAPE PLAYER—relaxing tapes;

PAPER TOWELS

SETUP

It is helpful to lay out a spread of paper of various colors to choose from, a box of pastels within reach of each woman, and a roll of masking tape for each woman.

PART II

Gender, Militarism, and Sexuality

CHAPTER 8

Translating/Transgressing/ Torture . . .

IRENE MATTHEWS

> *No one bears witness for the witness.*
> —PAUL CELAN

TRANSLATING

I had made an appointment with Rigoberta Menchú to meet 12th September, 1989 and discuss her book, *Me llamo Rigoberta Menchú y así me nació la conciencia*, "dictated" in 1982 and "authored" by Elisabeth Burgos.[1] I wanted to ask Rigoberta about a number of literary aspects of the book in connection with an academic conference called Translating Latin America.

Me llamo Rigoberta Menchú seemed to be a perfect text for discussion at a conference dealing with the ethics and esthetics of translation: it is a transliteration of a cultural history from oral into written form, and it is a "translation" of that history from its original *lengua memorial*— Quiché—into the language of colonialism, in this case *castellano*. Above all, among many themes and narrative threads, Rigoberta's story itself showed how the lack of a common language can be a *barrera étnica* to intercommunity survival, yet also how "interpretación" has commonly been synonymous with "traición"—betrayal—in a society built on greed and the power of violence.

So, I sat on a low wall and waited for Rigoberta Menchú in the central carousel of "Insurgentes" metro station in the heart of Mexico City, prepared to pick her brains and her memory about those political and literary focuses: whose idea was the original version of her book, was she happy with the translation, what did *she* think about the "place" of the "ethnographer," had the book been distributed in Guatemala, did she

have any control over or profit from the translations into yet other languages, etcetera.

Rigoberta arrived almost an hour late—she was very busy and I had
waited expecting that she might not show up at all. She wore what was to
become her "uniform" at gatherings around the world: an embroidered
huipil from her village, plus, in this instance, a pair of blue jeans; but the
usually smooth skin on her shiny round face was roughened and patchy
with nervous allergies and her dark eyes red and moist from lack of
sleep. We sought out an empty table in a local taco bar: an anonymous,
safely public spot. I had my tape recorder and notebook at hand, my copy
of her book with a hundred little yellow stickers in it, and a list of questions divided into sections of interest. I explained to her, quickly—she
had another appointment soon after mine—what my interests were. But
she asked *me* the first question: "What time are you leaving tomorrow for
allá ('there'—Guatemala)?" I explained I had changed my plane
ticket—the first leg of a research trip through Central America—from
Wednesday to Thursday, in order to be able to talk to her first without
worrying about packing and so on. "That's a pity—tomorrow a *dele-
gación* of *universitarios* is leaving from here on your plane to investigate
and protest the *matanzas*; have you seen the paper today?" I hadn't.

She showed me the headline: "Another 16 persons executed in
Guatemala by the death squads."[2] Among them, two more of the group of
thirty students and university professors from San Carlos University.
They had "disappeared" over the previous two weeks or so, and, now, six
recognizable bodies had turned up in the last two days. The entire committee of the Students' Union, which supported a recent massive teachers' strike, and which formed a part of the leadership of the consolidated
popular movements, had been wiped out. . . . except one: the general secretary. He had happened to be at a conference in Costa Rica the day the
others were picked up and had "disappeared." This young man, against
any normal sense of self-preservation, would be flying to Guatemala
with the Mexican group on 13 September as an act of solidarity for his
lost *compañeros*.

To Rigoberta, her young university friend represented the wasteful-
ness of another life potentially lost: she believed that a martyr's death
was not so important nor so useful as a live combatant. But for Rigoberta, an *exiliada*, he also embodied the ineradicable *deseo* and strength of
fighting in and for one's country. When she was in Guatemala in spring
1989—and her feeble cover there, like the student's, was publicity and
visibility—Rigoberta was threatened and attacked three times, a pair of

bombs concealed in two bouquets of flowers was delivered to her hotel for Mother's Day! She told me that she didn't feel the danger until afterwards, on the plane returning to Mexico: "the *orgullo*, the pride of dying in one's *patria* made her lose the perspective, the dimension, of risk" (IM 1989).

At Rigoberta's request, I had not switched on my tape recorder; I was hesitant even to take out my notebook. I felt alert enough and hysterical enough to register every word as if it were being carved into my own body. We talked about torture: many of the "disappeared" never reappeared, but many did, often unrecognizably disfigured. The strategy was not to hide the bodies, or pretend they were accidental deaths, but to produce them openly, obviously tortured and obviously executed: symbols of the authorities' impunity. After several years of studying the rhetoric and violence of war for my dissertation, I still could not fully comprehend the strategic rationale for torture other than as a *highly effective* means of mass terrorism or as a sort of tautological outlet for men brutalized by training in and under torture into perpetrating it themselves: an expression of both power and vengeance. Torture did not seem to fit into a projection of any sort of postwar harmony. Rigoberta Menchú, however, was much more of an expert than I in the theory and the practice of a "civil" warfare that targeted the people in the popular movements and those who might harbor them in the countryside. Rigoberta considered that the army "experts" were not merely arbitrary, sadistic *matadores* ("killers"), but a different—perhaps incomprehensible—type of professional. "If they are human," she pondered,

> for them it must be just like soldering two wires together, or like being a doctor or a psychologist. Torture is the intelligence arm of the police, the army. The army of every country ruled by a dictatorship has to be, in fact, a highly developed 'intelligence' of the people, a constant source of information on the desires, the goals, the hopes of the populace. This is a tactic, a strategy of war. For in Guatemala, there would be no other way to get this information, 'no sabrían golpear,' they wouldn't know how to 'lean on' these people, a people that is *sumamente discreto*—totally, utterly *discreet*. (IM 1989)

When Rigoberta wrote her book, she told me, "the wound was still huge, as huge as the experience of unnatural death—like a river in flood . . . the scar did not exist, but the wound did." According to the evidence in her book, she had lost one baby brother to malnutrition, another to asphyxiation in the plantations, another brother and her father and mother to torture and assassination. Seven years later, Rigoberta thought, maybe "la vivencia de uno (de una persona individual) es demasiado pequeña en comparación con los miles y miles de su pueblo, miles de muertos." [One's life, one individual life, is very small in comparison with the thousands and thousands of one's people, thousands of deaths.] In 1989, she could see the context—that is, she said, "The *context* is the *scar:* not in the sense that the wound is disappearing, but that it is leaving a trace that is never erased." At the same time, now, she saw that the struggle has advanced, that there was hope. "If there were no hope, I would kill myself right now. *The army keeps on killing as a response to the hope that one carries in one's heart"* (IM 1989).

Rigoberta's text, the story of an *utterly discreet* people lies a long way behind her; the book itself is a part of the scar over history that leaves both a trace of events and a context for them. Elisabeth Burgos "diría que Rigoberta es un producto de aculturación logrado, puesto que las resistencias que muestra con respecto a la cultura ladina constituyen la base misma del proceso de *aculturación antagonista"* (Burgos 1983, Prólogo 15; my emphasis). [Elisabeth Burgos would say that Rigoberta is a successful product of acculturation, in that the resistances she shows in respect to *ladino* (mixed indigenous and European) culture constitute the very base of the process of *antagonistic acculturation*.] My first question to Rigoberta about her book—aimed at unveiling that "antagonism"—was to have been, "what did she think of Elisabeth Burgos's consistent use of the term *'indio'* in the introduction and the prologue to her book?" The very term, its innate imperialism, and its connotation of "a people," in truth many peoples scattered through hundreds of tribes and groups and customs and languages over large areas of a vast continent, already implies a transgression of cultures as we "translate"—however benignly—"the other." But at least Elisabeth Burgos's "authorization" established a presence and a history. My jittery interviews with Rigoberta and "translation" of her words into my own (unpublished) notebooks proved, if anything, that—in comparison to Elisabeth Burgos—I was not much of an interlocutor, and far from a literary historian.

I didn't consider myself to be much of an international courier or a spy, either. Yet I met with Rigoberta Menchú again the next day, in another subway station, and she gave me some letters and papers to carry to a few *"compañeros"* remaining in Guatemala. I did not share Rigoberta's *"esperanza"* and I was also pretty scared of getting into serious trouble. But I could not refuse. Maybe later, I thought, I'll be able to talk to Rigoberta about her book.

TRANSGRESSING

> *This situation has been the same for five hundred years . . . we cannot wait another five hundred years.*
>
> —"ROSALINA"[3]

In 1999, after many years of rumor, leaks, and debate, David Stoll published his version of *Rigoberta Menchú and the Story of All Poor Guatemalans*. Stoll's text is the result of a decade's research in Guatemala, focused primarily on Chimel, the village where Rigoberta Menchú was born and raised, and on the communities nearby. The anthropologist concentrates on three areas of Rigoberta's first work, *Me llamo Rigoberta Menchú*, which he found to be most problematic: the eyewitness information regarding the abuse and deaths in her family that Rigoberta claims, the rivalries between different groups over tenure of particular parcels of land, and—on a much larger scale—the impression given in *I, Rigoberta Menchú* that most, if not all, Mayan groups in the Guatemalan countryside both had a sense of the injustice of the political system operative in the country and actively supported the guerrilla movements. The framework for David Stoll's concerns includes his findings, which suggest that Rigoberta was much better educated than she implied throughout her own text, and that she had a political agenda born not simply from her own experiences and those of her family, but through contact with "Marxist" militant groups she encountered when she fled to exile in Mexico in the early 1980s.

The Story of All Poor Guatemalans begins with a series of disclaimers, intended to anticipate and respond, no doubt sincerely, to the arguments of those who support Rigoberta's text and her award of the Nobel Peace Prize in 1992. The author poses a series of hypothetical questions: What if much of Rigoberta Menchú's story is not true? If part of the laureate's famous story is not true, does it matter? Why did such a catastrophe befall her village and her family? In answering himself, David Stoll hedges his bets: "It would be naive to challenge Rigoberta's account just because it is not a model of exactitude. Obviously, stories can be true even if they are selective in what they report" (Stoll 1999, ix).

On the question of the prewar situation in her village, Stoll admits and laments:

> Rigoberta told her [untrue] story well enough that it became invested with all the authority that a story of terrible suffering can assume. From the unquestionable atrocities of the Guatemalan army, her credibility stretched further than it should have, into the murkier background of why the violence occurred. The result was to mystify the conditions facing peasants, what they thought their problems were, how the killing started, and how they reacted to it.
>
> That a valuable symbol can also be misleading is the paradox that obliged me to write this book. (Stoll 1999, x)

So, *The Story of All Poor Guatemalans* sets out to redress the imbalances and contradictions that are somehow glossed over in *I, Rigoberta Menchú* when "the complexity of a particular life is concealed in order to turn it into a representative life" (Stoll, xi). Despite the particularity of his focus, Stoll claims that his work is "not a biography of the Nobel laureate," but an investigation into why Rigoberta's story "took the shape it did, as well as why it appealed to an international audience before being transmitted back home, where Guatemalans have made it a part of a national debate about who they are" (xi). Stoll's stated intention seems to be both expansive and politically objective; once again he uses a supposedly candid hypothetical question to establish his own perspective: "Must we resign ourselves to be apologists for one side or the other?" (x). With such a modest and nonpartisan claim, his text should fill in those gaps perhaps necessarily present when one book is chosen to exemplify the condition, heritage, and aspirations of an entire people (whether or not *I, Rigoberta Menchú* had that original intention).

The additional background material David Stoll provides on the conditions in the area proximate to Rigoberta's village of Chimel, and the inclusion of oral histories from other witnesses of the events of the worst years of the civil war, serve to offer an expanded context for Rigoberta's own story. Unfortunately, supportive critics of Stoll's work have tended to exaggerate both the significance of the "dubious" details he exposes, and the damage such exposure does to Rigoberta's text. In particular, both Stoll and those who endorse him have enjoyed lambasting (North American) academics who sympathize with or utilize Rigoberta's text and her status as a subaltern. At best, it is claimed, the intellectuals—mostly middle-class white folks—are unenlightened innocents, and at worst, Marxist-feminist partisans seeking evidence for anti-establishment manifestos.

Despite Stoll's stated desire to denounce the *use* made of Rigoberta's book, rather than the work itself; however, much of the critique supporting the deconstruction of *I, Rigoberta Menchú* centers on the very polemic that Stoll himself prefers to downplay in both his preface and in preambles throughout his text: the literal veracity of her account. But Rigoberta's text has perhaps been most broadly used not as a piece of historical or anthropological truth, but as an exemplar, in some ways an archetype, of a hybrid type of literature: an "ethnobiography" in Rosemary Feal's designation, or, more broadly, a *testimonio*. Testimonial literature has a long history and has recently taken on a life of its own in Latin America. In *testimonios*, biographical narrative and social consciousness are presented inside a historical framework; this combination is recognized to have a formal (literary) function as well as an informational content. In an essay overviewing the forms this hybridity takes, Marc Zimmerman suggests:

> By virtue of its collective representativity, testimonio is, overtly or not, an intertextual dialogue of voices, reproducing but also *creatively reordering historical events in a way which impresses as representative and true and which projects a vision of life and society in need of transformation.* (Zimmermann 1989, 1; my emphasis)

Rosemary Geisdorfer Feal, in turn, looks toward slave narratives for an earlier paradigm of the testimonial and suggests that while texts such as *Biografía de un cimarrón* by Miguel Barnet and *Me llamo Rigoberta Menchú* share some of the essential features of a self-representative literary form of autobiography, this does not guarantee either a whole truth or nothing but the truth. She claims:

> . . . the structure of autobiography of all types, most particularly those written within a literary tradition, intersects with the rhetorical devices found in novels. . . . at the textual level, the markers of historical reality and novelistic fantasy are indistinguishable. The difference may be perceived extra-textually only in that the story of the non-fiction novel is historical, whereas the story of the traditional novel is hypothetical. (Feal 1990, 100)

Rosemary Feal additionally views testimonials—and I agree with her hypotheses—as the product of a "heterobiographical pact"; so there may exist multiple *personas* as well as multiple narrative points-of-view in the final product. Both of these critics assume that testimonials may contain elements of fiction, albeit they are primarily based on fundamental truths and on personal experience. And most critics of the genre identify Latin American *testimonios* also by the political agenda usually present in them, often including a denunciation of the present system and an appeal for solidarity and for change. In order that such an appeal may have a generalizable import, material may be included that is drawn from common experience—verified through trustworthy informants or other substantial evidence—rather than restricted to the direct experience of the individual biolocutor.

David Stoll deals with "literary" interpretations by suggesting that anthropologists who follow the route of comparative literature analysts are slavishly "replacing hypothesis, evidence, and generalization with stylish forms of introspection" (Stoll 1999, 247).[4] In insisting on the singularity and the "personal responsibility" behind Rigoberta Menchú's words, David Stoll somewhat confusingly accuses her on the one hand, of oversimplifying, and on the other, of "mystifying" the story of her area and her time. Of his own respondents who had heard of Rigoberta's version, some replied to his enquiry (from twenty to thirty years after the events in question) by agreeing with the anthropologist that *I, Rigoberta Menchú* was a pack of lies; others did not query the United States researcher's elucidation of "the truth" but counter-argued that "it's the story of all of us." In itself, Stoll's hypothetical question about truthfulness invites a simplistically dichotomous response—scarcely the "evidence" he apparently needs to be able to generalize along the lines of his own formula for conservative ("scientific") anthropological research outlined above.

To those who read Rigoberta's story outside Guatemala and whose reading context differs greatly from her experiences and identity, a more significant question might be: without *I, Rigoberta Menchú*, would we know *anything at all* about Guatemala, its demography, its history, its customs, its socio-political place in the world scheme?[5] And, as a result of reading Rigoberta's text, are we "mystified"—that is, convinced by her simplified and partisan view of things? Or did our experience with her text persuade us to delve further and to notice brief newsflashes on Guatemala at the bottom of page eleven of whatever newspaper we read? Without the international success of her book, would Rigoberta have won the Nobel Peace Prize in 1992? Was the award of the prize to an "ethnic" Guatemalan, on the five-hundredth anniversary of the "conquest" of the Americas, a purely political, and therefore an inappropriate, gesture? Is there a larger, perhaps a pacifist, morality that escapes politics?

To those of us who do support or promote a pacifist solution to the problems of our contemporary world, Rigoberta's erstwhile advocacy of guerrilla tactics and armed activism disturbs our concept of a prize for peace. But, perhaps, if we read *I, Rigoberta Menchú* as an historical explanation of five hundred years of oppression and as a manifesto for strategies to avoid further arbitrary damage to a largely unpoliticized and primarily unarmed people, we may come to a more useful evaluation of the worth of her text than we would by dissecting her potentially libelous indictments of her neighbors. It is unfortunate that Rigoberta Menchú did not respond to David Stoll's requests that she read and comment on his manuscript; perhaps she preferred to spend her time on more urgent and useful issues.[6] But I believe it is even more unfortunate that an obviously experienced and committed anthropologist should have spent so much time re-researching a geographical and historical case study rather than using his expertise to reveal other aspects of a country still harboring too many socio-political "mysteries" that harm its own people.

TORTURE . . . TEXT

> *I don't call myself a "widow."*
> —NINETH DE GARCÍA[7]

In concentrating on the history of interfamily rivalries over land tenure, on details of exactly who of Rigoberta's immediate family died exactly what sort of brutal deaths, and on the fact that many villagers were as wary of the guerrilla fighters as they were of the military and the militias, David Stoll's book scarcely mentions in passing the sexual atrocities and crimes against women depicted in Rigoberta Menchú's book. Nor does Stoll discuss the information she gives of women acting on their own behalf and resisting violence, or indeed inciting retaliatory violence against their aggressors.

On the other hand, David Stoll does mention Juana Tum Cotojá on several occasions, and admits that "[h]owever improbable some of the details, there are two reasons to believe that Rigoberta's account [of her mother's kidnapping and death] is basically true" (Stoll 1999, 127). The account is credible because relatives told the researcher essentially the

same story, and secondly, according to Stoll, because "the army murdered thousands of helpless prisoners" (127) and therefore, by deduc-
tion, Juana Tum as well. In other words, Juana Tum's death is an
example of scientific proof: hypothesis, evidence, and subsequent generalization. David Stoll mentions that Rigoberta's mother was raped, but,
as elsewhere, makes no attempt to interpret rape or any other tactics of
the war, nor to assign any special significance to the treatment of women
prisoners and civilians. The term "rape" does not appear in his index.

Perhaps unsurprisingly, confirmation of the particular tortures that
Rigoberta's mother, that many women, were submitted to is left to two
other investigations conducted concurrently with that of David Stoll, but
not premised upon deconstructing the words of one witness-woman-
writer. In April 1998, the group led by Bishop Juan Gerardi and denoted
"Recuperation of Historical Memory," published a detailed report based
on the testimony of fifty-five thousand victims of political violence, three
quarters of whom were Maya. And in February 1999, backed by the
United Nations, the Commission for Historical Clarification (CEH) published its report after several years of research into the atrocities committed during the thirty-six years of civil war in Guatemala.[8] Based on
investigations in four key areas of Guatemala, the Commission concludes that approximately 93 percent of the killings and disappearances
registered in Guatemala were committed by members of the armed
forces or governmental militia organizations, some 3 percent by guerrilla
forces.[9] On 4 March 1999 the director of the Commission and principal
signatory of the report, Christian Tomuschat of Berlin (an experienced
and reputable German jurist), was interviewed on National Public Radio
in the United States. He confirmed that genocide, that is, the killing of
men, women, and children in Mayan communities targeted uniquely because of their ethnic identity, was committed by agents of the state, and
that rape was used in a systematic manner: most women were violated
before they were killed, this was "almost a compulsory stage . . . soldiers
looked upon women as objects to be looted."[10] Tomuschat told his radio
audience that the commission members had personally participated in
forensic examinations of human remains and in the interviewing of surviving witnesses. In his assessment of the "terrible, terrible" things he
viewed and learned, the director revealed that, for him, "the most terrible" incidents were "the mistreatment, the sexual attacks, the assaults on
women," the "most frightening evidence . . . showing how debased human
nature can become," turning men into "killing machines."

A fourth reason to believe Rigoberta Menchú's account of her mother's death does not derive merely from the fact that many similar atrocities were proven during the independent commissions' investigations into the devastations of the twentieth century, but from the historical continuity of the degradation of women in wartime, particularly when there is, or there is perceived to be, a difference in ethnic identity between conquerors and conquered. In the rest of this article, I read *I, Rigoberta Menchú*, not as a purportedly anthropological-sociological verity as David Stoll does, nor as a justification for United States' academic angst, but as a personal document on civil warfare, its techniques and its tragedies. Above all, woven into *I, Rigoberta Menchú*'s multiple, richly informative and denunciatory narrative tapestry is a graphic example of how the degradation of a mother's body might represent some of the fundamental, archaic, goals of warrioring: control and direction of the productive space, the implantation of ideology, and—not incidentally— injuring the "enemy" and subjugating other (men's) women.

I'll start with a quote, written by a man, that gives one historical precedent to the procedures of state terrorism. Writing in the sixteenth century as a Franciscan missionary and zealous inquisitor of the peoples of the Yucatan, Diego de Landa recorded his impressions of the Mayan Indian women he encountered and observed. They are good-looking, healthy, bronzed by the sun, clean, sweet-smelling, hard-working, and above all, "wonderfully good before they came to know our people" (de Landa 1975, 89). De Landa gives a number of examples of the Mayan women's "goodness," almost entirely posited upon their modesty and chasteness. He begins:

> The captain Alonso López de Avila, brother-in-law of the *adelantado* Montejo, captured, during the war in Bacalan, a young Indian girl who was a beautiful and charming woman. She had promised her husband, fearful lest they should kill him in the war, not to have relations with any other man but him, and so no persuasion was sufficient to prevent her from taking her own life in order to avoid being defiled by another man; and because of this they had her killed with the dogs. (de Landa 1975, 90–91)

This report from observations made in the easternmost province of Mexico suggests that (Mayan) women were naturally considered to be desirable spoils of war, and that war itself was used as an excuse to malign marital fidelity. Yet four hundred years after this particular "conquest" in Mexico, the way the Mexican Revolution was fought and written about betrayed it as a product of a different type of archaic, perhaps "Latin," ideology and custom. In this, the first popular revolution of the twentieth century, there were certain codes of behavior which, although often breached, were equally often upheld: while huge numbers of the general population were involved in the war, civilian deaths were still often assessed either as "accidental" or as "murder." And men and women were treated differently (although not necessarily "better" or "worse" than each other). The repeated waves of "conquest" and resistance in Guatemala[11] tell a somewhat different story: in the second half of the twentieth century, civil war took on a new perspective, no longer of "socially sanctioned" open conflict (Margaret Mead's words) but of a diffuse and generalized violence pitting unequal forces against each other: "overarmed militaries" on the one side, and on the other, traditionally unarmed civilian institutions: oppositional political parties, workers' unions, the indigenous community, the church, and the family. Jean Franco reminds us:

> These institutions owe their effectiveness as refuges to historically based moral rights and traditions. . . . Homes were, of course, never immune from entry and search but until recently, it was generally males who were rounded up and taken away often leaving women to carry on. . . . (Franco 1985, 414)

While this is a somewhat optimistic (and class-blind) assessment of the historical inviolability of the domestic—women's space and women's continuity—it points toward recent drastic increases in attacks on the home front (62 percent of the reported "disappeared" in Argentina's "Dirty War" were kidnapped from their homes, for example). Indeed, in Latin America, the eradication of civilian institutions—including patriarchal family structures and the home—has seemed an essential factor in the development and self-protection of militarized, authoritarian states. Traditionally, church and patriarchy were accepted coagents of the state but also occasional rivals to "government." When the state was relatively weak, these were the principal functioning social organizations, and when the state sought to reaffirm hegemonic power, they were absorbed or coerced into subordination or collusion, or, if resistant, identified as "enemies" under a declaration of war.[12]

The contemporary history of almost any country in Latin America might be culled for evidence of large-scale organized political violence as an alternative to other forms of civic persuasion, and for examples of women's involvement and resistance. The French critic and cultural commentator, Tsvetan Todorov, chose to epitomize his ethical examination of five hundred years of European influence on the Americas—*The Conquest of America*—in terms of women's violation; his work uses Diego de Landa's words as his epigraph and is "dedicated to the memory of a Mayan woman devoured by dogs."[13] The central aspect of the reference, is, of course, not just horrible violence, but the powerlessness of the woman, not only caught between the desires of two men but unprepared to fight, and, therefore, both choiceless and helpless when her "protector" is unavailable: her protection is as much ideological—a projection of a masculinist ideal—as actual. In "civil" times, (one hesitates to call not-war "peace" in our contemporary world) avoidance of rape and of death often depends on women being trained to defend themselves, physically and emotionally, on being capable of negotiating with their attackers, and, above all, on being scared enough and alert enough to avoid dangerous situations. In wartime, when many men are armed and in groups, when violence is sanctioned by the state and therefore not negotiable on a personal level, and when dangerous situations are usually unavoidable, survival is not so easy. Especially when "survival" is associated with degradation and betrayal.

In her book, Rigoberta Menchú relates how her mother—a local leader and midwife on call throughout the highland area to attend the sick, and childbirths—developed close ties early on with the "*compañeros* in the mountains . . . the *guerrilleros*, she loved them like they were her own children" (*IRM* 218). In Rigoberta's account, her mother will lose a surviving son from her already depleted biological family to the state terrorism of public and publicized torture in the open assassination—burning alive—of a group of "subversives": an incredible "performance" that recalls Inquisitional tactics and objectives. This scenario, combining political obtuseness and sadistic impunity, serves to instill fear in the onlookers forced to witness the event, but may also serve to unite the people in their anger and their will to organize and defend themselves. In the case of Rigoberta's mother, the death of her son incites in her the outrage necessary for overt action: ". . . she went to the women and said that when a woman sees her son tortured and burned to death, she is incapable of forgiving anyone and ridding herself of that hatred, that bitterness" (*IRM* 196).[14]

In reconstructing her mother's thoughts and aspirations, Rigoberta Menchú exemplifies two elements that epitomize "mothers" in warfare:

the courage that gives women the strength to remain "behind the lines" to protect their children, and to stimulate others into retaliation and resistance on the basis of that ultimate preservation. Rigoberta's mother proves to be as much a revolutionary as her father, her life is a *testimonio vivo*—a "living testimony"—to other women to show them how "they too had to participate, so that when the repression comes and with it a lot of suffering, it shouldn't be only the men who suffer . . . any evolution, any change that women didn't participate in, would not be a change, nor a victory" (*IRM* 196). The women of Guatemala birth and raise numerous children and take primary responsibility for running the home. Additionally, they—perhaps particularly the rural Mayan women—have taken on the tasks of raising domestic animals and working on the *milpas* as well as foraging for plants and roots to supplement a meager diet. They also often provide family income through domestic labor and by seasonal working on the coffee and cotton plantations where their small stature and nimble fingers, like those of their children, are particularly useful during the labor-intensive harvests. In wartime, the women's already present enterprising skills and communitarian spirit are further developed out of the urgency required by a sense of social responsibility during crisis: in order worthily to share a better future, the women must also directly share men's combat. So in Guatemala's "revolution," the classic structure of inter-state warfare—where men are recruited to protect (ideally) the women and children who are left behind to weep—is radically inverted. In *I, Rigoberta Menchú*, the Guatemalan women's willingness to confront the army is the result of a deliberate attempt to "read" the "rules" of men's war:

> It seemed at one time that the women and children might be shown more respect by the army because the army mostly kidnapped the men, especially the leaders of the community. So because of this it was decided the men should leave first and the women stay behind as the rearguard to face up to the blows. (*IRM* 127)

This nostalgic co-opting of the rules of "civilized" war does not, however, work in the diffuse violence of Guatemala's "low intensity" warfare under a military encouraged to despoil the countryside and its inhabitants. When the women and children are left behind as the "rearguard," they run risks equal to those of their men: of capture and death . . . and rape.[15]

Organized rape plays a special role in a policy of ethnocide; it violates the rules and customs of the group, spreads fear, morally and physically disintegrates the family and the community, and submits women to the most monstrous evidence of the power of violence. Torture and rape also serve to initiate the unwilling conscript: one of the "training techniques" of modern militaries—particularly those such as in Central America where they were likely to be involved in conflicts with guerrilla forces—is to brutalize new recruits through self-torture and, more often, through forcing them to collaborate in the abuse of captives and civilians. Dissension and mistrust "in the ranks" is quashed through group *ritualization* of torture, and particularly of rape, thus "guaranteeing to the company the solidarity required to sustain it as an effective . . . unit."[16] Torture and rape also reward, or appease, the professional warrior.[17] When Rigoberta's mother is captured, she is "raped by the town's high-ranking army officers" (*IRM* 198). She is taken to the military camp, where she is again raped by the officers commanding the troops. Her body is punctured and starved, she is tortured almost to death, resuscitated, and "then they started raping her again" (*IRM* 199). It is easy to read into this torture scene an instance of "gang rape taken to its pathological conclusion, where the torturers are competing with one another over who has control of the victim's body and what they do to it" (Wilden 1985, 70). And the logical conclusion, as happens here, is a God-like control over not just woman's body—her life—but also her death. One of the particular refinements of the technology of intelligence and oppression in modern Latin America, and particularly in Guatemala, is the extent to which the victims were tortured to death.[18]

Additionally, the forces of "conquest" (or control) in Central America were often comprised of young men co-opted from the indigenous population itself—although usually from groups or regions other than the ones allocated in the army—many of them orphans taken off the streets or raised in harshly authoritarian institutions. And the outraged body in *I, Rigoberta Menchú* is not that of just "any" Indian woman (although it might be almost every Indian woman). Nor does it merely represent, as the sixteenth-century version of conquest did, the common commodity exchange of women's marital fidelity versus the military ethic of rewarding the conqueror. In a country where women are still doubly colonized by their sex and their ethnicity, they were now being punished not because of their chastity, nor only to intimidate or humiliate their menfolk, but for the public nature of their own actions: for their assumption of a voice—unprecedented and unwelcome and insistent "noise" against the oppressive monologue of the warfare of state terrorism. This *mother's* body was punished for daring to stray away from her secondary identity and her home.

It takes a special stretch of the imagination to "explain" the (apparently) aberrational nature of male cruelties against the mother. Theorists have attempted to isolate a male tendency towards aggression through rereading classic philosophical and psychological parameters and studying girl and boy children. Nancy Chodorow's neo-Freudian analysis of individuation and separation is based on her argument that the asymmetrical "practice" of parenting projects masculine socialization through repression of the female and its relegation to the domestic sphere, in other words, the devaluation of woman-as-mother. In turn, Jessica Benjamin suggests how not merely separation but independence or self-identity requires a confrontation with an other that needs to be "created" in the unwilling domination that physical violence expresses, most often borne out (in a heterosexual and patriarchal society) as male-master and female-victim. If we combine and project these two masculinizing scenarios of empowerment and identification inside the military, we see how the debased woman, and particularly the debased mother—insufficient in herself to fulfill a "real man's" identification needs—"serves" under rape for men to recognize other men's manhood. So, woman in war, or perhaps women and war, become the embodiment of "the erotics of patriarchy."[19]

The increasing presence of women on active military service in "advanced" societies, such as the United States, may make it more difficult to accept separatist paradigms of masculine aggression. On the other hand, the continuing unease stimulated by overtly homosexual recruits suggests that old theories, or old fantasies, linger on. We are not obliged to accept the Chodorow-Benjamin model, of course, but it seems as though the Guatemalan military did. Imitation and secondariness are almost inevitable characteristics of an army that was a vital but precarious lynchpin in a society tottering interminably on successive schemes of dependent development—economic, political, and military. The soldiers in the Guatemalan army were themselves positioned very precariously on the ladder of social and sexual security. Klaus Theweleit observes that "the most common sign of upward social mobility is the acquisition of a woman from the social stratum to which the man has risen" (*Male Fantasies* 372). Given Guatemala's complex history of *mestizaje*, that may be the second step; the first is the denigration of the women in the soldier's own social stratum: the indigenous peasant women who don't speak Spanish (but who give birth to soldiers).[20] The capturing and torturing of this mother's body, then, might fill varying categories of "otherness" that conflate the imperialistic, masculinist, racist, and professional inversions of an "orphaned" military based on often reluctant recruitment and socialized into "selfhood" through techniques instilling fear, obedience, alienation, objectification, and brutality.

But, just as torture cannot and should not be reduced to mere military methodology or some sort of "torturology" (Michael Taussig's word), this mother's body is not "merely" a cipher of deathly transcendence or an abject symbol of repudiated ethics. Her daughter's text represents a living, breathing, maternal body that is inflicted with pain and humiliation and done to death as it is used to call her own *biological* children to present themselves morally and actually to the scene. The torture scenario is converted into a timeless scene of sacrifice. The mother's clothes are placed "on display" as a record of the event (her capture) and proof of her helplessness, her nakedness. Her family is invited to expose themselves in order to cover up their mother's "shame." In turn, her daughters (in consultation with an absent brother) must agree not to submit themselves to a certain death just like their mother's:

> We had to guard that suffering to ourselves, as a testament. . . . And so we had to accept that my mother was going to have to die, in any case. . . . The only thing left for us to hope was that they would kill her quickly, that she would no longer be alive. (*IRM* 199–200)

This terrible ethical dilemma involving the children's sacrifice of their own mother in wartime, announced as the account of a mother's courageous struggle against violence, is also, perhaps particularly, the story of a daughter's encounter with futility: "I never thought my mother would meet a worse death than my father" (*IRM* 210). A daughter's denial of a normally "attentive" response, her refusal to comply with the torturers' demands that she present herself, may have been the only way to break the cycle that was destroying her family—her father, brother, and now her mother—and her people. If the daughter had only *consented* (to her own certain death), might her mother have been spared? This daughter will never know the truth of her choice but lives on in "a panic" of dying like so many of her friends, of emulating her mother: "I wouldn't want to be a widow woman, and I don't want to be a tortured mother, either" (*IRM* 225). *I, Rigoberta Menchú*, and its evidence of and on "participating-mothers," underlines how complex is the nature of mothering, and daughtering, in wartime, when the ultimate goal of war—*injuring*—strains and ruptures forever the closest of all emotional and psychical bonds.

It is perhaps because of the intimidating intimacy of the mother-daughter bond that David Stoll balks from questioning Rigoberta Menchú's version of her mother's death.[21] Yet it scarcely matters whether the account in *I, Rigoberta Menchú* is accurate in every detail, or even eye-witnessed by the speaker. Indeed, Rigoberta excuses herself from witnessing the death of her mother because of her fears for her own safety: surely an even more telling indictment of the horror of this death than being "strong enough" to be present could imply. Rigoberta Menchú makes no overt, direct connection between the continuing cult of *machismo* in her society and the reactionary violence inherent in militarized politics. Nor does she reduce suffering to a single woman's experience. However, the strongly personal—and uncomfortable—identification between the individual woman who narrates the story and the perverse violence perpetrated upon the women who are narrated, leaves a more memorable and disturbing image in the mind of the reader than many other strictly historical or theoretical accounts do.

I had visited Guatemala many times before I read Rigoberta Menchú's book, and had read her book several years before I met her personally. I had listened to her talk in a number of public forums, in Mexico and in the United States, when her diminutive stature (she was often the smallest adult person on the platform, or in the room) seemed to be compensated by the force of her personality and her words: simple yet powerful. I returned to Mexico from Honduras several months after my conversations with Rigoberta in Mexico City's subway stations. Since then, I had traveled throughout a Central America laid waste once again by hurricane, earthquake, and war. In Nicaragua, I listened in horrified disbelief as the news came over the wires of the assassination of six Jesuit priests and their household staff in San Salvador—but, hadn't I chatted to one of them in a seminar at the university, only thirty-six hours earlier? In El Salvador I interviewed military officers, including one of the very few women of rank in the army, trying to understand the ethics and philosophy—and the training required—for carrying and using arms against a civilian populace. In Guatemala, I trotted obediently round the dank and threatening mountains at midnight, "escorting" young teachers and union leaders who supposed, or told me they supposed, that a foreign face from a neutral country might afford them some protection from the military patrols. I stepped cautiously around a small crater and over shards of glass and piles of plaster—the remnants of a small bomb hurled through the window—in GAM's supposedly "safe" headquarters. I listened carefully to instructions about signs of trouble and escape routes whispered fiercely at me in one venue after another—in schools, homes, bus stations, union offices.

The many women, and the men, I met in Guatemala's cities and villages confirmed and expanded the impressions I had gained from Rigoberta's book. All of them had lost many family members, some of them virtually every relative. As David Stoll mentions, "except for Amilcar Méndez [leader of CERJ], the best known leaders of the popular movement—Nineth [de García], Rosalina [Tuyuc], and Rigoberta—were women whose husbands or fathers had died in the violence" (Stoll 1999, 207).[22] Stoll omits pointing out that these strong, courageous leaders are also the survivors of many dead and disappeared *women*, their co-workers, friends, sisters, their mother in Rigoberta's case. Each of them has also survived threats and attacks against their own person. *I, Rigoberta Menchú* showed Guatemalan and foreign readers alike how elderly women (and even unusually old women, for Guatemala) could participate usefully in the defense of the villages; how very young girls *were* willing to choose between rape and death and volunteered to risk the first in order to protect their companions from the second; how despite indigenous resistance to methods of birth control imposed on them from outside, women were willing to research and use ancient methods of their own to abort babies conceived by force in soldiers' assaults. Not least, these fundamentally *discreet* women found strength and solidarity with each other in order to reduce or eliminate the shame involved in being violated by "the enemy."[23] It is not only because they are "targeted" less often than men that women can and do survive. In a patriarchal and patrifocal society, women may even find it easier than men to re-form different communities and to contest the autocracies of violence that still reign immune. Above all, I learned over and over how the women of Guatemala, Maya and ladino alike, were becoming conscious of their oppressed state and were learning how their new status—widows, un-married mothers, a *majority* of Guatemala's population— needed a new social contract to support them.[24]

In the years following the worst moments of military-political violence, the mothers and the grandmothers and the families of the disappeared bravely paraded the two-dimensional faces of lost husbands and lost sons and daughters, like a "moving cemetery," around the Plaza de Mayo in Argentina, in Uruguay, in Chile, and in El Salvador. There are few, very few, photographs of the indigenous women and men lost to violence over the centuries. The face and the words of Rigoberta Menchú represent them throughout the world. From Argentina, Eduardo Galeano responds to David Stoll's accusations against Rigoberta Menchú with a short list of other "dubious" recipients of the Nobel Prize for Peace—all of them "warrior-chiefs," none of them "Indians." Galeano wonders: in this upside-down world, why we are asking if Rigoberta deserves the prize. Surely the question should be, "Does the prize deserve her?"[25]

NOTES

1. As well as the "authority" (truthfulness) of *Me llamo Rigoberta Menchú y así me nació la conciencia*, the "authoring" (narrative responsibility) has a somewhat polemical history. The first two versions—in French and then Spanish (both in 1983)—included Rigoberta's name in the title but Elisabeth Burgos on the cover and title page, as author. The text was published in English by Verso in 1984, under the title *I, Rigoberta Menchú*, subtitled "An Indian Woman in Guatemala." This version shows no "author" on cover or title page; rather it is "Edited and introduced by Elisabeth Burgos-Debray" and "Translated by Ann Wright." In section 4 of a lengthy research and review article in the *New York Review of Books* ("Rigoberta Menchú and the Story of All Poor Guatemalans," 8 April 1999, 32–33), Peter Canby investigates the multiple versions of the first encounter between Rigoberta Menchú and Elisabeth Burgos, her Franco-Venezuelan "ethnobiographer."

2. "Otras 16 personas ejecutadas en Guatemala por los escuadrones," *La Jornada* (Mexico), 11 September 1989, 1.

3. Rosalina, director of Conavigua, in an interview with Irene Matthews, 20 September 1989. For my protection as well as hers, I was not told "Rosalina's" full name at our first meeting, although it was not difficult to discover. CONAVIGUA, *Coordinadora Nacional de Viudas de Guatemala* (the National Coordination of Guatemalan Widows) was consistently one of the most active and effective human rights organizations: The members of CONAVIGUA, primarily but not entirely women, formed the basis of the regular Guatemalan manifestations demanding information about the disappeared. Against a rapidly worsening situation in which even the civil patrols had been taken over by the army's worst assassins, CONAVIGUA (with some 14,000 members in 1996) was denouncing human rights abuses by the military, educating women left unprotected by the army's actions, providing daily essentials, and teaching women and children how to fight for survival.

4. David Stoll cites a number of literary critics—John Beverley and George Yúdice, among others—to support his principal demand for truthfulness, above all, in *testimonios*. His argument is somewhat tautological: "*I, Rigoberta Menchú* does not belong in the genre of which it is the most famous example, because it is not the eye-witness account it purports to be" (Stoll 242). But in her own text, Rigoberta Menchú frequently advises her readers that she herself has not *witnessed* certain events, but has details of what happened. Stoll himself balked at confronting "Latin Americanists" (mainly the same literary critics he cites) at their annual conference in 1990, since "if there had been an important reason to challenge [Rigoberta's] 1982 account," he would have done so himself, and "not through a third party quoting [him] for a minute or two"(Stoll 1999, 240).

5. John Beverley seems to presuppose some of Stoll's concerns, but in a much larger arena: he wonders whether more anarchic forms of emergent popular-democratic culture are preempted when texts such as Rigoberta's are posited as "a new form of literature," or made into "a new form of alternative reading to the canon" (Beverley 1989, 26). "Genre-fying" written texts certainly drags along problems of its own, but hardly competes with the "mass media" Stoll accuses of latching on to Rigoberta and thus forming, as well as disseminating, public interest.

6. The outcry in the press preceded the publication date of Stoll's book. Headlines included "Nobel Winner Accused of Stretching Truth," (the *New York Times*, 15 December 1998, International, 1); "Nobel laureate 'invented life story'," (the *Independent* (London), 16 December 1998, 13); "Nobel Prize winner 'told a pack of lies'," (the *Guardian* (London), 16 December 1998, 14). Rigoberta gave two press conferences early in 1999, in response to those advance notices. She is reported in *El País* as reminding us: "El premio Nobel de la paz no es premio Nobel de literatura. Este se lo dan a alguién que escribe libros. A mí no me lo dan por un libro. El de la paz es un premio simbólico por el papel jugado en el proceso de la paz." (*El País*, 24 January 1999, n.p.) [The Nobel Prize for Peace is not the Nobel Prize for Literature. The former is given to someone who writes books. They don't give me a prize for a book. The prize for peace is a symbolic prize for the role played in the peace process.] Robin Wilson takes a more measured approach to the polemic in "A Challenge to the Veracity of a Multicultural Icon," *The Chronicle of Higher Education*, 15 January 1999, A14–A16; and Peter Canby summarizes Rigoberta's New York press encounter in his *NYRB* article, 32.

7. Interview with Irene Matthews in the office of GAM (Grupo de Apoyo Mutuo, Mutual Support Group), Guatemala City, 22 September 1989. "No me llamo viuda," Nineth told me and added later in response to my question about gendering Guatemala's civil war: "Hombres son la mayoría del ejército, pero también la mayoría de los secuestrados . . . se han llevado mujeres pero no en la

magnitud de los hombres. Por ejemplo, tomaron a Fernando, pero me dejaron a mí." [Men make up the majority of the army, but they are also the majority of the disappeared. For example, they took Fernando (Nineth's husband, on 18 February 1984), but they left me.] I asked her if that might have been an accident; with a burst of malice she replied, "Les hubiera servido mejor tomarnos a los dos . . . estarán arrepentidos" [they'd have been better off taking the two of us . . . they must be regretting it]. Nineth de García has been an indomitable force for justice in the country since her husband's disappearance and was elected to Guatemala's civilian congress in 1995 (cf. note 25 below).

8. An uneasy truce was agreed upon in Guatemala in December 1996, with peace accords monitored by the United Nations. The CEH was established through the Accord of Oslo on 23 June 1994, "in order to clarify with objectivity, equity, and impartiality, the human rights violations and acts of violence connected with the armed confrontation that caused suffering among the Guatemalan people" (a). I cite here from the Internet version at: http://hrdata.aass.org/ceh/report/english/toc.html.

9. These figures are very close to those published in the earlier REMHI (Recuperación de la Memoria Histórica) report, which identified, by name, more than a quarter of the war's estimated two hundred thousand dead and disappeared, documented more than four hundred massacres, and found that the Guatemalan Army and associated paramilitary groups were responsible for ninety percent of the crimes and that guerrilla factions had committed less than five percent of the killings. Bishop Juan Gerardi Conedera, founder and director of the Guatemalan Archdiocese Office of Human Rights, was bludgeoned to death at his home on 26 April 1998, two days after the Human Rights Report was published. Peter Canby includes a brief overview of the REMHI report and its sources in his extended essay dealing with the Stoll/Menchú polemic in the *New York Review of Books*, 8 April 1999 [cf. esp. p 29]; Francisco Goldman writes a biography of the bishop and investigates his acolytes, his enemies, and his death in "Murder Comes for the Bishop," *The New Yorker*, 15 March 1999, 60–77.

10. In an interview with Terry Gross, "Fresh Air," 4 March 1999.

11. George Lovell (1988) identifies these conquests (in broad terms) as: (1) colonization by Spain; (2) local and international capitalism; and (3) state Terror.

12. In the case of modern Guatemala, where Mayan lifestyles of subsistence agriculture were seriously eroded both by the plantation system controlled by large landowners and by a series of legal enactments splintering traditional small farms, family cohesion stubbornly persisted in focusing on inherited patches of land, however tiny, inaccessible, or difficult to till. The displacement of large groups of peasants and their compulsory rehousing in "model villages" was, in part, an attempt to break that traditional loyalty to "the earth" with more govern-

able communality. The relationship of the people to the church has proved to be equally tenacious and unpredictable. In the 1950s and 60s, the Catholic Church introduced an expansive missionary program which, although initially conservative (intended to give the Catholic Church a more concerned community profile in the face of incursions by Protestant acolytes), eventually both raised Maya consciousness and promoted community self-reliance. According to W. George Lovell, by 1975, the agricultural, consumer, and credit cooperatives promoted by *Acción Católica* posed a direct challenge to the Guatemalan status quo. Lovell suggests that this expansion of community self-interest, in conjunction with the urgency of personally repairing ruined communities after the earthquake of 1976, provoked a major confrontation between community and state interests. (cf. Lovell, 1988, p. 444 and fns. 116–122)

13. After several hundred pages examining the semiotics of encounter and intervention, Todorov returns in his epilogue to the Mayan woman:

> A Mayan woman died devoured by dogs. . . Her husband, of whom she is the "internal other," already leaves her no possibility of asserting herself as a free subject: fearing he'll be killed in the war, he seeks to ward off the danger by depriving the woman of her will; but war will not only be an affair among men: even when her husband is dead, the wife must continue to belong to him. When the Spanish conquistador appears, this woman is no more than the place where the desires and the wills of two men confront each other. To kill men, to rape women: these are at once proof that a man wields power and his reward. (*The Conquest of America*, 246)

Todorov's comprehension of the "tragedy of the other"—woman as the place of desire between two men—is interestingly ambivalent. The husband "deprives the woman of her will," yet choosing "to obey her husband and the rules of her own society [. . .] she places all that remains to her of personal will in defending [herself against] the violence of which she is the object." A hopeless defense if she *has* no will since it has been prohibited to her; and, anyway, what sort of will-full "choice" weighs between rape and death? (But please see modern Guatemalan women's response to that "choice," below.)

14. This incident is one whose details David Stoll takes great pains to refute. He can find no other villager who remembers a group massacre of prisoners of exactly this nature, although "it was not rare for the army to humiliate and torture captives before they were killed, even in front of their families" (Stoll 69). He records, however, commentaries about a group of young men brought to the village and publicly assassinated by the military, probably including Petrocinio,

Rigoberta's brother. (see chapter 24 in *IRM*, 172–182; chapter 5 in Stoll 1999, 68–70.)

15. Despite the difficulties of gaining detailed reports from already traumatized victims, there is plenty of evidence of sexual assault during military campaigns in Guatemala. One report states: "one woman was brought to Rabinal and held in the *destacamento* (military detachment) for almost a month, was raped over 300 times, including twice by the lieutenant in charge, and in front of her father, who was tied up and held in the same room. She has stated:

> Night after night a group of soldiers would enter—sometimes ten, sometimes fifteen—and they would throw me down. One would strip me and they would do it over and over, and you can't say anything because they threaten to kill you. I had two nights when they left me alone because the soldiers went to a party to get drunk. But there were nights when I really suffered.

When she left the *destacamento* for the army (!) refugee camp, the same soldiers who raped her gave her five pounds of rice each to 'start a new life' [Americas Watch Report (1984): *Guatemala: A Nation of Prisoners*, 111].

16. This form of "solidarity" training has been broadly experienced and recorded: from Greece to China to Vietnam to Central America, widely cited in Susan Brownmiller (1975) and Anthony Wilden (1985). I quote here a "civilian" version from Michael Taussig's analysis of the "Culture of Terror" and the "Space of Death" among the Putamayos: an account of the atrocities against rubber workers in Colombia. (Taussig 1984)

17. The CEH ponders this procedure anew: "assaults on women [are] an official doctrine taught in military academies" (Tomuschat 1999).

18. It is tempting here to revert once more to historical precedence. Diego de Landa's apparently not unsympathetic sixteenth-century account of the Maya of the Yucatan veils his own interests there. An unusually assiduous inquisitor, he was in his day accused of using excessive methods—torture—to get information from the native peoples. In his introduction to "The Maya," A. R. Pagden tells us that de Landa bemoaned that "nothing could be extracted from an Indian without torture" and withdrew from all further investigations when prohibited to use that procedure. To prove his methodology, apparently, de Landa offered his own bishop a "practical demonstration of the efficacy of torture," an offer resulting in further investigations of de Landa's previous inquisitions (Pagden 1975, 14).

19. Jessica Benjamin writes on "The bonds of love: rational violence and erotic domination" in *Feminist Studies* 6:1 (Spring 1980). Nancy Chodorow writes on *The Reproduction of Mothering*. (See, in particular, ch. 10: "Post-Oedipal Gender Personality.")

20. In her conversation with me in 1989, Rigoberta—like Christian To-muschat ten years later—was particularly horrified by the treatment of mothers and of pregnant women: "El ejército tiene un tratamiento particular a la mujer, hasta mataron a mujeres y dejaron a la matriz afuera . . . es simbólico: la repro-ducción de algo diferente debe ser terminada" [the army has a special way of treating women, they even kill women and leave their womb exposed outside the body . . . this is symbolic: the reproduction of something different must be stopped.] (I.M. 1989). One might interpret as "political" Rigoberta's coda on the symbolic nature of this barbarity, but one might equally share her horror of such events as a daughter, a future mother, a woman, as any human being aware of the excessive degradation involved in training soldiers to carry out such deeds.

21. Perhaps unconsciously anticipating future doubts about the veracity of a scenario she admits not having witnessed herself, Rigoberta prefaces her account of her mother's death and torture with a disclaimer: "And I want to say in ad-vance that I have in my hands details of every step of the rapes and tortures suf-fered by my mother. I don't want to reveal too many things because it will risk the lives of some *compañeros* who are still doing a very good job" (*IRM* 198). The implication here is that there were some sympathizers spying inside the army and able to get information out to the villagers and guerrillas.

22. Stoll goes on to remark that two of the leading community groups in Guatemala—the Group for Mutual Support, and the Coordination of Widows—consist mainly of women, and women often played the leading role in rural orga-nizing, one reason being they were less likely to be killed. He continues, "although [women leaders] had little presence in some municipios, in others they obviously did, despite the army's warnings against them" (207). This seems somewhat illogical: *did* these women leaders run risks, or were they leaders sim-ply because they were "survivors of men?" Why would the army "warn against them" if the latter were the case? Jean-Marie Simon (1987) gives graphic details of abductions and assassinations among the population at large and among group leaders, including the founders of GAM. (cf. in particular 186–192)

23. In both Guatemala and El Salvador, the *campesinas "más listas"* (the "smartest") were often forced to seek the protection of one officer or soldier against the predatory claims of the rest. Rosalina Tuyuc, of CONAVIGUA lamented to me in 1989 of another "army whim" in which the widows of disap-peared village leaders are co-opted with promises of marriage ("playing on the 'weak side' of the *compañeras*"). On accepting, the women are then publicly rejected, denounced, and humiliated before their village, thus stripping them of any residual iconic significance. Or, simply, the women are also "disappeared," but with less risk of reclamation from the community if they are said to have run off with a soldier. One of CONAVIGUA's tasks was to reintegrate women into their communities with their status and dignity intact.

24. In 1995, Rosalina Tuyuc, Nineth Montenegro de García, and Manuela Alvarado took their places in Congress as members of a new liberal political party, the New Guatemala Democratic Front (FDNG). All three had spent many years in opposition to the government, on the front line of civil rights activism. "But the event also reveals one of the oddities of this [Guatemala's] politics," reports Edward Hegstrom. "Though Guatemala is still a male-dominated society, many of its important opposition political leaders are women" (*The Christian Science Monitor*, 16 January 1996, 7). Like so many other (male) commentators, Hegstrom remarks that "the women of the Guatemalan left have typically become politically active only after the men in their family have disappeared or been murdered." All three of these women received personal telephone and written death threats before taking office, but they are unlikely to run away; as Nineth de García told me ten years ago, "yo me muero aquí"—"I will die here, in my country, in Guatemala."

25. "Patas arriba: el mundo al revés discute ahora si Rigoberta merecía ese premio en lugar de discutir si ese premio la merecía." Eduardo Galeano writes the "Contratapa" in *Página 12* (Argentina).

REFERENCES

Benjamin, Jessica. 1980. "The Bonds of Love: Rational Violence and Erotic Domination," *Feminist Studies* 6:1(Spring), 144–174.

Beverley, John. 1989. "The Margin at the Center: on *Testimonio* (Testimonial Narrative)," *Modern Fiction Studies* 35:1 (Spring), 11–28.

———. 1993. "'Through All Things Modern': Second Thoughts on Testimonio." In *Critical Theory, Cultural Politics, and Latin American Narrative*, edited by Steven M. Bell, Albert H. LeMay, and Leonard Orr, 125–151. Notre Dame: University of Notre Dame Press.

Brownmiller, Susan. 1975. *Against Our Will: Men, Women, and Rape*. New York: Simon and Schuster.

Burgos, Elisabeth. 1985. *Me llamo Rigoberta Menchú y así me nació la conciencia*. Mexico: Siglo veintiuno.

Canby, Peter. 1999. "The Truth About Rigoberta Menchú." *The New York Review of Books*, 8 April 1999: 28–33.

Chodorow, Nancy. 1978. *The Reproduction of Mothering. Psychoanalysis and the Sociology of Gender*. Berkeley and Los Angeles: University of California Press.

de Landa, Diego. (c. 1566) *Relación de las cosas de Yucatán* (Mexico: Truay, 1938). [*Diego de Landa's Account of the Affairs of the Yucatan: The Maya*. 1975. Ed. and trans. A. R. Pagden. Chicago: J. Philip O'Hara Inc., 1975. I have cited the Spanish version and the English translation in Pagden: 89–91.]

Feal, Rosemary Geisdorfer. 1990. "Spanish American Ethnobiography and the Slave Narrative Tradition: *Biografía de un cimarrón* and *Me llamo Rigoberta Menchú*," *Modern Language Studies*, 20:1, 100–111.

Felman, Shoshana, and Dori Laub, M.D. 1992. *Testimony. Crises of Witnessing in Literature, Psychoanalysis, and History*. New York and London: Routledge.

Franco, Jean. 1985. "Killing Priests, Nuns, Women, Children." In *On Signs*, edited by Marshall Blonsky. Baltimore: Johns Hopkins University Press.

Galeano, Eduardo. 1999. "El Nobel y ella." *Página 12*. Argentina, n.d., n.p.

Goldman, Francisco. 1999. "Murder Comes for the Bishop." *The New Yorker*, 15 March 1999: 60–77.

"Guatemala: Memory of Silence," Report of the Commission for Historical Clarification, (accessed 5 April 1999) at http://hrdata.aaas.org/ceh/report/english/toc.html.

Hegstrom, Edward. 1996. "In Guatemala's Male-Ruled Politics, Activist Widows Break Into Congress." *The Christian Science Monitor*, 16 January 1996: 7.

Jonas, Susanne. 1991. *The Battle for Guatemala. Rebels, Death Squads, and U.S. Power*. Boulder: Westview Press.

Lovell, W. George. 1988. "Surviving Conquest: The Maya of Guatemala in Historical Perspective," *Latin American Research Review* (Vol. 23 2):25–57.

Menchú, Rigoberta. 1984. *I, Rigoberta Menchú. An Indian Woman in Guatemala*. Trans. Ann Wright. London: Verso.

Millett, David L. 1995. "An End to Militarism? Democracy and the Armed Forces in Central America," *Current History*, February: 71–76.

Simon, Jean-Marie. 1987. *Guatemala. Eternal Spring: Eternal Tyranny*. New York and London: Norton.

Stoll, David. 1999. *Rigoberta Menchú and the Story of All Poor Guatemalans*. Boulder: Westview Press.

Taussig, Michael. 1984. "Culture of Terror—Space of Death. Roger Casement's Putamayo Report and the Explanation of Torture," *Comparative Studies in Society and History*, 2:3 (July): 467–497.

Theweleit, Klaus. 1987. *Male Fantasies*, Vol. I. Minneapolis: University of Minnesota Press.

Todorov, Tsvetan. (1982) 1984. *The Conquest of America. The Question of the Other* (I have revised the translations). New York: Harper and Row.

Tomuschat, Christian and Albrecht Randelzhofer, editors. 1999. *State Responsibility and the Individual: Reparation in Instances of Grave Violations of Human Rights*. Martinus Nijhoff.

Yúdice, George. 1991. "*Testimonio* and Postmodernism." *Latin American Perspectives*, Issue 70, 18:3 (Summer), 15–31.

Wilden, Anthony. 1985. "In the Penal Colony: The Body as Discourse of the Other," *Semiotica* 54.1/2: 33–85.

Wilson, Robin. 1999. "A Challenge to the Veracity of a Multicultural Icon." *The Chronicle of Higher Education*, 15 January 1999: A14–A16.

Zimmermann, Marc. 1989. "*Testimonio* in Guatemala: Beyond *Díias de la Sevla* and Rigoberta Menchú," M/MLA, November: 1–10.

CHAPTER 9

Women and Militarization in Israel
Forgotten Letters in the Midst of Conflict

ISIS NUSAIR

INTRODUCTION

I started writing this paper in the spring of 1995. At the time, I was taking a class on Women and Militarization with Cynthia Enloe at Clark University, and one of the course requirements was to conduct an interview with a woman in which we analyze the militarization processes in her life. My friend Hilla happened to be visiting, and she agreed to work with me on this project throughout her one-week stay. We started working in traditional and nontraditional settings: in the office, around a meal, during a walk. Many times, while discussing other issues or through a sudden remembrance of a forgotten detail about militarization, a whole new chapter of our project evolved. Despite our long friendship, Hilla and I recognize our different ethnic, cultural and national backgrounds, she being a Jewish Israeli and I a Palestinian from Israel.[1] This realization enriched our debate on the subject of militarization of individuals and institutions in Israeli society, and could provide the reader with a comparative analysis of the nature of militarization in our lives.[2]

Hilla could not participate in drafting this paper because of lack of time, and because of our separate locations, her living in Israel and me studying in the United States. The paper provides a vertical and horizontal reading of our correspondence and of the footnotes. These two levels of narrative, vertical/personal and horizontal/academic are subsequently real/fictional.[3] They interweave continuously to form a certain meaning/presentation.

Dear Hilla

I was very glad to receive your letter and hear about the recent peace developments at home. Who could have believed that the 'historic' handshake between Rabin and Arafat on the lawn of the White House could have ever taken place?[4] Yet, despite the national and international peace euphoria, I could hear/read between the lines of your letter a lot of fear and suspicion. Maybe this is embedded in being a member of the Israeli society or maybe we have gone through a similar scenario before. I still remember General Ariel Sharon's invasion of Lebanon, named by the Israeli government as the Peace of Galilee Operation.[5] What peace were they talking about, who defines it, and whom does it serve? Could occupation of other countries ever bring peace? I guess it is about time we start naming things with their real names.

*   *   *

Dear Hilla,

Where to start and how to proceed in discussing the militarization processes of our lives? How can I move beyond the initial stage of asking the following questions? How is the construction of the Israeli collective identity created and maintained, and what role does the education system play? How do daily war practices shape and how are they shaped by rituals, symbols, values, tradition, and culture? What are the connections between the military and civil society? Who defines hi/story, who is left out, and how are past/present/future 'realities' constantly re/constructed? How do constructions of patriarchy, masculinity and femininity, and public/private spheres shape the nature of political discourse in Israel?

*   *   *

Dear Isis,

I think it is hard and quite impossible to differentiate between the state, society, and the military in Israel.[6] They are one for me. The army is like the Eighth Passenger, that science fiction story about a monster that grows inside you and threatens to control and kill everything. I decided not to go to the army because of the horror stories I used to hear from my scouts councilor, who, after finishing her service in the army, became a religious orthodox Jew. Maybe that is what she needed in order to remain sane. I became a vegetarian just like her. I wanted to avoid the control and humiliation of the military officers, maintain my independence, and not become an object like the others. Maybe I was not politically aware at the time, yet I strongly felt that the military institution is very patriarchal and not a place for me.

*   *   *

Dear Hilla,

I realize that my life is militarized, but I insist on surrounding the word 'militarization' with quotation marks. I, the alien creature who comes from 'nowhere' and could hardly feel any belonging or even be considered to belong to anything in this state,[7] stand in between the television shows, the daily newspapers, the education curriculum, the racist/sexist/egocentric/nationalist discourses which define a 'certain' relation towards me and witness/formulate my marginalization and consequently my 'militarization'.[8] Do you think that because of your 'pure Israeliness' you tend to see yourself as totally militarized, while I prefer the quotation marks around the word 'militarization' as around everything else in my life?

*   *   *

Dear Isis,

I remember my second grade participation in Memorial Day celebrations. It was 1972 and I was eight at the time. We came to school with white shirts, and read the names of the soldiers who fell in the wars of Israel. We glorified their heroism and sacrifice. We had a chance to meet the parents of the soldiers who died in these wars. I was surprised to discover, when attending Memorial Day celebrations at my son's school last year, that these celebrations are still the same. I came to realize that the militarization process is continuous, persistent, starts from an early age, and is defined by constructions/interpretations of daily and national events. From the moment you are born, they start feeding you the education about the need to love and protect your country. Many of the songs we learnt at school revolved around themes of friendship, bonding, religion, love of the land, and love mixed with blood. Now that I am reflecting back on my childhood days, I recall this song:

> Not because the color of the eyes is sky blue, I fell in love with
> him
> He is simply a combat soldier, no more and no less, and he is my
> soldier

The process of militarized education takes place not only at school, but at the scouts, in the street, and on the radio and television. It is a learning/construction of meanings about the national security and the protection of the homeland.[9] Yet, what happens when these meanings are militarized? Do our relations to them become militarized too? I remember how jumpy my previous partner became before he was called to the military draft. He could hardly control himself, and once he came out of control and attacked me. I know that his violence has a lot to do with the army, and me being his partner at the time involves me in this process, whether I want it or not. I realize that many people could isolate these incidents and see no connection between them and the military.[10]

*   *   *

Dear Hilla,

Could one isolate themselves from the process of militarization? Is it possible for a fish to live without water? I consider my life to be 'militarized' and this militarization is part of my memory and identity. I was born in 1967, the year of The Occupation. As a child, I could never understand why members of my community associate my birth with war. At age ten, I started envying children of the world for having a flag and a national anthem, and at age fifteen the Israeli army invaded Lebanon. That war shaped my political consciousness and made me realize the intensity of the intrusive nature of the Israeli military in my life. They were present in every little detail. They were in our house, on the radio, in the newspaper, and on the television screen boasting of their macho power and military elitism. My memory was bombarded with war images of occupying soldiers and slaughtered bodies scattered all over the place. I wrote in my journal about the war; I wrote short stories and essays, too. I could not participate in the public demonstrations against the war and against the Sabra and Shatila massacres in my hometown Nazareth. I could only peek through the window to witness it all.[11] A year after, my classmate and I prepared a lecture at school in memory of the Sabra and Shatila massacres. Our history teacher interrupted our presentation, and criticized our naiveté and lack of experience. He warned us against anything that will cause the security service authorities to put our names on their 'black lists'. I could not do anything then but cry secretly in my heart.

The following years brought more wars. War becomes part of the daily ritual of living. The war is here, unbearably heavy and disturbingly present, like a cloud sitting in my heart.

*   *   *

Dear Isis,

You wondered in your previous letter about whether I see an embedded contradiction in living a militarized life and in resisting the military service. Well, I believe that what gets to be defined by me and what gets to be defined by society is highly intractable. I remember aspects in my childhood which helped me resist serving in the army. My parents always emphasized the humanistic aspects of life. They also made me feel that, as a girl, I am worthy of something, and that I can do what I want. Now I realize that there were lots of double messages in their bringing me up, even though they never directly stated that they hated Arabs. My father was very angry when he heard that I was not going to the army. He himself has, since the 1973 war, managed to avoid the military draft. I do not know if his anger stemmed from not wanting me to be stigmatized. I perceived myself as having an 'antisocial' personality. I hung out with people who considered themselves and were considered by society as 'antisocial'. They looked, dressed, acted, talked, and thought differently.[12] When I wanted to enter a state institution, attend university, I had to redefine my relation to society. Suddenly, I became aware of what it means to serve in the army; it is an integral part of your life and curriculum. I was afraid that people would stigmatize me as being mentally ill for refusing to serve in the army.

Many of the skills that I learnt while studying social work have helped me find some kind of an equilibrium between my life and society.

It takes a while, and it is still hard. I need to negotiate it all continuously, especially when it involves people that are close to me, like my mother, partner, father, friends, husbands of friends, and children.[13] I realize now that there are things that I cannot change, and I am learning to live with them. I do not know, though, what price I am paying, yet I know that this equilibrium keeps me going.

*   *   *

Dear Hilla,

Throughout our correspondence we have been talking and writing in Hebrew, and I have been thinking in Arabic and translating our conversations into English. I wonder about the reasons behind the state's law obliging me to learn Arabic, Hebrew, and English since elementary school. By the time I graduated from high school, I was fluent not only in those three languages but also in the history, literature, and religion of the Jewish people in the diaspora and since the creation of the state of Israel.

In high school, I started designing my own parallel curriculum to that imposed by the Israeli Ministry of Education. They insisted on wiping out anything that has to do with the history and literature of the Palestinian people. I felt that they were wiping out my identity and existence. My self-designed extra-curriculum helped me understand the politics of learning in Israeli society. I learned how to bridge the gaps between my knowledge and life, and I learned the limits of the Israeli collective identity and my position in it as an outsider from the inside.

Making sense of the private/public resistance to the militarization processes in Israeli society

How could we make sense of the public and private resistance to militarization processes in our lives, and does this process differ among men and women, Jews and Palestinians? How does belonging to the state and constructions of our collective identities inform our resistance? Would our resistance be the same if we had served in the army, and what does it mean to resist a militarized mentality of occupation in a country drunk on victory and omnipotence?

*   *   *

Dear Isis,

I feel belonging and responsibility to the state. I get angry and do not agree with what is happening, but I feel I have an influence though. I know I am very weird. I like the country, the earth, the stones, but not the people. I see the average Israeli as a rude person, and that makes me sick. It is as if I have a garden and they would walk over my plants and would not even say "sorry." This is my relation towards the men, with women it is more complicated.

I see a way out of this situation. I think that our generation will grow and things will be all right. It will take time and lots of work, especially from women who participate in making the politics of the state. Then, things will start changing! You can already see some change. Since the signing of the Peace Agreement in 1993, the Arab character in educational textbooks is changing to the better and Islamic civilization is being introduced at Jewish schools.[14] I believe that there is a difference between my generation and my parents' generation. I was born and grew up in Israel, and that makes a difference. The state is already established, it is there. Feminist resistance is not easy in Israeli society.[15] It is to oppose something that the whole society is structured around. It is to harm the social morale. There is always a need to discuss thoughts and tender things. Resistance! Oh, well! Many times I feel not ready or do not want to resist. At times, I have political arguments with people and I can say what I want, and at other times I find it not useful to 'fight' back.

*   *   *

Dear Hilla,

I see resistance as a condition for living, a necessary act to negotiate my existence and define my identity. Early on, I understood that resistance is not a privilege, it is a state of living. It is a process of redefining the meaning and practice of politics in Israel. You do not look like an Arab, many of my Jewish classmates in the university always said. What should an Arab look like, I always answered. I do not always want to have a politicized life. It tires me, rips me apart, and steals the best moments of my life. Yet I know that there is no way around it. I have to live and resist simultaneously on different fronts. Growing up feeling and realizing my location on the margin of Israeli collectivity opens more space for me to resist. As an outsider/insider, I question my 'non-existence' by questioning back the prevailing notions of Israeli collective identity.

*   *   *

Dear Hilla,

Are you tired and hesitant because of the constant need to negotiate the contradictions of militarization? Are you tired because you have to fight on various fronts, or is it because you are 'alone' in your struggle? Can I, on the other hand, allow myself to be tired? I think that we need to collectively challenge and change the dominant hegemonic discourses about Israeli national security and its definitions of war and peace. It scares me, though, to think of anything in collective terms. Realizing commonalities and differences and providing a chance for equal representation of the usually underrepresented puts the boundaries of collectivity into question. Learning about the experiences of resistance of men and women in militarized societies in other countries provides a space for comparison and exchange. I hope that we can pool our resistance to support and strengthen each other. So that when you are tired of 'fighting', you can get strength from other resisting women.[16] I hope you have been sleeping well lately and your nightmares are fading away.[17]

EPILOGUE

I wonder why I find myself resisting ending this paper. Many of the questions raised in it are still open, and the vulnerability and pain of dealing with the embedded violence in militarization is not dealt with yet. Both Hilla and I have avoided speaking directly about the connections between militarization and public and private violence in our lives. Hilla's description of the average Israeli as walking over your garden without apologizing, of 'them' taking away your creativity and oppressing your development, and of the eighth passenger growing inside you until it controls everything suggest a strong sense of rape. When I told Hilla of this observation she said nothing but wondered about the meanings and ramifications of the intrusive and controlling nature of the private and public violence in militarized societies.[18]

NOTES

1. Hilla considers her being Jewish as problematic, for the state of Israel uses the term simultaneously to mean religion and nationality. Hilla does not define/identify herself as a Zionist. I, on the other hand, will refer to myself as a Palestinian from Israel and not as an Israeli Arab or an Israeli Palestinian. In my view, the notion of Israeliness holds a definition by the state of what is Israel and who is an Israeli.

2. According to Cynthia Enloe, militarism is a package of ideas about the army, while the military is the institution itself. Militarization is the process in which individuals or political systems either become increasingly dependent upon, controlled and affected by the military, or a process by which individuals and political systems adopt militaristic values, beliefs, and presumptions about human hi/story that enhances military ones. For more elaboration, see Enloe's *Does Khaki Become You? The Militarization of Women's Lives* (chs. 1, 8) and *The Morning After: Sexual Politics at the End of the Cold War* (chs. 8, 9). See also Sharoni's *Gender and the Israeli-Palestinian Conflict: The Politics of Women's Resistance* (chs. 3, 6).

3. What is real and what is fictional depends on the way the reading of this paper develops. Hilla and I did work on analyzing the militarization processes of our lives. I choose to present this project as a fictional correspondence between Hilla and myself. The letters written by Hilla are an exact transcription of my interviews with her. The real/fictional split could challenge notions about the personal/academic split, and definitions of "truth".

4. See Simona Sharoni's *Gender and the Israeli-Palestinian Accord: Feminist Approaches to International Politics* for an analysis of the gendered nature of peace and war in Israel.

5. General Sharon's invasion of Lebanon presumed canceling the existence of the Palestinian Liberation Organization in Lebanon in seventy-two hours. Israel occupies until today a fifteen-mile security zone in Southern Lebanon.

6. Errella Shadmi argues in *Women, Palestinians, Zionism: A Personal View*, that the main mechanism employed to achieve "national unity" is "compulsory Zionism," an uncompromising demand, enforced by means of a wide range of methods, to adopt the values, attitudes, and behaviors prescribed by Zionist ideology. Each and every Israeli, adds Shadmi, is expected to follow the socially approved and sanctioned norms and to be committed and loyal to the collective will. Pluralism, she argues, is possible only in so far as it does not threaten Zionist ideology, where the particular aspirations of the different and the deviant are ignored, and hence the voices of Palestinians, homosexuals, Sepharadic Jews, and women are silenced. According to Shadmi, new ideological boundaries were

established after the creation of Israel in 1948, based upon their common denominator, which revolved around three principles: God, Family, and Homeland. Thus the Zionist ethos, concludes Shadmi, was dramatically transformed: fundamentalism, nationalism, militarism, and phallocentricism became its key features towards the end of the 1970s and 1980s. For further elaboration on the subject see Mayer, *Women and the Israeli Occupation: The Context*; Chazan and Marfi, *What Has Occupation Done to Palestinian and Israeli Women*; Sharoni, *Homefront as Battlefield: Gender, Military, Occupation and Violence against Women*; Meyer, *Israel Now: Portrait of a Troubled Land*; Shapiro, *Land and Power: The Zionist Resort to Force, 1881–1948*, and Horowitz and Lisak, *Trouble in Utopia: the Overburdened Polity of Israel*.

7. The state of Israel was created in 1948 on the Zionist premise of land without people for people without land. According to Deborah Gerner, *One Land, Two Peoples: The Conflict Over Palestine*, many early Zionists operated under a set of illusions about Palestine that blinded them to the true situation: the illusion that Palestine was an almost empty land that could easily accommodate their dreams and aspirations, the illusion that the people already in Palestine would welcome Zionist colonization, and especially the illusion that any resistance to Zionism could be blamed on Arab politicians rather than on broad-based sentiment against the European immigration.

8. The Israeli media ignores/marginalizes Palestinians from Israel from its rhetoric (since they stand on the margins of the Israeli national/Zionist collective identity), and, if presented, the image is that of backward people. The education curriculum for Palestinians in Israel is determined by the Ministry of Education and completely ignores the history and literature of the Palestinian people. See Majed El-Haj, *Education for Democracy in Arab Schools: Problems and Missions* and Sammy Smooha, *Arabs and Jews in Israel: Conflicted and Shared Attitudes in a Divided Society*. Palestinian women in Israel are marginalized on the basis of being women in a patriarchal Palestinian society and on the basis of being Palestinians in a Jewish state. See Nabila Espanioly *Palestinian Women in Israel: Identity in Light of the Occupation*.

9. According to Kathy Ferguson, the agents of unification of the state of Israel are the state, the media, the schools, and the relentless unifying drone of the discourse of "national security". On this level, the centralizing forces work at corralling the diversity within Israeli life, and, thus, at reinforcing reigning claims to meanings. The dominant self-understanding is a particularly strident masculinity, a gendered underwriting of the central order. The dominant culture forces are threatened by the manyness of things, the differences, which put constant pressure on prevailing truth claims and self-understandings. The agents of unification attempt to tame the fractious dialogues, to marshal the selective re-

sources of history, geography, and culture around a single understanding of what it means to be an Israeli.

10. In Simona Sharoni's *Homefront as Battlefield: Gender, Military, Occupation and Violence Against Women*, the story of Gilad Sheman is presented. Gilad, a twenty-three-year-old Israeli Jewish man, doing his military service in Gaza, shot and killed in April 1989 a seventeen-year-old Palestinian woman, Amal Muhammed Hasin, as she was reading a book on her front porch. The regional Military Court convicted Shemen of carelessness in causing Hasin's death, but he was released after an appeal. Two years later, on 30 June 1991 Gilad Shemen shot and killed his former girlfriend, nineteen-year-old Einav Rogel. Sharoni sees this story as underscoring the complex relationship between sexism, militarism, and violence against women as interrelated in the private and public spheres of the Israeli life.

12. According to Tikva Honig-Parnass, in *Jewish Fundamentalism and Oppression of Women as Inherent in the Jewish-Zionist State*, in the course of the Zionist Movement's efforts to build the new secular national collectivity, it did not completely break away from Jewish Orthodoxy, but preserved religious myths and symbols among central symbols of Zionism—including the cardinal "commandment" of Zionism, immigration to Israel. The biblical connection to the land and the connection between the bible and present day life in the old-new land were strongly emphasized. Despite their attempts to invest the Bible with historical, philosophical, and mythological meaning, it has remained primarily a religious document and, as such, has had an impact on the nature of the political aspirations of the state. Even the most important holidays, which were and are celebrated in the state of Israel, are religious. Thus, the nucleus of the state symbols remain today Jewish-religious. The rest is but a thin veneer of what only appears to be secularism. For further information see Jehuda Reinhartz, *The Transition from Yishuv to State: Social and Ideological Changes*; Dina Porat, *"Attitudes of the Young State toward the Holocaust and Its Survivors: A Debate over Identity and Values"*; Myron Aronoff, *Myths, Symbols, and Rituals of the Emerging State*; Yael Zerubavel, *New Beginnings, Old Past: The Collective Memory of Pioneering in Israeli Culture*; Anton Shammas, *At Half-Mast: Myths, Symbols, and Rituals of the Emerging State: A Personal Testimony of an "Israeli Arab."*

13. Hilla's mother works in a civil company that sells its products to the army. Hilla's partner, according to her, suffers from a post-traumatic syndrome after serving in the army during the Israeli invasion of Lebanon. The husband of Hilla's best friend is an officer in a special army unit and Hilla's sons are obliged to serve in the Israeli army for three years by the age of eighteen.

14. For an evaluation of the Israeli government's education policies in regard to the representation of the "Arab" in educational textbooks, see Esther

Shiela and Deborah Koubobi, *The Contribution of Literature to Education for Democracy and Arab/Jewish Coexistence.*

15. According to Tikva Honig-Parnass, *Feminism and the Peace Struggle in Israel*, the feminist movement in Israel whose members are central activists in Women and Peace is characterized by an avoidance of coming to terms with the question of connection between the Jewish-Zionist nature of the state and the oppression of women in Israel. Thus, in their struggles on specific issues of women's oppression—whether in the legal/legislation sphere or that of culture and symbols—the feminists have avoided asking questions regarding the fact that this oppression is an inherent part of the structure of this society and of the Jewish-Zionist state in which they live. By means of its conceptualization of the oppression of women in Israel, it was possible to dissent from the 'national consensus' as women and to fight for the general feminist goal of a society where there is gender equality, without leaving the nationalist Zionist consensus. This created a paradox whereby the targets of the feminist struggle remained overly general and vague on the one hand, and on the other hand could be very concrete—when they involved questions like the abortion law, rape, and violence within the family. Specific targets such as these were attacked without acknowledging the connection between them and the structure and ideology of the state, which are the real factors responsible for the oppression of women in these spheres. See also Yvonne Deutsch, *Israeli Women against the Occupation: Political Growth and the Persistence of Ideology.*

16. Sharoni's *Gender and the Israeli-Palestinian Conflict: The Politics of Women's Resistance* concludes that there is a need to move beyond simply speaking about women's perspectives on the Israeli-Palestinian conflict and their struggles for a just and lasting peace in the region to include the complementary project of making men visible as men and exposing the discourse of militarized masculinity underlying the Israeli-Palestinian conflict and conventional writing about it.

17. Hilla recounted, throughout the work on this project, three nightmares. The first is about the Nazis controlling the world; the second about the Arabs controlling Tel Aviv, where Hilla is left alone with her mother and aunt; and the third about Netanyahu and Sharon (right wing Likud party leaders) controlling Israel's media and politics. It is worth mentioning that Hilla recounted her nightmares in 1995, a year before the rise of Netanyahu into power in Israel.

18. According to Errella Shadmi in *Occupation, Violence, and Women in Israeli Society*, violence is well-rooted in the Israeli society: Israel was founded on and continues to exist by virtue of armed force. Power and militarism, argues Shadmi, have become the lifeblood of Israeli culture, in which the history of the occupation has been deliberately concealed under cover of myths and alleged security considerations, in which the army is the place where political careers are

made, in which the soldier is the culture hero, and war stories the key literature, and in which coercion of various types—religious, ethnic, gender—has become the acceptable norm in political negotiations.

REFERENCES

Arab Association for Human Rights. 1990. *Palestinians inside Israel: An Unrecognized Minority.* Nazareth, Israel.

Aronoff, Myron. 1991. "Myths, Symbols, and Rituals of the Emerging State." In *New Perspectives on Israeli History: The Early Years of the State*, edited by Lawrence Silbertein, 175–192. New York: New York University Press.

Bowden, Tom. 1982. *Army in the Defense of the State.* Tel Aviv: University Publishing Projects.

Chazan, Noami and Mariam Marſi. 1994. "What Has Occupation Done to Palestinian and Israeli Women?" In *New Perspectives on Israeli History: The Early Years of the State*, edited by Tamar Mayer, 16–32. London: Routledge.

Deutsch, Yvonne. 1994. "Israeli Women against the Occupation: Political Growth and the Persistence of Ideology." In *Women and the Israeli Occupation: The Politics of Change*, edited by Tamar Mayer, 88–105. London: Routledge.

El-Haj, Majed. 1989. *Education for Democracy in Arab Schools: Problems and Missions.* Jerusalem: The Ministry of Education and Culture.

Enloe, Cynthia. 1988. *Does Khaki Become You? The Militarization of Women's Lives.* London: Pandora Press.

———. 1993. *Sexual Politics at the End of the Cold War: The Morning After.* Berkeley: University of California Press.

Espanioly, Nabila. "Palestinian Women in Israel: Identity in Light of the Occupation." In *Women and the Israeli Occupation: The Politics of Change*, edited by Tamar Mayer, 106–120. London: Routledge.

Ferguson, Kathy. 1995. *Kibbutz Journal.* California: Trilogy Books.

Gerner, Deborah. 1991. *One Land, Two Peoples: The Conflict Over Palestine.* Boulder, CO: Westview Press.

Honig-Parnass, Tikva. 1992. "Feminism and the Peace Struggle in Israel," *News From Within* 8:2–5. Jerusalem: The Alternative Information Center.

———. 1992. "Jewish Fundamentalism and Oppression of Women as Inherent in the Jewish-Zionist State," *News from Within* 8:6–12. Jerusalem: The Alternative Information Center.

Horowitz, Dan and Moshe Lisak. 1990. *Trouble in Utopia: The Overburdened Polity of Israel.* Tel-Aviv: Am Oved (in Hebrew).

Liebman, Charles and Eliezer Don-Yehia. 1983. *Civil Religion in Israel: Traditional Judaism and Political Culture in the Jewish State.* Berkeley: University of California Press.

Mayer, Tamar, ed. 1994. *Women and the Israeli Occupation: The Politics of Change.* London: Routledge.

———. 1994. "Women and the Israeli Occupation: The Context." In *Women and the Israeli Occupation: The Politics of Change*, edited by Tamar Mayer. 1–15. London: Routledge.

Meyer, Lawrence. 1982. *Israel Now: Portrait of a Troubled Land.* New York: Delcorte Press.

Porat, Dina. 1991. "Attitudes of the Young State toward the Holocaust and Its Survivors: A Debate over Identity and Values." In *New Perspectives on Israeli History: The Early Years of the State*, edited by Lawrence Silberstein, 157–174. New York: New York University Press.

Reinhartz, Jehuda. 1991. "The Transition from Yishuv to State: Social and Ideological Changes." In *New Perspectives on Israeli History: The Early Years of the State.*, edited by Lawrence Silberstein, 27–41. New York: New York University Press.

Said, Edward. 20 April 1995. Tufts University: Lecture on the Israeli-Palestinian Peace Process.

Shadmi, Errella. 1993. "Occupation, Violence, and Women in Israeli Society," *News From Within* 9:20-23. Jerusalem: The Alternative Information Center.

———. 1992. "Women, Palestinians, Zionism: A Personal View," *News From Within* 8:13–21. Jerusalem: The Alternative Information Center.

Shammas, Anton. 1991. "At Half–Mast: Myths, Symbols, and Rituals of the Emerging State: A Personal Testimony of an 'Israeli Arab'." In *New Perspectives on Israeli History: The Early Years of the State*, edited by Lawrence Silberstein, 216–224. New York: New York University Press.

Shapiro, Anita. 1992. *Land and Power: The Zionist Resort to Force, 1881–1948.* New York: Oxford University Press.

Sharoni, Simona. 1994. "Homefront as Battlefield: Gender, Military, Occupation and Violence Against Women." In *Women and the Israeli Occupation: The Politics of Change*, edited by Tamar Mayer, 121–137. London: Routledge.

———. 1995. *Gender and the Israeli-Palestinian Conflict: The Politics of Women's Resistance.* New York: Syracuse University Press.

———. 1996. "Gender and the Israeli-Palestinian Accord: Feminist Approaches to International Relations." In *Gendering the Middle East: Emerging Perspectives*, edited by Deniz Kandiyoti, 107–126. Syracuse: Syracuse University Press.

Shiela, Esther and Deborah Koubobi. 1988. "The Contribution of Literature to Education for Democracy and the Arab/Jewish Coexistence." In *The Education for Democracy and the Involvement of the Councilor.* 80–96. Jerusalem: The Psychological and Counseling Service in the Ministry of Education and Culture.

Silberstein, Lawrence, ed. 1991. *New Perspectives on Israeli History: The Early Years of the State.* New York: New York University Press.

Smooha, Sammy, 1989. *Arabs and Jews in Israel: Conflicted and Shared Attitudes in a Divided Society.* Colorado: Westview.

Zerubavel, Yael. 1991. "New Beginnings, Old Past: The Collective Memory of Pioneering in Israeli Culture." In *New Perspectives on Israeli History: The Early Years of the State*, edited by Lawrence Silberstein, 193–215. New York: New York University Press.

CHAPTER 10

Sudanese Women under Repression, and the Shortest Way to Equality

FATIMA AHMED IBRAHIM

EDITOR'S INTRODUCTION

Massive Sudan is also one of the most ethnically heterogeneous countries in Africa and the Middle East. The legacy of many colonialisms is a divided country, encapsulated by artificial boundaries that forcibly amalgamate "Arabs" and "Africans," Muslims, Christians, and other religions. Part of the bitter differences between "northern" and "southern" Sudan are perpetuated in the unequal regional development between the two regions. Such diversity makes generalizations very difficult. The imposition of colonial values and customs in the midst of this diversity was unsettling to gender relations.

In the more rural and less developed south, women and men relied for their political association on grassroots organizing and self-help, their organizations being forced to develop strategies to survive in the longest civil war in Africa. In an urbanizing, more economically developed central riverain and northern areas where British parliamentary institutions and legal codes prevailed until recently, people generally relied for their political association on hierarchical organizations such as nationalist and sectarian parties and their affiliates. The exception was the formidable Sudan Federation of Trade Unions, itself a hierarchically-organized and male-gendered collection of organizations. Northern women generally followed the pattern of men's organizations, forming auxiliaries, fronts, and affiliated organizations. Like southerners in general, however, women also formed neighborhood and commu-

nity cultural events where prefigurative politics reigned. These were rarely recognized by the established organizations as legitimate.

The strongest and best-known of the established women's organizations is the Sudanese Women's Union, which, for most of its forty-plus years of existence, has been headed by Fatima Ahmed Ibrahim, and affiliated (sometimes loosely, sometimes more tightly) with the Sudanese Communist Party (SCP).

The Sudanese Women's Union had branches throughout the country, and could boast of some 15,000 members in its heyday in the 1960s. Moving in and out of political good fortune, the Women's Union has been banned for many years of its existence. Now it is mainly an organization in exile, with only a clandestine vestige remaining in Sudan. But its leader, banished to England, remains a tireless campaigner against the current Islamist regime (in power since 1989). Fatima Ahmed Ibrahim is also a member of the SCP Central Committee and of the governing council of the National Democratic Alliance (a coalition of banned Sudanese political parties in exile). Eds.

Sudan is the largest country in Africa. It lies at the northeastern side of the African continent, is bounded by eight countries and has a total area of 2.6 million square kilometers. 70 percent of that area is agricultural land, pasture, and forests. The rest is either desert or semi-desert. The river Nile runs from south to north, and there are other water resources, among them the Red Sea. Sudan has a tropical climate and is a country rich in timber, cotton, rubber, gum arabic, sugar, gold, diamonds, precious stones, minerals, petroleum, livestock, wild life, cement, fruits, vegetables, fish, etc. The capital and the largest city in Sudan is Khartoum. In 1993, the population of the country was estimated at approximately 28.7 million. The Sudanese people include many races, cultures, and religions. The majority are a mixture of Arab and African, most of whom are Muslims, while one third are pure Africans, some of whom are Christians.

From 1821 to 1885, Sudan was under the rule of Turkish-Egyptian Imperialism, and from 1898 to 1956 under the rule of British-Egyptian Imperialism. During their stay in our country, the British made all the arrangements necessary to ensure that their policies and economic interests would be preserved long after their departure from Sudan, so that the country would continue to be a source of cheap manpower and raw materials, as well as a market in which they could sell their manufactured output. These arrangements are summarized in the following paragraphs.

The national economy was molded to become a primary producer and exporter of agricultural raw materials, and to remain a market for the manufactured goods produced in the West. To achieve this, every effort was made to impede any attempts to build up national industries. As part of their policy, the British did not attempt, even to a limited degree, to develop the Southern part of Sudan as they did the Northern regions. As a direct result of this deliberate policy, a situation arose which they used to instill hatred between the people of the South and of the North, and to deepen their ethnic and religious divisions. They made it appear as though the backwardness of the South was the responsibility of the Northerners, because they were Arab and Muslim. By keeping the South undeveloped and dividing us, they created a deep resentment by Southerners toward Northerners. Southerners began to associate Arabs and Muslims with domination and, therefore, with the history of slaving in the South. In addition, the British prohibited the teaching of Arabic and tribal languages at schools, and made English the only common language in Sudan. To further divide the North from the South, they forbade the people of the North to travel to the Southern part of the country without having been granted special permission. Thus, they succeeded in convincing the educated people in the South to fight for separation from the North. They trained and armed them and, as a result, a civil war broke out in 1955, just a year before the departure of the British troops in 1956. After independence was achieved, successive Sudanese governments in the North made no effort to develop the South and give its people their equal rights as citizens in order to solve the problem fairly and stop the war.

In 1957, the United States offered to give Sudan financial aid, but all the parties in the opposition and trade unions rejected it on the grounds that it was not needed and that instead of accepting the aid, the government should develop national resources and adopt a self-reliance policy. To avoid failing to accept the American aid offered, however, the prime minister of the Umma party government handed over the power to the army leader, General Ibrahim Aboud. Later on, Phillip Agee of the CIA revealed, in his book *Inside the Company CIA*, that the Americans had planned and executed that military takeover. Immediately, the military regime banned all political parties, trade unions, and our Sudanese Women's Union (SWU—the largest and oldest organization of women in the country); they then accepted the American aid. Many American economic advisors were sent to Sudan and started to direct our economic policy in particular, and our government policy in general. This marked the beginning of a deterioration in the economic situation of the country, and we are now drowned in debt. Evidently, a new form of imperialism found its way to our country soon after Sudan gained its political independence from Britain—this time in the form of economic advisors rather than military troops.

In October 1964, the Sudanese regained democracy through a great popular revolution. In 1969, Numairi seized power through a military coup, and in 1972 he gave the South the right to have a local government. Accordingly, the war stopped. In 1983, however, Numairi canceled his promises and the war started again. During that time, Dr. John Garang and his colleagues in the South founded the Sudanese Peoples' Liberation Movement (SPLM) and its armed wing (Sudanese Peoples' Liberation Army, SPLA). They adopted a new and more correct approach to the problem facing the Sudanese people, declaring that it was not the problem of the South, but indeed the problem of the whole of Sudan. Thus, Sudan's situation is not the responsibility of Islam or the people of the North, but the responsibility of the colonial and Numairi governments.

The Sudanese problem is an economic, political, cultural, and racial one, linked with democracy, human rights, and social justice. In 1989, the National Islamic Front (NIF) came to power by a military coup d'état, under the leadership of officer Omer El Basheer. In fact, El Basheer is but a mere mask for the real leader, Dr. Turaby. They declared Sudan an Islamic state and waged the war under a new slogan: "The Islamic Jihad." It is essential to note here, first, that there is no such thing as an "Islamic state" in Islam. This can be clearly proven by referring to verses of the Qur'an. Second, the declaration of such a state is a violation of democracy and human rights, because a third of the population is not Muslim. In addition, waging an Islamic war against the people of the South merely because they are not Muslims is against Islamic principles. This can also be proven by referring to verses from the Qur'an.

THE HISTORICAL BACKGROUND OF WOMEN'S SITUATION IN THIS SUDANESE CONTEXT

Women in Sudan experience repression even before they are born: at marriage ceremonies, the guests and relatives of the newlywed couple sing a popular song in which they wish the groom a baby son as his first child. After marriage, discrimination becomes even more apparent within the family house. The largest and most beautiful quarters are usually reserved for the man and his guests, and men are usually given the best food, while women eat the leftovers after the men have finished their meal. Girls are circumcised during their early childhood, to control sexuality and ensure virginity. This is done in the belief that the practice is an Islamic one, but this is not true. Young women are denied the right to choose their husbands and, in most cases, they are not even consulted about their marriage. Moreover, all family laws are designed in the man's favor, to give him the maximum advantage. Although the house is, falsely, called "the woman's kingdom," a husband can kick his wife out of her home at any time. He has the right to marry more than one wife, and the right to divorce his wife or wives. In the event of divorce, the "obedience law" forces the wife to go back to her husband if he changes his mind, irrespective of her interest and desire. Furthermore, women, as mothers, do not enjoy equal rights to those of men or fathers. The family laws grant women custody of their sons until the age of seven, and of their daughters until the age of nine. Until a few years ago, no law required the father to pay maintenance to his children after divorce. Ironically, even in the Southern region, where people are not Muslims, men often marry more than one wife. This is especially the case because women represent an important economic force and provide valuable work in agricultural and food production. Thus, the more wives a man has, the greater his wealth and, by the same token, the greater the number of children—a fact that gives him greater social status. Clearly, the indications are that traditions and economic benefits are more important and effective than religious beliefs.

Women also face repression and discrimination outside the domestic sphere, at the societal level. The percentage of women's illiteracy is 96 percent, while that of men is 86 percent. The British government started boys' education before girls' education, and to this day there are only half as many girls' schools as boys' schools at all levels. The majority of women do not have waged labor outside the home; the tiny minority who do are confined to nursing and teaching. Women get four-fifths of men's wages for the same kind of work, even when they have the same qualifications, and women are denied equal opportunities to training, promotion, pensionable service, and the right to a paid maternity leave. The monthly contract work arrangements make women's jobs less stable and they can be fired on short notice. In agricultural areas, on the other hand, women's work is considered as part of the man's work, and they do not get paid for the amount they carry out in the fields. In Western Sudan, for example, women do the vast majority of the agricultural work. After the harvest, however, a man may take the woman's income and marry another wife. This is why the percentage of wives killing their husbands is growing. This was also the women's situation before independence was achieved from British rule.

The Sudanese Women's Union (SWU) was founded in 1952. Because of a lack of experience, however, the Union started, at first, by promoting reforms and charity work. They soon realized, however, that these kinds of activities would not solve women's problems, eradicate illiteracy among women, or promote equality. Charity would never eradicate poverty. As a result, the Union introduced some changes in its tactics, by conducting a peaceful demand campaign to go side by side with other work the Union had already been doing, so as to put pressure on the government to change its policies and laws affecting women. Thus, a campaign to win women voting rights was launched in 1953, with the goal of transforming women's votes into a political force for which all parties would have to compete to win. To assist in that campaign, I and some of my colleagues started publishing *The Women's Voice* magazine to raise the awareness of Sudanese women. The majority of the executive members of the Union rejected our proposal that the magazine be published by the Union, as they considered it a big risk. As could be expected, the Union's demands for women's political rights were met with strong opposition from the Islamic Front, which is in power now, and from other Islamic groups, on the grounds that Islam does not allow women's participation in politics or, indeed, their equality to men in general. The Union realized that the best way to fight off this attack was to use the same weapons or arguments as our opponents— those of Islam itself—to defend women's rights. By studying Islam from its source, the Qur'an, we could prove that Islam neither prohibits women's involvement in politics nor their equality. Furthermore, it does not permit polygamy. It is the Islamic leaders who interpret Islam in a way that suits them. This argument was finally won by the Union, and the Sudanese women achieved the right to vote in 1954. The Union then continued its campaign to achieve the right for all women to stand for election.

FIGHT FOR DEMOCRACY

Our magazine succeeded in raising women's awareness. It explained the strong links between discrimination against women, democracy, human rights, and social justice. When our union was banned by the first military regime, it went underground and started to organize women to take part in the opposition to the military regime. Here, our magazine played a significant role and, eventually, women took part in the popular revolution which overthrew the military regime in 1964. This was the first time in our history that a mass of women took part in a political fight for democracy and human rights. After the success of the revolution, women were given the right to vote and stand for elections in 1965. Through this achievement, we pressed the Islamic Front into a corner and compelled them to face a difficult dilemma: Whether they accepted or refused women's rights to vote and stand for elections, they would end up losing. They accepted, however, and put forward as a candidate a Muslim sister who had stepped out of the executive committee of our Union on the ground that the mere demand for political rights for women was against Islam. We organized a campaign against the Islamic front, revealing the contradiction in their stand, which reflects the misuse of Islam. God has certainly not changed his religion! The Muslim sister failed and I succeeded and became the first woman member of Parliament in Sudan and Africa. Inside the parliament, I demanded the full equality of working women to men. Outside the parliament, we formed a committee of representatives of trade unions, students, youth organizations, and others, in support of working women. That committee organized a large campaign in support of the introduced legislation. As a result of that campaign, we achieved the following rights by 1968:

1.	The right for women to enter all economic spheres. As a result, women were able to enter the judiciary, diplomacy, armed forces, police, holding office, and even become judges in Islamic law, etc. They started to take part in public life, political parties, and all other activities inside and outside Sudan, such as participating in international meetings and congresses.
2.	The right to equal payment for equal work, and equal chances for training, promotion, and pensionable service.
3.	The right to a fully paid maternity leave for eight weeks, plus feeding hours for working mothers.
4.	The abolishment of the monthly contracted work arrangement for working women after marriage.

In the field of family laws, the result of our campaign, which was also based on women's rights in Islam, was as follows:

1. An act was issued, giving women the right to be consulted before marriage. If it could be proven that a marriage took place without the woman's consent, it could be dissolved by the court.
2. The abolishment of the obedience laws.
3. Women were given the right to get divorced in case of proven abuse, or even when wives had no interest in living with their husbands. (However, they added that the wife had to give her husband back the dower.)
4. Mothers were allowed custody of their sons until the age of seventeen, and of their daughters until their marriage.
5. Children were given the right to maintenance by their fathers, in the event of a divorce. But, they added, this should not exceed half of the father's income.

For all these achievements, our Union was awarded the United Nations Human Rights Prize in 1993, and thus became the first and only nongovernmental women's organization, to this day, to win that prize.

THE EXPENSIVE COST OF THESE ACHIEVEMENTS, AND THEIR ABOLITION

When Numairi came to power in 1969, he struck a deal with our Union, promising to put all the rights women had achieved into practice in return for Union support for his regime. In less than one year, however, he changed his mind and withdrew all that had been agreed upon. Instead, he offered to make me a Minister of Women's and Social Affairs. I refused his offer. My husband, who was the secretary general of all Trade Union Federations, also refused an offer to be made Minister of Labour. The result of that episode was the banning of the Union's activities in 1971, and in July 1971, Numairi executed my husband after torturing him. They arrested me on the same day and imprisoned me for two and a half years. After releasing me, I filed a case in the Supreme Court against Numairi and the ministers who tortured my husband. The next day, I was sent to a prison outside Khartoum and kept in a room with male criminals for three days, without food or water. The prisoners refused to eat or drink, expressing their solidarity with me. After three days, I asked for a judge. He came and ordered me sent to a hospital. The lawyers' trade union organized a silent march to the Supreme Court and handed over a memorandum of protest.

In 1983, Numairi sent me to an emergency military court, but before arriving at the court, he announced through all official media that I should be beaten and sent to prison for life. Thousands of people surrounded the court. The other Union's leaders were also subjected to imprisonment and expulsion for their work, for the first time in our history. Our Union went underground and started organizing women to take part in the struggle to overthrow the military regime and regain democracy.

In the same year, 1983, the Islamic Front entered Numairi's government and declared the application of Islamic laws. According to adultery laws, a woman is accused of committing adultery if she has so much as been seen in the company of a man from outside her direct family, even if that encounter takes place in public. The penalty for this offense was a fine of one hundred Sudanese pounds, plus eighty lashes and a prison sentence of one year. Wrongful convictions led to an increase in the number of suicides among women, especially as the accused were publicly humiliated in the media. This law is against the Islamic law, which makes it necessary to have four eye-witnesses in order to prove that adultery has been committed. The hidden purpose of passing this law was to make families stop their daughters from going out, to protect the family's reputation and honor. Another law was passed forbidding women from traveling alone.

NIF REGIME AND WOMEN'S DISCRIMINATION

Immediately after seizing power in 1989, the NIF regime dismissed most women judges, diplomats, army and female police officers, and women who held high posts in the civil service. Some NIF women members or sympathizers were left in their posts or were moved into more prominent positions later. They banned our Union and all other women's organizations, except the NIF women's organization. They issued new family laws, which deprived women, as wives, mothers, and daughters, of their rights. For instance, these laws give the father the right to marry off his daughter even if she is underage, and the right to stop and dissolve his daughter's marriage if he does not agree with the arrangement, irrespective of her wishes and choices. This is against Islam, which gives the woman the right to choose her husband and the right to divorce him. In addition, the NIF passed a decision considering our national costume, the toab, as not being Islamic. Now, Sudanese women had to wear the Iranian women's black chaddor. Our Union issued a declaration revealing the fact that Iran had given the NIF tens of thousands of these costumes free of charge, so they decided to make it compulsory for women to buy them, in order to gain profit. In addition, we pointed out that there is no verse in the Qur'an in which God mentioned that the Iranian costume is the Islamic one. As a result of our actions, the NIF withdrew their decision, but they made it compulsory for working women and female students to tie their heads and necks and wear a long dress or trousers under the toab, or else be dismissed.

On top of all that, the NIF regime fully implemented the World Bank and IMF structural adjustment program. As a result of this, the Sudanese pound fell in value. In 1976, a Sudanese pound was equal to three U.S. dollars. Now, after regular devaluation, it takes 2,250 Sudanese pounds to equal one U.S. dollar! The implementation of this program caused radical changes in the structure of our society. Despite the fact that we still have a primitive agricultural economy, the NIF and their structural adjustments created a wealthy parasitic capitalist minority class, consisting mainly of the billionaire leaders of the NIF. Our large middle class has disappeared, and the majority of our population lives in complete poverty, especially women and children in the South and Nuba Mountains. In addition, the people are suffering from famine, disease, displacement, poverty, and death because of the war. Finally, this regime is practicing ethnic cleansing and a slave trade.

WHAT IS THE SOLUTION?

In fact, there is no solution other than getting rid of this regime. In my opinion, all the conditions necessary for the success of a people's uprising are now in place. First, there is the economic destruction; second, the political crises which have reached their boiling point, to the extent that the regime is now completely isolated internally, regionally, and internationally; third, the public anger has reached a peak and manifested itself through demonstrations against the regime, in spite of its cruelty. The fourth condition is the national united leadership, which is now available and even better than in the past, because the SPLM and SPLA have joined the opposition under an umbrella called the National Democratic Alliance (NDA). All of them signed a historical agreement, which announces a complete separation between politics and religion, and forbids political parties based on religion. This agreement also promises to give the South self-determination, and to stop the war and form a government of representatives of all oppositional forces to implement a development program within five years and then run free democratic elections.

We Sudanese women, from the North and the South, decided to come together to fight for peace, democracy, social justice, human rights, and women's equal rights, through our women's organization and the Sudanese Women's Voice for Peace. We already organized, together with the youth organization, a peace caravan in 1996, which will continue to fulfill its aims. We are proposing a tribal conference to set up an agreement and a council to be able to put an end to the tribal armed conflicts and adopt peaceful solutions. Also, we convened a gender conference in the South to make a wide campaign for our full equality. We expressed our full support for the NDA, but at the same time we criticized it for isolating women from its organization and activities. None of these parties or trade unions represent women in their delegations—not even the Communist Party and the SPLM. This indicates the fact that women are the suppressed of the suppressed. All political parties open their membership to women only to help themselves during elections, by bringing women to vote for men to get into power. They may be generous by appointing one or two women as an example, to pretend that they have given women their rights in decision making. But they are always keen to choose women members of the ruling party, who are more loyal to them than they are to their own sex. For all this, we are fighting against the regime and at the same time putting pressure on the opposition to represent women in their organization. Despite difficulties and suffering, we are sure we will succeed in the end.

CHAPTER 11

Who Benefits?
U.S. Military, Prostitution,
and Base Conversion

SAUNDRA STURDEVANT

I want to work with several categories of inquiry during this article. But before I do that, I want to raise an issue of central concern to me. That concern is the very authenticity of the presentation itself. It is not necessary that I be here. Voices of women selling their sexual labor are those rightfully belonging here, discussing their lives and issues with us. We have reached the point in organizing where this is possible. The next step is to recognize this and to act in such a way as to make it possible for the women working in this labor market to be included in, to be the principles in these discussions.

There has and continues to be the assertions, taken seriously, that prostituted labor is the "oldest profession" on earth, is deplorable but can't be helped, and is in the "natural order of things." There is much discussion in feminist circles about the "right to sell one's body if one so chooses," versus "the selling of the woman's body is exploitation and is to be prohibited." These positions both have much to recommend them. Formally educated women in North America and North Europe are primarily the ones defining and defending these positions. Prostituted women are increasingly a part of these formulations.

Women in Third World countries selling their sexual labor or those faced with the decision of whether or not to enter that labor market are not part of the formulation of either position. They do not have the means of access, the documents for such discourse or the forums where such discourse takes place. Consideration might then be given to a possible third position in feminist discourse on this topic, one suggested by prostituted women in Asia themselves: "What about the right not to have to make one's way in the world by selling one's sexual labor?"

We need to look at why prostituted women in third world countries are not part of theoretical formulations and discussions. Those formally educated, who take an interest in the subject, are guided in their discussions by key documents found in books, journal articles, and papers presented at conferences. They are also frequently guided and informed by organizing work with prostituted women. But in order for the women selling their sexual labor to participate in theoretical discussions and formulations, key documents must be translated into their language(s). English is not their first language, and the often esoteric terminology of academic/activist discussion is not accessible to these women, who are the very subjects of academic/activist discussions. In reality, those trained in both languages are the ones who will have to do the translations, place the works in the hands of prostituted women, and learn, from the women, what makes sense to the women themselves.

What I have to say has been obtained directly from the women themselves, and I feel uncomfortable that it is still necessary for me to be the presenter of their stories. The subtext that flows with my photographs is from the life stories of women selling their sexual labor. These stories are excerpted from *Let The Good Times Roll: Prostitution and U.S. Military in Asia* (1993), which I co-authored with Brenda Stoltzfus. This is my attempt, working within the current forum, actively to include the women's voices. I see this attempt as a step along the path that will lead to the full participation of prostituted women in the discussion. As we proceed, I would like us to keep in mind this introduction and reflect on how our discourse might have been vitalized and deepened had we had such participation.

The first category of inquiry that I wish to deal with has to do with the economics of the bar and brothel areas outside U.S. military bases, and indeed outside bases of other nations' military establishments. The basic issue is: Why do women themselves benefit so little? The sale of women's sexual labor is at the base of a complex economy. There is the sale of the woman's sexual labor itself, which the woman usually has little or no say in agreeing to and of whose proceeds she receives very little. Those who gain economically from the transaction are the owners, managers, and employees of bars, brothels, liquor, grocery, and drug stores; the owners, managers, and workers in restaurants, short-order takeout establishments, clothing stores, tailors shops, stereo-sunglass-photographic equipment stores; the owners of hotels where short-time and all-night are

Figure 1. FILIPINA WOMEN WORKING IN OKINAWA
Rowena: I'm always teaching Sally. I'm always building up her inner strength. I tell her, 'Don't be afraid of papasan (bar owner). He can be frightened. Fight him. Watch what I do.' I answer back to our papasan. I fight. I said, 'You fight too. If you're afraid, he'll frighten you even more. He knows you're afraid.' Now she fights back.
Janet: I take care of myself even if there is trouble at the club because of that. I don't want to allow myself to be abused or exploited by another person and lose my self-respect. I show others that no matter what, they must respect me. I haven't changed my opinion of myself. I want to continue to respect myself so that others will respect me whether they are Americans or anyone else.

Figure 2. WORKING WOMEN'S LIVING SPACE
Madelin: I was eleven-years-old when I started grade one. I studied until grade
three, but did not finish. How could I? It was difficult. You go to school without
food, and nothing the teacher says stays in your head because of the hunger. I
also saw our poverty and decided I would not study anymore. I would work.

choices the purchaser of the woman's sexual labor make; the street shoe
shiners, street vendors, and numerous repair personnel. All depend directly on the sale of a woman's sexual labor.

So, too, do the taxi owners and others who convey the purchaser of
sexual labor and the woman to and fro. And there are the taxes, sales and
income, from these various commodities and work situations that are
paid to local and national government agencies. And when the woman is
no longer able to sell her sexual labor, alternative sources of work are
few. One that is common is the work of washing the sheets, bedding, the
uniforms, and undergarments of the military men and others. The point is
that the sale of women's sexual labor is at the base of an economic system of considerable proportions—true historically and true today.
Women seldom benefit financially. The power and the money are in the
hands of those buying and those running the businesses and of the governments gaining from such an arrangement.

Why, then, do women benefit so little? We are talking here about so-
called third world women. The work found in *Let The Good Times Roll*
focuses on the Philippines, Okinawa, and the southern part of Korea. The

Figure 3. STREET VENDOR
Lita: I thought about our situation. I agreed because he gave me money. I didn't
know how much it was because it was dollars. What I saw looked like a lot in
my eyes. Of course, I came from the province. I didn't know the value of dollars.
I really didn't want to, but he forced me. It was very painful. I bled. He tried to
undress me, but I wouldn't get undressed. There was a lot of blood on my
clothes. I sent the money to my mother. Maybe my mother thought it was my
salary as a maid. She didn't know I was now working in a club. She said we
were able to pay off some of the debt.

situation with respect to women selling their sexual labor to U.S. military
in these countries and in other parts of the so-called developing world, is
quite different in origin and motivation from that which informs the sale
of women's sexual labor in the so-called first world. Wars, empire expansion, and maintenance greatly intensified in the post-World War II period. In the Philippines, for example, logging has left standing only 10
percent of the original growth forests. With run-off from deforested lands
smothering the reefs, one is left with approximately 25 percent of the
coral reefs still alive. Farming, fishing, and living off the forest products
were ancient ways of life that have either been completely destroyed by
mal-development or highly marginalized.

The result is great internal migrations of peoples from rural to urban
areas. This is true of peoples forced off the land by mal-development that

Figure 4. LABANDERA/WASHING WOMEN
Glenda: I want other people to know that the life working in the clubs is difficult, especially for the women they call prostitutes. . . . the loss of sleep . . . if
you don't earn anything, there is no money for food...they get sick and have to
spend money on medicine. If you really look at it, they have great difficulties. It
is ugly. All different men have sex with you. It should be that only your husband
has sex with you, but in the bar, it's all different men. If it were possible, I
wouldn't do it. But there is nothing the women can do to earn a living. The work
in the club is dirty because you're not respected by the Americans. They really
look at you as pigs.

Figure 5. WOMAN WORKING IN THE BARRIO
Manang, mother of Lita: Before, our dream was to earn a living and buy good land, so that whatever happened to our family would be good. How could we do that? After two years, you have a baby. After three years something suddenly happens to your family. Whenever we had money, our children got sick. How could I do everything? My husband only worked as a farmer. When the corn was high, the wind was strong. Nothing. If the typhoons had not come, we would have had many crops. Even our house was destroyed. If it hadn't been for our children, we would not have survived. No matter what we thought to do, nothing worked. We had a *carabao* but had to sell it because of the poverty. Now we're old.

has greatly damaged the environment and ecology and resulted in the destruction of traditional ways of life. And it is true of those who stayed on in the rural areas, who were dispossessed of land, who turned to work for huge agricultural companies, both indigenous and multinational. We see them becoming subject to commodity marketing forces in the world. Impoverishment and great poverty become the norm. These people, too, add their bodies to the internal migrations to the cities.

The point is that a cheap, steady supply of expendable labor migrated to the cities. Although skilled in traditional modes of making a living in the agricultural/fishing/forest-based economy or on huge agricultural plantations, these people did not have skills marketable in the urban environment. Older members of the family, parents and grandparents, found it exceedingly difficult, if not impossible, to earn money in the cities. That task fell to the young members of the family, those also unskilled and ill-educated from the point of view of the demands of the urban economy. But the young have their labor power. Young men commonly find work at

Figure 6. CHILDREN IN THE BARRIO
Manang: When Lita came to Olongapo, I didn't know what would happen. I
agreed to let her come because I thought she would be working as a maid. My
niece is the one who brought her here. They didn't say right away what the work
was. She was still young. I said, 'Okay, so that you will be able to reach your
dreams of what you want to be.' Later, she wrote and said she had a steady
boyfriend, American.

the lowest level of hard physical labor. Young women most commonly
work as maids and as sellers of their sexual labor. The route of employment from maid to seller of sexual labor is the most direct for young
women. In addition to the hard physical work of being a maid, they find
that they are commonly required to provide sexual services to virtually all
the male members of the family in which they are employed.

With an economy where 70 percent of the population in the Philippines is under the absolute poverty line, great pools of young, cheap
labor were available for the bars and brothels catering to the military.
Creation of this cheap labor pool of female labor was well underway and
continued to intensify as the Vietnam War progressed. The Philippines,
principally the bar and brothel areas in Olongapo directly outside Subic
Naval Base, became the model rest and relaxation (r and r) for all of Asia
during the Vietnam era.

Figure 7. WOMEN AND CHILDREN IN THE BARRIO
Manang: I am ashamed, but I leave her alone if she wants to do this work. She said that she could earn a living. I'm the one who took care of this child who left me. Of course, you remember that you are a mother. You have many tears because of what went wrong. But we can't prevent them from doing what they want to do.

The second area of inquiry is the organization and administration of prostituted labor. Certainly the sale of women's sexual labor is part of a highly organized and institutionalized system. It is as necessary to the running of a military machine as weapons, munitions, military gear, communications systems, battle fatigues, and MREs. It doesn't just happen that bars and brothels filled with indigenous women of the country

Figure 8. SCAVENGING AT SMOKEY MOUNTAIN

Figure 9. CHILDREN OF SMOKEY MOUNTAIN
Lita: When I left the school, I sold *kalamay* (sweet rice). When it was all sold, I
climbed up to the garbage dump and scavenged for bottles. Our earnings for one
day were very small. Once I was almost run over by the bulldozer that pushes
the garbage. My foot accidentally got caught in the garbage. I couldn't get it out.
The bulldozer was coming closer and closer. I was caught in the moving garbage
up to my stomach. No one saw me because the roaring sound was loud and the
mound of garbage was large. It kept coming and coming. I didn't know what
would happen to me. I thought I was dead.

find their way to areas immediately outside U.S. military installations
around the world. It is not the case that "men will be men," of independent open-market entrepreneurial activity carried out by local males,
making money off the presence of U.S. military men. The existence of
bars and brothels directly outside U.S. military bases is orchestrated by
the U.S. civil and military authorities in the United States and those on
the ground in Asia. They, together with the political and economic
welders of political and economic power in the country, are directly responsible for the creation, organization, and management of the bar and
brothel areas. Congressional representatives who vote monies for appro-
priations and who laud U.S. military presence abroad make it possible
and give their patriotic approval.

The third area of inquiry focuses on the situation of the women since
the formal leaving of the Philippines by the U.S. military. In 1991, after
extensive organizing by progressive and nationalist forces in the Philippines, the Philippine Senate voted not to renew the Military Bases Agreement. The U.S. military consequently closed down Subic Naval Base,
Clark Air Base, and the smaller remaining bases. But in 1992, literally as
the United States was lowering the flag at Subic and departing, Admiral

Figure 10. APPROVED FOR U.S. FORCES

Figure 11. OLONGAPO SOCIAL HYGIENE CLINIC
Madelin: I had a friend in Manila who told me about a friend of hers in Olon-
gapo. I said, 'What's Olongapo?'
She said, 'There are many Americans there.'
'Americans? I've never seen an American. What's her work there?'
'Waitress. Do you want to come along?'
When I first arrived in Olongapo, I saw many Americans because there was a
ship. It was a large ship, a carrier. I was innocent. I didn't know what a carrier
was. When I saw all the Americans, I said, 'Where are we? In the States? We
didn't ride in an airplane.'
'Stupid! We aren't in the States. We are in Olongapo.'

Charles Larson, commander in chief of the U.S. Pacific Command, and General Liandro Abadia, the chief of staff of the Philippine Armed Forces, were concluding the Continued Access Agreement. This agreement allows the U.S. military the right to dock at some twenty-seven ports in the Philippines, and also grants landing rights to various airfields. It's a "pay as you go" agreement. When a ship pulls in, it pays for what it needs, and sailors and marines get liberty. These are its two major points. Although the U.S. press and U.S. congressional representatives have not acknowledged the existence of this agreement, newspapers and political figures in the Philippines have not been so retiring. Resistance in the Philippines to the Continued Access Agreement has been considerable. As a result, the U.S. military and civil authorities have not pushed for full implementation and have kept a low profile, porting a few ships each year and waiting for opposition to die down.

Figure 12. WOMEN AT WORK—MEN AT PLAY
Madelin: In my opinion, the U.S. Navy treats the women as a way to pass the time and do whatever they want. They have money, so they buy here and buy there. There are also sadists in the U.S. Navy. An American like that took me out once. He did things to me. I fought. He swore at me. I fought him. I would not allow myself to lose. I thought we might both die. He was choking me. I cried. I thought I was dying.

U.S. Navy ships occasionally dock in Olongapo at the former Subic Naval Base facility since its formal closing in 1992. And they dock at Manila. Shore leaves, r and r have continued, but the areas where sexual labor is now regularly sold have diversified. The sex industry in Angeles, the city outside former Clark Air Force Base, and in Barrio Barretto and Subic City, both short jeepney ride from Olongapo, are the major areas for r and r. Olongapo's sex industry continues but on a much smaller scale than these two areas. For example, the U.S. Embassy, Angeles City Social Hygiene Clinic, the Angeles City government, and the Bar Owners' Association of Angeles work together to coordinate bus trips for U.S. servicemen docked at Manila or at Olongapo to use the r and r facilities of Angeles. Explicit floor shows have returned. The social hygiene clinics are quite busy, with funding for AIDS testing coming through the U.S. Agency for International Development (AID). And, a new, virulent form of syphilis has become an additional cause for concern.

Alternatives to selling one's sexual labor are said to be more available than previously. Upbeat articles appear in The *New York Times, Washington Post, Wall Street Journal* announcing, "Fast Growth at Subic Free Port," "Democracy Isn't a Bar to Fast Growth," and so on. Total foreign investment in the Subic Free Port is estimated by the upbeat articles to vary from $1.5 billion to more than $2 billion. Aside from the question of the reality of this "Philippine Renaissance" and the public relations work implicit in the articles is that of the participation of Olongapo citizens, especially of former prostituted labor, in this announced economic boom.

With the closure of Subic Naval Base, the Philippine legislature created the Subic Bay Metropolitan Authority (SBMA). Until 1998, this governing body was headed by presidentially appointed former Olongapo City mayor Richard Gordon. The Gordon family had long been in control of the political and economic spheres of life during the many years of the Magsaysay Strip, r and r-centered economic growth. During those years Olongapo was dependent for its viability on the existence of an external body, U.S. Naval presence, and its purchase of women's sexual labor. In the post-base era, Olongapo is still dependent upon an external body, that of investors, primarily foreigners, who do not have a significant interest in the welfare of the people of Olongapo. Functionally, Olongapo's citizens remain in the same position as before.

Under Mr. Gordon, women who wanted to secure work from factories and commercial establishments within the SBMA had to meet three requirements: (1) they needed to have a volunteer certificate; (2) they had to be under thirty-five; and (3) have appropriate skills. A volunteer certificate is issued to a woman after she has worked without pay on the former naval reservation for a period ranging from three months to one year. Gordon decreed that local people who would do this clean-up, maintenance, and guard work would get priority in being considered for employment once foreign investors came in and set up factories. A number of women who had worked in bars and brothels did this work in hope of eventually obtaining a decent and well paying job.

To put in time as a volunteer is a time-consuming, nonpaying job. It is also expensive to maintain; while volunteering brings in no income, expenses may include transportation to and from the base, child care and support, and sending money back to the provinces for support of a woman's family. There are the additional and obvious economic considerations of rent, food, utilities, and health expenses. One needed to already have a secure economic base in order to be a volunteer. Furthermore, even if the woman had successfully dealt with these expenses and volunteered for the required time, had her certificate, and was under thirty-five years old, chances are that she remained unemployable. To his credit, the new chairman of SBMA, Felicito Payumo, has discontinued the volunteer requirement. The other requirements however, remain in place for most factories.

Having the third requirement, that of training and skills that would enable the women to work, is almost always lacking. The fact of the matter is that former prostituted women's aspirations of acquiring jobs in the new commercial and industrial complexes have remained in their dreams. Primarily this is due to the fact that the real-life situations of the women upon whose backs the base economy literally depended during base days were not taken into consideration when base conversion was implemented. This was the case even though the government funded extensive research on conversion, research carried out by women's organizations who consulted with prostituted women. Recommendations in the resulting reports are not visible in the implementation of conversion policy. Central to the issue of integrating former prostituted women into a post-base economy is their low level of education and lack of the third requirement, the training and skills that would enable them to work.

For the few former prostituted women who were able to acquire skills and gain employment in the factories in the industrial complex, wages are very low. The minimum wage law sets P127.00 per day, which is about five dollars. With current inflation rates and loss of value of the peso due in part to World Bank and IMF restructuring, minimum wage is

Figure 13. SUBIC BAY METROPOLITAN AUTHORITY
Glenda: I think that, if possible, it would be better to get rid of the base and give
better work to the women. Maybe they would accept that. Their situation is very
bad. They don't want the base to shut down because that's where they earn their
living. I understand. But I would like the women to be able to change so that
they wouldn't be in the bars all their lives.

not a livable wage. And many employers pay below the minimum during
the duration of the employee's training period, which may last from three
to six months. After the initial training period, the practice is to fire the
employee and hire others or rehire the same employee at the training
rate. In a tightly controlled SBMA, Mr. Gordon was able to successfully
prohibit labor organizing. Mr. Payumo indicates he will not stop such organizing, although he points out that if unions become strong, the investors will move and all employees will lose their jobs. As of February
1999, labor organizing was well on its way though not yet ready for open
confrontation.

The question of Who Benefits? U.S. Military, Prostitution, and Base
Conversion is one with a historical past rooted in mal-development and
the necessity of internal migration. Once that migration was accomplished, work in bars and brothels secured, the direct sale of the women's
sexual labor and the economic spin-offs therefrom formed the basis of
the economy in Olongapo outside Subic Naval Base. With conversion,

the women found this labor no longer marketable, and opportunities for training that would secure work in another sector of the economy were not open to them.

ACKNOWLEDGMENTS

Special thanks go to Brenda Stoltzfus, Alma Bulawan and staff of Buklod Center, The Philippines, in helping to prepare this presentation.

REFERENCES

Stoltzfus, Brenda and Saundra Sturdevant. 1993. *Let the Good Times Roll: Prostitution and U.S. Military in Asia*. New York: The New Press.

CHAPTER 12

Demilitarizing Security
Women Oppose U.S. Militarism in East Asia

GWYN KIRK AND MARGO OKAZAWA-REY

On September 4, 1995, two U.S. marines and a sailor based in Okinawa (Japan) abducted a twelve-year-old Okinawan girl as she was coming home from the store. They bundled her into the back of their rental car, taped her mouth, eyes, hands, and feet with duct tape, and took her to a deserted place. They beat and raped her, and then abandoned her. When she regained consciousness, she walked to the nearest home to call for help and later reported the incident to the police.

This violent crime outraged many Okinawans and revitalized opposition to the U.S. military presence in Okinawa. On their return from the Beijing Women's Conference later that same week, Okinawan women activists immediately organized around this incident. Seventy-one women from Okinawa had gone to Beijing to make connections with other Asian women and to share their experiences of living with U.S. bases for many years. Seven of the eleven workshops they presented concerned militarism and peace. Their preparation for the Beijing Conference, as well as the inspirational and energizing effect of this momentous international gathering of some 30,000 women, served them well upon their return. They organized a twelve-day street vigil in downtown Naha, the capital, drawing worldwide attention to the rape of this girl and, more generally, to the many incidents of violence against women by U.S. troops in East Asia. They played a central role in organizing a major demonstration attended by some 85,000 people (out of a total population

A version of this paper appeared in *Iris: A Journal about Women*, 39 (Fall 1999): 12–16.

Russia

Japan

Korea

Okinawa

China

Taiwan

Hong Kong

East Asia

Philippines

of one million). They started a new organization, Okinawa Women Act against Military Violence, to focus on the impact of U.S. military operations on women and children.

This particular rape prompted bitter memories of many other assaults on women and girls over a fifty-year period. Women who had never talked about this issue in public began to speak out. At a meeting in Berkeley, as part of the Okinawa Women's America Peace Caravan in February 1996, Mitsue Tomiyama said:

> What has happened recently has caused me to look back. When I was a child, U.S. troops found their way into residential areas. My mother and I would hide under the house to avoid being attacked and raped. . . . I remember some very beautiful girls in the neighborhood hitching rides to school on military trucks. One friend was pulled up on the truck and raped. She tried to get away. She jumped, or was pushed off the truck and died. Her mother was filled with fear and suffering. She only went out when she had to.[1]

In Korea, too, a particularly brutal incident galvanized strong public protest against the U.S. military presence there. On 28 October 1992 Yoon Kum E, a woman who worked in a bar that serves U.S. troops, was found murdered, her body mutilated. A group of feminists, human rights activists, students, and labor activists came together to organize public demonstrations and vigils in Seoul. As a result of their conversations and work together, they founded the National Campaign for the Eradication of Crime by U.S. Troops in Korea in October 1993 to document and publicize this issue.

These are just two well-known incidents out of thousands, many of them not reported. Women activists from Okinawa, Korea, and the Philippines who are dealing with the severe negative effects of U.S. military bases and port visits on host communities share the view that violence against women is an integral part of U.S. military attitudes, training, and culture (see Reardon 1985). Iva Hosaka, who works as a community liaison for the U.S. military in Okinawa, confirms this, although she said, "There are some people who would love to limit it only to the action of a few bad apples."[2]

ACTIVISM ON BEHALF OF WOMEN AND CHILDREN

In all three East Asian countries, women are working on these issues in three main ways: developing their own local organizing; uncovering what has happened in the past, through conversations, workshops, drama, and historical research; and making international connections through regional and worldwide networks. U.S.-based activists are working to publicize these issues in their country and seeking support from U.S. organizations and members of Congress.

In Korea, there are two centers for bar women. Du Rae Bang (My Sister's Place), an outreach project of the Korean Presbyterian Church, was started in 1986 with centers in Uijongbu (near Camp Stanley Army Base) and Dongduchon (adjoining Camp Casey), north of Seoul. The Dongduchon center closed in 1996, but was replaced that same year by Sae Woom Tuh. Both centers provide educational and counseling services for women, and education and night-care for their children. Du Rae Bang broke new ground by establishing a bakery as an alternative means of livelihood for former bar women. Sae Woom Tuh has started an herb project in which women sell fresh herb plants and handmade items like potpourri, and cards and paper from dried herbs and recycled milk cartons. Hyun Sun Kim, director of Sae Woom Tuh, emphasizes that the women working in the *kijichon* (GI Town) have tragic stories to tell, but stories of great strength also. There are examples of women pooling money to pay each other's debts to bar owners and so buy each other out of the bars. In the case of Yoon Kum E, another bar woman who knew the murderer waited outside the base for him and forced military police to arrest him. He still had blood on his white pants.

Han So Ri, an organization working for the eradication of prostitution in Korea and the protection of the rights of prostituted women, has grown out of the work of these centers. The Korea Women's Hotline, started in 1983, focuses on domestic violence. It established the first shelter for battered women in Korea, and in recent years has addressed the issue of militarized prostitution. The National Campaign for the Eradication of Crime by U.S. Troops in Korea, formed after the murder of Yoon Kum E, documents and investigates military crimes against Korean citizens. It arranges counseling for victims and advocates for compensation. It also advocates for significant revision of the Status of Forces Agreement (SOFA) between the United States and Korea, which governs the conduct of U.S. military personnel. At present, U.S. troops who commit crimes against people in host communities are rarely tried in local courts. Yu Jin Jeong, director of the National Campaign, writes:

> It can be said that crimes by U.S. troops continue because of the arrogance of the U.S. Army as an occupation force, the Korean government's submission to the U.S., and the unequal nature of SOFA. The

U.S. Army displays a certain arrogance in claiming that it came here to protect Korea and yet disrespects Korean citizens.[3]

In Okinawa, several projects have started since the rape in September 1995. The Rape Emergency Counseling Center Okinawa (REICO) counsels rape victims. Young Voice is a network for women in their twenties and thirties who are concerned about violence against women, women's work experiences, marriage, children, and women's sexuality. DOVE (De-activating Our Violent Establishment) addresses military issues from the perspective of high school and college students, women and men. In contrast to these antimilitary voices, some young Okinawans romanticize military personnel. They wear U.S. Army surplus uniforms and paraphernalia sold in local shops, and go onto the bases to hang out with young U.S. personnel. Yuka Iha, a founding member of DOVE, said:

> Some young people only know good things about the U.S. military. They think GIs are cool and that they are learning English from their American friends. Most teachers and leaders won't talk about these issues of violence against women, because it is considered a private matter. I'd like to talk about these things with other young people so that we can learn from each other.[4]

In the Philippines, several women's activist organizations are dealing with the long-term fallout from the U.S. bases, continued troop visits for rest and recreation, (r and r), (sometimes referred to as I and I—intoxication and intercourse), and the wider sex industry that has its roots in U.S. military occupation. The Buklod Center in Olongapo, near the former Subic Bay Naval Base, was established by bar women and community activists in 1987 as a drop-in center for bar women. The Center offered night-care services for children of bar women, temporary shelter, counseling, referrals, and other crisis interventions. Now Buklod provides informal education and training for former bar women and other poor women, educational scholarships for some Amerasian children of members, and a community clinic. Minda Pascual, a former bar woman in Olongapo, is active with BUKAL in Quezon City, working with women in prostitution. She introduced herself to students at American University, Kay Spiritual Life Center (Washington, D.C.) in October 1998 by saying:

> I used to work in the clubs for six-and-a-half years. I have two abandoned Amerasian children. I am one of the many women who have experienced violence at the hands of the USA. I'm now an organizer for

an NGO-BUKAL—which means United Women in the Streets. Women in the streets lost work when the bases left. We organize women. We conduct street visits. When women are arrested in the streets and go to jail, we conduct investigations, home visits, and counseling. We assist in maintaining their good health.[5]

Aida Santos, a veteran feminist organizer in the Philippines, reports: "There has been no government help for the many women who used to work in bars and clubs near the bases in the Philippines, or for their Amerasian children."[6] With others, she founded WEDPRO (Women's Education, Development, Productivity and Research Organization) to assist bar women who were left without livelihood when U.S. bases closed. WEDPRO drew up a redevelopment plan for the former bases that would benefit local people, but the government ignored it, preferring investment from Japan, Taiwan, Korea, the U.S., and Europe, which used local people only as cheap labor. Most new jobs in the hotels, duty-free shops, casinos, and factories on the former baselands are part-time or temporary, and low paying, sometimes below the minimum wage. WEDPRO has a field office in Angeles City, next to the former Clark Air Force Base. Together with Buklod, WEDPRO offers training in business skills, setting up micro enterprises, and getting access to loans. These organizations help to support women's co-ops, and are involved in public education and advocacy. WEDPRO conducts research on prostitution and sex-trafficking, and does health training in reproductive rights and sexually-transmitted diseases, including HIV/AIDS.

ORGANIZING ACROSS NATIONAL BOUNDARIES

Fifty-five women activists from Korea, Okinawa, mainland Japan, the Philippines, and the United States (including the authors of this article) gathered in Washington, D.C., 8–13 October 1998 for the second international meeting of the East Asia-U.S. Women's Network against U.S. Militarism, founded in Okinawa in May 1997 (Kirk and Okazawa-Rey 1998). We discussed the following issues:

- The many acts of violence committed by U.S. military personnel against local women and children.
- The dire situation of abandoned children of military fathers, raised by single Asian mothers and living with severe prejudice and discrimination.

- The lack of firm environmental guidelines for the cleanup of toxic contamination of land and water caused by U.S. military operations that compromise the health of our communities.
- The sexual harassment, physical violence, and emotional abuse perpetrated on women, as well as men, in the military by other military personnel, and sexual, physical, and emotional abuse by military personnel against their families.
- The diversion of U.S., Japanese, and Korean tax-payers' money from socially-useful programs to military funding.
- Military recruitment focused on poor and working-class African-American and Latino youth, including JROTC programs in public high schools in the United States.

Network members are teachers, students, writers, policymakers, and community organizers. Women from East Asia exchanged information with U.S. organizers and student audiences. We briefed officials at the State and Justice Departments, and Members of Congress and their staff. We coordinated plans for future activities in all our countries: lobbying policymakers, educating the public, planning our own research, and supporting women's projects.

REDEFINING SECURITY FOR WOMEN AND CHILDREN

Network members are arguing for a new definition of human security that puts the needs of women and children and the health of the physical environment at the center (see also Reardon 1998). To date, most of the advocacy and research conducted by the organizations mentioned here concerns violence against women and children. We recognize that the health effects of military contamination also need detailed investigation.

Women in Okinawa and the Philippines are documenting local people's observations of contamination on the bases or in surrounding areas. This includes chemical leaks, explosions, the deaths of animals, birds, and fish, and illnesses in children and adults. In Okinawa, a 1996 report on babies born to women living near Kadena Air Force Base showed significantly lower birth weights than those born in any other part of Japan, attributed to severe noise generated by the base.[7] At White Beach, a docking area for nuclear submarines, regional health statistics show comparatively high rates of leukemia in children and cancers in adults. In 1998, two women from White Beach who were in the habit of gathering local shellfish and seaweed in the area died of liver cancer. In the Philippines, drinking water from wells in the former Clark Air Force Base is contaminated with oil and grease. Independent researchers reported that at twenty-one of twenty-four locations, ground water samples contained pollutants that exceeded drinking water standards, including mercury, nitrate, coliform bacteria, dieldrin, lead, and solvents.[8] These contaminants persist in the environment for a long time and bio-accumulate as they move up the food chain (see Seager 1993, ch. 1 for a good discussion of military contamination).

The presence of U.S. bases predetermines national foreign policy in Korea, Japan, and the Philippines. Through treaties and agreements, the host governments are tied to U.S. foreign policy, its alliances, and enmities. Ruling elites also share U.S. economic priorities. Much opposition to the U.S. military in East Asia is based on nationalism and self-determination. Women's analysis and organizing also focus on the sexism and racism involved in U.S. military violence in Asian host communities, and the sexism of the East Asian governments who are complicit in letting such violence go on. They argue that eliminating gender inequalities, and specifically ending violence against women, must be a fundamental element of a demilitarized future. They challenge the conventional military notion of security: that the military protects ordinary people. On the contrary, they argue that the military harms many people, including women and children in East Asia who are victims of personal violence, hit-and-run accidents, or the severe noise and disruption of military training.

The U.S. military system also harms women in the military, many of whom experience sexual harassment, and women and children in military families where domestic violence is much higher than in civilian families.[9] The military disrupts local communities, damages local economies, and contaminates the physical environment wherever it is located. Military security has devastated inner-city communities in the U.S. by starving them of resources—public funds to rebuild their economies and infrastructure, as well as the talents and hopes of their young people who are condemned to long-term unemployment in neighborhoods destroyed by poverty, crime, and violence, or forced to seek opportunities elsewhere (Childs 1993).

Genuine security derives from the expectation that four fundamental conditions will be met:

- that the environment in which we live can sustain life;
- that our basic survival needs for food, clothing, and shelter will be met;

- that our fundamental human dignity, and personal and cultural identities will be respected; and
- that we will be protected from avoidable harm.[10]

Women in the U.S. need to work with women from East Asia and many other countries to redefine security. We need to link foreign policy issues and U.S. domestic concerns, showing similarities and continuities in our experiences, the underlying causes of military violence, and suggestions for activism—locally, nationally, and internationally.

THE U.S. MILITARY PRESENCE IN EAST ASIA

U.S. bases in the Philippines date from 1898, at the end of the Spanish-American War. The United States took over the Phillippines from Spain, the former colonial power, against concerted Filipino resistance, which the U.S. military put down with brutal force. With the overthrow of President Ferdinand Marcos in 1986 by the pro-democracy movement, a vigorous anti-bases campaign organized to close U.S. bases. In December 1991, the Philippines Senate refused to renew the base agreement, and the U.S. military withdrew (Bello 1991). The U.S. subsequently proposed a Visiting Forces Agreement (VFA) to cover situations when U.S. troops are in the Philippines for joint exercises or shore leave. The VFA gives access to Philippines ports and airports on all the main islands, as needed, for refueling, supplies, repairs, and rest and recreation (r and r). This is potentially far greater access than before, but under the guise of commercial arrangements and without the expense of maintaining a permanent workforce and facilities (Asia Pacific Center for Justice and Peace 1997). The Philippines Senate ratified the VFA in May 1999, but before it can go into effect, the Philippine government is seeking ways to make the United States responsible for the cleanup of former bases. Popular opposition to the VFA was expressed in huge public demonstrations in Manila, a special plea by Roman Catholic Cardinal Sin, and petition drives in the United States in the fall of 1998 and spring of 1999 (Reuters 98, Teves 1998).

Bases in Japan and Korea date from 1945, the end of World War II. Currently, there are some 37,000 U.S. troops in Korea and 60,000 in Japan, including 13,000 on battleships home-ported there (Department of Defense website). The islands of Okinawa, the southern-most prefecture of Japan, house thirty-nine bases and installations—75 percent of U.S. bases in Japan—although Okinawa is only 0.6 percent of the country's land area. 30,000 troops and another 22,500 family members are stationed in Okinawa (Okinawa Prefectural Government 1997).

Bases in these three countries were used for bombing missions during the Korean War, the Vietnam War, and the Persian Gulf War. They are used for training, refueling, repairs, and recuperation on an ongoing basis. The Pentagon's current objective is to be capable of fighting two regional wars at the same time. For planning purposes these are assumed to be in the Middle East and the Korean peninsula. This scenario assumes that 100,000 U.S. troops will be based in East Asia indefinitely (Department of Defense 1998). It also assumes that they will continue to have access to women and girls through officially-sanctioned r and r in the many bars, clubs, and massage parlors just outside the bases (Enloe 1993, Moon 1997, Sturdevant and Stoltzfus 1992). U.S. bases in East Asia are supposedly there for the "defense" of the region—that's what the host governments have officially agreed to. However, battleships based at Yokoska (Japan) were sent to the Persian Gulf in 1998, and troops in Okinawa were moved to a higher level "alert" at times during the various stand-offs and bombings of Iraq. Recently, parachute practice that usually takes place on a small island in the Okinawa group (Ie Jima) has been moved to Kadena Airforce Base on the main island. This flies in the face of the legal agreements the U.S. has with Japan about where maneuvers can happen, and the governor of Okinawa has recently complained about it. The reason, according to the U.S. military, is that it's too windy over Ie Jima and the military needs to get in more parachute practice, presumably to facilitate operations in Kosova and Serbia.

NOTES

1. Interpreted by Carolyn Francis; notes Gwyn Kirk.

2. Quoted by Andrew Pollack, "Marines Seek Peace with Okinawa in Rape Case," *New York Times*, 8 October 1995, p.Y3.

3. *Cases of Crimes Committed by U.S. Militarymen* (Seoul, Korea: The National Campaign for the Eradication of Crime by U.S. Troops in Korea, nd) pp. 3–4.

4. Interview with Yuka Iha, *Okinawa*, an English-language newsletter. Rachel Cornwell, ed. Okinawa Christian Center. Issue #6, May 1997. p.6.

5. Interpreted by Maria Carisa Lamar; notes Gwyn Kirk. Minda's experience of working in Olongapo is part of "For the Boys: Filipinas Expose Years of Sexual Slavery by the U.S. and Japan," Sheila Coronel and Ninotchka Rosca, *Ms.* Nov./Dec. 1993. pp. 11–15.

6. Report to the founding meeting of the East Asia-U.S. Network against U.S. Militarism, Okinawa, 1–4 May 1997.

7. Research Study Committee of Aircraft Noise Influences to Health, *Summary of the Second Interim Report of the Field Study on Public Health around U.S. Bases in Okinawa*, March 1998.

8. Asia Star Weston International report to Clark Development Corporation quoted in *People's Task Force for Bases Clean Up Update*, Sept. 1998, p.2. Recently (Spring 1999), the Philippines Commission of Human Rights has taken up the issue of military bases' cleanup. They have taken a toxic-land case, filed by 421 families, to the U.N. Human Rights Convention in Geneva (E. Torres, "RP files toxic-waste case vs. U.S. before U.N. body," *Today Newspaper*, 17 April 1999). A forensic expert at the Commission of Human Rights has called for the immediate relocation of families housed at an evacuation center at Clark Field (formerly Clark Air Base) after studies in the area confirmed that the presence of mercury and nitrate wastes far exceeds standard levels set by the World Health Organization (reported in the *Philippine Star*, 17 May 1999, p.2). The authors of this article believe this is the first time that the issue of cleanup of former military bases has been taken up as a human rights issue, or brought before a United Nations body.

9. As shown by the powerful documentary, *The War at Home*, screened on CBS's *60-Minutes*, 17 January 1999.

10. This Human Security Paradigm has been developed by Betty A. Reardon, director of Peace Education, Teachers College, Columbia University.

REFERENCES

Asia Pacific Center for Justice and Peace. 1997. "The Pentagon Tries Again: The Quest for Military Access to the Philippines," *APC Focus* (10) 1–2.

Bello, Walden. 1991. "Moment of Decision: The Philippines, the Pacific, and the U.S. Bases." In *The Sun Never Sets: Confronting the Network of Foreign U.S. Military Bases* edited by Joseph Gerson and Bruce Birchard, 149–166. Boston: South End Press.

Childs, John Brown. 1993. "Toward Trans-Communality, the Highest Stage of Multiculturalism: Notes on the Future of African-Americans," *Social Justice: A Journal of Crime, Conflict, and World Order*: 20 (1-2) 35–51.

Department of Defense 1998. "The United States Security Strategy for the East Asia-Pacific Region." http://www.defenselink.mil/pubs/easr98/index.html

Enloe, Cynthia. 1993. *The Morning After: Sexual Politics at the End of the Cold War*. Berkeley: University of California Press.

Kirk, Gwyn and Margo Okazawa-Rey. 1998. "Making Connections: Building an East Asian-U.S. Women's Network against U.S. Militarism." In *The Women and War Reader* edited by Lois A. Lorentzen and Jennifer Turpin, 308–322. New York: New York University Press.

Moon, Katharine. 1997. *Sex Between Allies: Military Prostitution in U.S.-Korea Relations*. New York: Columbia University Press.

Okinawa Prefectural Government. 1997. *U.S. Military Bases in Okinawa*. Okinawa: Okinawa Prefectural Government, Military Base Affairs Office.

Reardon, Betty A. 1985. *Sexism and the War System*. New York: Teachers College Press, Columbia University.

————. 1998. "Gender and Global Security: A Feminist Challenge to the United Nations and Peace Research," *Journal of International Co-operation Studies*: 6 (1) 29–56.

Reuters, 1998. "Thousands protest U.S.-Philippines military accord." 16 Sept. In 1998 *Common Grounds: Violence against Women in War and Armed Conflict Situations*, edited by Indai Sajor. Quezon City, Philippines: Asian Center for Women's Human Rights.

Seager, Joni. 1993. *Earth Follies: Coming to Feminist Terms with the Global Environmental Crisis*. New York: Routledge.

Sturdevant, Saundra and Brenda Stoltzfus. 1992. *Let the Good Times Roll: Prostitution and the U.S. Military in Asia*. New York: New Press.

Teves, Oliver. 1998. "Philippines Mark U.S. Base Rejection." Associated Press Wire Service, 16 Sept.

OTHER RESOURCES

Organizations

Buklod Center, 23 Rodriguez St., Mabayuan, Olongapo City 2200, Philippines. Fax: 065 047 223–5826.

Du Rae Bang (My Sister's Place), 13/1 116 Kosan-dong, Uijongbu, Kyonggi-do, Korea 480–060. Phone: 0351–841–2609.

National Campaign for the Eradication of Crime by U.S. Troops in Korea, Rm 307, Christian Building, 136–46, Yunchi-Dong, Chongno-Ku, Seoul, Korea, 110–470. Fax: 82–2–3673–2296.

Okinawa Women Act Against Military Violence, 405, 3–29–41, Kumoji, Naha, Okinawa, Japan. Fax: 81–98–864–1539.

Sae Woom Tuh, 483-034 Kyunggi-do, Dongduchon City, Saeng-yun 4 dong 541–39 11/4, Korea. Fax: 82–351–867–3031.

Survivors Take Action Against Abuse by Military Personnel (STAMP), 500 Greene Tree Place, Fairborn, OH 45324. Phone: (937) 879–9304; Fax: (937) 879–2359.

WEDPRO, 14 Maalalahanin St., Teachers Village, Diliman, Quezon City 1101, Philippines. Fax: 632–921–7053. E-mail: wedpro@qinet.net

Films

Olongapo Rose concerns military prostitution in the Philippines. Women Make Movies, 462 Broadway, # 500R, New York, NY 10013. Phone: 212 925–0606. Fax: 212 925–2052. E-mail: orders@wmm.com

The Women Outside and *Camp Arirang* concerns military prostitution in South Korea. Third World Newsreel, 335-38th St. New York, NY 10018. Phone: 212 947–9277. Fax: 212 594–6417.

Toxic Sunset concerns military toxics in the Philippines. ArcEcology, 833 Market St., #1107, San Francisco, CA 94403. Phone: 415 495–1786. E-mail: arc@igc.org

World Wide Web

Asia Pacific Center for Justice and Peace. www.apcjp.org

Japan Coalition on the U.S. Military Bases. http://www.coara.or.jp/~yufukiri/e-index.html

Japan Policy Research Institute. http://www.jpri.org/

Sexual harassment and domestic violence in the military. <http://military-woman.org> and <http://userpages.aug.com/captbarb/violence.html>

CHAPTER 13

Women's Politics and Organizing in Vietnam and Cambodia

KATHRYN McMAHON

Vietnam and Cambodia, neighbors with a history of intertwined politics, can be characterized by differences as much as similarities; for instance, Vietnam's stable socialist state contrasts sharply with Cambodia's precarious coalition governments negotiated after elections of 1993 and 1998. The Vietnam Women's Union, founded in 1930, has a complex organizational structure and an eleven million formal membership, while Cambodia's women's movement is characterized by small, energetic, nongovernmental organizations. After the Vietnamese invasion and occupation of Cambodia in 1979, there was an attempt by the Vietnamese-backed Cambodian government to organize a Vietnam-styled Women's union in Cambodia. The relative failure of top-down organizing efforts contrasts both with the mass-based Vietnam Women's Union and grassroots organizing in Cambodia.

Vietnamese and Cambodians struggle with legacies of decades of war, and women of both countries face daunting political, economic, and social realities; it is not possible in a short essay to present a truly representative account of their struggles. However, it is possible to indicate some of the major issues. Women of Vietnam experience rural poverty, ecological and health damage due to dioxin used against rural National Liberation Front areas during the U.S. war, and a double burden of outside jobs and domestic work. Representation in the National Assembly has declined from a high of 32.3 percent in 1976 to only 18.5 percent in 1992 (Tran and Le 1997, 155). Prostitution and trafficking of women and children, increased reports of domestic violence and migration from the countryside to cities accompany the economic and social impacts of privatization as part of market-based economic reforms. Reforms have included IMF mandated cutbacks in government programs including food subsidies, health care, and other services important to the welfare of women. It would be a mistake to assume that the problems facing women in Vietnam were somehow a result of failure of the women's movement. Historically, "the Vietnam Women's Union cannot be faulted. It continues its efforts . . . to mobilize public support, and to intervene in situations of obvious injustice" (Marr 1981, 250).

Cambodian women also face consequences of decades of war, including the genocidal regime of 1975-79 and subsequent years of a civil war just ended with the death of Pol Pot and the capitulation or capture of the last major leaders of the Khmer Rouge. As in Vietnam, women suffered violence, displacement, and loss of family members in the years of war. Unlike women in Vietnam, Cambodian women struggle with high rates of illiteracy and clear wage discrimination. Women of the two countries share problems with domestic violence and lack of political representation. In Cambodia, as of 1997, there were only seven female members of parliament out of a total of 122 legislators, even though women constituted 58 percent of voters in the 1993 elections (UNDP 1998, iii–xii). As in Vietnam, women in Cambodia are responsible for domestic work while also economically active as farm labor, small shopkeepers, street vendors, and factory labor. There is a growing problem of trafficking of women and girls in Cambodia. "The greatest part of the trafficking for commercial sexual exploitation takes place within the country, but a large number of Cambodian children are also trafficked into Thailand and many Vietnamese girls are trafficked into Cambodia" (UNDP and Ministry of Planning, Kingdom of Cambodia 1998, 29).

During the 1980s, attempts in Cambodia to develop a national women's association met with little success due to lack of resources, failure to mobilize popular support, and inability to address the needs of women in rural villages. In contrast, during the French and American wars, with resources limited and in the face of severe repression, the Vietnam Women's Union was able to recruit members from all strata of society. By organizing from the village level, the Union has continued to build and maintain its base to this day. Women of Cambodia mobilized popular support and took to the streets in coalitions during the early 1990s, demonstrating for a democratic constitution which would give equal legal rights to women. Their efforts were successful, and active, effective nongovernmental women's organizations continue their work among urban poor and rural women.

VIETNAM

Organizing of the revolutionary Vietnamese women's movement began in the 1920s when debates on the question of women became a way to encode political commentary in the context of colonial censorship. These debates "became primary vehicles for arguing about topics that could not be addressed forthrightly, in particular the meaning of freedom and the best way of achieving it" (Tai 1992, 90–91). The precursor of the Women's Union was established at the founding of the Indochinese Communist Party (ICP) in 1930; under various names, it has remained the "organization responsible for the political mobilization, education, and representation of Vietnamese women . . . organized at every level of society beginning with the village" (Tetreault 1996, 40). It took its present name when:

> On 11 September 1945, only nine days after establishment of the Democratic Republic of Vietnam, the first general conference of the Women's Association for National Salvation was convened, and before the end of that year women were fighting and dying to defend the Republic in southern and central Vietnam. . . By the end of 1946, more than one million women had joined the women's association or other Viet Minh affiliates and the association was reorganized, becoming the Vietnam Women's Union (Marr 1981, 248).

Until the partition of Vietnam in 1954, the Women's Union was the major women's organization. Though illegal, by the end of the French war it had nearly three million members (Eisen 1984, 123).

After partition, the Diem regime repressed the union in the south, which was reformed in 1961 as the Union of Women for the Liberation of South Vietnam. By 1975 it had approximately two million members. The Women's Union in the north had at least five million members by 1975. Both unions were organized at the level of village or commune, district or province, and at the national levels. In June 1976, the two organizations merged; the new central committee included all of the representatives of the two preexisting Central Committees (Eisen 1984, 119–136). In May 1982, the National Women's Congress met and elected a new Central Committee and the first president of the Women's Union, Madam Nguyen Thi Dinh. Madam Dinh had been a general during the war, second in command of the People's Liberation Armed Forces. She was known as the general of the Long-Haired Army because of her leadership in organizing women during the Ben Tre uprising of 1960 against the Diem regime (Young 1991, 66–67, Dinh and Elliot 1976, 62–77).

Union membership is open to any woman over sixteen years of age, to special interest groups (for instance, national minority groups, religious groups), and to women's sections within trade unions; dues are nominal. Except for workers who become members through their trade unions, membership is direct. The union publishes books and a national women's magazine, has a weekly television show, and has an international relations department, which maintains relations with women's organizations worldwide. Its research department conducts policy-related research, and conducts leadership training at cadre schools, which teaches women from the local level to act in leadership roles and to conduct training projects (legal, health, midwifery, small-scale income-generating) for poor rural women. The national budget comes primarily from membership dues, sales of publications, and income-generating projects owned and operated by the union. The union receives a small subsidy from the government, and since the trade embargo has been lifted and normalization of relations with the United States is underway, there is modest international funding available for specific health and small-scale rural development projects.

Current union identified priority areas include: 1) poverty; 2) health and education; 3) problems related to rapid commercial development— immigration to cities, urban poverty, a growing commercial sex industry, women's labor rights, industrial health issues and environmental issues,; and 4) HIV and the growing AIDS epidemic. The primary focus for poverty alleviation, health and education is rural women and the "family economy," with an emphasis on small-scale development and income-generating projects. 94 percent of adult women take part in economic production, and 75 percent of them work in the agricultural sector.

In order to increase cash incomes for rural women, the union has developed women's savings groups at the provincial, district, and city levels. Women pool savings and grant loans to members at low-interest rates; interest accrues to the fund. Funds have come from the Bank of Agriculture, from UNDP, and UNIFEM. In addition, the union has established a National Fund for Hunger Elimination and Poverty alleviation; fund-raising campaigns include the use of television, radio, newspapers, and women's magazines. One example was the "Savings for Poor Women Campaign," which designated Ho Chi Minh's birthday as the "Day of Savings for Poor Women." Loans were to be provided for one year to start vending or marketing, chicken or fish raising, or vegetable growing for market. On the first day of the campaign in Hanoi, office workers raised 250 million dong. Special priority for loans was given to widows, ethnic minority groups in mountain areas (the poorest areas of the country), sex workers, and HIV-infected women. Popular support of the campaign signifies a high level of social solidarity among Vietnamese women.

Other union projects include: vocational training programs at the grassroots level; free health care clinics offering immunization, basic health care and family planning; campaigns to alleviate malnutrition in children, including help with growing fruits and vegetables and education about maternal and child nutrition; education and policy-related research and advocacy concerning environmental protection; work in both rural and urban areas to provide wells, potable water, and information about basic hygiene, and family planning clubs for women committed to having no more then one or two children. The clubs offer support with child rearing, nutrition and child care information, group social activities, and opportunities for education. Leadership training and campaigns to increase women's participation in decision making and election to public office include a goal of 20 percent representation in the National Assembly. The union represents women in government, designs new laws, supports candidates for elected office, serves to protect women's rights, and ensures implementation of policies important to women.

Ideologically, the union's emphasis is on strengthening family and reconstituting cultural traditions in the face of commercialism and international culture industries, while educating for economic development. These "traditions" have their roots in pre-colonial matrilineal leadership organization and the roles of women during the revolution. Current discussions concerning gender and social change are complex in Vietnam; questions of tradition, modernization, the concept of family or the social role of the mother are discussed in a manner characteristic of Vietnamese social and intellectual discourse, placing the present period in the context of Vietnamese history (Pelzer 1993, 311). For instance, the image of the nurturing mother is widely used in Vietnam. However, the model for Vietnamese women is the antithesis of the western concept of the mother, who stayed in the background in a supporting role. The category, mother, includes national heroes such as Madam Nguyen Thi Dinh who, as a field general, "nurtured" her young National Liberation Front soldiers to effectiveness. Also, the National Liberation Front used a family strategy between cadres and villagers, including organizing older women into "Foster Mothers' Associations" to serve as surrogate mothers to young guerrillas (Tetreault 1996, 46–47). In Vietnam, the mother in the social "family" is represented in terms of her agency and is not relegated to the private sphere.

CAMBODIA

During the Khmer Rouge period from 1975–1979, Cambodians experienced the death of over a million people. More men than women were killed by the Khmer Rouge, and men died in the subsequent war, leaving women a reported 65 percent of the adult population. Emerging from the Pol Pot period, people experienced food shortages and the difficulties associated with the destruction of roads, schools, places of worship, and the economic infrastructure of the country. Many women had experienced the loss of husbands and other family members. Women had to bring up young children and sometimes orphaned children of relatives as well. The Khmer Rouge period also left deep psychological scars. Many women had terrible experiences and some witnessed their husbands or children being shot, clubbed, or starved to death (Women in Development 1995, 5–6).

In 1979, women went to their home villages to find houses destroyed and rice-fields ravaged; 85 percent of the Cambodian population live in rural areas and 65 percent of the farming population are women. Difficulties were compounded by the U.S.-led economic and trade embargo between 1979-1992; the embargo left Cambodia internationally isolated and included the denial of U.N. development aid. In order to maximize scarce resources, starting in 1979, villagers were divided into "solidarity groups" consisting of between ten and twenty families. Efforts were made to ensure that each group had a comparable number of adult men, tools, and work animals. The crops produced were divided among the members, according to the amount of labor performed. The "solidarity group" system enabled women without family or material resources to survive (Women in Development 1995, 8).

A national women's organization called the National Association of Women for the Salvation of Kampuchea was founded in 1979 by the Vietnamese-backed government in Phnom Penh; also formed was a national Youth Association, which had a special section for young women. The Women's Association's main activity was to explain to women workers and peasant women the policies and programs of the government. Every woman was considered a member of the association, which had a small national budget. For many years the association did not have a well-organized or -financed program to assist women at the village level, though it did have representatives throughout the country. Although members did attempt to raise money to help women whose husbands had died or been disabled in the war, in most parts of the country the impact of the Women's association was not felt, and many women did not trust the Association because of its inability to offer effective assistance (Boua 1992, Women in Development 1995, 21–27).

The Women's Association used part of its small budget to establish a Department of External Relations, which maintained links with women's organizations in other countries, especially socialist countries, but also India, France, Australia, Japan, and progressive international organizations. The association also produced a twice-weekly radio program dealing with political and women's issues, which gave advice in the areas of health, child care, and agricultural production. There were also a small number of women who held positions in the top echelons of government. In 1991, in the ruling People's Revolutionary Party, there was one woman in the political bureau of the party central committee, which had twelve members. Significantly, out of 10,000 members of the party, approximately 5 percent were women (Boua 1992).

In the late 1980s and early 1990s, several international humanitarian organizations helped design and fund programs through the Women's Association, which helped to identify areas of crucial need and facilitated assistance programs. Projects included sewing workshops, silk weaving, cow banks, and assistance with family food production. However, input by international organizations was small and barely began to address the needs of women in the aftermath of war, the devastation of the Pol Pot period, and the internal displacement during the continuing conflict between the Phnom Penh government and factions fighting from the Thai border areas (Boua 1992).

Persistent poverty and hardship, especially among families headed by widows, were inadequately addressed by the Women's Association. Also, women's involvement in policy-making inadequately responded to the urgent needs of rural women, who made up the majority of the work force. Following the withdrawal of Vietnamese troops in 1989 and the United Nations Transitional Authority's establishment of a transitional government in Cambodia in 1992 (which led to the drafting of a new constitution and national elections in 1993), the Women's Association was disbanded. During this period, a number of nongovernmental groups were formed out of a popular struggle for a democratic constitution.

There were public campaigns, national debates, demonstrations and marches comprised of coalitions, which included monks, students, and emerging grassroots women's organizations. There are now a number of active nongovernmental women's organizations.

Groups working on behalf of women include KHEMARA, one of the largest and most highly funded groups (thanks to other international agencies), which promotes equal status under the law and works for implementation of those laws that offer protection for women's rights. KHEMARA has also developed cooperative projects for women in the marketplace, including a small loan program. Khmer Women's Voice Center produces videos and a weekly radio program. Cambodian Women's Development Association is one of the lead organizations in the struggle against trafficking of women and girls; they recently organized a collective for sex workers. Organizations work as partners to promote equity for women in development policies and education, health care projects, and human rights.

At the state level, a Secretariat of Women's Affairs was formed in 1993; using the former Women's Association network, it recruited staff for each province. Its effectiveness has been limited by a very small budget and political instability at the state level, which led to armed conflict between the Cambodian People's Party (CPP) and FUNCINPEC (the royalist party) and a CPP coup in July 1997. Seen as unstable because of political tensions, the secretariat (elevated now to ministry level) has had limited input from international agencies, which prefer to support nongovernmental organizations.

CONCLUSION

The Vietnam Women's Union has been organized for nearly seventy years of challenging history. Vietnam's transition to a market-based economy, including commercial development and rapid social change, brings urgent issues to the forefront: urbanization, women's health and safety, workers' rights, and the poverty of women in rural families. Trafficking in women and children has grown as a result of persistent poverty and the concurrent growth of the commercial sex industry. HIV/AIDS education has become a national priority in the context of growing concern in a country with a health care system in need of resources. Women's political representation at the state level remains a priority along with the development of leadership in a younger generation for whom the wars of liberation are but stories told by elders.

Women have legal equality under the constitution, and the state continues to draft laws ensuring the protection of women's rights. The union works to ensure implementation of laws and has a powerful influence on policymaking. However, women are still not adequately represented in the economic and political structures of the country. The union is the lynchpin of the struggle for political representation, since virtually every woman who has achieved a position of authority in the Vietnamese government has been a Union member (Tetreault 1996, 40). Women have achieved equality in education and employment, and if a woman feels that she has been discriminated against because of her sex, she can raise the issue in public without fear of retaliation.

Daughters still defer to parents, and wives often defer to husbands, but, as David Marr has pointed out,

> If a woman chooses to disagree with her parents, husband, or male co-worker, she is no longer at an automatic disadvantage. She can seek support from her teachers, from local Women's Union representatives, or from Party officials. Largely for this reason, few parents dare to pressure a daughter entirely against her will. A husband who abuses his wife risks stern rebukes from outside. A wife, if she wishes, can institute divorce proceedings at no special penalty to herself (1981, 249-250).

Gender equity within the family is not a reality for most women; those with responsible positions are often still seen as naturally better suited for child care and domestic work. The image of the nurturing mother can be a figure of social and political agency, or, with increasing privatization, a woman who accepts a double burden without complaint. The union's influence through leadership, its television programs and publications might challenge those ideological assumptions that perpetuate the subordination of women.

As a result of the struggles of women's organizations working in coalition in the early 1990s, Cambodia's constitution now has progressive legal provisions regarding the rights of women. The National Assembly has drafted laws such as the Law on Abortion, the Law on Domestic Violence, and the Law on Trafficking, which further protect women. However, implementation and enforcement are problematic. Courts tend to favor men in judgments, and with a higher level of illiteracy (only 55 percent of women are literate), women are less likely to know the law and are more easily intimidated. Female representation in the weak judicial system is low; out of 110 judges in Cambodia only eight are women; of forty prosecutors, none are women (UNDP 1998, iv–v).

Cambodian women also face discrimination in education and employment, and they are poorly represented in political and economic structures. For instance, as of September 1998, no women were ministers in government, no women were provincial governors, and no women were secretaries of state in any ministry. Women also face inequality in families; in a recent survey, 16 percent of married women reported physical abuse resulting in injury (UNDP 1998, iii–xii). This is in spite of the fact that traditionally women enjoy a relatively high social status. Khmer kinship is bilateral, and there has been a preference in Khmer society for young couples to live with the parents of the wife, giving her the protection of her kin. The high levels of domestic abuse speak to the damage to the social fabric that years of war, social, and economic displacement have effected.

Women's organizations continue to work in coalition to organize women on their own behalf in order to address the above issues. The development of a more stable state, as well as a viable Ministry of Women's Affairs, could create an opportunity for nongovernment organizations to promote women's rights, consolidate their gains, and move ahead on more solid ground. Progress in areas of grassroots research and advocacy for policy change, coalition building with local human rights groups and international organizations, and effective organizing is impressive given that women's groups are small with few stable funding sources. Consistent international support is important in helping to ensure that women's organizations, human rights organizations, and the Ministry of Women's Affairs can work together to effect the implementation of laws on women's behalf and to advocate for human rights of women and equity in development.

REFERENCES

Boua, Chanthou. 1992. "Challenges Facing Cambodian Women." Panel presentation for Cambodian Network Council Conference, 4 July 1992 at Long Beach, California.

Eisen, Arlene. 1984. *Women and Revolution in Vietnam*. London: Zed Books.

Marr, David. 1981. *Vietnamese Tradition on Trial 1920-1945*. Berkeley: University of California Press.

Nguyen Thi Dinh, and Mai Elliot. 1976. *No Other Road to Take: Memoir of Mrs. Nguyen Thi Dinh*. Ithaca: Cornell University Southeast Asia Program.

Pelzer, Kristin. 1993. "Socio-Cultural Dimensions of Renovation in Vietnam: Doi Moi as Dialogue and Transformation in Gender Relations." *In Reinventing Vietnamese Socialism*, edited by William S. Turley and Mark Selden, 309–336.

Tai, Hue-Tam Ho. 1992. *Radicalism and the Origins of the Vietnamese Revolution*. Cambridge: Harvard University Press.

Tetreault, Mary Ann. 1996. "Women and Revolution in Vietnam." In *Vietnam's Women in Transition*, edited by Kathleen Barry, 38–57. New York: St. Martin's Press.

Tran Thi Van Anh and Le Ngoc Hung. 1997. *Women and* doi moi *in Vietnam*. Hanoi: Woman Publishing House.

UNDP. 1998. *Cambodia Human Development Report 1998*. New York: United Nations.

Women in Development. 1995. *Cambodia's Country Report*. Phnom Penh, Cambodia. Xerox.

Young, Marilyn. 1991. *The Vietnam Wars 1945-1990*. New York: Harper Collins.

CHAPTER 14

Women in Command
A Successful Experience in the
National Liberation Army of Iran

SORAYYA SHAHRI

I am very grateful for this opportunity to address this gathering. I am hopeful in the course of my remarks that I can provide the answers to some of your questions.

The women's movement of Iran has a long history. At the turn of the century, women were active in the movement for freedom in Iran. They organized themselves and provided logistical support. During the Constitutional Revolution in 1906, the system of monarchical despotism was transformed to constitutional monarchy.

During the anti-shah movement, there was a sharp increase in the number of women who joined organizations seeking to gain freedom through armed struggle. Although their numbers were still limited during this era, for the first time, women were arrested, tortured, and imprisoned by the dreaded secret police, SAVAK.

As the momentum of the anti-shah movement picked up, demonstrations erupted across Iran, involving millions of people. Again, there were striking numbers of women among them. This process culminated in the overthrow of the shah's regime. For a short while afterwards, when freedom actually did prevail in Iran, the opposition political organizations were able to operate freely in society. In an extraordinary manner, women took to political activism. Of course, there was also a fundamental reason: from day one, the Khomeini regime began to discriminate against and suppress women.

I was a supporter of the Mojahedin, the leftist resistance to the Shah's regime. As I became acquainted with their views, I began to involve myself in the political warfare. I started out selling newspapers and collecting contributions for the Mojahedin. In those days, Mojahedin women and girl activists were a new phenomenon in Iranian society.

When the era of peaceful political opposition drew to a close, and the need for resistance became apparent, women members of the Mojahedin took on a variety of responsibilities in the bases. In the prisons, other women put up a heroic resistance against vile treatment. In direct contrast to society, where women had no rights and were of no account, in the prisons they were tortured and tormented twice as brutally, precisely because they were women.

For example, one of the most savage methods of torture for women is rape. The Khomeini regime set up certain units, called residential units, to suppress women political dissidents. There, the regime retaliated against women who had committed the unforgivable crimes of demanding freedom and refusing to submit, by having them continuously raped by its Revolutionary Guards. We have women in our organization, and in our army, who emerged from these cells. Today, years after their imprisonment, they still have not recovered emotionally. In some cases, these women became vegetables, but to the last they refused to abandon their beliefs.

The record of resistance by women in the prisons of the Khomeini regime is a source of pride in our nation's history. We do not even know yet the full dimensions of their ordeal. That will have to wait, until that day when the prison doors are opened wide, and the truth is revealed in the light of day.

Thus, Iranian women kept pace with the progress of the movement, and were present in every arena. They played out their role in the best, most responsible manner. When the National Liberation Army (NLA) was formed in 1987, the women of the Iranian Resistance found a new arena in which to overcome new trials. I would like to speak to you a little about the days when women first made their way into the NLA.

Women were first active in support units in the NLA. During this stage, which did not last long, they were busy in the transport, supply, administrative, and similar units.

Next, women became involved in providing backup for military operations. To accomplish this, we first formed women's brigades in the NLA, which was then an infantry army. Within their brigades, women combatants ran all of their own affairs, from servicing their equipment to mechanical repairs. They were trained separately from the male combatants. After they had learned the ropes, they began to take over the logistical support for the military operations, first with mortars and then artillery guns.

The next stage was for women to actually take part in the operations. In spring 1987, the NLA launched its first major operation, code-named "Shining Sun," in the southern province of Khuzistan. Women were organized into two separate brigades, and, for the first time, took the field and fought face-to-face with Khomeini's forces on the front lines. The enemy's forces were shocked to find themselves captured by one of the women's brigades. Scenes of their capture, their surprise evident for all to see, were featured in some of the world's leading newspapers. Despite all the objections you have heard, women were fighting on the frontlines and reality was laid bare. Like their male counterparts, the women of the NLA demonstrated they were capable and qualified.

The women's brigades, now veterans of a full-scale military operation, were merged with the male brigades. These units took part in the "Forty Stars" operation together, during which the strategic city of Mehran in western Iran was conquered. One of the Khomeini regime's best-armored units was destroyed, and billions of dollars in tanks and weapons were seized as booty. Fifteen hundred of the regime's soldiers were taken prisoner.

Immediately after this operation, only a week later, the National Liberation Army staged the "Eternal Light" operation. "Eternal Light" was the NLA's largest operation and penetrated 150 kilometers into Iran. The fighting raged over four days. Two cities were liberated, and the NLA reached the gates of Kermanshah, the largest city in western Iran. The Khomeini regime suffered 55,000 casualties in this operation, the first in which women commanded many divisions and brigades. The operation, and in particular the fighting spirit of the NLA's women, had a tremendous impact.

Twelve hundred NLA combatants were killed or went missing in "Eternal Light," many of them women—women of various ages, women with children. One older woman died, along with her daughter and son-in-law. And of course, there were many young women who fought courageously against Khomeini's revolutionary guards. In one case, three women combatants of the NLA held off a force of 6,000 for hours, until their ammunition ran out. Before dying as martyrs to their cause, they killed hundreds of the regime's guards.

The regime, until after it was all over, was convinced that it was facing a squad or brigade hunkered down in bunkers. Afterwards, of course, it found only three women.

Up until this time, the NLA was essentially an infantry army. After "Eternal Light," our army began to evolve into an armored force. In truth, this stage was equivalent to all the earlier stages of the NLA's formation.

The point to notice is that although our army resembles a classical army, as far as our methods and our combatants' motivations are concerned, we are unlike any classical army in the world. For that reason, instead of taking long years, our evolution into an armored force took only two years.

This process was undertaken with the creativity, encouragement, and constant supervision of Maryam Rajavi, who was then the NLA deputy commander in chief. Of course, this is a whole discussion in itself, but I wanted to give you an idea of how, under these high-pressure conditions, we simultaneously introduced women into the emerging armored apparatus.

At first, to be truthful, no one except Mrs. Rajavi believed it could be done. First, a group of commanders, men and women, checked out the theory in the field. The top female commanders in the NLA sat in tanks and tried to learn how to use them. The first answer that Mrs. Rajavi received was that the task was impossible, but she was not convinced. She sent another individual to study the job, our martyred sister Zahra Rajabi. Zahra was a woman of formidable determination, effort, and creativity. Physically, she was very strong. She declared war on the tank, and she won. Mrs. Rajavi said, "If one woman can do it, then all women can do it." And thus, the women of the NLA began to undergo training in the armored divisions.

In the beginning, the women were generally unwilling to take coed courses. Hence, a group of women commanders had to first undergo the training process, master the materials and skills, and take on the training of the other women in separate classes. But after the first group of women had graduated from the training courses, the "tank taboo" was shattered and coed classes were formed.

Actually, the women performed much better in those classes than their male counterparts, even in practical trials. Their initial foot-dragging was a product of their view of themselves as the weaker sex. After this concept was proven wrong, they no longer resisted the training and, thus, did much better in practice. Of course, the same applies in theory, but I will not go into that, because theory is something that women discovered long ago.

We also passed through several other stages while making full participation by women a reality. One stage involved the NLA's airborne division, another the operational commanders, who draw up battle plans, and another involved introducing women into the general command. One by one, we overcame the mind blocks resulting from the women's lack of faith in their own capabilities and unwillingness to take on the responsibility of command and operational planning (where hundreds of lives are

at risk). If it were not for Mrs. Rajavi's constant advice and encouragement of each combatant, we never would have made it.

In truth, she was the first woman to shoulder the burden of leadership.
She did not run from the problems and effort that task requires. She was
the only one who believed that women can take part in every task. As I explained in our transition to an armored force, she never gave up in the face
of others' lack of faith. She did whatever it took to resolve the conflicts.

We have been blessed with the presence of this innovative woman in
the leadership of our movement, and we have found the proper path of
our struggle. The experiences of each and every one of us confirm that if
we had not been engaged in a torturous struggle, and had not had this
leader as our role model, we could never have conquered our own disbelief and achieved true faith in the practical equality of men and women.

What actually sets Mrs. Rajavi apart is that she has brought an entire
generation of women with her along her path. The jobs that our women
perform in the army have certainly been taught in other armies of the
world. And there have always been the few exceptions, women who even
flew combat missions in wars, including the last war in Kuwait. But these
were only a few women who, for whatever reason, had the desire and
personal ability to overcome all the inherent difficulties.

In our movement, this was not the case. We had women from every
walk of life, all social classes, all ages and levels of education. They
wanted freedom, but had few feminist ideas. Our pilots were scared of
the very idea of flying. Our tank commanders were afraid to fire their
cannons. Our unit commanders said, "We were not cut out for this!" For
many of them, when they joined the freedom movement in Iran, they
thought martyrdom under torture lay at the end of the road they had
chosen.

But in the harsh resistance against the anti-woman regime of
Khomeini, they became convinced that it was imperative that women be
introduced into every arena. And they realized that if they did not emerge
victorious from each of these arenas, they would not be capable of overthrowing the Khomeini regime and establishing peace and justice in their
homeland.

Because the enemy is antihuman, because the enemy uses the most
inhuman means to crush his opponents, we had to become the antithesis
of Khomeini—to the marrow of our bones and in the depths of our souls.
Otherwise, we would not be able to go on with the struggle. We should
not submit to our enemy, even in our most secret thoughts.

Mrs. Rajavi's greatest achievement lies right here. She declared war
on the Khomeini mentality, hidden deep in the minds of the most enlight-

ened sector of Iranian society. These were people who, in theory, were absolutely convinced of the equality of women and men and opposed to any form of discrimination. But deep inside, and in practice, they were the opposite. It was these ideas and perceptions that prevented the progress of the struggle.

We have focused here on the issue of women. But let it not go unsaid that if the men in our movement had not made the conscious decision to accept the command of qualified women, this experience would have been a failure. At first, it was no easy task for these men to take orders, even from women who had proven themselves qualified. But we worked on this problem, we did not ignore it. We discussed it at length, and of course Mrs. Rajavi also taught the men that liberation from patriarchy and belief in the equality of women with men were also imperative for men. They had to annihilate the idea that their own sisters, mothers, and daughters were less than human, were somehow second-class. They had to fight against that notion, and in doing so, they would achieve their own humanity and internal unity.

For example, for me and other officials and commanders, it was so much easier to use one of the male officials or commanders in delegating responsibility or choosing a commander for a unit or post. Men had more experience, sometimes more maturity, and a military record. They did not have all the problems a woman would have in taking on the responsibility.

But in truth, this was simplistic, and it did nothing to solve the problem. In its own way, it meant the exclusion of women. But then the movement as a whole stood up to the idea of male dominance, and we firmly confronted gender suppression at every turn without, of course, ignoring the individual's qualifications and commitment. In the military, there are no joking matters.

Recognizing the need for expansion, our movement and our army saw in practice that women who can overcome their lack of faith in themselves and discover their own capabilities, make worthy, efficient commanders. Of course, their potential, motivation, and sense of responsibility are greater than a man's, because they are like a spring that has been compressed; all of a sudden, they are free.

To shatter the notion of male superiority, which bound the hands and feet of our men and women, we voluntarily ended our marriages in divorce so that no one had any responsibility to anyone or anything but the all-out war on the Khomeini regime. Our women chose to take this path to disengage themselves from what the world defined as being a woman, the weaker sex, and to disengage themselves from their traditional role, in which, to be recognized, they required the existence of a husband.

In the same fashion, the men, to rid themselves of the notion that they owned their wives, body and soul (and it was these men who inspired the women to strive), had to recognize their wives' right to choose between a life of resistance and a private life. They had to learn to look upon women not as women, but as equal human beings.

In this way, our women and men were physically helped to step outside of their traditional roles and to consciously declare war on ideas that they had automatically brought with them from society.

In a year's time, with the start of the Persian Gulf War, the Iranian Resistance's bases in Iraq became vulnerable to a continuous bombardment unprecedented in history. The seriousness of our situation and conditions of war in which we found ourselves were such that we could no longer condone the presence of our children in the bases. Everyone was sent into the bunkers, and everything was transported underground. We had prepared ourselves for very difficult conditions and did not want our innocent children, not yet at an age to choose their destinies, to be scarred. Thus, all combatants, mothers and fathers, sent their children out of Iraq to safety, where they were taken in by relatives and Resistance supporters. This was a major operation completed at great expense in time and money.

And so you see that the men and women combatants of the National Liberation Army of Iran have given up everything in their struggle to establish peace and democracy in their homeland. They are striving to overthrow the antihuman regime ruling their nation. We have paid an enormous price to make our women's equality and our nation's freedom realities. Of course, our women dedicated themselves and vowed to pay the price of their own and their people's freedom, because no one will ever hand freedom on a silver platter to Iran's women or men.

CHAPTER 15

Conversion

HABIBA METIKOS

I feel a pain in my heart when the phrase "life in exile" comes to my mind. You are interested in my life in exile, but I must mention the wonderful life I had before in order to compare my present and past life. I was an intellectual, I worked, I was married. I had a daughter, and I lived in the most beautiful city in the world, as you guess, in Sarajevo. On the 11th of April, my present painful life started. My twelve-year-old daughter and I left all that meant life to us. Some strange people broke our life as if it were a glass and we were just two pieces who had to set off to make up a whole someplace else. That day we could leave only by taking a plane to Belgrade. What a paradox! To be a refugee means to be driven from one's home, but then not all refugees are equal: Serbian refugees can go to Serbia, Croatian to Croatia, and Muslims, nowhere. I am one of those.

We came to Belgrade. I dared not pronounce my name because it is a Muslim name. War in Bosnia got worse and worse and my stay in Belgrade became unbearable. I decided to send my only and longtime expected child to my cousin's place in Canada. I went to Germany to stay with friends. Both of us could not survive together in one place, because we didn't have enough money. I thought that conditions in Sarajevo would improve and that we would soon return. My husband stayed in

Excerpted from Mertus, Julie, Jasmina Tesanovic, Habiba Metikos, and Rada Boric, eds. 1997. *The Suitcase: Refugee Voices from Bosnia and Croatia.* Berkeley and Los Angeles: University of California Press.

Sarajevo. That day, 9 May 1992, was probably the hardest day in my life—that was the day when my child went out into the unknown world. I looked at the departing plane for a long time. It seemed that the little black dot in the sky would stay there forever.

Ten days later I went to my friends' house in Germany. I had met those people fifteen years ago at the seaside in my country. They had come to our place in Sarajevo, and now I came to theirs during the worst point in my life. Since I was not the rich lady anymore, they treated me differently. I worked in their restaurant, cleaning and cooking for eighteen to twenty hours each day, just for food and a place to sleep.

One month later, I decided to go away. The only place I could go was Zagreb because I had some relatives there. So I went to Zagreb. My child's life in Canada had become complicated, and I needed to bring her to Zagreb too. She did not have a round-trip air ticket, but a few kind people lent me the money and my girl arrived. Then, life took a turn for the worse. At that time, my mother died in Sarajevo. She was everything to me since my father had died when I was young. Her death was extremely hard on me. I couldn't call my husband at all, because the phone lines didn't work to Sarajevo.

In Zagreb, I again dared not pronounce my name because the only important thing was to have a Croatian birth certificate, which only pure-blooded Croats can get. That's how you can get work, a passport, and put your child in a school.

A Croatian birth certificate became my obsession. After a year I found a priest who didn't refuse to convert me and my daughter to the Catholic religion. I paid for it of course, because you cannot take on a new faith for free. I was infinitely happy; I thought we wouldn't be hungry and without clothes anymore; we had had nothing to live on until then. I swore allegiance to my new Catholic God, I forgot my Muslim one, who had brought me all that pain. But my birth certificate didn't bring me happiness because the name written on it wasn't Croat but Muslim. The authorities just spat on my one-year strain and I had nobody else to spit on but myself. I couldn't get a job because I wasn't a real Croat.

Our position became worse every day. I stood in line for clothes and food: we were fasting. And then God finally accepted the birth certificate of my daughter and we managed to put her in a school where people were more tolerant, maybe because she had a name which was universal and quite frequent in Croatia.

Wandering around, by chance, I came upon a women's center, for victims of war and violence. I started working there, helping other refugee women. And that is when the worst period of my life ended. I found myself in the women's organization and I found the strength not only to survive but to find myself. Those girls, Croatians, were like all other Croats except they weren't nationalists. They wanted to help every woman. I felt like a human being again and my faith in people was restored.

CHAPTER 16

The Passage

VINKA LJUBIMIR

This is not the first time I sit to this—in front of a blank computer screen, deadline ahead of me. And then . . . nothing. Words do not come to me. All I keep thinking is that my story is not anything special, that many other people have lived through worse. For me, a lifetime has passed between the last peaceful summer at home in Dubrovnik and today. I am in the U.S. now, and yet another one of my friends is suggesting that I write the story down. I write as I remember—a jumble of scenes.

We discussed among ourselves the possibility of a war years before it actually started. The Serbian-controlled media said that the city was filled with Ustashas (the state-supported Croatian forces allied with Hitler in World War II and responsible for grave war crimes) and that they presented a threat. We wanted to believe that the city's beauty was going to save it. We could not imagine that in Europe, again, for the third time in the twentieth century, bombs were going to fall on civilians, that there were going to be massacres, that rape was going to be employed on a large scale for territorial gains. Although we saw all the warning signs, we tried to live as if the situation would not deteriorate that far. But it did.

On 1 October 1991, bombs destroyed our transmitters, food supplies, water and electricity installations. We were besieged. Each day

Excerpted from Mertus, Julie, Jasmina Tesanovic, Habiba Metikos, and Rada Boric, eds. 1997. *The Suitcase: Refugee Voices from Bosnia and Croatia*. Berkeley and Los Angeles: University of California Press.

was a long struggle for survival. After four days of incessant shelling, some of us decided to take advantage of the Red Cross ferry that promised to bring us to safety.

THE JOURNEY

Day 3, afternoon

My stomach was writhing in my body with the worst seasickness of my life. I put a wet piece of cloth on my face and lay on my side, being as still as possible, trying to calm my frightened body. The bed was damp, one of those very narrow bunk beds in a typical third-class accommodation on Adriatic passenger ships. The mattress was rank with months of refugee service, rank with fear. Under my nose, only a few inches away from my face, were the feet of the other woman in the bed, a nurse, five months pregnant. Since there was not enough room, we lay two to a bed, so her feet were near my face, and her head was near my feet. Every so often, she would moan a painful sound from her chest. Every so often, she would throw her heavy body across mine and lunge to a small sink in the corner of the cabin to throw up.

On the other lower bunk bed there lay the four-day-old baby. It did not move throughout most of the first leg of the journey. All of us in the cabin had been evacuated from St. Blaise hospital in Dubrovnik. The baby had been sent to safety along with its two-and-a-half-year-old diabetic brother and its mentally retarded mother. From time to time the boy gave instructions to his mother: "Take me up; take me to the bathroom; give me water!" which she would obediently and lovingly fulfill.

This little boy, Ivan, was our hero, taking care of himself, his mother, and his brother. The first time he needed insulin, he approached me and said, "Help me, I need an injection!" He was aware that his mother was not able to do it under the circumstances. Another nurse among the women gave him the insulin. We stared at the little arm, our eyes open, not blinking.

The captain of the ship had left all of his supplies in Dubrovnik. He had expected to stop for food on the way. But once he set sail, he was warned not to stop. In the cabin we dug through our bags for food, taking stock. Ivan's mother had bread, two of us had fruit. We saved as much as possible, because we did not know how long our trip would be.

Day 3, night

Soon after we docked in Zelenika, the ship was met by a brigade of Montenegrin Red Cross ambulances. About five hundred people felt they would not survive the trip and were allowed to disembark. Meanwhile, JNA soldiers came on board, with machine guns on their shoulders, searching every cabin. They were very thorough, precise, yet apathetic. They looked under our beds, poking their guns to see if anyone was hiding there. Under the terms of our passage, no men between eighteen and sixty years of age were allowed to leave the city. All the men who could walk were marched onto the dock, in teeming rain, and left to stand in line. They stood for hours as they were questioned, one by one. A few were taken away.

No one knew exactly what was going on, but through word of mouth we managed to get the most important news. We felt trapped in our places and it was very painful not to know what was going on. Those who didn't suffer from seasickness went from cabin to cabin, bringing news. We found out we were sailing from Zelenika the next morning.

Day 4, morning

The ship's engines woke us at dawn. We turned north, having passed the JNA inspection. Even in the rough weather, we expected to reach Korcula, our next stop, within several hours. We were promised a safe harbor, water, food, and medical supplies, but again we learned we would not be allowed to dock. It was still safe in Korcula, and many people on board had planned to remain there, rest with their relatives or friends, and be close to Dubrovnik. The disappointment was enormous.

The captain's voice came over the loudspeakers again: "I have food for only two hundred meals on board. I have to make a decision how to divide it justly and to avoid panic. We have approximately 3,500 passengers on board. My idea is to put a high price on the food so fewer people will crowd into the restaurant. If anybody on this ship has a better idea, please come forward and let me know." No one had and the food was expensive.

Day 4, daytime

The sea was calmer, so we started talking among ourselves. The main topic was where and how we would live after we got off the ship. At that time we did not know whether the new country we voted for, Croatia, would be recognized as a country or not, what the price would be that we would have to pay for separation.

All the children accepted their hunger; they did not even take a second piece when offered. Preoccupied with thinking about how to make the most of what we had, I handed Ivan a jelly sandwich by mistake. "I don't eat this," he said, looking at me with his big smart eyes. I could not believe there was such perfect sense in the middle of all the humiliation and confusion and despair. For a moment nobody spoke or moved. I know that for everyone there his alertness and simple dignity was a sign of hope that life might somehow continue normally.

THE DESTINATION

Day 4, daytime

We climbed to the top deck, only to see an army cruiser in the distance, following the ship. There was a very old man sitting on a top deck bench, looking at the sea. He had a black coat on and was leaning on a cane. His white hair, as well as his beard, were flying in the wind, but his face was expressionless. Only his eyes occasionally searched for something in the distance. People would stop to ask him if he was all right, but he would reply in short sentences that he wanted to be left alone. It was cold up there, and somebody brought a blanket to cover his legs.

I knew many of the women on board. Some of them were my colleagues, neighbors, relatives, and friends. I kept looking for my friend, a medical doctor, who was working all the time during the trip. She had to disembark her grandmother at Zelenika, because she had lost too much liquid with the seasickness and would not survive the rest of the journey. Her parents, however, stayed with her on the ship. At the beginning of the fighting in the Dubrovnik area in autumn that year, the army had burnt their house in the village of Grude, with their dog still inside. The family had already spent months as refugees in Dubrovnik shelters. When I saw my friend on the deck, she was behaving like an automaton, performing perfectly, completely detached from her feelings. There were many who needed her help. There were three deliveries. Two healthy babies and one stillborn were born.

Day 4, night

It was past midnight. My hands were hurting with the heaviness of the luggage I carried down the narrow, steep steps of the ferry, stepping over people and children, to the car department area. Our little group organized itself almost perfectly, trying not to spend any more energy than necessary. Those with children had to be helped because it was impossible to take care of all the things at the same time. Somebody had to carry, others were taking care of the children.

As the people approached the exit, the area in the ship's belly started getting more and more crowded. Finally, there was no more room. We were all standing there, squeezed among our dirty luggage, the wounded, and the crying children. But there was also an immense silence and patience. We had been preparing ourselves for this moment.

THE MEMORIES

Day 1, evening

The feeling in your arms when hugging your mother good-bye. The way you feel her body tensed under the layers of clothes, her soft and fine skin under your fingers, the look in her eyes: many unspoken prayers and the desire to live.

I couldn't decide whether to stay or go. Mother said, "Go."

My mother decided to stay. "I am not leaving," she said, and I knew the decision was final. It was the night two nights before our departure. The air was filled with smoke of the harbor burning. The fire was so big that it made such a light you could see almost as in the daylight, although you were on the other side of the peninsula embracing the harbor.

THE DEPARTURE

Days of exile

To get out of the city was not at all easy. First, you needed to make the decision. Then, you needed a lot of luck. Your name had to be listed on a list made by the Red Cross. Many people stayed because they were so afraid of bombing that they could not risk leaving their shelter to reach the ship. Some others were not ready to wait for the transport for hours and risk being hit by the shelling. The waiting seemed to them much worse than the day-to-day suffering in the shelters.

War taught us a lot. How people change completely, in unexpected and sometimes even unexplainable directions when exposed to it. How the fear makes people irrationally greedy. It is difficult to resist becoming greedy. It is almost like an instinct. To possess, to hold on to something.

In shelters, to hold on to somebody. To hold on to your prayer, even if you never prayed before. To hold on to your principles. Then, to give up your principles for the possession. Many know that if they leave, nothing will be there for them to come back to. It will be stolen, taken away, destroyed, burned. To some, their things had meant their life. Old paintings, memories caught in photographs, things they shared together with the dear ones. Their lives would not be complete without these things, and they were prepared to live through all that could come.

THE MORNING BEFORE THE DEPARTURE

Day 3, morning

In the morning we finally had the information that the ship had come in. We had been prepared for the departure since very early in the morning, but we had to wait for hours. On the way to the harbor, we saw a man looking at us while the driver (of the ambulance Vinka and others were traveling in) turned along the curve on the road. The man lifted his hands up to his forehead in a gesture of despair. His eyes were fixed on a woman in the ambulance. "That's my husband," she shouted, and waved. He just kept his eyes pasted on the ambulance. He had a completely lost expression on his face.

I'm holding a four-day-old baby in my arms. "Please, hold the baby," said a nun to me, handing me a small, light-green bundle containing a small, helpless body. "His mother is retarded, and the other kid is a diabetic," she said, and hugged the other child. I had already boarded the overcrowded ambulance in the basement hospital garage after more than thirty-six hours of waiting there for a ship to take us out.

Our vehicle was among the last to reach the ship. The rain was still pouring. I carried the baby in, put him on a piece of luggage, and then started going back for the rest of my stuff. I almost did not make it. The doors were already closing. The captain had a deadline to respect that the JNA (Yugoslav National Army) had imposed on him, and he was already late. During the embarkation, the JNA promised to hold their fire.

Days 1 and 2

Those hours were filled with anxiety. Would we be able to get to the ship, to get on it, to sail out? We spent time keeping the children calm, talking to each other, worrying.

During the waiting, little things made a difference, like a comforting word, like a sandwich that was handed to me by one of the woman doctors. Her calmness and kindness stayed with me for hours like a shield against all the mess around me. Some of the people gathered there could not communicate—they were in a state of shock. One of them was my friend whose apartment served as a point of strategic defense and where a couple of fighters had died the previous night.

THE ARRIVAL

Day 4, night

The machines came to a stop. The people in the ship were waiting, silent, motionless, for the ship to open its huge belly and let us out. There were so many people that we were afraid that somebody could be hurt. Over the loudspeakers we were warned to wait and to let the first-aid crews carry out the wounded first. It was raining desperately, the same as on the day we embarked in Dubrovnik.

NEW YORK, N.Y., UNITED STATES OF AMERICA, JUNE 1994

(Although sporadic fighting began earlier, the siege of Dubrovnik began the day after Vinka left Dubrovnik, on 2 October 1991. The JNA bombardment of the UNESCO-protected town—called one of the most beautiful and historic cities in the world—flared on 23 October and again on 11 November, continuing throughout the month of December. Unlike the earlier JNA attacks on Vukovar, which were largely ignored by the press, the JNA's shelling of Dubrovnik and the burning and looting of nearby villages drew intense condemnation from the international community.

While a January 1992 agreement calmed the area for a while, Serb shelling continued into May 1992, and it wasn't until 20 October 1992, that the Yugoslav army abandoned its siege of Dubrovnik. Even after that date, however, the city and its surroundings came under periodic attack.

After Vinka wrote this in the United States, she returned to Croatia where she is a psychologist and researcher. She also works on projects to rebuild the destroyed villages near Dubrovnik and to support local refugees (Mertus et al. 1997, 54).)

PART III

Nonviolent, and Not-Nonviolent, Action against Patriarchy

CHAPTER 17

The Kitchen Cabinet

JULIE MERTUS

Everyone loves a scandal. Few people understand how the global women's movement works. That's why you never heard about our remarkable dinners at The Restaurant in Huairou.

News from the women's conference was dominated by matters of a more sensational sort: Would Hillary speak? Do the Chinese know how to run a world conference? Will women attending the meeting be harassed?

Was there more? You had better believe it. These were, after all, 30,000 women activists from around the world. They were accustomed to difficult travel, getting wet in the rain, getting things done against obstacles. And they had plenty of experience creating unusual alliances in unexpected places.

In many parts of the world, being a women's rights activist means having your phone tapped, your mail read, your meetings infiltrated, and your children harassed. In countries without freedom of speech, it means holding meetings in dark flats, passing out photocopied brochures that will later be confiscated by police, being called into the police station and lectured after attending foreign or even local conferences. In countries at war, it means teaching girls how to read in bomb shelters, hiding your sons from the army, waving antiwar placards in the town square, and passing out humanitarian aid with refugee groups. In countries in poverty, it means ladling out milk in the mornings, learning new farming techniques in the afternoon, teaching women how to operate small businesses in the evening, and fighting environmental degradation and structural-adjustment policies on the weekend. In countries riddled with fundamentalism and national chauvinism, it means finding a way to join forces with every oppressed minority group in the struggle to survive.

The women's gathering in China was not what Western human rights groups expected. Representatives of such organizations, new to women's rights, stumbled about uncomfortably, uncertain where and when "real work" would begin. Amnesty International, for instance, has lagged ten to twenty years behind women's groups in Latin America and elsewhere. Unless women conferees attacked the repressive policies of China, the amnesty types presumed, we were either ill-informed or just plain stupid.

But most of us had not come to turn the World Conference on Women into a World Conference on China. We had come to unite for women's human rights. I had come to the NGO Forum from my Belgrade post to search out "unusual alliances." In Huairou, many unusual groupings of women had come together pragmatically to get work done: lesbian-rights activists and Tibetans, Sudanese, Rwandans, Bosnians, and proponents of reparations for "comfort women," Islamic reformists, pro-choice advocates, and opponents of female genital mutilation. These seemingly unlikely combinations might have looked odd to an outside observer. To women working side-by-side for human rights, however, it was all in a day's work.

Or an evening's repast.

The Restaurant is a privately-owned Chinese restaurant that I chanced upon with a small group of women from "the former Yugoslavia" the day before the NGO Forum started. Seated in tiny rooms, secreted away in all corners of a haphazard collection of buildings, we were served cheap, delicious food by a friendly family staff. We never asked how much anything cost—no matter how much we ordered, the price was always the same. We couldn't find anything half as good, so we kept coming back, bringing in more and more friends. Soon the place was overflowing with regulars, all of whom were "related" to us in one way or another: the Russians in one room, Ukrainians in another, lesbian-rights activists next door, French musicians in a corner room, human rights activists in the karaoke bar, human rights educators in the long room at the back with the lizards on the ceiling, Spanish-speaking delegates in a room near the patio, and of course, always, a large group of "former Yugoslavs."

"I am really surprised that the women from the former Yugoslavia haven't had more of a presence at this conference," more than one journalist remarked to me over the course of the conference.

"Oh?" I would reply. "Have you been to 'The Restaurant'?"

No one ever planned anything, but night, after night women dropped in for dinner from Croatia, Bosnia, Serbia proper, Kosovo, Macedonia, and, by the end, Slovenia. These women cared deeply about what was happening in their countries—but while the rest of the world debated peace in the Balkans, they joined in singing early pioneer songs over sweet-and-sour fish, teasing one another about which songs are now too "nationalistic." A Bosnian woman, perhaps too sad to add her own voice, usually listened somberly while the other women sang one song after another—Bosnian, Croatian, Serbian, Albanian, Macedonian, and, yes, even Yugoslav songs.

The owner of The Restaurant beamed, watching the scene from the doorway of the evening's "former Yugoslavia" room. "I am going to rename my restaurant 'Yugoslavia'!" he exclaimed. No one barked at his geopolitical incorrectness. Instead, a young woman from Belgrade borrowed a pen from an Albanian woman and scrawled a sign, "Former Yugoslavia Caucus." A Slovenian woman taped it to the door. Women passing by from other rooms looked in with curiosity.

I already knew that such informal get-togethers of women from all parts of the former Yugoslavia were far from unusual. Over the past three years, I had watched these women meet with other women whenever they could. With telephone lines cut and roads blocked and transportation within ex-Yugoslavia unsafe, that chance was often provided by outsiders who paid for their trip to a neutral third country. But on those occasions, participants were obliged to do what their hosts wanted. At The Restaurant, where every woman paid her own tab from her own separately-obtained grant, no one was obligated to do anything. As a result, The Restaurant meetings ended with perhaps the most concrete, self-initiated proposal ever to arise from such an encounter: the beginnings of a joint declaration and a December or January follow-up meeting in Vienna or Budapest to plot future cooperation. "To Christmas together!" the women toasted. No one thought twice about whose Christmas—Catholic or Orthodox.

Next time women of the world unite, we should not settle for so repressive a host country . . . but we should definitely pick as good a restaurant.

CHAPTER 18

Ritual as Resistance
Tibetan Women and Nonviolence

BENINA BERGER GOULD

Buddhist Nun Song from Drapchi Prison

Looking out from Drapchi Prison
There is nothing to see but the sky.
The clouds that float in the sky
I wish I were my parents.
We the imprisoned friends
Are like the flowers of the Norbulingka
No matter how severe the hail and frost
Our linked arms cannot be separated
The white cloud from the east
Is not a patch that is fixed—
The sun from the behind the clouds
Will certainly appear one day.
We feel no sadness.
If you ask why,
Even if the day's sun sets,
There is the moon at night.[1]

TIBET AND THE MEANING OF RESISTANCE

To name what is going on in Tibet as a "cultural holocaust" and to bear witness to the indoctrination, torture, and forced exile of the Tibetan people is essential.[2] To examine *resistance*[3] from the unique Tibetan perspective and to represent the voices of the women who have been active in the nonviolent resistance movement in Tibet and in the exile communities is the main purpose of this chapter. What motivates my activism in this movement is the *hope* that someday all Tibetans will be free to return to their country, either to live or visit. The collective unconscious for all of us suffers from the atrocities inflicted on others, even if the "others" are not in your own family.

Tibet has been occupied by the Chinese Communists since 1949. The indoctrination of the Tibetans has always posed a particular problem for the Chinese, because the Tibetans could not understand the Chinese language. In order to spread mass information and further the transformation of Tibet into a socialist society with a socialist consciousness, a new language was needed. A new lexicon of the Tibetan language that included Chinese was developed in order to promote and publish communist propaganda.

> When the Communists entered Tibet they were immediately confronted with problems of how to promote and develop socialism. . . . One of the major problems was how to communicate socialist ideas and propaganda to the masses. . . . The major resistance to the development of communism was not the resistance of guerrilla fighters or the Tibetan army: it was the objective sociocultural conditions in Tibet . . . The problem was not only that Communist ideology was alien to Tibetans, but that there were no linguistic means of communicating the Communist ideals and concepts to them . . . thus since the 1950s, the Tibetan language has undergone fundamental changes in order to adapt to the prevailing political ideology. The Chinese also realized early on that the effectiveness of the printed media was limited by the extent of illiteracy in Tibet. From the beginning the Chinese used radio broadcasts as a method of disseminating information and propaganda (Shakya 1994, 157–158).

Exile, torture, and prison[4] are threats whenever the Tibetans demonstrate or choose to worship publicly, as has been their practice for over 2,000 years. Leaving Tibet is the only choice for many who want their children to be brought up in a traditional Tibetan culture. Even this does not assure that the families in exile will be able to carry on the traditions of the Tibetan culture through the next generation.[5] Little is known about the families who remain in Tibet; they rarely escape having some of their family members imprisoned and beaten.[6]

Despite this, there remains a group of women and men in Tibet and in the exile communities in India who continue to practice nonviolent resistance:

> the Chinese were intent on making religion seem laughable, and many children were sent to China to become good Communists with Chinese hearts and Chinese souls. Influential women were compelled to disseminate Chinese propaganda among their less well-educated sisters. But where it was possible, they continued to show *resistance* (Dechen 1991, 93).

What is unique about the Tibetan resistance movement is that the religious belief system of Buddhism is combined with the political, nationalistic system. It is as if the Dharma and the Politics are the same.[7] Resistance for the Tibetan people is intricately laced into the rituals of everyday life by belief in the dharma. "This complex term in Sanskrit, when used in Buddhist contexts, may signify either a thing or phenomenon in general (as is 'all dharmas are empty of self-nature') or the teachings of the Buddha."[8] Also, a religion is dharma in the sense that it holds persons back or protects them from disaster. "Any elevated action of body, speech, or mind is regarded as Dharma because through doing such an action one is protected or held back from all sorts of disasters. Practice of such actions is practice of Dharma" (Hopkins 1975, 23). The practice of the teachings of the Buddha provide refuge for all sentient beings and through the practice of the dharma, it is believed that all people will be protected from evil, wrongdoings, and death.[9]

The interdependence of dharma and nationalism is the basis of the resistance movement, and the rituals enacted by the Tibetan people reflect this mutuality:

> the religion of the Tibetans occupies a central place in current protest. Demonstrations are led by monks and nuns, and Tibetans have come to see political protest as religiously sanctioned action. But it is the ethical aspects of Buddhism as a religion—rather than its magical elements—that predominate in current protest. The demonstrations draw on traditional forms of Buddhist practices ordinary Tibetans understand and value. Buddhism offers Tibetans assurance about ultimate religious ends as well as effective means to realize those ends through individual behavior (Schwartz 1994, 22).

Five major rituals—circumambulation, prostrating, mantra recita-
tions, tsampa throwing, and lighting incense—were thought (by the Tibetans) to be acceptable religious practices to the Chinese before and
after the cultural revolution. However, the use of these ritual symbols,
combined with political action, made Tibetan religious practices threatening to the Chinese, and these practices are now punishable by imprisonment, beatings, and torture. The monks and nuns, by combining
common protest movement techniques (such as screaming independence
slogans, carrying the Tibetan flag, and showing the exiled leader's pictures (in this case the Dalai Lama) with these religious actions, angered
Chinese authorities. Formally acceptable religious acts became nationalist ones of rebellion.

The Tibetan resistance movement, although unique in its symbolic
ritual as political action, is suffering. On the local level, many monasteries and nunneries have been destroyed, the usual places for prayer and
political protest are decreasing, and, on the larger societal level, the massive influx of Chinese settlers into Tibet has made the Tibetans a minority in their own land. "NonTibetans now control a large segment of all
levels of the local economy. . . .Tibetans in Lhasa have complained about
this flood, arguing that . . . Tibetans cannot compete economically with
the more skilled and industrious Han and Hui . . . and they expect to become increasingly marginalized, both economically and demographi-
cally" (Goldstein 1997, 95). The danger of the Tibetans losing their
national identity is greater now than ever before.

China's current constitution, adopted in 1982, protected "legitimate
religious activities," but the Chinese Communist Party (CCP) remains
fundamentally hostile to religion. Methods of undermining religion include:

1. educating Tibetan youth to abstain from Buddhist practices
2. persistent disseminating of antireligious publications
3. banning photos of religious prayers or texts
4. restricting liturgical practices and monastic education
5. maintaining security officers and informants on the premises of
   religious institutions
6. enforcing compulsory political education sessions in the monasteries and nunneries
7. expelling monks and nuns who have refused to repudiate Tibetan independence

8. arresting and torturing those suspected of involvement in nationalist activity. (TWA UN 1996, 3:3)

TIBETAN WOMEN AND NUNS' RESPONSES TO THE INVASION: "THE PERSONAL IS POLITICAL"

Traditionally, Tibetan women enjoyed a higher social status then their
counterparts in many other Asian societies. They were not subject to
footbinding, arranged marriages, or a one-child policy. They also played
an active part in the affairs of family and society. "However, as in most
traditional societies, women were considered inferior to men. The very
name by which they were known (*kiemen* or *kye-mi*), translated literally
to mean 'inferior birth' or 'lower birth,' defined the Tibetan Buddhist belief that to achieve nirvana, it was necessary to be male; thus a common
prayer among women was 'may I reject a feminine body and be reborn a
male one.' It is not surprising that a nomad chieftain would state that 'in
our land it was considered a great misfortune not to have a child, moreover a son, to carry on the family life.'" (Grunfeld 1996, 19).

The traditional Tibetan autobiography was written by enlightened
monks and lamas and their life stories reflected the times they spent med-
itating or in retreat. These "rangnam" or "full liberation stories of oneself," were written in the traditional manner of Tibetan Buddhism.[10]
There has also been a genre of autobiographies written by women, but
generally these were about women of the ruling class and they were not
distinctly political.[11]

The history[12] of the Tibetan Freedom movement as told by Tibetan
women,[13] appears in many brief versions, most of which have not been
accessible to the West.[14] Most of the lay women's reports are about early
uprisings in March 1959. Lhamo Yangchen, a participant in the people's
uprising at the Norbulingka on the 10th of March, 1959, and in subsequent events, gives just such a personal account:[15]

> On the 11th, the representatives announced that a great Sang Sol—a
> purification ritual in which incense is burned and tsampa[16] is thrown in
> the air to disperse evil elements—would be held at Tsomon Ling.
> Everybody was invited to give donations or contributions for special
> prayers to be said at all the monasteries around Lhasa to prevent the
> Chinese from occupying Tibet. Many people went to Tsomom Ling to
> make offerings. Most of the workers on that day were women—people

brought prayer flags that they had made and the women were kept busy stitching them onto rope.

. . . Among the organizers on that day, there was one very striking women called Pamo Kusang. . . . She had encouraged people to come to the Norbulingka and to be very wary of the Chinese and their traps and led the women in chanting slogans.

On the 11th at Tsomon Ling, she encouraged women who were helping there to lend their weight to the cause of freeing Tibet from China. They agreed to hold a meeting the following day and asked two women to come from every courtyard. . . .

During that meeting we passed resolutions and each representative was allocated a district to go to inform the women of a public meeting to be held . . . on the large ground below the Potala Palace, called Drebu Lingka.[17]

Recently a Tibetan nun, Ama Adhe, who was released from a Chinese prison after twenty-one years, published her memoirs. She is the first woman to consciously tell a combined story of the "dharma and politics." What distinguishes Ama Adhe's book is that the story she wanted to tell was as much about the brutality and injustices of the Chinese as it was about her own monastic life.[18]

Throughout my imprisonment, I always tried to pray to my tutelary deity—Dolma, the protectoress—but as time went on, I found it increasingly difficult to concentrate on the long twenty-one verse prayer that my father had taught me. Perhaps due to starvation clouding the mental faculties . . . (i)t was also impossible to pray in my free time without being interrupted either by guards or by other prisoners (Adhe 1997, 121).

As ordained "holders of the Dharma" nuns, like monks, have played a powerful role in the resistance movement, motivated by the religious life and by their commitment to the survival of the Tibetan people and culture (Havnevik 1994, 259). In Buddhist tradition and traditional Tibet, male monasticism has been dominant, so nuns have suffered marginalization in several respects. Traditionally, nuns have been less educated, did not receive financial support from home, nunneries were usually subbranches of important monasteries, and monks or yogis were often abbots in nunneries. The resistance movement for the nuns has provided a way to make meaning of their lives by creating change on the national level as well as in the politics of the monastic orders. On the societal level, they are dedicated to saving their people and culture. On the local level, nuns are concerned with changing their status in monastic life so that monks are not the authority. They want women to receive more education, financial support, and social prestige for joining a nunnery. They are "political nuns" and through their actions and activities provide a powerful model of a "change agent" for all women.

There are no records before 1959 of organized political activity by nuns within Tibetan society. But since 1959, they have played a "prominent role in resistance to the Chinese occupation" (Schwartz 1994, 99). In most of the demonstrations that have taken place in Tibet since the autumn of 1987, young nuns have been very active . . . about 50 percent have been arrested" (Havnevik 1994, 259).

"Through political protest, nuns are thus in a position to change Tibetans' perceptions of their status and gain respect. Tibetans see nuns assuming the same burden of political responsibility as a concomitant of their clerical status as the monks" (Schwartz 1994, 102).

POLITICAL ORGANIZATION: FORMATION OF THE TIBETAN WOMEN'S ASSOCIATION

Rinchen Dolma Taring reports that, in 1952, under the supervision of General Chang Ching Wu's wife, it was suggested that all official ladies should form a *Patriotic Women's Association* to support the nation's activities. "Everybody looked at everybody else and the Shap-pes wives had to speak. They said . . . first we must consult the Kashag, as we have had no public women's activities before and have no experience. . . . Two of the Shappes wives, Ngapo Tseten Dolkar and Shasur Lhacham were asked to consult the Kashag, who reported to the Dalai Lama. Soon his holiness gave permission for us to organize the Lhasa Patriotic Women's Association and I was compelled to join it. The Patriotic Youth Association was being started simultaneously, under other Chinese leaders" (Taring 1970, 213).

Even before the first major women's uprising in 1959, Tibetan women were very active in the resistance movement. Their activities were violent and guerrilla-like in warfare and did not reflect political organization, except by class. In 1956, Dorjee Yudon, wife of the chieftain of the upper Naryong area of Kham, led her warriors into battle, inspiring the whole region. There were nine other chieftains in the Naryong area of Kham, one of whom was a powerful nun. She ruled the area of

Narog until Tibet lost her independence in 1959. She administered the whole area and was helped by two male subjects, one dealing with local law and order and the other with the Central Government.

The first wave of the nonviolent resistance movement began formally in March 1959, when women visibly organized political actions. During this time, the Dalai Lama fled Tibet, and the Tibetan Women's Association, a nongovernmental, nonprofit organization, was founded in Lhasa, Tibet. When it was begun, its influence was mainly nonviolent and the rebellions mirrored this philosophy.

"On March 12th, 1959, the first major political action by an organized body of Tibetan women took place in Lhasa to oppose the forced occupation of their country by the Chinese. This is known as the Tibetan Women's Uprising" (Russell and Singeri 1992, 29). Two nuns were among the leaders of this women's revolt in Lhasa. According to the Tibetan Women's Association report of 1995, an "estimated 3,000 women met publicly at the Drebu Lingka, the ground below the Potala Palace, and in a spontaneous movement of solidarity among ordinary laywomen and nuns, the women of Lhasa staged several peaceful protests demanding that the Chinese leave Tibet. On 19 March, at least 5,000 women gathered to make offerings and prayers and lead a procession to the Indian Consul General to ask that he help intercede against the encroaching Chinese army. One of the outstanding leaders of the Women's Resistance Movement of March 1959 was Pamo Kunsang, a mother of six. She inspired many women with her courage and determination. In spite of being behind bars, she did not lose her convictions and became a legendary martyr for Tibetans" (Flag for Tibet 1996, 1).

The second wave of organized political activity occurred from 1965-1977, during the cultural revolution, and saw women as natural leaders. There was a mix of nonviolent and guerrilla warfare. It was also the time of greatest religious oppression. Tibetan Women's Association was less active during this time and not as influential in supporting nonviolent action. Trinley Choedon, executed in 1969, was believed to have led a guerrilla organization stretching from Mount Kailsh to Kham. Pema Dechen, said to have led a rebellion of 30,000 guerrillas, was also publicly executed. Ama Adhe, Ani Pachen, and Rangzen Amala are the nuns who bear witness to this period of struggle for Tibet's independence.

The third period was during the 1980s and took a distinct shape in the form of only nonviolent activities and demonstrations. Monks and nuns were the major initiators during this time, seeing that their position as women and men without families made them more able to bear the toll of political leadership. While nuns were the most active female dissidents in Tibet, laywomen also initiated protests and hid fugitives. The Tibetan Women's Association was officially reactivated in 1984 in the exile community of Dharmasala, India.

Since 1995, American, European, and Tibetan women have worked together in the nonviolent resistance movement. The Tibetan women, in solidarity with women from America and Europe, strategized their moves at the Beijing Fourth Women's Conference through informal meetings and the Internet prior to meeting in China in August 1995. "Communication is critical and the greatest ally for small, underfunded organizations is the Internet. The Tibetan community must continue to develop and expand its expertise in electronic communication in order to maintain its edge in international relations" (TWA UN 1995, 28).

Most recently, the Tibetan and American women involved in the movement have focused their work on testifying to the United Nations about the forced sterilization and torture of Tibetan women. On 4 March 1999 "Losang Rabgey, a Tibetan who holds Canadian citizenship, said she had been given permission to address the commission as one of five speakers on behalf of a nongovernmental taskforce on women and health, but was told in the last minute she could not testify. . . . 'I was told the reason I could not speak is that my name is recognizable as Tibetan and it might offend the Chinese and would jeopardize our nongovernmental status in the future.' " Janice Mantell, executive director of the International Committee of Lawyers for Tibet, said it was "unacceptable that a United Nations body entrusted to promote the human rights of women cannot hear from a participant because her ethnic identity is a politically sensitive issue. 'Tibetan women are subjected to systematic violence in the form of forced or coerced sterilization and abortion, including late-term abortion' " (TibeAction ICLT, 1).

GENDERING OF NONVIOLENT RESISTANCE

Nonviolence as a political policy, not unlike militarism, has been primarily dictated by the philosophy and belief systems of men. Gandhi defined the resolution of conflict as "absence of conflict" (Nakhre 1982, 2). For Gandhi, the Bhagavad Gita was the major scripture from which he built his nonviolent theory of Satyagraha. "Gandhi did not see Satyagraha as a movement for independence nor a technique of political action. . . . Satyagraha is a spiritual force, a potent, viable source of energy that belongs to all individuals, though few are aware of it (Easwaran 1972, 148).

The Dalai Lama was influenced by Gandhi and traveled to India while in charge of the Tibetan government. While there the Dalai Lama visited Rajghat, the site of Gandhi's cremation. He stood on the grounds and wondered "what wise counsel the Mahatma would have given me." At that moment, the Dalai Lama felt that Gandhi's advice would be to follow the path of peace. The Dalai Lama determined at that time that he could never associate himself with acts of violence. He was in his early twenties when he made this resolution, and he has never wavered from it. (Ingram 1990, 6). On 21 September 1987 the Dalai Lama, steeped in Buddhist tradition and influenced by Gandhi, presented his Five Point Peace Plan for Tibet during an address to members of the U.S. Congress. The plan called for the establishment of Tibet as a sanctuary of peace, ensuring human and democratic rights for the Tibetan people, and protecting the whole of the Tibetan plateau as an ecological preserve. Two years later on 5 Oct. 1989 the Dalai Lama won the 1989 Nobel Peace Prize.

While doing research on women and resistance, I found only a small number of women who had "taken the chance" to develop an ideology of power and nonviolence. Hannah Arendt is one of these voices: "Political action, acting in concert with one's peers according to new ideas generated from the group itself, is for her one of the highest forms of self-expression and self-fulfillment. When people act politically together they experience power. Power according to Arendt defines it as the ability to act in concert. When a group is organized and all members freely agree to engage in a certain action, they are powerful. Parekh describes Arendt's notion of power as the 'ability to secure another's energetic cooperation and support' " (Presbey 1993, 247–8).

The demonstrations at Greenham Common in England in 1985 offer an excellent example of the power of cooperative action. The goal of the women who took action around the nuclear silos at Greenham was nonviolent revolution. When I visited the base camp outside London, I saw the camps surrounding the nuclear base as an unforgettable example of nonviolent moral outrage and concern for the planet. Establishing camps and staging demonstrations so close to nuclear silos required courage and a deep moral conviction that went beyond merely saying that one was for peace.

Petra Kelly, from West Germany, is another important voice in the development of a theory of power and nonviolence. She states, "When we talk of nonviolent opposition, we do not mean opposition to parliamentary democracy. We mean opposition from within parliamentary democracy. Nonviolent opposition in no way diminishes or undermines representative democracy, in fact it strengthens and stabilizes it. It is expressed in all kinds of local groups operating outside parliament, in work councils, and other self-governing bodies. Nonviolent opposition is one way, among others, of forming political opinion within that infrastructure" (Kelly 1988, 312).

Sara Ruddick believes that women come to the belief of nonviolence as "maternal thinkers" concerned with the care of the earth and its inhabitants because of the ability to procreate (Ruddick 1990). Carol Gilligan suggests that women are organized around interconnectedness with others and that, for women, the moral imperative that emerges is an injunction to care—a responsibility to discern and alleviate the "real" and recognizable trouble of this world (Gilligan 1982).

Tatyana Mamonova, from the former USSR, agrees with Ruddick and Gilligan that women are altruistic. "She gives life and appreciates life" (Mamonova 1988, 55). Svetlana Alliluyeva (also from the former USSR) and Petra Kelly speak to the ecology of women's position on earth. "Everything on our tormented earth that is alive and breathes, that blossoms and bears fruit, lives only by virtue of and in the name of Truth and Good" (Alliluyeva 1988, 282). "The earth has been mistreated, and only by restoring a balance, only by living with the earth, by employing soft energies and soft technologies can we overcome the violence of patriarchy" (Kelly 1988, 311).

Petra Kelly also exposes the dilemma of equality. "When women fight for equal status with men, they run the risk of joining the ranks in times of war. We are so conditioned by masculine values that women often make the mistake of imitating and emulating men at the cost of their own feminism" (Kelly 1988, 311).

The actions of women in nonviolent warfare have been significant in many Asian countries and deserve to be written into existing resistance ideology. In Vietnam, Chan Ngoc Phuong, a Buddhist nun, eloquently describes the resistance movement with others nuns and monks in her book, *Learning True Love: How I Learned and Practiced Social Change in Vietnam*. In Burma, the movement for nonviolence is led by the incredibly brave and noble Aung San Suu Kyi, a Nobel Peace Prize recipient.

What addition to the discourse on nonviolent resistance can Tibetan women make? What can we learn from the Tibetan laywomen and nuns that we can apply to our work?

Religion and politics are embedded in the social life of Tibetan people. It is the basis of their identity. TWA holds regular ceremonies to cultivate a religious spirit among the Tibetan people, especially among the younger generation. TWA also sponsors Tibetan cultural traditions and is contributing to the educational development of Tibetan community. On all levels of the individual and society this organization is active in supporting the religious beliefs of its people. By supporting existing religious beliefs that are consistent with nonviolence, the Tibetan women are essentially teaching people how to be "political."

The Tibetan women give us a political movement that is a combination of spiritual, cultural, and social belief systems that are nonviolent. It does not "resist" anything.

> When you are in the face of incredible adversity, if you have the option of reacting violently and if you chose not to, it doesn't mean you are inactive. You can be active and nonviolent. And I think that is the more difficult route . . . much more so because it's quite common to want to react with equal violence or more. (Devine 1993, 43).

Women around the world are not innocent victims, but active members of nonviolent movements to end injustice in occupied lands. Tibetans build their nonviolent resistance on a base of prayer, cultural activities, and rituals that reflect a deep sense of the spiritual. By staging demonstrations, using printed material, forming pro-independence groups, passing information to exiles or foreigners, criticizing the government in public or private, and carrying the Tibetan flag and pictures of the Dalai Lama, Tibetan women have developed nonviolent action and ritual. They present a major force in history through the power of nonviolent actions combined with their deep spirituality that infuses every moment of their lives.

As Eva Herzer, president of International Committee of Lawyers for Tibet states:

> If the world community does not support Tibet's nonviolent struggle and assist in bringing about a negotiated solution for Tibet, it cannot, with any sense of credibility, protest violent international conflict and terrorism. Tibet can become the model for peaceful dispute resolution or it can become the symbol for why only violence leads to success. (Herzer 1996, 7)

It can only benefit all of us if nonviolent resistance is rewarded and given the power it deserves, not only as a legitimate political movement, but also as a psychological and philosophical mind-set that is as popular as our belief system in the "aggression of mankind."

CONCLUSION

The spirit of the Tibetan people is threatened, because in Tibet the Tibetan people have been deprived of their cultural and religious freedom. As more and more monasteries and nunneries are burned and destroyed there are fewer places for public display of ritual and protest. Indoctrination forbids teaching of the Buddhist religion and speaking the Tibetan languages in schools, breaking down the transmission process that has gone on for over 3000 years. According to Tibetan Buddhist practice, if customary rituals, such as prayers and chanting, circumambulation, prostrations, tsampa throwing, and incense burning are forbidden, the Tibetan culture and religion is lost and resistance as a movement and protection of all sentient beings as a prophecy will die. When Tibetans are deprived of their language and religious and moral education, and when they are forced into exile, the culture becomes threatened.

"The courage of Tibetan woman is a lesson for us all, but the question is how long we can continue to hold out? Can we survive as a distinct race under a Chinese policy of Sinification that aims to make us a minority in our own country? How can we offer resistance to genocide (Dechen 1991, 93)?"

It is my belief that if the Tibetans are presented as people who are not just a part of the Shanghri-la syndrome[20] that has long stereotyped this country, but as a land and people with the full complexity of any group and nation, the political issue of Free Tibet will receive more attention in the world of international security and foreign policy. The important issue is not to do away with the myths and our fondness for Tibet, but to "search for the real Tibet, beyond representation" (Lopez 1998, 9). It is imperative that we understand as completely as possible the ability of the Tibetans to stand so defiantly, without violence, in the face of extermination as a culture and as a people. This knowledge will then be available to benefit all human beings everywhere.

ACKNOWLEDGMENTS

I would like to acknowledge Eva Herzer, President, Barbara Green, Co-Chair of the Women's Committee, Lisa Tracy, Board Member, Khando Chazotsang, Yangchen and Tseten Khangsar, and all members of the International Committee of Lawyers for Tibet, for their encouragement to prepare this article and to Linda Blum, Librarian at the Carl G. Rosberg International Studies Library at Berkeley for her technical support and to

Tenzin Lhadon Gould for her patience and compassion while her mother focused elsewhere.

NOTES

1. This song and many others have been reproduced on a tape from #1 Prison of the Tibet Autonomous Region (TAR). This song (#13) is a solo sung by a Buddhist nun. Her voice was modified on the tape to protect the identity of the source. In October 1993, fourteen nuns in Drapchi Prison, the largest in Tibet, made a recording of freedom songs on a tape recorder smuggled into the prison with the help of a nonpolitical prisoner. The songs are a testament to the suffering and agony of Tibetan political prisoners that the Chinese claim do not exist. "Although the punishment for singing freedom songs in prison is severe, it is believed that political prisoners in Tibet continue to sing them today as a source of comfort and inspiration to each other and in their never-ending defiance of the Chinese occupation" (Parr 1998, 19). Although I do not know the name of the nun who wrote this particular poem, despite the great risk involved, each of the women stated her name on the recording.

2. Bearing witness is essential from a global, as well as personal, viewpoint. What allows me to bear witness from these two perspectives is that my religious beliefs—my concern with meaning in life—and my writing are a manifestation of my moral outrage with our world in crisis. From a global perspective, it is necessary to let others know what is happening to our sisters and brothers of oppressed and war-torn countries. On a personal level I, like many other women, must "demonstrate solidarity, sympathy, and identification with the suffering victims of war" since to "open oneself to the world signifies a stance of accountability" (Brenner 1997, 175). This identification with the "Other" as Levinas claims is made possible because "the other is in me and in the midst of my very identification . . . the very relationship with the other is the relationship with the future. My contact with the other extends me beyond myself" (Levinas 1989, 176). "My being for the other is not a function of compassion, but rather a function of absolute necessity, as the other is a part of my inner self but also a part that extends my 'I' beyond the limits of my self" (Brenner 1997, 177).

3. Resistance discourses have been criticized for "lacking an ideology" yet many writers are struggling with interpreting resistance in the context of political movements. Lorentzen looks to the Salvadoran model of liberation theology. She explores "women's prison writings from El Salvador as resistance in themselves . . . and links liberation theology with testimonio from women's prison" (Lorentzen 1998, 193). Mahoney and Yngvesson investigate "how subjects expe-

rience . . . relationships of power" in order to "explain what impels them to resist domination and to make change." They look at recent research in developmental psychology and in particular the work of D. W. Winnicott for "an understanding of motivation and the processes by which subjects come to want to conform or resist" (Mahoney and Yngvesson 1996, 246). Ann Maria Alonso uses historical memory to understand resistance and analyses discourses of resistance among the Serranos, the non-Indian inhabitants of the Sierra Madre of the state of Chihuahua, Mexico. In a recent book, Margaret Weitz highlights the role of women in the French Resistance Movement.

4. "The Tibetan Centre for Human Rights and Democracy released its new publication entitled "Tales of Terror: Torture in Tibet," which describes widespread torture practices under Chinese rule. The personal accounts in the report reveal that the Chinese authorities continue to abuse human rights on the worst scale. "Political prisoners are at the greatest risk of being tortured, many . . . have died whilst in detention or within a few months of release on medical parole." (Tibetan Bulletin Mar.–Apr 1999, 13).

5. "Postmemory is a powerful form of memory precisely because its connection to its object or source is mediated not through recollection but through an imaginate investment and creation. . . . Postmemory characterizes the experience of those who grow up dominated by narratives that preceded their birth, whose own belated stories are displaced by the stories of the previous generation, shaped by traumatic events that can be neither fully understood nor re-created. . . . Children of exiled survivors, although they have not themselves lived through the trauma of banishment and the destruction of home, remain always marginal or exiled, always in the Diaspora. 'Home' is always elsewhere. . . . Camus writes that 'a homeland is only ever recognized at the moment of its loss,' and this sense of loss, the feeling of exile and misplacement, is the central theme of his life and work" (Judt 1998, 97).

6. In my household there are two Tibetan women doctors who came here from Tibet. The mother still is afraid to talk about what happens in Lhasa, and the daughter can only relate the brutalities to her aunts and uncles. Little is known about this group of people and I hope to do more in-depth interviews for a follow-up to this article.

7. For *some* Tibetans the integration of politics and dharma is not a solution. "Politics have always been a problem in Tibet. It began when the lamas started to rule the country. This development started in approximately the thirteenth century. Prior to that, it had been possible to find purely spiritual teachers. . . . But then something went wrong, and this needs to be fixed again. No one will be able to achieve this unless a person like Karmapa tries to do it" (Rinpoche Topga 1997, 23).

8. This glossary of terms was prepared by Richard Barron and Katherine Pfaff as an offering to Sakya Jetsunma Chime Lunding.

9. An example of this is the Dedication Prayer from the Sakya lineage:

> . . . May I liberate beings from the
> ocean of existence where the wave
> birth, old age, disease and
> death roll violently.

> . . . By whatever merits I have gained
> by hearing and teaching of the
> Mahayana Dharma, may all
> beings be worthy of the pure and
> precious Dharma.

> Through this power . . .
> may . . . all the harm inflicted
> upon beings be
> destroyed from the root.

10. An excellent book on "liberation and esoteric autobiographies" has been written by Janet Gyatso. A tradition of Tibetan autobiographies has existed "prior to and uninformed by modernity and/or the West; in fact, it is difficult to find any extra-Tibetan influence to account for their genesis at all . . . unlike the nonliterate cultures often studied by anthropologists, Tibetan religious culture has been a very literate one since the eleventh century . . . lay and monastic, wealthy and poor, male and female (though many more males than females)" (Shakya 1985, 102).

11. An example of this is the autobiographical account of Lady Jamyang of Tibet. "Raised in a loving family of moderate affluence, she enjoyed frequent contact with monks and nuns, and her way of life and education were pervaded by the spirit of Buddhism. Her childhood was one of good cheer, and of innocence, by Western standards, of naiveté . . . She had the unusual good fortune to receive a fine education from an early age." (xiii).

12. "The most attractive aspect of New Historicist practice is its commitment to what Clifford Geertz . . . calls 'thick description,' in which an event or an anecdote is "re-read . . . in such a way as to reveal through the analysis of tiny particulars the behavioral codes, logics, and motive forces controlling a whole society. . . . Thick description allows me to use my training to a different purpose, not to identify the markers of a literary consciousness, but to read the trace

of a human person constructing her identity in her historical, social, cultural, and gendered place" (Buss 1996, 86).

I use "thick description" as a way to relate to oral histories of women from a historical, social, cultural, religious and political place. I choose this terminology because it crosses the boundary of disciplines without using only male or female formalization of each discipline.

13. There has been much criticism of bringing third world voices into American discourse by more privileged women: "A subfield of feminist discourse has expressed doubts as to the legitimacy and advisability of writing about other, less privileged women . . . The most critical point is not that we reap material and social benefits from their stories, but that we help to disseminate their views and that we do so without betraying their political interests as narrators of their own lives" (Ong 1995, 353–4).

14. "(i)n spite of Tibet's relative isolation and lack of visitors, considerable information about it was available to the serious scholar . . . This situation was to last, more or less, until 1950. The victory of communism in China in 1949 and the subsequent creation of a strong central government in Beijing for the first time in over half a century was to have its repercussions in Tibet—and around the rest of the world. In universities throughout the West and especially those in the United States, scholars were prevented from putting forward views that could be construed as pro-Communist. Scholarship on Tibet degenerated into the taking of sides: black and white, wrong and right, good and bad" (Grunfeld 1996, 4).

15. The vignettes in this section are from a cultural magazine, *CHO Yang*, which I brought back from Dharmsala, the exile Tibetan community in India. The source of text and translation is not cited. The narratives do represent a more political then "enlightenment" text.

16. Tsampa, or roasted barley flour. is the national food of Tibet, and the throwing in the air of handfuls of tsampa is done on special anniversaries and holidays. It symbolizes "offering to the gods" and is designed to "ensure the future welfare of the person being celebrated" (Barnett 1996, 253). This is another example of Tibetan religious traditions, "expressing nationalistic symbolism." In later demonstrations in 1989, the Chinese government declared tsampa throwing and incense burning to be illegal. They became political crimes and could result in up to three years in prison. By calling tsampa throwing a political crime, the Chinese, in fact, recognize the "religious and political identity as one." According to Barnett, "the Tibetans had led the Chinese state into an arena rich in symbolism where, step-by-step, the ideology of Chinese liberalization was stripped of value and exposed as rhetoric" (Barnett 1996, 253).

17. The route for the "women's uprising" was to the Jokhang Palace. This represented a strong political symbolism of the joining of the religious with the

political. March came to represent, later in the eighties, many anniversaries of other significant uprisings and that month is always chosen to demonstrate for Tibetan independence. Paying attention to anniversaries is another strong message about the importance of ritual in the Tibetan political arena.

18. The Dalai Lama wrote in the introduction to Ama Adhe's book: "Hers is the story of all Tibetans who have suffered under the Chinese Communist occupation. It is also a story of how Tibetan women have equally sacrificed and participated in the Tibetan struggle for justice and freedom. As she herself says, hers is the 'voice that remembers the many who did not survive' " (Tapontsang 1997, vii).

19. "On March 22 there would be a twenty-four hour blockade of the base . . . On that day, 150 women chained themselves together across the gates; thirty-four later appeared in court, charged with obstructing the highway. . . . Greenham remained queen of the peace camps. Its preeminence was assured by the increasingly imminent arrival of Cruise missiles, there, rather than anywhere else" (Liddington 1989, 237).

20. I agree with Donald Lopez's concept of the Shanghri-la syndrome, by which "Tibetan Buddhist culture has been portrayed as if it were itself another artifact of Shangri-La from an eternal classical age, set high in a Himalayan mountain kept outside of time and history" (Lopez 1998, 7). In fact, a view of Tibet as perfect and idyllic can work against its political goal of sovereignty as a Tibetan Autonomous Region (TAR). Tibet needs to be seen in its full complexity in order to be taken seriously in the West by all people, not just Buddhist practitioners and their friends. Lopez goes on to say that Tibet, "like any complex society, had great inequalities, with power monopolized by an elite composed of a small aristocracy, the hierarchs of various sects (including incarnate lamas), and the great Geluk monasteries. The subordinate members of the society included nonaristocratic laymen, non-Buddhists, and women" (Lopez 1998, 9).

REFERENCES

Alliluyeva, Svetlana. 1988. "Twenty Letters to a Friend." Trans. Patricia McMillan. In *Women on War: Essential Voices for the Nuclear Age*, edited by Diane Gioseffi, 280–282. New York: Simon & Schuster.

Alonso, Ana Maria. 1992. "Gender, Power, and Historical Memory: Discourses of Serrano Resistance." In *Feminists Theorize the Political*, edited by Judith Butler and Joan Scott, 404–425. New York: Routledge.

Barnett, Robert, ed. 1996. *Tibet: Cutting off the Serpent's Head—Tightening Control in Tibet*. Human Rights Watch.

Becker, Norma. 1988. "Strategies for Peace." In *Women on War: Essential Voices for the Nuclear Age*, edited by Diane Gioseffi, 284–286. New York: Simon & Schuster.

Brenner, Rachel Feldhay. 1997. *Writing as Resistance: Four Women Confronting the Holocaust*. University Park: Pennsylvania State Press.

Buss, Helen. 1996. "A Feminist Revision of New Historicism to Give Fuller Readings of Women's Private Writings." In *Inscribing the Daily: Critical Essays on Women's Diaries*, edited by Suzanne Bunkers and Cynthia Huff. 86–103. Boston: University of Massachusetts Press.

Butler, Judith and Joan Scott, eds. 1992. *Feminists Theorize the Political*. New York: Routledge.

Dechen, Pema. 1991. "The Oppression and Resistance of Tibetan Women." In *The Anguish of Tibet*, edited by Petra Kelly, Gert Bastian, and Pat Aiello, 92–95. Berkeley, CA: Parallax Press.

Devine, Carol. 1993. *Determination: Tibetan Women and the Struggle for an Independent Tibet*. Toronto: Vauve Press.

Easwaran, Eknath. 1997. *Gandhi the Man: The Story of His Transformation*. Berkeley: Nilgiri Press.

Feuerstein, Georg. 1998. *Tantra: The Path of Ecstasy*. Boston: Shambhala.

Flag for Tibet. 1996. *March 10 Women's Resistance Movement: History of Tibetan Women Freedom Fighters*. Internet, 1–2.

Forche, Carolyn, ed. 1993. *Against Forgetting: Twentieth-Century Poetry of Witness*. New York: W. W. Norton.

Gilligan, Carol. 1982. *In a Different Voice: Psychological Theory and Women's Development*. Cambridge, Mass.: Harvard University Press, 1982.

Goldstein, Melvyn. 1997. *The Snow Lion and the Dragon*. Berkeley: University of California Press.

Grunfeld, Tom. 1996. *The Making of Modern Tibet*. New York: East Gate.

Gyatso, Janet. 1998. *Apparitions of the Self: The Secret Autobiographies of a Tibetan Visionary*. Princeton: Princeton University Press.

Havnevik, Hanna. 1989. *Tibetan Buddhist Nuns: History, Cultural Norms, and Social Reality*. Oslo: Norwegian University Press.

———. 1994. "The Role of Nuns in Contemporary Tibet." In *Resistance and Reform in Tibet*, edited by Ronald Barnett, 259–265. Indianapolis: Indiana University Press.

Herzer, Eva. 1996. "International Committee for Lawyers for Tibet Attends Bonn Conference," *Tibet Brief*, Fall/Winter.

Hirsch, Marianne. 1998. "Past Lives: Postmemories in Exile." In *Exile and Creativity: Signposts, Travelers, Outsiders, Backward Glances*, edited by Susan Rubin Suleiman, 418–446. Durham: Duke University Press.

Hopkins, Jeffrey, ed. and trans. 1975. *The Buddhism of Tibet*. Ithaca: Snow Lion.

Ingram, Catherine. 1990. *In the Footsteps of Gandhi*. Berkeley: Parallex Press.

International Committee of Lawyers for Tibet Report. "Tibet/Action at UN." March 15, 1999, Berkeley, California.

————. "Violence against Tibetan Women," March 10, 1995, Berkeley, California.

Jansen, Eva Rudy. 1990. *The Book of Buddhas: Ritual Symbolism Used on Buddhist Statuary and Ritual Objects*. Holland: Binkey Kok Publications.

Jamyang, Sakya. 1990. *Princess in the Land of Snows: The Life of Jamyang Sakya in Tibet*. Boston: Shambhala.

Judt, Tony. 1998. *The Burden of Responsibility: Blum, Camus, Aron, and the French Twentieth Century*. Chicago: University of Chicago Press.

Kelly, Petra. 1988. "Women and Ecology." In *Women on War: Essential Voices for the Nuclear Age*, edited by Diane Gioseffi, 309–316. New York: Simon & Schuster.

Levinas, Emmanuel. 1989. *The Levinas reader,* edited by Seán Hand. Oxford, UK; Cambridge, MA, USA: Blackwell.

Liddington, Jill. 1989. *The Road to Greenham Common*. Syracuse: Syracuse University Press.

Ling, T. O. 1972. *A Dictionary of Buddhism*. New York: Charles Scribner & Sons.

Lopez, Donald S. Jr. 1998. *Prisoners of Shangri-La: Tibetan Buddhism and the West*. Chicago: University of Chicago Press.

Lorentzen, Lois Ann. 1998. "Women's Prison Resistance: Testimonios from El Salvador." In *The Women and War Reader*, edited by Lois Ann Lorentzen and Jennifer Turpin, 192–202. New York: New York University Press.

Mahoney, Maureen and Barbara Yngvesson. 1996. "The Construction of Subjectivity and the Paradox of Resistance: Reintegrating Feminist Anthropology and Psychology." In *The Second Signs Reader*, edited by Ruth-Ellen Joeres and Barbara Laslett, 245–274. Chicago: University of Chicago Press.

Majunpuria, Indra. 1990. *Tibetan Woman Then and Now*. Lashkar, Gwalior, India: M. Devi.

Mamonova Tatyana. 1988. "Women's Active Role." In *Women on War: Essential Voices for the Nuclear Age*, edited by Diane Gioseffi, 55. New York: Simon & Schuster.

Nakhre, Amrat. 1982. *Social Psychology of Nonviolent Action: A Study of Three Satyagrahas*. Delhi, India: Chanakya Publications.

Neier, Aryeh. 1998. *War Crimes: Brutality, Genocide, Terror, and the Struggle for Justice*. New York: Times Books.

Ong, Aihwa. 1995. "Women Out of China: Traveling Tales and Traveling Theories in Postcolonial Feminism." In *Women Writing Culture*, edited by Ruth Behar and Deborah A. Gordon, 350–372. Berkeley: University of California Press.

Parr, Tracey. 1998. "We Sing a Song of Sadness, We Sing it from Drapchi," *Tibet Envoy*, Sept., Vol. 3:19–21.

Phuong, Chan Ngoc. 1993. *Learning True Love: How I Learned and Practiced Social Change in Vietnam*. Berkeley: Parallex Press.

Presbey, Gail M. 1993. "Hannah Arendt on Nonviolence and Political Action." In *Nonviolence, Social and Psychological Issues*, edited by V. K. Kool, 247–248. Albany: State University of New York Press.

Ruddick, Sara. 1989. *Maternal thinking: Toward a politics of peace*. New York: Ballantine Books.

Russell, Philippa and Sonam Lhamo Singeri. 1992. "The Tibetan Women's Uprising." In *The Voice of Tibetan Religion and Culture No. 5 Cho Yang*, edited by Pedron Yeshi and Jeremy Russell, 51–60. Dharamsala: Department of Religion and Culture, Central Tibetan Administration.

Schwartz, Ronald. 1994. *Circle of Protest*. New York: Columbia University Press.

Shakya, Tsering. 1994. "Politicisation and the Tibetan Language." In *Resistance and Reform in Tibet*, edited by Ronald Barnett, 157–165. Indianapolis: Indiana University Press.

Suu Kyi, Aung San. 1991. *Freedom from Fear*. London: Penguin Books.

Tapontsang, Adhe. 1997. *Ama Adhe: The Voice that Remembers the Heroic Story of a Woman's Fight to Free Tibet*. As told to Joy Blakeslee. Boston: Wisdom Publications.

Taring, Rinchen Dolma. 1970. *Daughter of Tibet: The Autobiography of Rinchen Dolma Taring*. London:Wisdom Publications.

Tibet/Action at UN. 15 March 1999. International Committee of Lawyers for Tibet.

Tibetan Bulletin. 1999. "The Official Journal of the Tibetan Administration." March–April Vol. 3. #2.

Tibetan Women's Report on the United Nations Fourth World Conference on Women, 1995. April, 1996, Dharmsala, India.

Topga Rinpoche. 1993. "Letter." In "Religion and Power in Old Tibet," *Buddhism Today* 3:22–28.

Weitz, Margaret Collins. 1995. *Sisters in the Resistance: How Women Fought to Free France 1940-1945*. New York: John Wiley & Sons.

Wu, Harry. 1998. "My View on the Tibet Issue." In *Tibet through Dissident Chinese Eyes*, edited by Cao Changching and James D. Seymour, 91–96. New York: East Gate.

CHAPTER 19

The Impact of Women in Black in Israel

GILA SVIRSKY

> *Never doubt that a small group of thoughtful,*
> *committed citizens can change the world. In-*
> *deed, it's the only thing that ever has.*
> —MARGARET MEAD

These words from Margaret Mead have been facing me across my desk for many years and have often given me heart when change seemed hopeless. Women in Black as a movement seems to have been sustained by this thought, or by one like it. But how did the change actually come about, and what role did Women in Black play in making it happen?

MAKING PEACE AN OPTION

What turned the situation around—from Palestinians and Israelis trying to clobber each other into submission into negotiating peace?

I believe the dynamics were as follows: The Palestinians in the territories, crushed under the burden of the occupation, began their popular uprising, the *intifada*. The violence of the *intifada* woke up the Israeli people to the evils of the occupation. Not only did it send a message of Palestinian suffering, it also brought suffering into the homes of the Israelis. Since, with several exceptions, army service is compulsory for all Israeli Jewish young men and women, almost every household began to feel the effects of the violence—death, injury, or the terror of being killed or injured. Simultaneously, the Israeli peace movement began to flourish, motivated both by (a) a sincere desire to end the repression of another people; and (b) a desire to stop the violence turned against Israel. The years of *intifada* created an intolerable situation inside Israel, and the Israeli government was searching for a way to end it. Force had proven ineffectual. Meanwhile, the peace movement was continuously battering the government and the public with its message that holding onto the territories was a liability and that the Palestine Liberation Organization (PLO) was an acceptable partner for negotiations. It fomented discontent with the status quo and the Greater Israel policy, and created a climate of legitimacy for compromise with the PLO.

The final factor that made peace possible, in my opinion, began with the Gulf War. Yasser Arafat took the side of Saddam Hussein, who lost the war. As a result, Arafat lost considerable financial support from the wealthy Arab Gulf states who had rallied against Saddam. Arafat was about to lose power to his rivals within the PLO when Rabin won the election in Israel and offered him a way out—making peace. Rabin and Peres knew that Arafat was in a vulnerable position and they could strike a good bargain with him at this moment. Arafat had no choice. Either he made peace, hoping to mobilize support for this from the Palestinians and the wealthy Gulf states—or he would lose his power base. The Palestinians had, by then, had their fill of intifada. Arafat chose peace.

What was the role of the peace movement? It legitimized the options to resolving the quandary, options that previously had been unpalatable to Israelis: It maintained that compromise was fine. It said that Arafat was no hero, but he was the one with whom to negotiate. It agreed that a Palestinian state is a viable option. In short, the peace movement guaranteed support to the government for entering into negotiations with Arafat. It was, thus, one critical component in a chain of factors.

IMPACT WEARS MANY FACES

The Women in Black vigil was one part of the tidal wave of seventy-four peace organizations that mobilized Israelis to demand peace. Singers sang peace songs, writers wrote books, lobbyists leaned on Knesset members, organizations documented human rights violations, some soldiers refused to serve in the territories, and many others went to demonstrations, marches, teach-ins, civil disobedience actions, and vigils, week after week after week. All of us together made the difference. All the protest work during this period contributed to creating the public climate that made possible the choice of peace by the politicians and countered the message of a Greater Israel that had dominated the Israeli agenda until then.

In the discouraging old days, before Oslo became a concept, not just a city, it was easy to disparage the effect that any of us was having. But now with the hindsight of the peace process, we can be more realistic about our impact, and we can ask ourselves, more usefully: What was the

contribution that each group made to the tidal wave of protest? Specifically, what was the unique contribution of Women in Black to creating the
climate for peace? I think the place to begin is with the woman herself.

Impact: Personal Transformation

The founding Women in Black were already highly political animals
who had been involved in organizing for years. For most of us, however,
donning black and standing on the vigil brought about a profound personal transformation. You could not stand on this intense vigil for six,
seven, or eight weeks—not to mention six, seven, or eight years—without being significantly altered. In what ways?

First, standing on the vigil politicized women who had not previously been politically involved. Reactions to our vigil (by bystanders,
friends, or family) made it incumbent upon us to have a more informed
response ready for them. Now we were educating ourselves about the issues, reading about and discussing them, attending political lectures, giving political activity a higher priority in our lives than activities that had
previously consumed our attention and devotion. Second, participation
in the vigil radicalized our thinking. It made us more critical of the comfortable views of the liberal camp, more skeptical of official positions,
leading us to shift our votes from the centrist Labor Party to the liberal
Meretz, or from liberal Meretz to progressive Hadash. Discussions
among ourselves—and communication with women peace activists from
other countries—raised our consciousness to more progressive solutions,
leading us to eschew military and violent solutions to political problems,
to adopt a more human rights perspective, and to repudiate the glorification of the army, one of Israel's holiest cows. And, third, participating in
the vigil was a tremendously empowering experience. A woman who
continued to stand through the anger and fear we evoked, through the bitter cold and broiling sun, through the seeming hopelessness of change—
had to have honed the strength inside her. It increased a sense of
determination, of belief in self, of powerfulness.

Related to these changes was the increased appreciation for feminist
formats and values—cooperative decision–making, power-sharing, support for the weaker links in social networks. Not every woman on the
vigil would agree to be labeled "feminist," but all were persuaded by the
feminist process and moved closer to a feminist perspective.

Once you have several thousand women feeling politicized, radicalized, and empowered, it is not surprising to find them having an effect on

others. The following categories suggest some audiences where the impact of Women in Black was—and was not—absorbed:

Impact: Immediate Circles

Inevitably, women who are more politicized and more radicalized will have an impact on their immediate environment away from the vigil, and so we did. Women as mothers, teachers, nurses, social workers, secretaries, doctors, librarians—all the many audiences we encountered in our personal lives—were exposed to our thinking. We, the great army of nurturers, now served up politics with your dinner. My two daughters became Women in Black. Some of our elderly mothers started coming to the vigil. Our schoolchildren were captive listeners to our message of ending political violence (couched within more neutral material). The ripple effect of our presence, thousands of secret agents who refused to sit still for inhumanity and violence, could only be felt in ever-widening circles.

Impact: Jewish Constituents in Israel

Although there was a flowering of peace organizations in Israel following the outbreak of the *intifada*, this subsided as the initial shock of the violence wore off and burnout took its place. Throughout the period of the Likud government and even more so during the Labor government, the right wing dominated the streets—posters, stickers, flyers, buttons, demonstration, marches. You could barely find a major intersection in the main cities without a few right-wing activists holding their favorite slogans aloft. Throughout this period, Women in Black was the only group that made a consistent effort to counter the pro-occupation barrage, to keep the message of peace out on the streets. Peace Now held rallies, some with very large turnouts, but these were few and far between. Women in Black were "the most persistently visible of campaigners" (Silver 1991, 16). We did not let the public slip into inattention. "Their constant presence is a clear and unavoidable reminder of the issues at stake" (Schrag 1990, 10). We were there to remind other Israelis, who were discouraged by the visibility of the right wing, that the voices for peace had not been silenced.

Peace groups also had dynamic effects on one another. The radical groups kept nipping at the heels of the more centrist organizations, pushing them to keep up, to assume more daring postures, to take greater risks. Women in Black was itself urged into more courageous positions by the seasoned radicals of the Women and Peace Coalition, and by the reactions of the authorities and outsiders to us. Peace Now was the largest mixed-gender peace organization, and its reputation for moderation gave it credibility. When the PLO (in December 1988 at a conference in Algeria) declared its renunciation of terrorism and, implicitly, its acceptance of a Jewish state beside the Palestinian state-in-the-making, Peace Now was free to espouse the positions of negotiating with the PLO and two states for two peoples. Peace Now's approval gave the seal of *kashruth* to these former taboos, and won over many more mainstream supporters than the radical groups ever could.

One odd offspring of Women in Black that must be mentioned is the "Women in Green" movement. At some point during the *intifada* when the nationalist right was dominating the streets, a group of extremist right-wing women became the focus of considerable media attention. Dubbed "Women in Green" by the media in reference to their green hats and frank allusion to us, these women hardly resembled Women in Black in other ways. They espoused a religiously fundamentalist vision of Israel and pursued it by staging unruly demonstrations against peace, which occasionally ended in arrests on charges of disturbing the peace or violating police orders, and once for squatting on Palestinian land. Not surprisingly, most members of Women in Green deny any connection to feminism, though they are not beyond a cynical use of feminist slogans to achieve the desired effect: "This junta [the Labor government] is raping the Jewish people" (Sugarman, Zacharia, and Grynberg 1995, 15). Thus, Women in Black begat a rebellious "daughter-movement," to counter our effect.

A more natural and friendly successor to Women in Black is the organization Bat Shalom (Daughter of Peace), which opened its doors in March 1994 in an effort to devise new strategies for the women's peace movement in Israel. Bat Shalom is further evidence that women realize the crucial role they can play in advocating for peace.

Impact: International

Long before the Madrid peace conference and very long before the current peace negotiations, Palestinian and Israeli women were taking part in international conferences for peace, including the "peace tent" at the Nairobi Women's Conference. Detailed peace treaties were hammered out between Israeli and Palestinian women in Jerusalem, Brussels, New York, Italy, Malta, and Geneva years before the men figured out how to do it in Oslo. True, these women did not have the weighty burdens of office to consider, but the question still arises, why were "enemy women" sitting together to negotiate years before the men?

First, it should be said that during the years of the *intifada*, this was not the work of the vigil, but of the larger Women and Peace Coalition. In this body, the more radical women set the tone. It was the Coalition that maintained contacts with the European organizations of women for peace, signed international peace agreements with the Palestinians, held aloft slogans that were light-years ahead of "End the Occupation," and staged demonstrations that left more moderate women, sometimes literally, gasping for air: "With the first joint Palestinian-Israeli women's march in December 1989—in which both groups were tear gassed by Israeli soldiers and police—the movement secured its place in the avant-garde of the Left" (Katz, 1995, 20). Virtually all members of the Women and Peace Coalition were also Women in Black, and it often suited the drama of the occasion to dress in black for these events.

The internationalist feminist approach of these women made it possible—and quite natural—to reach across borders and even across so-called enemy lines. This was not a woman's natural predilection for peacemaking, but the ideological commitment of women to a vision of international peace. It did not come from instinct, but from socializing and educating each other over the years. Being outside establishment politics was an asset in taking a more critical perspective of them.

Whether through the coalition or directly, the links of Women in Black with women's peace organizations around the world were a two-way street of support and sustenance. We drew inspiration from each other. "Women in Black gained prestige as its name spread; it became a model for the international women's movement for peace" (Katz, 1995, 20). And the international women's movement for peace become a model for us: "Belonging to the circles of feminist women throughout the world who struggle against violence and who work to promote a political-cultural alternative, which will include the experience of women, gives me the strength to continue in work that is often perceived as hopeless" (Deutsch, 1994, 6). The impact of our activity in Israel was amplified by the dozens of Women in Black vigils that formed all over the world, some in solidarity with our cause and others taking a stand about their local issues. From the brochure of the Asian Women's Human Rights Council based in Manila:

> We are the Women in Black—a movement that has inspired groups of
> women in different parts of the world to stand in their own towns and
> cities, at street corners, in market squares, and other public places—for
> one hour every week—dressed in black—silently protesting the many
> forms of violence, which are increasingly becoming intrinsic to our
> everyday realities in our different cultures and communities (Asian
> Women's Human Rights Council, 1995, 1).

And one more testimony to our impact from an international source:

> It is clear that there is a particular power to this quite simple gesture.
> Just the intensity of response that it can provoke—to say nothing of the
> way it has spread among women internationally, or the effect it can
> have on participants—is enough of an indication of that. Probably the
> effectiveness of any symbolic protest action depends on the extent to
> which it can shake our traditional mental categories. The Women in
> Black phenomenon does that . . . these Women in Black were standing,
> blatantly, in the middle of the public world—visible, unavoidable, in-
> escapably political (Helwig 1993, 8–9).

Impact: Palestinians

One of the important audiences for Women in Black was Palestinians. It
was important for them to know that there are Israelis with whom a real
peace can be made. This was as important for the Palestinian trucker,
who delivered a crate of cucumbers to the vigil at Kibbutz Nahshon so
that his son could learn "that not all Israelis are border guards, soldiers,
police, or tax collectors," as it was for Arab political leaders. President
Mubarak of Egypt and Hanan Ashrawi, the former spokesperson of the
PLO, have both mentioned Women in Black in the context of taking
heart from the peace camp in Israel. It was important for us to tell the
Palestinians, to tell Arabs in general, and to tell the world at large that not
all Israelis support the occupation policies of the Israeli government, and
that some of us also yearn for a just peace.

Impact: Passersby

And finally, the angry passersby. Here, of course, we had no impact at
all. I have no illusions that there was a single person who disagreed with
us who became convinced of our views by seeing us stand there. They

were not our target audience. We did not stand on the vigil to convince Likud voters to vote Labor, nor did we hope to convince Shamir to forfeit his vision of a Greater Israel. These were obviously impossible tasks.

What we did attempt to do was create a constant sound of peace, a soprano continuo, demanding reconciliation. Women in Black and other peace organizations, together, encouraged and gave voice to the growing body of Israelis who had enough of war and suffering. We were the voice of the silent public who would rather sit at home than be on the streets holding up signs. We represented the Israelis who wanted peace, but were too well-mannered (or constrained by jobs or family) to raise their own voice. Our silent protest served as their voice, demanding peace on behalf of us all.

Women in Black were the conscience of Jerusalem and Tel-Aviv and Kibbutz Nahshon and the thirty-six other places in Israel where we stood. We were not Cassandras, wailing our prophecies of doom to an inattentive public. We were heard, though it wasn't always pleasant for those listening. Week in and week out, year in and year out, Women in Black did not allow the Israeli public to forget the occupation and its brutal consequences. And ultimately, the impact was felt through all these ripples, our personal and our public lives, pulsing through Israeli society and the world at large.

PEACE. PEACE?

And, finally, the question of peace. If you walk through the streets of modern post-Oslo Israel, particularly through the streets of Jerusalem, that beautiful but cursed town seething with intensity and suffering, you will see a variety of stickers on the cars. Bumper stickers are where the silent majority and the silent minority express themselves best. During the days of the *intifada*, the only stickers extant were "Greater Israel," "Hebron Forever," "The Nation is with the Golan," and the like. Peace stickers were rare, as their presence would invite a passing political adversary to slash the tires, "fold" the wipers, or simply "key" the paint job. Not anymore. Today, you can gauge the climate that favors peace by a long line of blue squares, sun clouds passing through a clear blue sky, with one word only on them: "Peace"—a beautiful production of the Peace Now movement. And there are stickers saying "Yes to Peace, No to Violence," a sad allusion to the many terrorist incidents that continue to plague both Israelis and Palestinians by extremist forces. I saw a picture of Rabin on one sticker: "In his death, he left us a legacy of peace." I wish a legacy of peace—one even deeper than Rabin's—really were on the doorstep: not a state of nonbelligerence, but a peace that fuses the concepts of shared land, shared destiny, and shared struggle for a better life. But we still seem to be some way off from this.

The conflict in the Middle East, while rooted in conflicting claims to the same territory by two nations, is fueled by the many parties who have an interest in keeping the enmity alive. In Israel and the Arab countries, these parties include religious fundamentalists, right-wing politicians who feed off the fear, liberal governments with reactionary policies, the military establishments, and the international arms industry. Some of these parties foment violence deliberately, while others don't even realize that their actions, in the interests of "security," foster the kind of fear that leads to aggression. Developing, testing, and carrying a big stick is an invitation to get hit.

I wish I could end this story by saying, "And now there is peace and we are living happily ever after," but I cannot. No matter when I stop this story, it will not have an unequivocally happy ending. A true reconciliation of hearts and minds is still distant in the Middle East, battered and scarred by years of hostility. Open borders and a "new Middle East" will not come about in my lifetime. As an optimist, I am hoping that it will come about in my children's lifetimes, but as a realist, I think that they will continue to suffer from the fallout of a century of ill-will between two otherwise wonderful nations. Now in their twenties, my daughters have already lived through (though not all their friends have made it) the Scuds of Saddam, the bus-bombs of Hamas, and, as I finish this writing, katyusha rockets of the Hezbollah in Lebanon exploding on my younger daughter's kibbutz.

The price of war and violence is fierce and often irreversible. I can only pray that my daughters and all our children have absorbed the lessons of hope, the will to persist, and a sense of the power of committed citizens. Efforts to make peace can exact a very high price, but their rewards are immeasurable.

WOMEN IN BLACK: A BRIEF HISTORY

Women in Black was founded in Jerusalem in January 1988 to protest the occupation by Israel of the territories it had gained in the 1967 war. Our tactic was to stand for one hour every Friday afternoon at a major intersection in Jerusalem dressed in black and holding signs saying, "Stop the Occupation" (in Hebrew, Arabic, and English). The idea caught on in

Tel Aviv and Haifa and, thereafter, at a total of thirty-nine crossroads throughout Israel. The Jerusalem vigil was always the largest of the Israeli vigils, though we were almost only Jewish women there. In other vigils around Israel, there was a sizable representation of Palestinian women who are citizens of Israel. I estimate that we were roughly about 5,000 during the heyday of the movement in Israel (1988-91).

A few months after Women in Black was founded in Jerusalem, we heard of solidarity vigils in other countries. First, it spread to Italian women. Then there was a flowering of these groups with slightly different emphases in each place. In some cities (Amsterdam, London, Melbourne, Sydney, etc.), the groups were mixed Jewish and Palestinian, and they struggled to develop a dialogue and find a common language with each other, at the same time jointly protesting the Israeli occupation. From New York we even received newsletters from a North American coalition of these vigils called the "Jewish Women's Committee to End the Occupation."

In late 1990, several months before the Gulf War, which began in January 1991, the idea of these vigils really took on a life of its own. Women dressed in black, calling themselves "Women in Black," formed vigils in many countries, now having nothing to do with the Israeli occupation. In Germany, Women in Black in Munich, Cologne, Berlin, Wiesbaden, and elsewhere originally protested the Gulf War and sale of chemicals by German firms to the Iraqi regime. After the war, German Women in Black broadened their mandate to protest neo-Nazism, xenophobia, racism against migrant workers, and other German problems. Women in Black in south India protested Hindu fundamentalism, which treated women badly. There were Women in Black in San Francisco to protest apathy about the homeless, Women in Black in Italy to protest war and organized crime, and Women in Black in Australia to protest domestic violence. To this day, Women in Black in Belgrade is a heroic group, courageously protesting their government's violently militant and racist policies in ex-Yugoslavia. Some of these groups have never even heard of Women in Black in Israel where it began. The Women in Black vigil at the U.N. conference in China in August 1995 had participation from several thousand women from many countries and was organized by the Asian Women's Human Rights Council based in the Philippines and India.

Women in Black is still alive and well in a number of countries, many groups are now completely dissociated from the original concept. Since the peace process began in the Middle East, only four small vigils in Israel continue to stand regularly. Nevertheless, Women in Black in Israel serve as a symbol of the nonviolent protest of women against war and an inspiration to the groups that follow, cast indelibly in the minds of many as the conscience of this country.

—May 8, 1999

REFERENCES

Asian Women's Human Rights Council. 1995. *Women in Black: A Gathering of Spirit.* Bangalore, India.

Deutsch, Yvonne. 1994. And Peace Shall Multiply Like Mushrooms. Unpublished essay.

Helwig, Maggie. 1993. "Wearing Black for the Enemy," *Peace News*, November, 1993, 8–9.

Katz, Shira. 1995. "New Agendas of the Women's Movement for Peace: To Be or How to Be?" *Challenge*, May–June, 21.

Schrag, Carl. 1990. "Staking a Claim for Peace: Grassroots Peace Movements in Israel," *Israel Scene*, April/May, 8–12.

Silver, Eric. 1991. "What Now for Peace Now?," *The Jerusalem Report*, March 7, 16–17.

Sugarman, Margo Lipschitz, Janine Zacharia, and Daniel Grynberg. 1995. "A Chronology of Hate", *The Jerusalem Report*, November 30, 15.

CHAPTER 20

Feminist Resistance to War and Violence in Serbia

LEPA MLADJENOVIC AND DONNA M. HUGHES

*They have been ceaselessly killing, torturing,
and raping for a year and a half already. They
have banished more than three million lives.
They manipulate women. Blackmail men. They
spread hate, destruction, and death; we are left
without words to express our horror and anger.
They have separated streets, classrooms, families, cities. They are drawing lines on mountains
and corridors through the countryside . . . Fascist leaders of Serbian politics threaten us with
war in Kosovo, Macedonia, and Serbia. Meanwhile, they have stopped all electricity, water,
and telephone systems in Bosnia-Herzegovina.
People die by the minute.*

—WOMEN IN BLACK

*War in Kosovo is escalating. The civil popula-
tion is suffering more and more. The number
dead, wounded, refugees, kidnapped, and expelled is increasing day by day.*

—WOMEN IN BLACK

An earlier version of this paper, entitled "Feminist Resistance in Serbia" by
Donna M. Hughes, Lepa Mladjenovic and Zorica Mrsevic appeared in the *European Journal of Women's Studies*, Vol. 2, 1995: 509–532.

INTRODUCTION

Since 1991, the Socialist Federal Republic of Yugoslavia has been torn apart. The Serbian regime, headed by Slobodan Milosevic, has instigated hatred, ethnic cleansing, and war throughout all the former republics and provinces of Yugoslavia. Throughout this same time, feminists in Serbia and Croatia have worked on peace activism and solidarity among women. While all the nationalist leaders have engaged in words of hatred and supported ethnically defined national identities and statuses, militarism, and killing, the feminist women's groups have founded antiwar and feminist movements.

This paper will describe the conditions and factors influencing women's lives in Serbia, and the ways women have organized to resist state and interpersonal violence and assist one another. To resist nationalism, sexism, and war, feminists founded antiwar organizations and crisis lines, counseling centers, and shelters for women and children. With activism and civil disobedience, they have transformed women's desperation and anger into action. In Belgrade, Serbia, since 1990, feminists have created the SOS Hotline, Women's Lobby, Women's Parliament, Women in Black, the Women's Studies Research and Communication Center, the Autonomous Women's Center Against Sexual Violence, the Center for Girls, two Women's Houses (shelters for battered women), a feminist publishing house called "1994," the Incest Trauma Center, the Counseling Center for Women, two houses called "Lastavica" (which means the Swallow) for single women refugees from Krajina, "Women on Work," an organization that supports women's enterprise initiatives, "Out of the Circle," an organization that supports women with disabilities and their families, and "Bibija," the Roma Women's Center.[1]

BACKGROUND

The Socialist Federal Republic of Yugoslavia was a multinational, socialist, Central European state madeup of six republics—Slovenia, Croatia, Bosnia-Herzegovina, Montenegro, Macedonia, and Serbia—and two autonomous provinces within Serbia—Vojvodina and Kosovo.[2] Throughout the 1980s, nationalism among the republics grew, spurred on by the fall of Communism in Eastern and Central Europe. In May/June 1991, Croatia and Slovenia declared their independence from Yugoslavia. The Yugoslav National Army, led by Serbian leader Slobodan Milosevic, resisted these moves for independence. In Slovenia, the fighting lasted ten days before the Yugoslav National Army withdrew, leaving Slovenia an independent nation. In Croatia, the war was longer and bloodier. In September 1991, in an effort to stop the fighting, the United Nations imposed an arms embargo on all the former Yugoslav republics, which gave the Serbian-controlled Yugoslav National Army far greater military strength. Local militant ethnic groups and nationalists attempted to seize control of the land where their populations were concentrated. Possessing greater military force, Serbs seized the area inhabited predominantly, but in no way exclusively, by Serbs. In January 1992, a peacekeeping plan, enforced by United Nations troops, was accepted.

In April 1992, just as Bosnia-Herzegovina declared its independence from Yugoslavia, the Yugoslav Army, along with Serb nationalists, launched the war in Bosnia-Herzegovina. Of all the republics in former Yugoslavia, Bosnia-Herzegovina was the most ethnically mixed. Although the conflicts have been driven on all sides by nationalism, it was the Serbs who initiated "ethnic cleansing," a term used to describe the forceful removal or killing of civilian populations. The efforts to create nationally or ethnically pure territories have meant that the wars are aimed primarily at civilian populations. According to the United States Committee for Refugees, "In Bosnia-Herzegovina, the most extreme elements of the nationalist Serb community—aided and abetted by their patron in Serbia—have chosen to wipe out, liquidate, remove, rather than to live with, those who are somehow 'different.' Their methods are crude, but effective: artillery barrages of civilian centers, forced population movements, appropriation of property. Those who survive and are not driven out face imprisonment, rape, and the forced separation from family. . . . Nationalist Croat forces and, to a lesser extent, troops of the mostly Muslim Bosnian army, have also committed violent, heinous acts" (Winter 1993).

At the end of 1995, escalating ethnic cleansing, mass killings, and the violation of "safe areas" for refugees prompted the North Atlantic Treaty Organization (NATO) to launch air strikes against Bosnian Serbs. All parties eventually negotiated an agreement to end the war. The Dayton Peace Accord called for Bosnia to be partitioned into a Bosnian Serb republic and a Croat-Muslim federation. After 1989, when the Yugoslav government revoked the autonomous status of Kosovo, the Serbian-headed regime put into a place a system of apartheid against the ethnic Albanians, who make up ninety percent of the population. In autumn 1990, the Albanian language was banned, and people speaking Albanian in public could be jailed for two months. Workers in state institutions

were required to sign a loyalty oath to Serbia. The majority of people refused and consequently were expelled from jobs. Many ethnic Albanian
businesses were forced to close. In 1992 and 1993, ethnic Albanian students were expelled from schools. As a result, schooling systems were
established by ethnic Albanians in private homes, cellars, and unheated
buildings. From 1989 to 1998, the system of apartheid and human rights
violations increased. In response, ethnic Albanians developed parallel institutions to meet their needs, such as schools, medical care, trade, and finally, their own army, the Kosovo Liberation Army (KLA).

As other wars in former Yugoslavia ended, the Serbian nationalist
regime turned their attention back to Kosovo. The repression of the ethnic Albanians by Serbian police increased, generating further nationalist
activities and organization among the ethnic Albanians. On 28 February
1998, Serbian-controlled Yugoslav Army troops and Serbian police entered Kosovo to squash the Kosovo Liberation Army, harass ethnic Albanians, and start ethnic cleansing in this region.

As in Croatia and Bosnia, the targets of Serbian paramilitary and
military forces were often civilian populations. According to the Kosovo
Information Center, from 28 February to July 1998, 266,729 ethnic Albanians were forced out of their homes and 269 villages attacked by
heavy artillery (Mladjenovic July 1998; Belgrade Feminists 27 July
1998). "Killing of Albanian people and looting of Albanian villages is
permanent and increasing. People are attacked in forests, while their villages are burned to the ground. They have no way out. The border with
Montenegro is blocked, the border with Albania is mined. A few go to
Macedonia, and some to Bosnia and Herzegovina. Most Albanian
women, children, and men are hungry, exhausted, sick, homeless,
desperate, terrorized, trapped, blackmailed, humiliated, if they survive.
Around 130,000 are without any roof, in the open, and the cold weather
is here" (Mladjenovic September 1998).

During the summer of 1998, 350,000 ethnic Albanian people,
mostly women, children, and elderly people were expelled from their
homes. The KLA reciprocated by targeting Serbian policemen and police stations, and kidnapping ethnic Serbs.

NATIONALISM IN SERBIA

In Serbia the Communist leadership did not want to lose power through
democratization, so they used ethnic nationalism to manipulate people
and create a popular base for their continuing control. They succeeded

in pulling Serbs toward Serbia and pushing others toward their own nationalist groups, who then chose independence to escape growing Serbian nationalism (Denitch 1994, 184).[3] Largely through mass rallies and state-controlled media, people were taught to hate those who were different.

"It all began with 'sweet' stories about national states, national rights, life within ethnic boundaries" (The Women's Parliament 20 May 1992, 48). Nationalism was constructed as a highly imagined community inhabited by people whose identities had little to do with accurate history, geography, or real attributes (Denitch 1994, 187). Over several years, old unresolved ethnic and national conflicts were given new life. Specials were shown on TV about Serbian history that recounted the victimization of Serbs. For example, the Serbian popular press retold stories of Croatian war crimes against Serbs during World War II (Denitch 1994, 176). As tales of the Serbian defeats and victimizations were rejuvenated with new emotion, all "Others" became potential threats to Serbia—ethnic Albanians in Kosovo, Slovenes in Slovenia, Croats and Muslims in Croatia and Bosnia-Herzegovina.

At the beginning of the wars in Slovenia, Croatia, and Bosnia, there were all-day media programs against the "enemy," whose identity changed as the war moved eastward (from Slovenia, to Croatia, to Bosnia, to Kosovo). Every night, before and after the TV news, there were extra segments of pictures of dead or tortured people with an accompanying commentary on "what the enemy has done to innocent Serbs." As nurtured animosities grew, opportunists exploited the conditions. "The specter of nationalism was thus awakened. Profiteers, gangsters, and murderers grabbed the opportunities offered by it. A state of general uncertainty, endangerment, and mistrust was created. Paranoia has become our everyday reality" (The Women's Parliament 20 May 1992).

A "cleansing" of the culture initiated by Serb officials removed books, films, and works of art created by those who were not Serbs. Singers, artists, and actors who were not Serbs were banned and harassed. Finally, most of them left the country. Textbooks were rewritten to include the nationalist view of history.

Beginning in Fall 1991, textbooks for elementary and secondary school in the Republic of Serbia had to include a "detailed account of wars, exterminations, tortures, destructions of people" (Imsirovic and Cetkovic 1991, 18).[4] The ideology of "brotherhood and unity," used for forty-five years to hold Yugoslavia together under Communism, disappeared. Some people with non-Serb names removed their nameplates from their doors. Many people had to conform to nationalist ideology in order to keep their jobs and live in the community.

NATIONALISM, MOTHERHOOD, AND WOMEN'S REPRODUCTIVE RIGHTS IN SERBIA

The nationalist ideology of the Serbian leaders calls for women to do their duty to the country by having more babies and by willingly sacrificing their sons. Mythic figures are evoked to coerce women into supporting nationalist goals, while the lawmakers are changing the constitution and laws so that women will have no choice but to comply. "In tandem with the cult of blood and soil, the new Serbian nationalists also summoned to life the symbolic mediaeval figure of mother Yugovich—the long suffering, brave, stoic mother of nine, offering her children up to death in the defense of the fatherland. Maternity is now to be seen as an obligation, not as a free option for women; the sexuality of women has to be controlled and reduced to procreation" (Zajovic December 1991, 26).

Militaristic nationalism insists that Serbian women must have more babies so that the nation will be able to defend itself in war. One politician said, "I call upon all Serbian women to give birth to one more son in order to carry out their national debt." Following the war in Slovenia, another politician said, "For each soldier fallen in the war against Slovenia, Serbian women must give birth to one hundred more sons" (Zajovic December 1991, 26).

Abortion has been readily available to women in Serbia by special law since 1951. In the new constitution of 1974, abortion was guaranteed as a human right by Article 191 of "Free Parenthood." This article protected "the human right to decide about the birth of one's own children" (Mladjenovic and Litricin 1993). In April 1992, a new constitution was formed for the "Third Yugoslavia."[5] It eliminated Article 191 on "Free-Parenthood." Nationalists called for legal restrictions on abortions by comparing the number of abortions to the number of soldiers killed in the war.

There is little education available on birth control and there is not a consistent adequate supply of contraceptives. The international sanctions imposed against Serbia for its aggression in the other republics has prevented contraceptives from being imported. By 1994, one pharmaceutical company in Serbia was manufacturing birth control pills, but the supply has been intermittent and the quality varies. The IUD is used, but without proper care. Contraceptives, such as the diaphragm and sponge, are unavailable. One woman said she had only seen a diaphragm once in her life.[6] Although condoms are available, men don't like them and often refuse to use them. Withdrawal is still frequently used as the only form of birth control. Pregnancy is a constant fear for women. As summarized by Stanislava Otasevic, a physician at the Autonomous Women's Center Against Sexual Violence, "No one is educated. Women are not consulted. No one speaks with them."[7]

ETHNIC CLEANSING, RAPE, AND WAR CRIMES

"Ethnic cleansing" is a term for the mass expulsion, killing, and raping of people. In this war it has been carried out mainly by Serb paramilitaries and the army. These acts meet the legal definition of genocide—the attempt to destroy, in whole or in part, a national, ethnic, racial, or religious group. Many civilians were, and are being killed, others were, and are being forced from their homes to become refugees or into concentration camps.

In the wars of ethnic cleansing in Croatia and Bosnia-Herzegovina, sexual abuse and violence against women were central in the planned policy of "ethnic cleansing." When the Yugoslav Federal Army shelled cities in Bosnia, maternity hospitals were targeted. Special concentration camps were set up to rape and prostitute women; these hotels and prisons were called rape camps by survivors. In Vogosca, near Sarajevo, Bosnia women with Croat and Muslim names were killed after they were raped; in Foca, the Serbs held women for months in an indoor sports arena where nightly men would come with flashlights to make their choices for rape; at Omarska, women were forced by Serb soldiers to work during the day and were raped according to a schedule, once every four nights (Gutman 1993).

From the start of the war in Bosnia in 1992, Serbian paramilitary forces committed systematic rape against Muslim and Croat women. Later, in spring 1993, Bosnian Croat nationalists adopted the strategy to create an ethnically pure Croatian sector (Gutman 1994). Forces of the predominantly Muslim government of Bosnia have also been charged with atrocities, but these do not appear to be government policy as with the Serbs. Women of all nationalities have been raped, but Muslim women have been disproportionately among the victims, and Serbian paramilitaries disproportionately among the rapists (Stiglmayer 1994).

Also implicated in the sexual abuse and prostitution of women are the United Nations "peacekeeping" forces (Gutman 31 October 1993; Bernstein 21 June 1993).

Forced impregnation has also been a weapon of nationalism and ethnic cleansing in the campaign of violence against women in Bosnia. In this constructed ideology, the ethnicity of a baby is the same as its father. Serb soldiers and paramilitary troops who raped women told them that they would give birth to "little Chetniks," or Serbian soldiers, who would grow up to kill them. Other Croat or Muslim women were told that if a woman carries a Serbian baby, then she, too, is Serb (State Commission for Gathering Facts on War Crimes in the Republic of Bosnia and Herzegovina October 1992). Some women were held in rape camps in Bosnia until their pregnancies were so advanced that they would not be able to obtain an abortion (Tresnjevka 28 September 1992). Since the goal of ethnic cleansing is the creation of an ethnically and nationally pure population, the forced impregnation of non-Serb women has required some twists in thinking in Serbian nationalist ideology.

REFUGEES IN SERBIA

"You can go anywhere in the world but home" said Milka Zulicic, economist and refugee from Sarajevo living in Belgrade (Statement made at a workshop at the Third International Meeting of Women in Black, Novi Sad, Serbia, 4–6 August 1994). She is Montenegrin, but keeps her husband's Muslim name, although he has been dead many years. In February 1993 she sent her oldest son, age twenty-one, to Montenegro by train to get food from relatives living there. When the train passed near the border of Bosnia, a group of unidentified men entered the train and asked for identification. Zulicic's son and eighteen men with Muslim names were removed from the train. None of them has been seen since. It is thought that the leader of this paramilitary unit is a member of the Serbian Parliament. Now, Ms. Zulicic is an active member of Women in Black and waits with her other son for immigration visas to somewhere else in the world.

Traditionally, refugees are thought to be those who have "fled," but the refugees who have become politically active in Belgrade clearly and forcefully state that they are those who have been "expelled." They were forced to leave their homes and regions by military aggression. All would like to return home. Instead, they are forced to apply for and await immigration to receptive countries all over the world. The implication is that they will never, or at least not in the foreseeable future, return to their homes or homeland.

According to the Serbian Commissariat for Refugees and the Red Cross of Serbia, at the end of 1993, there were 559,000 registered and 150,000 unregistered refugees in the territory of the Federal Republic of Yugoslavia.[8] As with most refugee populations, they are predominantly women and children. Of the adults, 84 percent are women. A sizable percentage of the children are without parents, because their families in Bosnia-Herzegovina sent them to Serbia to be safe with relatives or friends for what they thought would be a short period of time. A number of these children have been sent since to live in orphanages or refugee camps. Over 95 percent of the refugees live with relatives or friends; only 4.8 percent live in refugee camps, which are old barracks and dormitories away from the population centers, with no transportation

In some cases women are resorting to prostitution to feed themselves and their children. Due to the unpopularity of the Serbian regime, aid from humanitarian sources has been scarce. Refugees are often harassed and made to feel guilty for being a burden. Fights often break out in schools between refugee and local children.[9] Refugees are also subject to nationalistic harassment because they speak with a Bosnian accent. Some women say they are afraid to speak in public.

In 1995, the Croatian army "ethnically cleansed" eastern Slavonia of its Serbian population, driving over 100,000 people from this region in Croatia into Serbia. Milosevic relocated many of these refugees in Kosovo to add more Serbs to the predominantly ethnic Albanian population.

FEMINIST ORGANIZING AND RESISTANCE TO NATIONALISM AND MILITARISM

Feminism Prior to the Wars

Compared to those of the other former Communist countries, the borders of Yugoslavia were more open, allowing international communication and exchange of ideas, one of which was feminism. The first presentation of contemporary feminist ideas was at a Croatian sociological association meeting in 1976. The first feminist conference, *The Woman's Question: A New Approach*, was held in 1978 at the Student's Cultural Center in Belgrade. The purpose of the meeting was to introduce the ideas of feminism and begin to challenge socialist patriarchy and the assumption that women's struggle was synonymous with class struggle

(Papic 1995). Inspired and motivated by this meeting, "Woman and Society" discussion groups formed in Zagreb and Belgrade.

In 1986, feminists in Belgrade defined their organization, "Women and Society," as feminist. The Yugoslav governmental organization, The Conference for the Social Activities of Women, condemned this move and accused the group of being an "enemy of the state," "pro-capitalist," and "pro-Western." The group operated independently without state institutional or financial support (Mladjenovic and Litricin 1993). The growth of feminist groups was also hindered by the Communist doctrine that everyone must work together for change. Many of the women did not want to exclude men. When men came to meetings, they always wanted to know why the group only talked about women. The fear of women-only groups was a challenge to creating feminist organizations.

The feminist group in Belgrade held workshops and public discussions on violence, abortion, sexuality, worker's rights, psychiatry, and medicine. On International Women's Day, 8 March, they did research on the streets of Belgrade by stopping women and asking them ten questions about their lives. Five years later, on the same day, women in Belgrade founded the SOS Hotline for Women and Children Victims of Violence.[10]

Feminist organizations have supported democratization in Yugoslavia. In 1990, the first multiparty elections were held in Yugoslavia. In that year, feminists formed four women's organizations. In the summer of 1990, women from different nonnationalistic parties formed the Women's Lobby to create a space for women's critical voices and to influence public opinion and the policies of the political parties in the election. The Women's Lobby took a strong stand against nationalism because of the nationalists' call for women to have more babies for greater Serbia. On 5 December 1990 the Women's Lobby issued a call to voters, "Do not vote for the Serbian Socialist Party, Serbian Radical Party, Serbian People's Renovation, and all other nationalist, fascist, warrior parties" (Women in Black, 17 December 1992, 101).

As the elections approached in the fall 1990, women formed the Women's Party, ZEST (an acronym for Zenska Stranka, the Z stood for women, E for ethics, S for solidarity, and T for tolerance). The women saw a need for a women's party because "[a]lthough legally equal and free, women have for decades been living the life of second-rate citizens and unrealized and subjected individuals in the family and society alike" (The Women's Party 1990). ZEST had three Principles of Activity: (1) "For democracy and against all forms and aspects of discrimination and authoritarian power and authority in society"; (2) "For peace, tolerance and cooperation among nations and peoples"; (3) "For quality of life as a crucial aim of development." With the aim of improving the lives of women, they organized public discussions about housewives, women artists, and work. As militarism grew, they lobbied the parliaments of the republics to negotiate a peace (Cockburn 1991).

The election resulted in a Serbian Parliament with only 1.6 percent women (the lowest percentage in Europe), so women formed the Women's Parliament on 8 March 1991 to monitor new laws that pertained to women (Mladjenovic and Litricin 1993). Throughout 1990 and 1991, women's groups organized and participated in protests calling for women's rights and a demilitarization of Yugoslavia.

During the time the women's groups were forming and evolving, nationalism was intensifying, forcing women's groups to decide where they stood. The Women's Lobby and Women in Black took antinationalist stands and said so publicly. ZEST, the Women's Party, disbanded because of conflicts over nationalism. The SOS Hotline for Women and Children Victims of Violence made a policy of nonnationalism that created conflicts among the volunteers. Eventually, some of the women with nationalistic views left, but some stayed and remained silent (Mladjenovic and Litricin 1993).

Transformation of Women's Lives

The end of socialism, growing nationalism, and eventual war with the intent of creating a Greater Serbia through ethnic cleansing had a life-transforming effect on many women. For many women, in many ways, their lives would never be the same. Zorica Mrsevic observed how her life changed from 1990 to 1994:

> I have been a witness to how easily what has been socially constructed can be destroyed. Within a few months practically everything was changed. All the rules of the game are now different. Institutions that we believed would exist forever don't exist anymore. All that I had invested myself in is worth nothing. We became miserable. In the previous time, we lived an easy life—not on a high standard, but somehow, everything was easy—to go on holiday, to get a flat from the institution where you worked, to buy new clothes, to eat whatever you wanted, to have fun, to visit restaurants, to travel abroad, to have free medical care. Now we spend practically all our earned money only for food.

Our clothes and shoes, as well as our health and good moods, come from the previous time. The winter of 1993/1994 was the hardest in my life. We lived by eating only potatoes and beans, and we had to spend our life savings to buy that. Our salaries were between ten and twenty DM per month.

Slavica Stojanovic was not a feminist before the war. With tears, Slavica described the pain she lived in at the beginning of the wars. "For one year I woke up as if someone had grabbed me. I didn't know what to do. It was as if I were having a heart attack."[11] She was in crisis at the beginning of the war, because she didn't know what to do, but felt a strong sense of responsibility to Yugoslavia:

My grandmother lived under the Austro-Hungarian rule, and out of the experience of her youth she despised inter-ethnic conflicts that were provoked by rulers who had vested interests in creating animosity. My grandmother remembered the enthusiasm of the time when Yugoslavia was founded as a multi-ethnic country after World War I. She lived near the Italian border in the early years of fascism and openly opposed it. At the beginning of World War II, she lived in Zagreb and was forced to leave because she was Serb. She came to live in Belgrade, and her house was bombed in 1941 by the Germans and again in 1944 by the Americans. Until her death, a few years ago, at age ninety, she called herself 'Yugoslav.' It was her political choice. I was raised with these ideas. When this war started, I had to make a distinction between the values I wanted to retain from 'Yugoslavia' and the material/territorial idea of Yugoslavia.[12]

In keeping with these values, Slavica turned to translating Virginia Woolf into Serbo-Croatian. She started teaching courses on women's literature in the Women's Studies Center. Later, she co-founded the Autonomous Women's Center Against Sexual Violence and, in 1994, started a feminist press called "1994." Slavica says that she "doesn't care for borders." Like Virginia Woolf, she says, "The whole world is my country. I want to work for values that are more open than nationalism. When Slovenia and Croatia wanted independence, I supported unity, but that meant I supported the war. I wanted to support unity, but I needed to respect their choice for independence, and I couldn't support crimes. I had political doubts about the motivations of some people who wanted separate states.

Because populations in the republics are so mixed, I knew that separating Yugoslavia would be very difficult and risky. I am not happy with the nationalistic states with their patterns of domination."

Another woman said that, prior to 1990, she published research papers, but growing nationalism, war propaganda, and eventual war compelled her to change the focus of her work and life.

> I felt lonely and frightened among men and my colleagues. I needed strongly to be surrounded by women. First, I joined the Women's Studies Research and Communication Center because it was a form of scholarship that was closest to my previous work, but with a feminist approach. Soon after this, I realized that this was not enough, that violence against women is very widespread, and I needed to do more than stay in my room with my books and my computer. That was a luxury that belongs to another time. More practical and less theoretical work was needed, so I joined the SOS Hotline and the Autonomous Women's Center Against Sexual Violence. During this time I realized that I was a lesbian, so my life in the women's groups is not only a scholastic adventure, but the adventure of my life.[13]

Feminist Resistance to War

Women were the majority of the organizers of, and participants in, the peace movement in Belgrade. Prior to the outbreak of war in the Yugoslav republics, women formed organizations against mobilizations for war. In March 1991, several women's groups from Slovenia, Croatia, and Serbia, collectively called Women for Peace, issued a statement calling for "a peaceful and negotiated solution to all controversial issues," and a "demobil[ization] of all reserve police units in all republics and provinces" (Lokar et al. March 1991, 1). Throughout the spring and summer of 1991, the Belgrade Women's Lobby took part in peace demonstrations, issued weekly calls for an end to bloodshed, and criticized media programs that promoted nationalism and violence against women. After the start of the war in Slovenia, the Belgrade Women's Lobby appealed to the federal government: "We ask that the units of the Federal Army unconditionally withdraw to their barracks. The youth did not go to serve in the military in order to impede the separation of any ethnic group from Yugoslavia. A Yugoslavia maintained by force is useless to everyone" (Belgrade Women's Lobby July 1991, 3).

The Mothers' Protest—1991

During the summer of 1991, women concerned about their sons in the Federal Yugoslav Army organized protests against the war. At the beginning of the war, all regular soldiers belonged to the Yugoslav National Army, whose responsibility was to stop moves for independence by Slovenia, Croatia, and Bosnia. Croat mothers did not want their sons fighting with Serbs to prevent Croatia's move for independence, which would put their sons on the "wrong" side of the war. Serb mothers did not want their sons fighting in Croatia, a land that they didn't perceive belonged to them anymore. The women used their role as mothers to express concern for their sons and call for peace. The women stated their opposition to the war: "We refuse that our sons become the victims of senseless militarists. It is not clear what are the goals for which we should sacrifice our sons. Our sons have been deceived: they have to participate in a war for which they are not the least bit responsible, in a war that has not even been declared. That they should give their lives for imperialist purposes is the project of politicians. It is a disgrace to win a fratricidal war" (Mothers of the Soldiers of Belgrade 20 July 1991, 8).

The first large protest against the war was held by several hundred parents, mostly mothers of conscripted men, in the Serbian National Assembly in Belgrade on 2 July 1991. In their statement they said, "The protests of mothers is a feminine spontaneous reaction to the disgrace of the civil war" (Mothers' Movement July 1991, 7). Repeatedly, throughout the summer, in letters to officials and public statements, the mothers called for an end to the war and a return of their sons.

At the end of August 1991, approximately a thousand parents, mostly mothers, from Croatia and a few from Bosnia-Herzegovina attempted to protest in front of the General Headquarters of the Yugoslav National Army. They were forced to move to the soldier's barracks. To enable such a large gathering, forty buses were used to bring the women from Croatia to Belgrade. The leaders of the group, Mothers for Peace, from Zagreb, had the Croatian flag as a sign of their organization. Lepa Mladjenovic attended the protest and participated with mixed feelings:

> I was very excited. The first night, the auditorium of the soldier's barracks in Belgrade was packed with women. It was amazing. Never before in this male space had there been such a scene. At the front of the auditorium, on the podium, were the "fathers"—the army officers. The women were sitting everywhere, talking and eating. At one point,

women from the villages in Croatia stopped listening to the men and started to softly sing a tender old Croat song. In contrast to the fathers in uniform with their hard strict military culture, the women's voices were from another world. On the other hand, at that time, if more than twenty women got together, I had to wonder how did it happen. It usually meant that some larger political thought or organization stood behind the event.

While Mladjenovic was excited and moved by large numbers of women coming together to protest the war, she recognized that some women acted with the support of men whose goal was their own nationalism and interest in preventing the Federal Yugoslav Army from intervening in their move for independence.

The Mothers' Protests were the first public resistance to the wars. Since the political tradition of fifty years of communism had suppressed people's rebellious motivations, the Mothers' Protest was important in breaking that tradition. Also, the Mothers' Protest contained a general peace message. The Mothers' Protest was a good use of the patriarchal belief that mothers are supposed to save men; this enabled the mothers to stand against authority. Unfortunately, the nationalist ideology was much stronger than their peace protests. Later, the statements of the mothers implied that their sons should be fighting for their own "blood and soil" if necessary. These sentiments slowly grew into pro-Serb and pro-Croat nationalist ideologies and peace was forgotten.

Women in Black, Belgrade

By the fall of 1991, feminists dissatisfied with the character of the anti-war protests decided to found another organization. The Israeli group, Women in Black, who wore black and protested in silence their country's treatment of the Palestinians, inspired the women. Women in Black made its first appearance in Belgrade on 9 October 1991. In their first public statement, the activists defined themselves as an antinationalist, antimilitarist, feminist, pacifist group who rejected the reduction of women to the role of mothers.

> The work of women in peace groups is presupposed; it is invisible, trying, women's work; it's a part of 'our' role; to care for others, to comfort, aid, tend wounds, and feed. The painful realization that the peace movement would, to some extent, also follow a patriarchal model

caused a serious dilemma for feminist-pacifists. We wanted our presence to be VISIBLE, not to be seen as something 'natural,' as part of a
woman's role. We wanted it to be clearly understood that what we were
doing was our political choice, a radical criticism of the patriarchal,
militarist regime and a nonviolent act of resistance to policies that destroy cities, kill people, and annihilate human relations" (Women in
Black 1993, 23a).

Another political aim of Women in Black is to strengthen the solidarity among women who have been separated by guns and borders. "We
are the group of women who believe that solidarity is one of the deepest
values of our existence, that active solidarity between women is the force
and the tenderness by which we can overcome isolation, loneliness, traumas, and other consequences of hatred. We are the ones who come out in
the public with our bodies and our visions of the world without war, rape,
violence, and militarism" (Women in Black, 10 June 1992, 50). Every
week Women in Black protested the wars by putting on black clothes and
standing silently in the Republic Square in Belgrade. "We are the group
of women who stand in silence and black every week to express our disapproval against war. We have decided to see what is the women's side of
this war. Women wear black in our countries to show the grief for death
of the loved ones. We wear black for the death of all the victims of war.
We wear black because the people have been thrown out of their homes,
because women have been raped, because cities and villages have been
burned and destroyed" (Women in Black, 10 June 1992, 50).

The feminists also shifted the philosophy and approach to protesting
the war. The statements and writings became more overtly political and
analytically feminist. "The militarization of former Yugoslavia has
meant the imposition of military values, and militaristic language; a cult
of necrophilia (expressed in slogans as 'the frontiers of Serbia are where
Serbs are buried'); and acceptance of political and moral totalitarianism"
(Zajovic December 1991).

With the establishment of the more radical Women in Black, a political shift in analysis and naming occurred—Serbian nationalism is seen
as a motivating force, and the Serbian government is named as the aggressor. "We say that the Serbian regime and its repressive structures
(Federal Army and paramilitary formations) are responsible for all three
wars, in Slovenia, Croatia, and Bosnia-Herzegovina. The Serbian regime
leads wars in the name of all citizens of Serbia. This way all the citizens
become the hostages of their imperialistic politics" (Women in Black, 10
June 1992, 50).

Long before the atrocities of the Serbs came to international attention, Women in Black issued a statement calling for an end to war crimes. In October 1991, the Women's Parliament and the Belgrade Women's Lobby issued a statement "Against War Crime," in which they listed acts which are war crimes, including: inhuman treatment of civilians, inflicting bodily harm, torture, prostitution, rape, stealing or destroying the property of others, including historical and cultural monuments, and the destruction of cities, towns, and villages. They reminded people that Yugoslavia had signed all United Nations conventions and agreements, including the Geneva Convention on war (Women's Parliament and Belgrade Women's Lobby 9 October 1991, 21). In 1992, Women in Black called for the naming of war crimes and the prosecution of perpetrators (Women in Black, September 1992, 83).

The feminists in Belgrade have maintained the position that all survivors of rape be recognized, but stated that many more rapes have been committed by Serbian forces. "The feminists of Belgrade and Serbia do not support the position about symmetrical suffering. They are conscious that the more powerful and better armed military-political forces of Karadzic in Bosnia (the army of the Serb's Republic) have the largest number of rapes on their consciences. How many exactly, it will be difficult to know, even after the war. The high percentage of Muslim women raped in the war in Bosnia is not a reason to forget the suffering of women of other nationalities and religions, atheists, or those claiming no particular nationality" (Women in Black, 28 October 1992, 92a).

By the end of 1993, Women in Black had been protesting in the streets for two years. In that time they acquired a jaded view of peace plans and international interventions. At this point, the Dayton Peace Accord, which would bring peace in Bosnia, was still two years away. In their New Year's Message of 1994, they had only universal condemnation for all parties:

> The sanctions imposed by the [United Nations] Security Council do not affect only those who have caused them: the militarist Serbian regime and its partners, the new elite of war-profiteers, whose worldwide bank accounts are safe and sound. The so-called international community has, moreover, given political support to this regime by legalizing the results of its conquests and ethnic cleansing in Bosnia and elsewhere. . . . We mistrust a 'peace' based on 'deals' made by the nationalist-militaristic elites who have caused this war. We mistrust the so-called mediators who use peace slogans to fan war and ethnic hatred; they are part of the same old patriarchal militaristic machinery.

We no longer harbor the illusion that the international community will not apply the logic of violence and the right of the stronger" (Women in Black, 27 December 1993, 15).

Women in Black continued to wear black and stand in the streets until after an enforced peace was brought to Bosnia. During 1997, they supported and participated in the grassroots democracy movement in Serbia. The situation looked more hopeful for the first time in many years. But Slobodan Milosevic was not about to be maneuvered out of power by democracy. He refused to accept the results of the election and soon had control of the government again. When Serbia renewed the violence in Kosovo, Women in Black, working with other pro-democracy, human rights, and anti-violence groups, organized protest rallies.

On 19 September 1998, the government banned the antiwar rally Against War. Women in Black issued a statement: ". . . by banning this protest, the regime in Serbia proves its policy of isolation, xenophoby [sic] and confrontation with the world. With this repressive act, the regime also shows its determination for war, hatred, destruction, and violence against all who think the opposite, even against an indeed small group of citizens, who, from 1991 until today, raise their voice against all kinds of violence" (Women in Black, et al., 19 September 1998).

Nine days later, threats to Women in Black and other groups that spoke out against the Serbian regime were issued in the Serbian Parliament. At this time, NATO had threatened to bomb Belgrade in order to force the Serbian regime to stop the police and military aggression in Kosovo. Vojislav Seselj, previously a war criminal in Croatia and Bosnia and now the deputy prime minister, responded with self-annihilating nationalism and threats to retaliate against peace activists, whom he referred to as "Serbia's inner enemies":

We should take the U.S. threats very seriously, but we must not be frightened. We will have an enormous number of victims and great material damages, but we don't have a spare fatherland. We must fight at all costs; no matter by whom we are attacked. Our determination to defend ourselves by all means should prove that if they want to attack us, they should withdraw their supporters. . . . [the United States should] withdraw their quislings, like members of the Helsinki Committee for Human Rights, Belgrade (Intellectual) Circle, and Women in Black, and not leave them as hostages. Maybe we cannot reach every airplane, but we will grab those who are close to us (Women in Black, 30 September 1998).

In response to these threats, the Women in Black issued their annual statement, "Seven Years of Women in Black Against War: 9 October 1991 to 9 October 1998." This time, the annual report was in the form of a confession of their guilt for seven years of activism for peace, freedom, and democracy for all people in former Yugoslavia:

> I confess
>
> to my longtime anti-war activity;
>
> that I did not agree with the severe beating of people of other ethnicities and nationalities, faiths, race, sexual orientation;
>
> that I was not present at the ceremonial act of throwing flowers on the tanks headed for Vukovar, 1991 and Prishtina, 1998;
>
> that I fed women and children in the refugee camps, schools, churches, and mosques;
>
> that I sent packages for women and men in the basements of occupied Sarajevo in 1993, 1994, and 1995;
>
> that for the entire year I crossed the walls of Balkan ethno-states, because solidarity is the politics which interests me;
>
> that I understand democracy as support to anti-war activists/friends/sisters—Albanian women, Croat women, Roma women, stateless women;
>
> that I first challenged the murderers from the state where I live and then those from other states, because I consider this to be responsible political behavior of a citizen;
>
> that throughout all the seasons of the year I insisted that there be an end to the slaughter, destruction, ethnic cleansing, forced evacuation of people, and rape;
>
> that I took care of others while the patriots took care of themselves (Women in Black, 9 October 1998).

FEMINIST RESISTANCE TO VIOLENCE AGAINST WOMEN

The SOS Hotline

The founders of the feminist anti-violence movement in Serbia view violence against women and children as a social and political issue, not as the private interactions between men and women, or within the family. The movement and organizations working against violence against women grew out of the feminist movement established in Serbia, Yugoslavia in the 1980s. The first SOS Hotline in the Socialist Federal Republic of

Yugoslavia opened in 1987 in Zagreb, Croatia. Following this the women in Belgrade, Serbia tried for several years to establish a similar crisis line, but the authorities were suspicious of this work and refused to grant them space and resources. After persistent effort, on 8 March 1990, International Women's Day, the SOS Hotline for Women and Children Victims of Violence opened in Belgrade.

The original mission of the SOS Hotline for Women and Children was threefold: (1) to assist victims of violence through a hotline; (2) to make visible to the public the existence, seriousness, and reality of men's violence against women and children; and (3) to initiate institutional change to bring about more prompt, serious, and sensitive response to victims of violence (Mrsevic and Hughes 1997). From 1990 to 1993, the SOS Hotline was the only feminist organization that women and children could contact for assistance concerning violence against women, their friends, or family.

The Group for Women Raped in War

In December 1992, women from the SOS Hotline founded the Group for Women Raped in War. Their aim was to support women raped in the war with basic needs, such as food, clothing, medicine, money, and friendship. They wanted to create solidarity among survivors of sexual abuse in war so the women could regain their autonomy and self-esteem. The Group for Women Raped in War wanted to help the women through the procedures of medical institutions and refugee organizations. They looked for women in hospitals where survivors went to have abortions or await delivery of babies. Sometimes, they received referrals from doctors, but there was poor collaboration since state institutions' interests were different from those of the Group for Women Raped in War. Medical personnel in gynecological wards treated women who were raped as "guilty victims." Survivors of war rape were treated the same way, unless they were Serbs—then the hospitals had a nationalist interest in their stories of victimization. Serb officials used the testimonies of the rapes of Serbian women to support their claim that Croats and Muslims were the aggressors. Thus they used women's bodies and pain in support of nationalism. In May 1993, while volunteers from the SOS Hotline sat in the hospital with a depressed rape survivor who had just had a painful second trimester abortion, the doctors were photocopying her story and preparing to take it to the European Parliament.

The Group for Women Raped in War supported the women's decisions in whatever they chose to do: go back to parents, leave the country, stay in Belgrade, find work and, for some, keep their babies or give them up for adoption. The Group for Women Raped in War's political goal was to make visible the systematic and genocidal rape of women with Muslim and Croat names by Serb soldiers. The media in Serbia never covered these rapes, and the Serbian public could remain unaware of the ethnic cleansing, concentration camps, and systematic rapes organized and carried out by Serbs in Bosnia.

The Autonomous Women's Center Against Sexual Violence

The Group for Women Raped in War founded the Autonomous Women's Center Against Sexual Violence. With the financial support of organizations from Europe and the United States, the center opened on International Human Rights Day, 10 December 1993. In their opening address, founders said, "We wish to stress once again that women's rights are human rights, that human rights are above national interests, and that the state must not kill its citizens" (Women's Lobby, 10 December 1993). The founders of the Autonomous Women's Center Against Sexual Violence are women who refuse to be bystanders to the destruction of people, whether they live in their own neighborhoods or in other parts of former Yugoslavia. The women refuse to be victims, although some have been victimized.

The Autonomous Women's Center Against Sexual Violence was created for all women who have survived rape and sexual abuse, whether from war zones or from neighborhoods in Belgrade. The center set up a multiple approach to sexual violence. They analyzed and responded to rape at the individual, social, and political level. Their goal is to respond to the emotional needs of the rape survivor, and to comprehend and condemn the use of sexual violence as a method of keeping women powerless in society and as a political and military weapon of war and ethnic cleansing.

The center has an SOS rape hotline and individual counseling, and in autumn 1994, the center organized support groups for survivors of sexual abuse. Women come to the center from several different populations and backgrounds. The center sees women coming from war zones and local women who have been sexually assaulted. Mothers of children who are being sexually abused have called for assistance, and teenage and adult incest survivors call or visit the center to talk about their abuse. Young women (ages sixteen to twenty) from the Belgrade Maternity House frequently come to the center to find support. These women are waiting to deliver babies. Some of these pregnancies are the result of rape, but many of the women become pregnant from boyfriends and then are rejected by their families because they are not married. Also, refugee women and children come to the center for humanitarian supplies and personal support.

For several years, the Autonomous Women's Center was the only women's drop-in center in Serbia that organized women's counseling, worked on women's rights campaigns, networked with different women's groups in the country, and had an ongoing public campaign to "make sexual violence against women socially visible." An additional aim of the center is to maintain communication with feminists and activists against violence toward women in Croatia and Bosnia-Herzegovina.

Growth of Women's Movement—1995 through 1998

The SOS Hotline and the Autonomous Women's Center Against Sexual Violence provided the training ground for many feminists in Serbia who have expanded the women's support and anti-violence work by founding many other organizations in Belgrade and throughout Serbia, including Kosovo. Although patriarchal cultural traditions and the totalitarian political climate in Serbia make the rise of women's organizations difficult, the feminist movement against all types of violence has spread to towns and cities outside Belgrade. At the end of 1998, there were initiatives in seventeen towns that are part of the feminist network. The Belgrade groups supported the new organizations with written materials, education, and exchanges of experience.

Two new women's centers were formed that gave support to victims of violence—the Incest Trauma Center and the Counseling Center for Women. Two houses called "Lastavica," meaning "the Swallow," were established for single women refugees from Krajina, an area of northern Croatia that was "ethnically cleansed" of Serbs at the end of the war. "Women on Work" is a new organization that supports women's enterprise initiatives. "Out of the Circle" supports women with disabilities and their families. In addition, "Bibija," the Roma Women's Center, was formed.[14]

NATIONALISM, MILITARISM AND VIOLENCE AGAINST WOMEN

The nationalist hatred generated in Serbia has increased the violence against women also. In the autumn of 1991, the SOS hotline started receiving calls from women who were battered after men watched the TV news in which there were stories filled with hatred for "the enemy." Women said the men became enraged after listening to and watching the nationalist propaganda and beat women as a way to avenge their wounded national pride. Some women reported that they were beaten for the first time in their lives after the men watched one of the nationalist reports on Serbian victims of war. Women reported that their husbands cursed the Croats and Muslims in Croatia and Bosnia-Herzegovina while beating them. In most of these cases the ethnicity of the woman was the same as her partner. In cases where the ethnicity of the man and the woman was different, the man beat the woman, claiming, "Our five minutes has come," meaning that this was the man's opportunity to be the victor for his ethnicity for a short period of time (Mladjenovic 1992, 55).

Men who were in the Yugoslav army or paramilitary groups returned to Belgrade traumatized, angry, and violent. They brought the weapons they had used in fighting and used them to threaten or harm women. Since the beginning of the wars, weapons are kept in many homes. Pistols, hand grenades, and automatic weapons have become part of households. "Some of the men who came back from the front (from regular army or paramilitary battalions) continue massacres in their homes: they abuse women, beat their children, sleep with machine guns under their pillows, rape their wives while they are sleeping, destroy the furniture, scream, swear, spit, and accuse" (Mladjenovic 1992, 54).

Women report an increase in men's alcohol abuse, which increases their violence to women and children. Men, who participated in paramilitary groups that loot houses and businesses as part of ethnic cleansing, are angry and violent because they have not received the material rewards they thought they would. The men expect and demand emotional understanding and support from the women around them, and see their wives as someone on whom they can displace their rage.

The longer the wars continue, the more tolerance and acceptance there is for violence as a way of resolving conflict or gaining control. Since the wars, violence is legitimated in Parliament, streets, and homes, with the result being an increase in violence against women in the streets and homes. In Serbia, nationalism and militarism have become dominant ideologies in society.

Women's groups that have formed to resist war and violence bring a feminist analysis to Serbian nationalism and men's violence against women. They see parallels between men's defense of their private abuse of women in their homes and Serbia's defense of the violence perpetrated against people of other ethnicities inside the borders of former Yugoslavia. Serbian President Milosevic resists international intervention in his war against ethnic Albanians in Kosovo, especially the presence of peacekeeping troops, by claiming that Kosovo is Serbia's land, and that the violence, as with men's violence against women and children, is an internal and private matter in which outsiders should not intervene. Feminist groups in Belgrade point out that both private and state violence stem from patriarchy.

> Patriarchy considers that men's violence in the family is a 'private family matter'—this ideology of privacy permits violence in all other domains of society. When the SOS hotline for women and children calls the police to intervene in violent scenes, a violent husband standing beside his bruised wife claims, 'This is my wife, it is my issue.' Policemen, also with male understanding, confirm that it is a 'family matter.' That is exactly the model for how the first man of the ruling regime leads the war in Kosova: 'Kosova is an internal problem of Serbia' (Independent Women's Groups in Belgrade, 22 May 1998).

NO ENDING

In 1994, we wrote that an ending could not be written for this paper because the story of feminist resistance in Serbia was far from over. In 1994, as the paper was sent to the publisher, the city of Bihac in Bosnia was being destroyed by Serbian artillery. It is now April 1999 as we write an update for this paper, and still an ending cannot be written. As this update of the paper is sent to the publisher, Serbian police, military, and paramilitary units are emptying all of Kosovo of ethnic Albanians. NATO is dropping bombs on Belgrade, Novi Sad, Karljevo, and on Pristina and other sites in Kosovo and Montenegro. We can only hope that the words of Women in Black, written in 1994, still apply: "Women will remember, women are telling each other stories of the reality we live in, and we are witnesses of many crimes for which this regime is responsible. Women, our friends from all parts and states of the former Yugoslavia, are still telling us about the suffering they went through and what is happening to them now. Nationalism didn't separate all of us; a stream of trust still exists between women of all names" (Women in Black, 5 October 1994).

NOTES

1. "Roma" refers to the nomadic people, originally from India, who migrated to Europe and are known colloquially as "gypsies." (eds.)

2. In 1989, the Serbian government removed the autonomous status of Kosovo and Vojvodina. (The spelling of the name as "Kosovo" is Serbo-Croatian. It is spelled "Kosova" in Albanian, the language of the 90% of Kosovars who are ethnic Albanian. eds.)

3. The history leading up to this conflict is long and complicated and beyond the scope of this paper. For a more detailed discussion see Meg Coulson. 1993. "Looking Behind the Violent Break-up of Yugoslavia," *Feminist Review*, No. 45, pp. 86–101; Maja Korac. 1993. "Serbian Nationalism: Nationalism of My Own People," *Feminist Review*, No 45, pp. 108–112; Bogdan Denitch. 1994. *Ethnic Nationalism: The Tragic Death of Yugoslavia*. Minneapolis: University of Minnesota Press.

4. In 1994, The Centre for Anti-War Action in Belgrade published *Warfare, Patriotism, and Patriarchy: The Analysis of Elementary School Textbooks*, which analyses the messages to students about patriotism, national (ethnic) relations, prejudices, war, peace, and gender (Rosandic and Pesic 1994).

5. The "first Yugoslavia" was the kingdom of Serbs, Croats, and Slovenes formed after World War I, and the "second Yugoslavia" was the Socialist Federal Republic of Yugoslavia formed after World War II.

6. Personal communication to Donna M. Hughes, July 1994.

7. Personal communication to Donna M. Hughes, July 1994.

8. Following the war in Slovenia, 37,000 Serbs left Slovenia and registered as refugees in Serbia. During the war in Croatia, tens of thousands of Serbs fled to areas of Croatia under nationalist Serb control, while 160,000 people (almost all Serbs) left Croatia and registered as refugees in Serbia. All figures are quoted from the U.S. Committee for Refugees (September 1993), which relied on The Commissariat for Refugees, Republic of Serbia. In 1993, The United Nations Human Rights Commission (25 May 1993), basing its figures on Red Cross reports from each country, reported that within the territory of former Yugoslavia there were the following numbers of refugees: 985,000 in Croatia, 87,000 in Krajina, 469,000 in Serbia, 2,280,000 in Bosnia-Herzegovina, 60,000 in Montenegro, and 32,000 in Macedonia.

9. Personal communication from teenage boys to Donna M. Hughes, July 1994.

10. The first SOS Hotline was founded in Zagreb, Croatia on 8 March 1988.

11. Personal communication to Donna M. Hughes, August 1994.

12. Personal communication to Donna M. Hughes, July 1994.

13. Personal communication to Donna M. Hughes, September 1994.

14. Details on these organizations could not be included in this update of the paper because one of the authors is under bombardment in Belgrade. She is engaged twenty-four-hours a day in providing support services to women.

REFERENCES

Belgrade Feminists. 1998. "Kosova-Report from Belgrade Feminists." 27 July.

Belgrade Women's Lobby. 1991. "Appeal of the Belgrade Women's Lobby against Violence and the War in Slovenia." In *Women For Peace Anthology*, edited by Women in Black (1993). Belgrade: Women in Black. (Henceforth cited as *Anthology* 1993).

Bernstein, Dennis. 1993. "Answers Needed to Charges of U.N. Misconduct in Bosnia," San Francisco, 21 June. Pacific News Service.

Cockburn, Cynthia. 1991. "A Women's Political Party for Yugoslavia: Introduction to the Serbian Feminist Manifesto," *Feminist Review* 39:115–159.

Coulson, Meg. 1993. "Looking Behind the Violent Break-up of Yugoslavia," *Feminist Review*, 45:86–101.

Denitch, Bogdan. 1994. *Ethnic Nationalism: The Tragic Death of Yugoslavia.* Minneapolis: University of Minnesota Press.

Gutman, Roy. 1993. "U.N. Troops in Bosnia Reportedly Visited Serb-Run Brothel (Sarajevo)." *Newsday*, 31 October (New York).

———. 1993. *A Witness to Genocide: 1993 Pulitzer Prize-Winning Dispatches on the "Ethnic Cleansing" of Bosnia.* New York: Macmillan Publishing Company.

———. 1994. "Foreword." In *Mass Rape: The War Against Women in Bosnia-Herzegovina*, edited by Alexandra Stiglmayer, ix–xiii. Lincoln: University of Nebraska Press.

Independent Women's Groups in Belgrade. 22 May 1998. "Statement."

Imsirovic, Jelka and Nadezda Cetkovic. 1991. "Women's Protest against Careful Nourishing of the Patriarchal System of Values—The Consequence of which is Always War—In the textbooks for elementary and secondary school in Serbia." 12 August. In *Anthology* 1993.

Korac, Maja. 1993. "Serbian Nationalism: Nationalism of My Own People," *Feminist Review* 45:108–112.

Lokar, Sonja. Women's section SDP, Belgrade Women's Lobby and Feminist Group "Women and Society." 1991. "Women for peace." March. In *Anthology* 1993.

Mladjenovic, Lepa. 1992. "Violence against Women." In *Anthology* 1993.

Mladjenovic, Lepa and Vera Litricin. 1993. "Belgrade Feminists 1992: Separation, Guilt, and Identity Crisis," *Feminist Review* 45:113–119.

Mladjenovic, Lepa. July 1998. "Kosova."

———. September 1998. "Fascism and War in Serbia and Kosovo."

Mother's Movement. 1991. "Mother's Movement." July. In *Anthology* 1993.

Mothers of the Soldier of Belgrade. 1991. "To the Public Opinion of the Federal Secretariat of Defense, the Senior Head of State of the Serbian Government and the Yugoslavian Presidency." 20 July. In *Anthology* 1993.

Mrsevic, Zorica and Donna M. Hughes. 1997. "Violence against Women in Belgrade, Serbia: SOS Hotline 1991–1993," *Violence Against Women: An International Interdisciplinary Journal* 3, 2:101–128.

Papic, Zarana. 1995. "Women's Movement in Former Yugoslavia: 1970s and 1980s." In *What Can We Do For Ourselves: East European Feminist Conference, Belgrade, 1994*, 19–22. Belgrade: Center for Women's Studies Research and Communication.

Rosandic, Ruzica and Vesna Pesic. 1994. *Warfare, Patriotism and Patriarchy: The Analysis of Elementary School Textbooks*. Belgrade: Center for Anti-War Action and Association.

State Commission for Gathering Facts on War Crimes in the Republic of Bosnia and Herzegovina. 1992. "Sexual Crimes of the Aggressor in Bosnia and Herzegovina," Bulletin No. 1. 31 October. Sarajevo: Republic of Bosnia and Herzegovina.

Stiglmayer, Alexandra. 1994. "The Rapes in Bosnia-Herzegovina." In *Mass Rape: The War Against Women in Bosnia-Herzegovina*, edited by Alexandra Stiglmayer. Lincoln: University of Nebraska Press.

Tresnjevka Women's Group. 1992. "Report." 28 September. Zagreb: Tresnjevka Women's Group.

U.S. Committee for Refugees. 1993. *East of Bosnia: Refugees in Serbia and Montenegro*. September. Washington D.C.: National Council for Nationalities Service.

United Nations Human Rights Commission. 1993. *United Nations Human Rights Commission Report on Refugees*. 25 May. Zagreb.

Winter, Roger P. 1993. *East of Bosnia: Refugees in Serbia and Montenegro*. September. Washington D.C.: U.S. Committee for Refugees, National Council for Nationalities Service.

Women in Black. 1992. "Women in Black against War." 10 June. In *Anthology* 1993.

———. 1992. "Women in Black Against War." September. In *Anthology* 1993.

———. 1992. "Women in Black against War: A Call for Action," 28 October. In *Anthology* 1993.

————. 1992. "Women in Black against War." 17 December. In *Anthology* 1993.

————. 1993. "Women in Black." In *Anthology* 1993.

————. 1993. "New Year's Message To Feminist and Pacifist Groups." 27 December. In *Women For Peace*, edited by Women in Black (1994). Belgrade: Women in Black.

————. 5 October 1994. "Women in Black: Three Years of War—Against the War."

Women in Black, Helsinki Committee for Human Rights in Serbia, Antiwar Campaign, Group 484, Center for Antiwar Action, Belgrade Circle, Autonomous Women's Center Against Sexual Violence, Yugoslav Committee of Lawyers for Human Rights, Multinational Society of Bosnians and Herzegowinians in Belgrade. 1998. "Banning the Antiwar Rally in Belgrade." 19 September.

Women in Black. 1998. "Opening of New Hunting Season on 'Undesirables.' " 30 September.

————. 1998. "Seven Years of Women in Black." 9 October.

Women's Parliament. 1992. "Session IV." 20 May. In *Anthology* 1993.

Women's Parliament and Belgrade Women's Lobby. 1991. "Against War Crime." 9 October. In *Women for Peace Anthology*, edited by Women in Black (1992) Belgrade: Women in Black.

Women's Party-ZEST. 1991. "Appeal on Behalf of Peace Initiative." 5 July. In *Anthology* 1993.

Zajovic, Stasa. 1991. "Militarism and Women in Serbia." December. In *Anthology* 1993.

CHAPTER 21

Gender, Nationalism, and the Ambiguity of Female Agency in Aceh, Indonesia, and East Timor

JACQUELINE SIAPNO

*It is difficult to start a revolution, more difficult
to sustain it. But it's later, when we've won, that
the real difficulties will begin.*
—GILES PONTECORVO,
"THE BATTLE OF ALGIERS"

This article examines the complex and often contradictory configurations of female agency, nationalism, modernity, and gendered opposition in Aceh and East Timor—two historically and culturally distinct nations fighting for independence from the Indonesian state. I focus in particular on the ambiguity of female agency in the nationalist movements for independence and the ways in which rural women's political agency is different from the path chosen by male nationalists and urban, Jakarta-based, cosmopolitan Indonesian feminists: in short, political agency beyond the nation-form and organized movements. In *Race, Nation, Class: Ambiguous Identities*, Etienne Balibar argues that wherever powerful lineal, tribal, or kinship solidarities still exist, the formation of the nation is incomplete (Balibar 1991, 102). While Balibar's work is not explicitly feminist—though in the same article he makes the argument that "nationalism has a secret affinity with sexism" (1991, 102)—I wish to use it here for my own feminist purposes. In East Timor and Aceh, this "incompleteness" has, on the one hand, opened up radical possibilities for belonging. On the other hand, it has also instituted a new form of community that privileges men and marginalizes women. I argue that in comparison to powerful, resilient kinship solidarities, which are matrifocal and egalitarian, the new nation form has constructed a "national personality" (to use Balibar's term) in which women's identity is ambiguous, if not marginal.

Following the important critical work on the contradictions between feminism/nationalism and the gendering of the national imaginary by, in particular, Elliston (1999), Balibar (1991), Anderson (1983), McClintock (1995), Jayawardena (1986), Enloe (1989), Yuval-Davis and Anthias (1989), Mohanty, Russo, and Torres (1991), and Parker et. al (1992), my analysis explores the following questions: why is it that the nationalist movements in Aceh and East Timor are predominantly male (not necessarily dominated by men, but predominantly male in membership), and why is it that women (compared to young men) are not as passionately inclined to join the independence movements or to enlist to "die for" the nation? This question is especially important at this time when the Indonesian government has suddenly announced, in late January 1999, that East Timor will be granted independence by January 2000, and when the Acehnese and West Papuan nationalist movements are demanding independence with increasing forcefulness. This paper critically examines the projects of well-meaning male nationalists and urban feminists whose definition of "feminism" is confined to modern, organized movements—for example, *Gerwani* and the *Organizacao Popular de Mulher Timor* or (OPMT) founded in Dili in 1975 (Wieringa 1995; Aditjondro 1999)—and occlude forms of female agency that do not conform to their particular definition of "feminism."

Feminist analyses of nationalist movements have tended to begin from the assumption that women are universally subordinated in all nationalist movements, and that "no nation in the world gives women and men the same access to the rights and resources of the nation-state" (McClintock 1995, 353). The absence of women in nationalist movements is interpreted as something foreboding, negative, and dangerous: ". . . nationalisms are, from the outset, constituted in gender power, but, as the lessons of international history portend, women who are not empowered to organize during the struggle will not be empowered to organize after the struggle. If nationalism is not transformed by an analysis of gender power, the nation-state will remain a repository of male hopes, male aspirations, and male privilege" (McClintock 1995, 385).

I argue here that women's relative absence and peripheralization in these nationalist movements may not be a marker of female subordination and marginalization. If the women themselves consciously choose not to participate, their absence may be due, for example, to the fact that they were not present from the movement's inception, or not actively enlisted to participate. It is a widely known fact that even though Acehnese and East Timorese women have been, and are, incredibly active in the struggles for independence, there are very few women members of nationalist movements such as Aceh Merdeka or RENETIL (*Resistencia Nacional dos Estudantes de Timor-Leste*). It may be useful to explore mechanisms, practices, and spaces outside the discourse of nationalism where women exercise power, independence, and agency, in order to understand women's disinterestedness, ambivalence, even animosity, toward nationalist organizations. Lila Abu-Lughod, in her reading of Spivak, Visweswaran, and the contradictory politics of feminism, modernity, nationalism, and post-coloniality, writes: "Spivak in a famous essay has questioned the very possibility of recuperating subaltern voices, including those of women. Visweswaran, in response, in a more cautious way has explored the special difficulty of recuperating the voices of any but middle-class and elite women in the study of nationalism" (Abu-Lughod 1998, 24). This argument for looking at discursive formations outside nationalism and nationalist movements is not new. It appears in the critical scholarship of the Subaltern Studies group (Chatterjee 1993, 1986, Guha and Spivak 1988, Spivak 1988), and, in the Philippine context, in an important essay by Reynaldo Ileto, "Outlines of a Non-Linear Emplotment of Philippine History" (1988). Ileto argues that historians— in particular leftist historians—have a tendency to look for political agency in modern forms of political organization, such as nationalist movements, political parties, and so on. Formations outside progressivist organizations are somehow "backward," "outmoded" (in colonial history, a form of "banditry"), because they are not organized in a way that is comprehensible and assimilable to the thought of the Euro-American historian. Ileto writes, "The concept of development is still understood as a universal 'given'—the 'given,' for example, of any text emanating from the national government and its technocrats. Surprisingly enough, even the critics of government and the technocratic elite, whether of the right or left in the political spectrum, while pointing out distortions and misapplications, fail to escape the very discourse of development" (Ileto 1988, 130). He further adds that while the left "look upon the masses as the real 'makers of history,' the masses are not allowed to speak" (Ileto 1988, 135).

The drive to write about the suffering of those "who have no history" is by no means limited to leftist historians and human rights workers. In a critique of scholars who are bound to this narrative of suffering in writing about peasant movements, Benedict Anderson writes that this comes "out of a profound moral impulse to show that the people of these peasant movements somehow did not die or suffer in vain. Historians look at these movements and see that almost invariably they were crushed, very often quite horribly, and so the idea of writing books about them is a way somehow to rescue them from the obliteration or silence they suffered in real life. But what is rescued is their suffering more than their thought" (Anderson 1977).

My argument is based on fieldwork in Aceh in 1992, 1993, and 1996 (for a total of fourteen months over a four-year period) and on extensive interviews with East Timorese in the clandestine movement in Java and Bali (in 1992 and 1993) and with East Timorese refugees in Portugal (1994). Having carried out several years of fieldwork among Acehnese and East Timorese communities and having a strong personal commitment to the struggles for social justice and democratization in these two regions, I would argue that female agency and power in these communities are not explicitly articulated in modern, progressivist, political movements or coalitions—such as the predominantly male nationalist movements and the predominantly urban, Jakarta-centered women's movements—but rather in more indigenous forms of local feminism and exercise of power that are not often examined in Euro-American analysis of gender agency. In other articles that I have written (Siapno, 1994, 1995, 1997), I have argued that if we were to look only at modern progressivist political organizations (NGOs, human rights groups, women's groups), and nationalist movements, and if we were to focus mainly upon the "nation-state"—and thus upon politics—rather than culture or noetics (i.e. literary, oral traditions, ethnography of rituals and spaces) or forms of social organization and community outside the nation-state—it would indeed be very difficult to find female power and agency in these societies. Unfortunately, most human rights reports and nationalist documents on Aceh and East Timor, while crucial in supporting political struggles and calling for international solidarity, tend to portray the commonality of victimhood rather than the diverse, contradictory local articulations of female political agency, which, in some ways, derail the agenda of organized movements. The most important point I wish to make is that women in Aceh and East Timor have participated actively in the struggles of their times, though perhaps not in publicly visible positions or overt forms of opposition. They have not been passive and silent. Their "absence" is a function of historiography, which places too much emphasis on organized, political movements and the nation-state.

Deborah Elliston, an anthropologist who conducted fieldwork on gender and politics in Polynesian nationalism (Elliston 1999) provides a compelling argument about Polynesian women's ambivalence about, and opposition to, the nationalist movement against French colonialism (in particular the antinuclear movement). She argues that the categories that Euro-American feminists use to examine social processes—such as gender, race, class, and sexuality—may not be very helpful in analyzing other societies, in particular, societies where there is a relative absence of gender hierarchy. Instead of assuming that gender, race, class, and sexuality are already meaningful, we may find it useful to look at differences that are locally meaningful—such as matrifocality, generation, rank system, place of origin, kinship, land tenure—indigenous maps of social relations in that particular society. Elliston addresses the questions of why it is that the nationalist movement appeals primarily to young men, and how men and women talk about the desirability of independence in different ways. Her analysis of gender and politics in Polynesian nationalism is particularly relevant to East Timor and Aceh in that both societies, though patrilineal in terms of kinship, are primarily matrifocal—that is, either they are mother-centered, or the older women in the house (the grandmothers, mothers, aunts, and older sisters) have the strongest influence in important decisions. In her comparative study of matrifocality in Indonesia (in particular Java, Aceh, and Minangkabau), Nancy Tanner describes the following distinctive features of matrifocal systems: (a) The role of the mother is structurally, culturally, and affectively central; and (b) this multidimensional centrality is legitimate. Where these features coexist, the relationships between sexes is relatively egalitarian; both women and men are important actors in the economic and ritual spheres (Tanner 1974, 131). During my numerous interviews and personal communications with male nationalist leaders in East Timor and Aceh, they underlined the central, dominant if not totalizing, power of their mothers, grandmothers, and older sisters when it came to important family decisions. I would argue that in Aceh, due to this relative power and autonomy in terms of ownership of land, control of the household, family, and local village affairs, Acehnese women do not suffer the same anxiety as women elsewhere concerning their peripheralization in modern nationalist movements.

Two different and unconnected groups, Dutch administrators and Muslim feminists such as Fatima Mernissi, have been perplexed by the contradictions and syncretism between *adat* or customary law (in particular matriarchal *adat*) and Islam in Aceh. The generalization that men and women are extremely unequal in virtually all Muslim societies is contested by Fatima Mernissi, who argues in her book, *The Forgotten Queens of Islam* (1993), that what she calls "Island Islamic societies,"

and in particular Aceh, are unusual in terms of women's access to political power compared to Middle Eastern societies. Aceh was already a cosmopolitan center of Islamic learning when it was ruled by a succession
of four Acehnese female heads of state in the seventeenth century: Tajul
Alam Safiatuddin (r.1641–75), Nur Al-Alam Nakiyyat al-Din Shah
(1675–78), 'Inayat Shah Zakiyyat al-Din (1678–88), and Kamalat Shah
(1688–99). Writing about the four female rulers who governed Aceh in
the sixteenth century, Mernissi writes, "They (the female rulers) reigned
despite the fact that their political enemies had imported from Mecca a
fatwa that declared that 'it was forbidden by law for a woman to rule' "
(Mernissi 1993, 110).

In Sylvia Tiwon's fuller investigation of the process of the Dutch
colonial state's domestication of matriarchal societies for purposes of
taxation, she argues that, from the Dutch perspective, "the notion of
communities centered on matrifocal households was inimical to the required development of individual, alienable property" and "militates
against contractual relationships": ". . . matrifocal households ('matri-
archies') [were] inimical to a proper (read: Western capitalist) process of
individuation of males as property-holders and citizens who are able to
engage in the common contractual relationships that form the basis of
national societies—societies needed for a nation-state to exist. . . . The
defeat of matriarchal *adat* (construed as the deficient equivalent of the
law—the paradox is inevitable and shows the limits of the discourse of
law) works against the possibility of contractual relationships and thus
militates against the originary social contract that marks the superiority
of Western states" (Tiwon 1997, 21–24).

In the Acehnese context, the failure of Dutch policy to effectively
tax and colonize the Acehnese through coercive force was then shifted.
On the advice of Snouck Hurgronje, then advisor for Native Affairs,
Dutch hegemony was imposed by the introduction of Western-style secular schools. The purpose of these secular schools was twofold: "to
emancipate the Muslims from their religion" (Hurgronje cited in Steenbrink 1993, 89) and to assimilate the Acehnese into more politically effective arrangements of the family and household (for purposes of
taxation), based on male property holders as heads of the family.

THE LIMITS AND CONTRADICTIONS OF "FEMINISM" AND "WOMEN'S SOLIDARITY"

In many ways, 1998, the year Soeharto resigned after being in power for
thirty-two years (1965-1998), was a "year of living dangerously" (this is

also the title of a famous speech by Soekarno, first president of the independent Republic of Indonesia and organizer of the Bandung Conference in 1955). Children broke away from their rich, conservative, bureaucratic or corporate parents to protest in the streets—and were brutally shot by the military; wives broke away from their domineering husbands to protest about violence against women (public and private) as a political and international issue; young women who were raised to be pious and demure overflowed into the streets in militant crowds, sleeping overnight in Parliament, and shouting "Hang Soeharto." In recent years, there has been a proliferation of women's groups and NGOs in Jakarta, and to some extent in Aceh and East Timor. One of its most effective forms is "internet activism," in particular the listserv of women's networks and groups throughout Indonesia (perempuan@egroups.com). "Gender" has become a popular focus for international funding agencies in their efforts to strengthen civil society in Indonesia, partly because it is a "safe" issue in the sense that the government and military do not seem to think that women's issues are a threat to national security or the state. One of the most active women's NGOs in Aceh decided to use the name "Flower," a very feminine, unthreatening name to disguise its real political objectives (personal communication with Fatimah Syam, 1998). However, there continues to be a "problem" (articulated by male nationalists in both East Timor and Aceh), regarding the disengaged, ambivalent, peripheral, sometimes antagonistic relationship that women have towards independence movements.

The errant and insurgent forms of gender agency in Aceh and East Timor that resist integration into a progressivist national feminist agenda based in Jakarta present a serious challenge to any form of totalizing feminism—whether imperialist, state, global, or national. A recent personal communication from a young Acehnese woman in her mid-twenties, who comes from a rural poor, strongly Islamic background and who completed training and internship with several Jakarta-based feminist organizations, includes the following: "*Mengenai lingkungan perempuan elite di LSM Jakarta, saya bergaul baik dengan mereka. Mereka baik, pintar, berani, profesional dan punya banyak jaringan internasional. Mereka tidak pilih bulu dalam bergaul, tapi beberapa diantaranya yang menganut paham/prinsip feminisme radikal—ada yang memilih hidup dengan seorang pria tanpa nikah, free sex. Karena mereka pikir itu tubuh mereka, mereka berhak menikamati selama tidak menganggu kepentingan orang lain "why not." Tapi saya pikir itu hak mereka memilih jalan hidup seperti itu, yang penting buat saya bisa bergaul dengan mereka, saling share memperoleh ilmu dari mereka dan yang penting*

tidak ikut memilih jalan hidup dan prinsip seperti itu, habis perkara."
[About the elite women in NGOs in Jakarta, I have a very good relationship with them. They are kind, smart, courageous, professional, and have
a lot of international network connections. They are not elitist or selective in their social relationships, but there are those among them who follow a radical feminist principle—there are those who choose to live with
men outside marriage, practicing free sex. Their feeling is that it is their
body, they have the right to enjoy, as long as they are not bothering someone else, why not. But while I agree that it is their right to choose this
kind of path, the important thing for me is to be able to interact with
them, share ideas, gain knowledge from them, but most importantly not
follow the path and principles they've chosen, that's all.]

For the middle-and upper-middle-class urban-based Jakarta feminists, "radical feminism" and politicization mean rebelling against patriarchy through sexual autonomy and working towards liberating the
female body from oppressive moral prisons—monogamy, taboos against
pre and extramarital sex. In another part of this young woman's letter,
she writes that what she is really most involved with is fund-raising to assist the thousands of widows and orphans in Aceh whose husbands and
fathers were killed and disappeared by the Indonesian military. She
writes that she was also thoroughly involved in volunteer fact-finding
missions investigating hundreds of cases of rape and violence against
women in order to put government and military officials responsible for
these heinous crimes on trial.

The most common example of resistance to "national sisterhood" is
the contempt for Kartini, the Indonesian national heroine. Acehnese
women and men have only antagonism towards Raden Adjeng Kartini
(1879–1904)—an enlightened Javanese nationalist and feminist who
wrote eloquently about women's emancipation. This strong rejection of
Kartini may be useful in terms of our analysis of why it is that Acehnese
and East Timorese women are not particularly enthusiastic about forging
"solidarity" only along the lines of gender and sexuality with Jakarta-
based Indonesian feminists.

Acehnese peoples' hatred of the Indonesian government is manifested in Acehnese claims that the Javanese are "immoral." Thus Kartini
is delegitimized as an improper heroine. During my fieldwork, the question often raised was "Why Kartini? Why was she the one chosen to be
the most important national heroine commemorated on Ibu Kartini Day?
So many Acehnese women—Teungku Fakinah, Pocut Bahren, Tjoet
Meutia—led military troops to fight the bloody war against the Dutch,
but they were not made into national mothers." All kinds of people (men

and women, but especially women), ranging from university lecturers, young girls, housewives, and *ulama*, who were open-minded on other issues, expressed what seemed to me to be extreme contempt for Kartini about whom they know little. She has come to symbolize the worst aspect of "Javanese colonialism"—domination by an ethnic group that would enforce its cultural hegemony by reducing local histories and languages to one homogeneous event.

In "Models and Maniacs: Articulating the Female in Indonesia," (1996), Sylvia Tiwon provides an analysis of the contradictions and paradoxes of the New Order's appropriation of Kartini as a "model national mother figure." Kartini herself never wanted to get married, and she died after childbirth without ever having performed the naturalized female role of mothering. Tiwon also pointed out to me the possibility that Acehnese men are contemptuous of Kartini because she wrote vehemently against misogyny in Islamic societies, in particular Java. Kartini devoted her life to advocating women's education and to building schools for girls. She also wrote in a powerful voice against misogynist practices (e.g. forcing girls into marriage at fifteen, polygamy, the practice of seclusion of girls in Java). These feminist ideals of Kartini are lost on Acehnese women, who are given only the domesticated New Order regime's version of her work. To them she has come to symbolize "Javanese colonialism." (Despite the fact that most rural Acehnese have never been to Java and have limited contact with Javanese, except with transmigrants and the Indonesian military, they have formed very strong antagonistic opinions and stereotypes of "the Javanese.") Kartini is despised by Acehnese men, meanwhile, because she is perceived as not Islamic enough and perhaps, too, because her emancipatory ideals threaten Islamic patriarchy.

Before I turn to an analysis of gendered opposition in East Timor and Aceh, it will be useful first to position the politics of gender within the context of neocolonialism and resistance, examining mechanisms put in place by the state in its attempts to integrate and co-opt the East Timorese and Acehnese into Indonesian state institutions and the national economy.

INDONESIA AS A "NEOCOLONIAL POST-WESTERN COLONIAL STATE": THE CASES OF ACEH AND EAST TIMOR

My analysis of the use of religion as a political tool by the Indonesian state and, at the same time, as a symbol of cohesion by local opposition secular forms of female agency and collective organization. Instead of focusing on secular movements, we should, perhaps, be looking at women's participation in liberation theology and in mosque/Islamic movements.

In both Aceh and East Timor, the Indonesian state uses religion as a political tool in the co-optation of opposition, the criminalization of independence movements, the subversion of trials of the justice system, the exploitation of natural resources, and in many human rights violations (see for example Taylor 1991; Kell 1995). (In another project, I provide a more extended analysis of the parallel patterns of violence under Indonesian neocolonialism in both Aceh and East Timor to demonstrate that these are not the isolated acts of undisciplined soldiers, but a centralized, institutionalized system of terror and surveillance [Siapno 1997].) Sympathetic observers of the Indonesian colonization of East Timor have tended to portray the war in terms of a religious conflict—a Muslim majority suppressing and forcibly integrating a Catholic minority—especially because the independence movement in East Timor has the strong backing of the church and has taken a formation similar to the liberation theology movements in Latin America. In his introduction to *East Timor at the Crossroads: The Forging of a Nation,* Peter Carey writes: "In this oppressive situation, where the very life of the church is threatened by the ubiquitous presence of what seems, to most Timorese, a Muslim military occupation, parishes, especially those run by East Timorese priests, cannot function in the normal sense of Christian Community" (Carey and Bentley 1995, 11).

The religious conflict argument becomes problematic when we turn to Aceh, where a "Muslim military occupation" is oppressing a Muslim community. In this case, we have to look elsewhere for the socio-political, economic, and historical justifications for neocolonialism. In Aceh, as in East Timor, it is the religious leaders, the *ulama,* and religious institutions who present the most formidable opposition to the state and the military.

Benedict Anderson proposed, with regard to the case of East Timor, that twenty years of "modern colonialism," with its rapid pace of economic development, forms of torture, and more elaborate mechanisms for imposing Indonesian cultural hegemony and eliminating dissent, have produced more violence and, as a consequence, a higher degree of consciousness of East Timorese cultural identity than 350 years of "traditional colonialism" under Portuguese rule. He writes:

"What the government did not understand was that its policies were astonishingly similar to those of the later Netherlands-Indies colonial regime and were bound, in the long run, to have parallel consequences. In the two decades between 1900 and 1920, the Dutch educated far more natives than they had done in the three previous centuries of their presence in the archipelago; they systematically invested large sums in 'development', especially in communications, transport, and infrastructure; and they created an elaborate police apparatus for surveillance and repression. Precisely out of the nexus between these transformations was born an Indonesian nationalism that ended Dutch rule in 1949" (Anderson cited in Carey and Bentley 1995, 145).

In the case of Aceh, the feeling of exclusion from the secular, post-independent nation gave a similar impetus to the emergence of a strong nationalist consciousness, a consciousness that finds social cohesion in Islamic identity. In articulating a theoretical framework for the analysis of power and neocolonialism in Indonesia, a comparative study of Aceh and East Timor demonstrates that the pattern of violence in Aceh is not an anomaly but part of a centralized policy. The comparative analysis also casts the "religious conflict" in a different light, presenting religious opposition as an alternative to the secular nation-state. Thus, religious forms of opposition are perhaps the most effective and ubiquitous forms of mass representation and participation in East Timor and Aceh.

GENDER AGENCY IN ACEH AND EAST TIMOR

In contrast to the male nationalist strategy of frontal attack through armed insurgency, female strategies against the Indonesian military have taken a more hidden, non-self-promoting form. As I noted earlier, this silence has often been confused with absence. During meetings I attended, at which Acehnese and East Timorese male nationalists eloquently spoke about historical injustice and rallied for organized resistance to the Indonesian military, women remained silent. For example, on one occasion in Aceh, I was invited by male elite leaders to come to a meeting to speak with some women whose husbands and brothers had been killed by the Indonesian military. The women had gone to the male elite to ask for help in protecting them from further harassment from the military. Throughout most of the evening, the men spoke for and on behalf of the women. In an East Timorese meeting, one outspoken woman defiantly challenged: "We'll start speaking in your meetings when you start cooking the meals for these meetings."

At the same time, according to accounts of the most recent violence in Aceh and East Timor, the worst forms of military repression (referred to by journalists, human rights workers, Acehnese and East Timorese) are those directed toward women: the "kampung janda" or "village of widows" (John Pilger 1995, film), rape by the military (in some cases mass rapes), sexual harassment, and torture. In her interviews with Acehnese women whose husbands had been killed by the military, Kerry Brogan writes, "Two years after his death, some soldiers approached Maya and started sexually harassing her. They asked where her husband was, but she was too scared to reveal that he was dead for fear that this would leave her vulnerable to further harassment from the military . . . She described what happened to her husband without displaying much emotion. But when we asked what life was like for her now, she immediately began to cry, perhaps because the day-to-day hardships are easier to grieve over than the inexplicable death of her husband" (Brogan 1997, 4).

In my interviews with Acehnese and East Timorese women, it was the profound grief and the heavy burden of social, financial, family, and practical responsibilities—in many unquantifiable ways the consequence of political violence—which aroused the strongest emotions. In the negotiations between the Indonesian military and the families of the victims, it is usually women who have the courage and initiative to demand explanations for military atrocities. It is also the women who are forced to come up with strategies to support their children in the event that their husbands are arrested or "disappeared," or extra-judicially executed. Acehnese and East Timorese women think of the Indonesian military as their "special enemy."

Furthermore, one Acehnese woman told me that as a consequence of her husband's murder, she and her children were stigmatized by their community, which feared that any kindness shown toward them would be interpreted by the military as sympathy for the independence movement. She has six young children. In order to protect them from further intimidation by the military, she managed, through the help of relatives, to distribute her children, one by one, to different families all over Aceh, changing their names and identity. Her story shows a common pattern for many of the Acehnese women who were at the meeting I attended. In contemporary Aceh, Acehnese women have been doubly silenced—by political institutions and by the military—but, more trenchantly, by their own male elite leaders who tend to monopolize representation in the name of the struggle for "independence." Thus, while in Aceh and East

Timor, it is predominantly the women who go through the laborious processes of negotiations with human rights lawyers and the military to seek the release of their male kin, many of them go through these struggles silently. While male political prisoners become "heroes" for "insulting the state," the activity and tremendous burden of responsibility, not to mention the suffering, of their wives, sisters, and mothers often goes unacknowledged.

It was, for example, the Acehnese women who initiated the local, national, and international campaigns demanding justice and the end to state violence in Aceh. They demanded meetings with President Habibie, military officials, the press and media, and women's groups in early 1998 for redress of grievances. It was also the women who initiated the formation of voluntary teams to investigate the mass graves and human rights violations in Aceh. They gathered more than 17,000 volunteers from different sectors of society.

In a recent conference on East Timor, a representative of the Women's Organization, "Organizacao da Mulher Timor" (OMT), based in East Timor, presented a historical analysis of the women's movement, state violence, and the struggle for independence, detailing some of the most critical issues that need to be addressed as a consequence of armed conflict: "As women are a specific group of war victims, in July 1997, a forum for communication among women was formed by a group of women activists. This forum was established because there is no institution that takes care of women victims or acts to improve the conditions of women. The forum is concerned with:

1. war widows
2. women prisoners and ex-prisoners
3. women who have been victims of rape and
4. wives of political prisoners (FITUN 1998, 6)."

A different kind of example of the ambiguous articulation of female agency, which breaks from conventional narratives of female victimization, has to do with women whose husbands are in prison. In conventional human rights reports we are given testimonies of wives who faithfully struggle for the release of their husbands from prison. I was surprised when I met women who did not occupy the role of "suffering wife." In the beginning of my fieldwork, I interviewed an Acehnese woman whose husband had been in prison for three years. He was accused of secretly providing funds to Aceh Merdeka and sentenced to thirteen years in prison under the subversion law. When I asked his wife, "Do you miss him?," she gave a most unexpected reply: "No, it is better when he's in prison because I have freedom. I have freedom to do whatever I want—to see my friends, go *mengaji* (reading the Qur'an)—without having to worry about being home before he gets home. When he gets out of prison, I go back to my old life. I won't be able to go out much. He never took me with him when he went out." (Interview with an Acehnese woman, now a widow, of a very prominent Acehnese political prisoner, 1996).

Before I met this woman, it had never occurred to me that a wife might not necessarily suffer while her husband was imprisoned for "subversion." On the contrary, she might benefit from it: what is freedom for him means imprisonment for her. His imprisonment grants her freedom. Like other women in political movements for independence where women's participation is marginalized, Acehnese women tend to have a profoundly cynical, if not contemptuous attitude towards Aceh Merdeka male leaders who claim to be struggling for democracy but who, in fact, do not practice democratic values in their own homes.

THE PRODUCTION OF "EXCELLENT HOUSEWIVES" AND DOMESTICATED WOMEN THROUGH PKK

The culture of servility imposed under the New Order, through "Javanization," has enormous implications for issues of identity, cultural nationalism, and class formation all the way down to a level that might initially be considered trivial, such as clothes. The Indonesian "national dress" for women, for example, is the Javanese *sarung* and *kebaya*, which emphasize femininity and are designed for demureness and immobility. This is in sharp contrast to traditional Acehnese female clothing, a pair of trousers called "*luweu tham asèe*" (dog-chasing trousers), which enables women, not only to be mobile, but to be able to chase dogs, something that cannot be done in a sarung and kebaya. Women's clothes may seem to be a minor issue, but it is in this arena that the production of a "national Indonesian woman," and, by extension, Indonesian national identity, is strongly articulated. When I attended the graduation ceremony of young women friends who had just finished their undergraduate degree at the Universitas Syiah Kuala in Banda Aceh, I was struck by the uniformity of their clothes, given that Aceh is known for its ethnic diversity in clothing.

Even though they wore different colors and types of textiles, they were required to wear one thing—the Javanese sarung and kebaya. By contrast, Acehnese men are required to wear, not Javanese dress, but Western dress: coat and tie, white shirt and black pants. I also noted that during official government functions, Acehnese men tend to wear Acehnese traditional clothing (*topi meunkutop* and *bajèe hitam*). In terms of clothing, then, it is the woman's body that becomes the vessel for the symbolization of an Indonesian national identity.

The central government also exercises its power through the PKK. The *Pendidikan Kesejahteraan Keluarga (PKK)*, literally meaning "Family Welfare Guidance," is a national program implemented down to the lowest-levels of Indonesian society. Families and communities in Acehnese villages are given explicit direction on how to build healthy, happy families. When I lived in West Aceh (Aceh Barat), I was able to observe KKN (*Kuliah Kerja Nyata*) university students from Banda Aceh attempt to implement the PKK Program in rural villages. The Universitas Syiah Kuala decided to send 1,300 undergraduate students to that regency, considered to be one of the poorest and most "backward" regencies in Aceh. The purpose of the KKN program was twofold: to expose urban university students to the poorest rural villages in Aceh and to have the students help implement state development programs such as PKK and urban ideas about development. Thus the university system and the KKN program in Aceh are not autonomous, but are used as an extended arm of the government in implementing state ideology. The students arrived with all kinds of ideas—building a community center, for example—but never asked the people of the village for their input. When the students leave such a situation, it is "as if it never happened" (Chiangkun 1985).

The monolithic conception of the household imposed through such programs as PKK is very different from existing conceptions of household in rural Aceh. The practice of giving the parent's home to the daughters produces communities in which the owners of houses and land are women, their sisters, and female related kin. In his analysis of household relations in Aceh, James Siegel writes: "Every married woman owned her own house and the land on which it stood, provided she had been *geumeklèh* from her parents. No men owned houses. If parents had no daughters, their house was sold, following the death of the second parent, and their sons divided the proceeds" (Siegel 1969, 141). Thus Acehnese find PKK values limiting, to say the least. Training women to become good "housewives" is profoundly contradictory to matrifocal values, which greatly transcend the subordinate and subordinated role of house-wife.

CONCLUDING REMARKS

In this essay, I explored the "problem" of women's peripheralization and relative absence in the nationalist movements in East Timor and Aceh, despite the vigorous efforts of male nationalists to enlist them. I argued that if we limited our analysis to membership in national collectivities and active participation in national struggles, then, at best, we would come up with women playing the lowly role of "maidservants" and "helpmates" to nationalism and male nationalists. Indeed, women in Aceh and East Timor have a long history of fierce independence of spirit and a long genealogy of powerful female ancestors, in addition to the more contemporary insurgent articulations of female agency and power on all fronts, including many outside the discursive space of nationalism. Limiting our analysis to the nation-state and to the realm of modern politics and organized movements would render them "absent" or "silent"—because that is not where they have staked their claims.

On the contrary, they seem to have a profoundly ambivalent, if not suspicious, attitude towards these predominantly male, hierarchical or urban-based organizations. It is not my place to make a judgment about whether or not this is a good thing, or to romanticize female peripheralization in national politics, for if women are marginalized in the process of nation-building, then the emergent nation-state will remain, as McClintock argues, "a repository of male hopes, male aspirations, and male privilege" (McClintock 1995, 385). Yet as someone who has strong and longstanding personal commitments to helping in every possible way in the struggle for social justice in these two regions, especially in the field of girls' and women's education, I would argue that it is indeed crucial to advocate women's participation at all levels and on all fronts, and to have a broad, inclusive definition of "feminism." However, my main contention is that it is arrogant to begin from the assumption (an unspoken, but pervasive assumption among urban cosmopolitan feminists) that women in Aceh and East Timor are somehow "backward" (*kampungan*) because they have shown very little interest in joining "modern," NGO-type, progressivist, political organizations (whether feminist, nationalist, or leftist). Indeed, as Abu-Lughod argues, we shouldn't romanticize the emancipatory possibilities of modernity and modernization theory, but be suspicious "about the way modernity is so easily equated with the progress, emancipation, and empowerment of women . . ." We should also ask "not just what new possibilities but what hidden costs, unanticipated constraints, novel forms of discipline and regulation, and unintended consequences accompanied such programs" (Abu-Lughod 1998, vi).

> *A luta continua em todas as frentes. (The struggle continues on all fronts.)*

ACKNOWLEDGMENTS

My research in Indonesia, Aceh, and East Timor in 1992 and 1993 were funded by grants from the Luce Grant's-in-Aid at UC Berkeley and the SSRC Pre-Dissertation Fellowship. The dissertation fieldwork for twelve months in 1996, from which most of the data in this article is based, was funded by SSRC and the American Council of Learned Societies Dissertation Fellowship. In Indonesia, my research project was sponsored by *Lembaga Ilmu Pengetahuan Indonesia* (Indonesian Institute of Sciences) and the *Majelis Ulama Indonesia/Aceh*. The people I have met in Aceh, East Timor, and Indonesia have taught me a lot. They are, without doubt, the kindest, warmest people I've ever met and, despite overwhelming military and political odds, have not lost hope that they will be free some day. This essay is dedicated to my family of real friends, my home in the world in Aceh, East Timor, and Indonesia, who continue to struggle for justice with remarkable integrity and courage in the face of so much violence. I also wish to thank the members of the residential seminar "Gender and Citizenship in Muslim Communities" at the Humanities Research Institute at the University of California, Irvine, who not only gave me critical insights into the contradictions between feminism and nationalism, but offered comfort, friendship, and inspiration.

REFERENCES

Abu-Lughod, Lila, ed. 1998. *Remaking Women: Feminism and Modernity in the Middle East*. Princeton: Princeton University Press.

Aditjondro, George. 1999. "Women as Victims versus Women as Fighters: Redressing the Asymmetrical Focus of the East Timorese Activists' Discourse." Paper presented to the Conference on "East Timorese Women and International Law," 20–24 January 1999 in the Portuguese Parliament Building, organized by the Associacao Portuguesa de Mulheres Juristas and the International Platform of Jurists for East Timor, Lisbon, Portugal.

Al, Chaidar, Sayed Mudhahar Ahmad, and Yarmen Dinamika. 1998. *Aceh Bersimbah Darah: Mengungkap Penerapan Status Daerah Operasi Militer (DOM) di Aceh, 1989-1998.* Jakarta: Pustaka Al-Kautsar.

Amnesty International. 1995. *Women in Indonesia and East Timor: Standing Against Repression.* London: International Secretariat.

Anderson, Benedict. 1977. "Millenarianism and the Saminist Movement." In *Religion and Social Ethos in Indonesia,* edited by Mitsuo Nakamura, Mohamed Slamet, and Benedict Anderson. Clayton, Victoria: Monash University Press.

————. 1983. *Imagined Communities: Reflections on the Origin and Spread of Nationalism.* London and New York: Verso.

————. 1998. *The Spectre of Comparisons: Nationalism, Southeast Asia and the World.* London and New York: Verso.

Balibar, Etienne and Immanuel Wallerstein. 1991. *Race, Nation, Class: Ambiguous Identities.* London and New York: Verso.

Bianpoen, Carla. 1999. "Reflections on International Women's Day: Indonesia's Women are Moving Ahead," *The Indonesian Observer,* 8 March 1999.

Brogan, Kerry. 1997. "The Forgotten Costs of Counter-Insurgency in Aceh," *Inside Indonesia.* March 1997.

Carey, Peter and G. Carter Bentley, eds. 1995. *East Timor at the Crossroads: The Forging of a Nation.* New York and London: Cassell and the Social Science Research Council.

Chatterjee, Partha. 1986. *Nationalist Thought and the Colonial World: A Derivative Discourse?* London: Zed Books.

————. 1993. *The Nation and Its Fragments: Colonial and Postcolonial Histories.* Princeton: Princeton University Press.

Chiangkun, Witthayakon. 1985. "As if It Had Never Happened," (A short story). In *The Mirror: Literature and Politics in Siam in the American Era,* edited by Benedict Anderson and Ruchira Mendiones. Bangkok: Editions Duang Kamol.

D & R. 1998. "Focus: Resistensi Perempuan Aceh." 31 January 1998, 44–51.

de Araujo, Fernando (Secretary-General of Resistencia Nacional dos Estudantes de Timor-Leste). 1992. "Mengapa dan Untuk Apa Aku Berjuang." Defense Statement (Pleidooi) to Indonesian Court. Pengadilan Negeri Jakarta Pusat.

————. 1998. "The Similarity of East Timor and Aceh under Soeharto/ABRI Dictatorship." Paper presented to conference on "Years of Living Dangerously: The Struggle for Justice in Aceh, Indonesia Beyond Soeharto," at New York University, 12 December 1998.

de Oliveira, Ivete. 1998. "Kekerasan Negara Terhadap Perempuan TimTim." Manuscript circulated through the Internet.

Elliston, Deborah A. 1999. "Geographies of Gender and Politics: The Place of Difference in Polynesian Nationalism." Public presentation, Department of Women's Studies, at University of California, Irvine, 18 February 1999.

Enloe, Cynthia. 1989. *Bananas, Beaches and Bases: Making Feminist Sense of International Politics.* Berkeley and Los Angeles: University of California Press.

Guha, Ranajit and Gayatri Spivak, eds. 1988. *Selected Subaltern Studies.* New York: Oxford University Press.

Gusmao, Jose Alexandre Xanana (Commander of CNRT-FALINTIL). 1995. *Timor-Leste: Um Povo, Uma Patria.* Lisboa: Edicoes Colibri.

————. 1998. "Interview with MATRA," *MATRA Magazine.* Jakarta. December 1998,16–26.

————. 1999. *"Mensagem do Ano Novo."* Document circulated through the Internet.

Hamzah, Jafar Siddiq. 1998. "Political Violence in Aceh." Testimony to the House Committee on International Affairs, Subcommittee on International Operations and Human Rights, 7 May 1998, Washington, D.C.

Husarska, Anna. 1999. "Bitter Lessons for Kosovo, East Timor," *Los Angeles Times,* 11 February 1999, B11.

Ileto, Reynaldo. 1988. "Outlines of a Non-Linear Emplotment of Philippine History." In *Reflections on Development in Southeast Asia,* edited by Lim Teck Ghee. Singapore: Institute of Southeast Asian Studies.

Jayawardena, Kumari. 1986. *Feminism and Nationalism in the Third World.* London: Zed Press.

Kell, Timothy. 1995. *The Roots of the Acehnese Rebellion, 1989–1992.* Ithaca: Cornell Modern Indonesia Project, No. 74.

McClintock, Anne. 1995. "No Longer in a Future Heaven: Nationalism, Gender and Race." In *Imperial Leather: Race, Gender and Sexuality in the Colonial Contest.* New York and London: Routledge.

Mernissi, Fatima. 1993. *The Forgotten Queens of Islam.* Minneapolis: University of Minnesota Press.

Mohanty, Chandra, Ann Russo, and Lourdes Torres, eds. 1991. *Third World Women and the Politics of Feminism.* Bloomington: Indiana University Press.

Organizacao de Mulher Timor (OMT). 1998. "A Chronology of East Timorese Women's Lives," in *FITUN: A Bulletin of East Timor from Praxis,* 17, 3–6, October.

Parker, Andrew, Mary Russo, Doris Sommer, Patricia Yaeger, eds. 1992. *Nationalisms and Sexualities.* New York: Routledge.

Pilger, John. 1995. *Death of a Nation: The Timor Conspiracy.* Film. Film for the Humanities and Sciences. Box 2053, Princeton, New Jersey 08543-2053.

Reid, Anthony. 1988. "Female Roles in Pre-Colonial Southeast Asia," *Modern Asian Studies* 22, 3.

Saad, Hasballah M. 1998. "Pelanggaran Hak Azasi Manusia di Aceh (Selama Berlakunya DOM 1989–1998)." Paper presented to the Seminar on "Democratization in Indonesia and the Question of East Timor," at Universitas Paramadia Mulya, Jakarta, 30 Nov.–1 Dec. 1998.

Sears, Laurie, ed. 1996. *Fantasizing the Feminine in Indonesia*. Durham: Duke University Press.

Setiyardi, Mustafa Ismail, Zainal Bakri. 1999. "Tragedi Lhokseumawe dan Referendum," in *Tempo*, 25 January 1999.

Siapno, Jacqueline A. 1994. "Gender Relations and Islamic Resurgence in Mindanao, Southern Philippines." In *Muslim Women's Choices: Religious Belief and Social Reality*, edited by Camillia Fawzi El-Solh and Judy Mabro. Oxford: Berg Publishers.

———. 1995. "Alternative Filipina Heroines: Contested Tropes in Leftist Feminisms." In *Bewitching Women, Pious Men: Gender and Body Politics in Southeast Asia*, edited by Aihwa Ong and Michael Peletz. Berkeley and Los Angeles: University of California Press.

———. 1997. *The Politics of Gender, Islam and Nation-State in Aceh, Indonesia: A Historical Analysis of Power, Co-optation and Resistance*. Ph.D. diss. University of California, Berkeley. Published by University Microfilms International.

Siegel, James. 1969. *The Rope of God*. Berkeley and Los Angeles: University of California Press.

Spivak, Gayatri. 1988. "Can the Subaltern Speak?" In *Marxism and the Interpretation of Culture*. Chicago: University of Illinois Press.

Steenbrink, Karel. 1993. *Dutch Colonialism and Indonesian Islam: Contacts and Conflicts, 1596-1950*. Amsterdam and Atlanta: Rodopi.

Syam, Fatimah. 1998. Personal Communication.

Tanner, Nancy. 1974. "Matrifocality in Indonesia, Africa and Among Black Americans." In *Woman, Culture and Society*, edited by Michelle Rosaldo and Louise Lamphere. Stanford: Stanford University Press.

Taylor, John. 1991. *Indonesia's Forgotten War: The Hidden History of East Timor*. London: Zed Books.

Tiwon, Sylvia. 1996. "Models and Maniacs: Articulating the Female in Indonesia." In *Fantasizing the Feminine in Indonesia*, edited by Laurie Sears. Durham: Duke University Press.

———. forthcoming. "Reconstructing Boundaries and Beyond." In *Reconstructing Conceptions of the Household in Indonesia*, edited by Ratna Saptari. Leiden, The Netherlands.

Traube, Elizabeth G. 1986. *Cosmology and Social Life: Ritual Exchange among the Mambai of East Timor*. Chicago and London: The University of Chicago Press.

Wieringa, Saskia. 1995. *The Politicization of Gender Relations in Indonesia: The Indonesian Women's Movement and Gerwani Until the New Order State*. Ph.D. Dissertation, University of Amsterdam.

Yuval-Davis, Nira and Floya Anthias, eds. 1989. *Women-Nation-State*. London: Macmillan.

CHAPTER 22

Maria Stewart, Black Abolitionist, and the Idea of Freedom

JENNIFER RYCENGA

The bold, dramatic figure of Antigone has inspired radical women across the ages by her (fictional) defiance of arbitrary state power. The similarly bold Maria Stewart[1] (1803–1879) is less well-known, despite her real-life achievements. Even when her place as the first American-born woman to give a public speech to a mixed audience of men and women is acknowledged, the full and dangerous revolutionary context into which she emerged, and which she helped shape, is often overlooked. So while many worlds separate Sophocles' Antigone from the work and thought of Maria Stewart, what connects them is vital to feminist revolutionary philosophy.

Both the retelling of Antigone's defiance of Creon and Stewart's daring female voice condemning slavery, sexism, and racism, were enunciated in key post-battle moments. For Antigone this came after the battle for Thebes, while for Stewart it occurred in 1831, in the first month after Nat Turner's nearly successful slave rebellion had been quashed by the Virginia militia. Because they were in a "frontline" situation, they each risked their own safety by taking action. They also had to take action in a way that was integral to thought; most crucially, by indicating how they related to the violence that preceded their speaking. Here again, they share a perspective: Antigone and Stewart refused to condemn violence, but also didn't engage in it themselves. Instead they transformed the abstraction of metaphysical realms—the divine or the gods—into the realm of their own action.

What I want to do by bringing these two figures into dialogue with each other is to follow a dialectic of revolutionary feminism and humanism. There is a significant political contrast between them, which elucidates questions faced by feminists today. Stewart transcends Antigone both by *surviving*, and by pushing the work of her slain "brothers" forward. I will examine the contradictions in Antigone's stance, which leave her merely effecting ritual closure, by drawing on Hegel's treatment of Sophocles' play in the *Phenomenology of Mind*. I will explore central dimensions of Stewart's historical setting, then demonstrate the complexities of Stewart's thought through her 1831 essay "Religion and the Pure Principles of Morality."

HEGEL AND ANTIGONE

My suggestion that Sophocles' representation of Antigone unites activity and thought is indebted to the strengths and weaknesses of Hegel's reading of Antigone in *The Phenomenology of Mind*. Hegel's Antigone surfaces in his discussion of the dialectics of ethical order, a section that contains a substantial amount of explicit sexism in its descriptions of the family and in sexist dichotomies based metaphorically in the opposition of male and female. But despite this unpromising setting, Hegel's analysis of Antigone illumines both her ethical glory and the limitations of her response to conflict.

In Sophocles' play, Antigone's two brothers, Etiocles and Polynices, are struggling over their late father Oedipus' throne. Etiocles has been reigning as king, but reneges on his promise to alternate years on the throne with Polynices, who gathers a military force to challenge his brother. In the ensuing war, the two brothers slay each other in battle. The new king, their uncle Creon, proclaims his first official act: honoring his predecessor Etiocles with full state honors in burial, while insisting that Polynices' corpse remain unburied, "left to be eaten by dogs and vultures, a horror for all to see" (Sophocles, 131). Knowing the ordinance, Antigone manifestly and obviously attempts to bury Polynices; she is arrested and condemned to death. In defense of her actions, she cites higher, divine laws, which she believes override arbitrary human laws, and defies Creon to his face:

> (Your) order did not come from God. Justice, that dwells with the gods below, knows no such law. I did not think your edicts strong enough to overrule the unwritten unalterable laws of God and heaven, you being only a man (Sophocles, 138).

Not surprisingly, the play has been a touchstone for those who oppose injustice and the inflated self-importance of the state.[2]

Hegel's analysis of the conflict between Antigone and Creon betrays his deep ambivalence toward Antigone. He begins his examination with Antigone representing the lower world—nature and the realm of the family—while Creon stands for the emerging social structure of the city, a "higher" world of culture. Given Hegel's confidence in historical advance, both György Lukács and the American Marxist-humanist philosopher Raya Dunayevskaya note that "Hegel should certainly have been against Antigone . . . But he isn't" (Dunayevskaya 1977). Hegel cannot suppress his admiration for Antigone. He sees that Creon and Antigone are equals, and their contradiction—in which each has aligned her/himself rather inflexibly with what s/he feels is the ultimate law—is an evenly matched battle, which marks the end of a historical period, rather than a fully new stage of history (Hegel 1807, 492).[3]

Thus, detailing the conflict between Creon and Antigone, Hegel characterizes it as

> an unfortunate collision of duty merely with reality . . . the ethical consciousness . . . at once proceeds either to subdue by force this reality opposed to the law which *it* accepts, or to get round this reality by craft. Since it sees right *only* on its side, and wrong on the other, so, of these two, that which belongs to divine law detects, on the other side, mere arbitrary fortuitous human violence, while what appertains to human law finds in the other the obstinacy and disobedience of *subjective self-sufficiency*" (Hegel 1807, 486, emphasis added).

Antigone and Creon, representing the principles—divine law versus human law—are irreconcilable, and each is stoutly resolute in her/his own self-contained totality. Each is so secure in self-righteousness that force or subterfuge will be used to achieve what they see as ethical. While Hegel clearly sides with the objectivity of human law, because its meaning is "open to the light of day" (Hegel 1807, 486), both sides are indicted by their equally bullheaded single-mindedness. Furthermore, this mutual obstinacy is seen to be symbiotic, resulting in a dialectic dead end. This finds expression in the mutual destruction that occurs to them once each side has taken action (Hegel 1807, 492). The abstract absolutes of each protagonist's chosen ethical system break down in the exercise of individuality in action: once you act, you are guilty of breaking some one's law.

Hegel also gives an elaborate justification of Antigone's famous speech claiming that a brother means more to her than a parent or a husband and children (see Sophocles, 150). Hegel lays out three family relations: husband and wife, parent and child, and brother and sister (Hegel 1807, 474–476). The first two relations are structurally unstable because they are fundamentally transient: their power relations change over time. But the brother/sister relation he sees as stable, devoid of sexual tension. While Hegel is patently wrong in this assumption of asexuality between siblings, what he is trying to do here dialectically is important to grasp: he is searching for a relationship between men and women which has some mutuality and equality in its very structure.[4] As Dunayevskaya says, elevating the sibling relationship, as Hegel does, because of a perceived equivalence, has some feminist resonance, since its underlying logic is that a brother, being on "the same level as you . . . brings out the greatness in both of you" (Dunayevskaya 1977).

Feminist scholars have been impatient with the masculinist dichotomies that Hegel employs in this section of the *Phenomenology*. There have been elaborate discussions of this as the nadir of his views on women. Patricia Mills has been especially prolific in her deconstruction of Hegel's Antigone, claiming it ignores relations between women (Antigone-Ismene), and silences the individual initiative of Antigone's actions (Mills 1996, 75–77). But when she maintains that "Hegel's dialectical theory becomes a closed system," which "always meant domination," I feel she has missed the creativity of subject in Hegelian dialectics (Mills 1996, 84). My approach, as a Marxist-humanist, will be to discover the dialectic of Hegel's Antigone as it is expanded *outside* of the texts, in the "untidy affirmation" of gritty reality.[5] Action is louder than fiction.

For this purpose, there shines the luminescent example of Maria Stewart, standing between her two brother-comrades: David Walker and Nat Turner:

> The act . . . is the realized self. It breaks in upon the untroubled stable organization and movement of the ethical world. . . . It becomes the process of negation, . . . which engulfs in the abyss of its bare identity divine and human law alike (Hegel 1807, 484).

Maria Stewart's action was decisive, self-activated, and innovative, beginning with the simple act of speaking *at all*.

MARIA STEWART: BIOGRAPHICAL AND HISTORICAL CONTEXT

Maria Stewart is best remembered as the first recorded American-born woman to give a public speech in the United States. She addressed a "promiscuous audience" of male and female, Black and white, in Boston's Franklin Hall, on 21 September 1832. That she was a free Black woman, a widow, and effectively penniless at that time, makes this historical achievement even more impressive.

Maria Stewart was born a free Black woman in 1803; after being orphaned at a young age, she was raised in a clergyman's family (Houchins 1988, 3–4; Richardson 1987, 28–29).[6] She was a domestic worker from the age of fifteen until her marriage. She was part of a small Black community in Boston (less than two thousand people) in the 1820s.[7] Her husband, James, worked as a ship's outfitter—this fact, and the religious beliefs of the couple, apparently brought them into contact with a used clothing store merchant, the Black Abolitionist author, David Walker.

In 1829, filled with anger at slavery and emboldened by revolutionary developments around the globe, David Walker had issued his *Appeal to the Coloured Citizens of the World*. This stirring pamphlet, exhorting in the tone of a Hebrew prophet, indicted slaveholding white America in no uncertain terms. The pamphlet reached Southern ports, possibly with the collaboration of people like James Stewart who may have sewn it into the pockets of Black sailors.[8] Once the pamphlet started circulating widely, the contagious force of the "idea of freedom" sparked a countering horde of tyrannical responses:

> The governor of North Carolina denounced it as 'an open appeal to their [the slaves'] natural love of liberty . . . expressing sentiments totally subversive of all subordination in our slaves'; the mayor of Savannah wrote to the mayor of Boston requesting that Walker be arrested and punished, and Richmond's mayor reported that several copies of *Walker's Appeal* had been found in the possession of local free Negroes; the governors of Georgia and North Carolina submitted the pamphlet to their state legislatures for appropriate action; and the Virginia legislature held secret sessions to consider proper measures to prevent the pamphlet's circulation. Finally, four southern states—Georgia, North Carolina, Mississippi, and Louisiana—seized upon the pamphlet to enact severe restrictions to cope with such 'seditious' propaganda (Litwack 1961, 234).[9]

The laws strengthening prohibitions against black literacy were especially insidious, including free blacks as well as slaves.[10]

Following the publication of Walker's *Appeal*, a rapid sequence of tragedies struck Maria Stewart. First, her husband, James, died in December of 1829, then David Walker himself died under mysterious circumstances—many at the time believed he had been poisoned—in June of 1830.[11] Greedy, dishonest white lawyers compounded Stewart's sorrows by cheating her of her late husband's estate.[12]

1831 is, by any account, a pivotal year in abolitionist history. William Lloyd Garrison commenced publication of his newspaper, the *Liberator*, in Boston, while in the South, in explicit response to Walker's pamphlet, harsh laws were passed, as noted above. But the event that proved to be the greatest catalyst was Nat Turner's slave revolt in Southampton, Virginia. Turner's mixture of religious vision, jeremianic prophecy, and keen military strategies combined to make this rebellion a near success.[13] However, his forces were defeated, and he went into hiding for two months, from late August to late October, when he was captured. After a sham trial, at which Turner neither denied his actions nor pled guilty since, as he said, he did not believe his actions were guilty ones, he was condemned and executed in early November.

With this setting in mind, Maria Stewart's multivalent relation to battle becomes clear. In the first days of October, while Nat Turner was still on the lam, and the young Abolitionist movement was divided on how to respond, Maria Stewart walked into the offices of Garrison's *Liberator* with her manuscript entitled "Religion and the Pure Principles of Morality, the Sure Foundation on Which We Must Build." Less than two years after her husband's death, and a year past Walker's, Stewart found her voice, and the sound of liberation modulated to a new feminist key.

MARIA STEWART'S NEW VOICE: PHILOSOPHIC THEMES

While many Southerners blamed Walker's pamphlet for inciting Turner's rebellion, Walker had always retained an interesting ambivalence on the question of violence: it is not clear whether he is calling for slave insurrections, or if he is simply predicting their inevitability. As Stewart will later do, Walker plays on two themes in relation to destruction of the given order. The first is religious: that God will wreak vengeance on the unjust. But God cannot do this without agents of his will. For instance, one passage from the *Appeal* says:

> O Americans! Americans!! I call God—I call angels—I call men, to witness, that your DESTRUCTION *is at hand*, and will be speedily consummated unless you REPENT (Walker 1965a, 108, his emphasis).

It is left unclear whether God, angels, and men are mere *witnesses* or operative *agents* in the destruction of the slavocracy.

The second theme of resistance that Walker, Garrison, and Stewart all draw from is the example of the American Revolution itself. Walker quoted extensively from the Declaration of Independence, then warned white America that their sufferings under the British crown were not "one hundredth part as cruel and tyrannical as you have rendered ours under you" (Walker 1965a, 143). Walker, and his "student" Maria Stewart, stress the ongoing development of history. Their sense of history resonated in Boston, where the American Revolution was still alive in memory and memorials, and they did not hesitate to relate this to revolutionary movements around the globe. But there was a larger temporal narrative for Walker's and Stewart's thought: the biblical God's actions in history.

Up to 1831, most white opposition to slavery had come from pacifist Quakers and Mennonites who totally renounced violence. Some of them reluctantly acknowledged the righteousness of Walker's anger, but almost all of them, including William Lloyd Garrison, hedged on supporting the entire document. While there was communication between antislavery forces in the North and slaves in the South, the veritable tyranny imposed on the activity of the slaves in the South dictated a vast gap between the strategies of Walker and Nat Turner. Turner's revolt was qualitatively different from Walker's pamphlet, since its violence was patent: the revolt resulted in the loss of about sixty white lives and over two hundred black lives. For the fledgling Abolitionist movement, Turner's revolt posed a strategic trap. To support Turner unconditionally could be seen as incitement. To condemn Turner wholesale would be to play into the hands of the racist ideologies that described Blacks as savages and animals.

It is at this moment that Maria Stewart arrived, with a new voice—that of a Black woman who refused to condemn either of her brothers—Turner or Walker. Her remarkable writing of 1831 *is* the dialectic moving: instead of burying her brothers, she extends their work. There are three crucial dimensions to highlight from the essay that Garrison published in the *Liberator*. First, Stewart consciously and precisely adopts the authoritative voice of a religious prophet. In this capacity she

uses biblical texts in quite creative ways. Second, Stewart must tread a
fine line concerning the safety of her people, herself, and the advocates
of abolition. To achieve this, she both sincerely affirms her Christian religion and uses it as a *code;* like Walker before her, she "veiled (her) call to
arms in millenialist language" (Sernett 1985, 188). Third, her sense of
the inevitability of Black freedom is not limited to the end of slavery. She
is keenly aware that the debilitating effects of Northern racism are part of
the same system that produced the slavocracy; she recognizes that totally
transformed human relations are needed, not merely tepid reforms.[14]

When word of Nat Turner's uprising reached Boston in the first days
of September, city Blacks proclaimed a day of "humiliation and prayer"
and begged God for "the prolonged life of all strenuous advocates for the
cause of the bleeding sons of Africa" (Turner 1999, 37).[15] Despite his
Quaker misgivings about violence, Garrison's response to the rebellion,
printed in the *Liberator* in early September, suggests that he understood
what motivated Turner:

> Ye accuse the pacific friends of emancipation of instigating the slaves
> to revolt. Take back the charge as a foul slander. The slaves need no in-
> centives at our hands. They will find them in their stripes—their emaci-
> ated bodies—in their ceaseless toil—in their ignorant minds—in every
> field, in every valley, on every hill-top and mountain, wherever you and
> your fathers have fought for liberty—in your speeches, your conversa-
> tions, your celebrations, your pamphlets, your newspapers—voices in
> the air, sounds from across the ocean, invitations to resistance above,
> below, around them! What more do they need? Surrounded by such in-
> fluences, and smarting under their newly made wounds, is it wonderful
> that they should rise to contend—as other 'heroes' have contended—
> for their lost rights? It is *not* wonderful (Nelson 1966, 30, emphasis
> Garrison).

While it cannot be proved that Stewart was at the city prayer day, or that
she read that particular issue of the *Liberator*, it seems highly likely that
she did.[16] So she would not have brought her essay to Garrison's office *if*
she intended to simply condemn Turner's action.

Furthermore, far from condemning righteous acts of violence
against oppression, Stewart, following Walker, uses the American Revolution as "a model from which . . . blacks as well as whites were entitled
to draw inspiration" (Richardson 1987, 17).[17] She pointedly compares
the situation of the slaves to a reconquest of the United States by Great

Britain, and then reapplies the logic of the American Revolution to Black women:

> Possess the spirit of independence. The Americans do, and why should not you? Possess the spirit of men, bold and enterprising, fearless and undaunted. Sue for your rights and privileges. Know the reason that you cannot attain them. Weary them with your importunities. You can but die if you make the attempt; and we shall certainly die if you do not (Houchins 1988, 17; Richardson 1987, 38).

Stewart is calling on Black women to pursue freedom unendingly, at all costs. It is not accidental that this appears in this first essay, when Stewart is standing between her two late brothers, Walker and Turner. The need for women to speak, to act, and to think ("*know* the reason . . .") is made manifest by Stewart's breaking silence. Seventeen years before the Seneca Falls Women's Rights Convention would compose its Declaration of Sentiments as a literal gloss on the Declaration of Independence, Stewart uncovered the relevance of the American Revolution to the liberation of women.

MARIA STEWART IN HER RELIGIOUS CONTEXT

As a deeply religious woman, who had recently undergone a full "conversion" experience of the type common during the Second Great Awakening, Stewart uses biblical language and allusions with ease. With its claim of equal access to divine power for each individual, the Second Great Awakening had unintended social consequences: it fueled the rhetoric of political struggle for equality on the basis of gender and race, as even a cursory glance at the documents of Seneca Falls or the American Anti-Slavery Society demonstrates. Stewart speaks with spiritual authority, rebuking the evil and exhorting the downtrodden to an unending self-development.

America, during the Second Great Awakening, was in the midst of a millennial fever, which could seem alternatively ironic or properly apocalyptic to Blacks. As Albert Raboteau points out concerning Stewart's context:

> Her words were addressed to an America that projected itself as the probable site of the coming Millennium. . . . From the perspective of slaves, and of free blacks like Maria Stewart, America was Egypt, and

as long as she continued to enslave and oppress Black Israel, her destiny was in jeopardy. America stood under the judgment of God, and unless she repented, the death and destruction visited upon biblical Egypt would be repeated here (Raboteau 1994, 12).

The centrality of the exodus narrative in the religious creativity of Blacks, both North and South, is well-known. Stewart unhesitatingly drew from the Book of Revelation, to which "she unfailingly returned as to a *cantus firmus* to sustain all of her melismatic flights . . . (finding) its emphasis on the written word, on didactic prophecy, and on the cataclysmic destruction of the forces of evil" to be a source of "justification for what secular authorities might well have considered inciting to riot" (Richardson 1987, 17–18). Equally incredible is her self-identity, as a woman, with the prophetic voice, in particular her echoes of Jeremiah.

Her adoption of Jeremiah's role is politically charged, since Jeremiah lived in a time of political disaster, when Judah fell to invaders, leading to the Babylonian captivity of the Jews. Jeremiah had prophesied this calamity, based on perceived national backsliding from God's ways. He was also a prophet who stressed his own personal loneliness and persecution. But for all his calling attention to the individual, it is very much to the larger community within where his concern rests. The one area where the prophet is unremittingly alone is in his calling: he is chosen directly by God and cannot refuse this vocation (Jer. 1:4–10). In this calling, there is a specific dual movement of destruction and creation: " I have this day set thee over the nations and over the kingdoms, to root out, and to pull down, and to destroy, and to throw down, to build, and to plant" (Jer. 1:10).

More crucially, given Stewart's context, is that the Book of Jeremiah served the Abolitionists with some of the strongest biblical texts against slavery.[18] In one passage (Jer. 34:8–22), the treachery of slave owners is detailed. During a siege, the slave owners had decided to follow a long-ignored biblical injunction to release their slaves after an allotted time; this most likely served their self-interest in a time of crisis. But once the siege was lifted, the slave owners reneged on the agreement and re-enslaved their fellows. Jeremiah is livid at their hypocrisy:

> thus saith the Lord; Ye have not hearkened unto me, in proclaiming liberty, every one to his brother, and every man to his neighbor; behold, I proclaim a liberty for you, saith the Lord, to the sword, to the pestilence, and to the famine; and I will make you to be removed into all the kingdoms of the earth. (Jer. 34:17)[19]

Stewart was not alone in finding Jeremiah a kindred spirit; but what makes Stewart's use of him unique is twofold: her certainty of being similarly called by God, and the fact that she is a woman thus called.

Self-authorizing power was almost the only kind available to Blacks and women. While the Black church had myriad institutional forms in the North, it is worth noting that Walker and Stewart (like Turner), lacked official credentials as preachers.

> The most radical black preachers were unconcerned about conforming to the expectations of white society. God, they felt, had called them and no one but God himself could revoke that call. . . . The best example . . . is the famous Nat Turner. *No church authorized him to preach* (Sernett 1975, 99, emphasis added).

When this lack of external authorization is perceived as subversive when coming from Black men, how much more is it transmuted when it is in the voice of a Black woman? Stewart's speaking functions as a creation of context, rather than a mere intervention into what exists. As Sue Houchins surmises, self-confidence in her relationship with God—and identity with God's movement in history—naturally led Stewart to a creative rejection and recasting of received gender roles (Houchins 1988, xxxiii).

Like Jeremiah, Stewart uses her prophetic voice to express both judgment against the hypocrisy of the nation and admiration for its ideals. They parallel each other in that their prophecies of doom are conditioned by the nation's *potential* to be righteous. Compare Stewart's statement here with Jeremiah's:

> O America, America! Thou land of my birth! I love and admire thy virtues as much as I abhor and detest thy vices; and I am in hopes that thy stains will soon be wiped away, and thy cruelties forgotten (Richardson 1987, 43).[20]
>
> If you return, O Israel—Yahweh's word—To *me* return,
>
> If you put your vile things aside, Nor stray from my presence, Then might you swear, 'As Yahweh lives,' Truthfully, justly, and rightly; And the nations by him would bless themselves, And in him exult (Jeremiah 4:1–2).[21]

Of course, there is a difference when that prophetic tone is *intoned* by a woman; apparently, many of Stewart's contemporaries couldn't hear her message because of her gender. Her "farewell address" of 1833 included a spirited defense, based in cross-cultural and biblical precedents, of women's rights to speak (Houchins 1988, 76–78, Richardson 1987, 68–70). James Horton speculates that her language and her departure from Boston in 1833 was prompted by Black males upset at her sharp exhortation:

> Black women who spoke on behalf of abolition and civil rights were applauded by their men. There were limits, however, to the public chastisement that these men were willing to endure, especially from a woman who questioned their manhood, even one whom they admired in other respects (Horton 1993, 109–110).

Following Jeremiah's lead, Stewart's self-confidence in her relationship to God comes from being, quite literally, a mouthpiece amplifying God's voice:

> for wise and holy purposes, best known to himself, he (God) hath unloosed my tongue and put his word into my mouth, in order to confound and put all those to shame that have rose up against me (Houchins 1988, 75).

Such a claim is open to criticism, and indeed, some readers have found her tone to be haughty and unsympathetic to her audience, but these characteristics are prototypical of the prophetic model (see Hinks 1997, 254; Horton 1993, 109–110; O'Connor 1954). The question, which I am pursuing, is not the theological truth or falsity of her claim, but what she enacts from this position. Her political use of this religious experience is an original contribution that dwarfs even her vanguard role as a speaker.

STEWART'S PROPHETIC QUILT OF THEMES

To illustrate Stewart's rhetorical, religious, and political strategies, I will draw from a single paragraph, near the end of "Religion and the Pure Principles of Morality." In this thickly concentrated quote, Stewart juxtaposes themes so quickly that her encoded comprehension and support of Turner's revolt is difficult to detect, at first.

She begins with a bold reading of the Book of Revelations:

> O, ye great and mighty men of America, ye rich and powerful ones, many of you will call for the rocks and mountains to fall upon you, and

> to hide you from the wrath of the Lamb, and from him that sitteth upon
> the throne; whilst many of the sable-skinned Africans you now despise,
> will shine in the kingdom of heaven as the stars forever and ever
> (Houchins 1988, 19; Richardson 1987, 39).

The biblical reference here is to Revelations 6:16. The preceding verse
(6:15), however, states that *"every bondman, and every free man . . .* said
to the mountains and rocks, Fall on us, and hide us from the face of him
that sitteth on the throne." Given that the biblical text indicates that doom
will fall on free and slave alike, Stewart's recasting of the passage to in-
voke the vengeance of God on slaveholders alone indicates her religious
agility and the prophetic politics undergirding her interpretation.

Next, she segues into a political theme: white American support for
white revolutionaries:

> Charity begins at home, and those that provide not for their own, are
> worse than infidels. We know that you are raising contributions to aid
> the gallant Poles; we know that you have befriended Greece and Ire-
> land; and you have rejoiced with France, for her heroic deeds of valor.
> You have acknowledged all the nations of the earth, except Hayti
> (Houchins 1988, 19; Richardson 1987, 39).[22]

In this bold attack on white racist political hypocrisy, she is following the
lead of Walker, who had cited the same examples. But the context has
been radically altered: this reads differently *after* Nat Turner's rebellion
than before. When she implies that America should support her own revolutionaries, and black revolutionaries worldwide, in addition to supporting white Europeans, she is clearly including the slave revolts of the
South. The dialectic concerning violence begins to emerge here. Valor
against tyranny (which can include violence) is *not* unjustified when
wielded by those who are *realizing* a metaphysic of *justice.* Turner's action had thrust white American hypocrisy out of the abstract and into the
"untidy" reality of bloodshed.

When Stewart resumes, she refines her logic, demonstrating that violence is not a monolithic concept:

> and you may publish, as far as the East is from the West, that you have
> two millions of negroes, who aspire no higher than to bow at your feet,
> and to court your smiles. You may kill, tyrannize, and oppress as much
> as you choose, until our cry shall come up before the throne of God; for

I am firmly persuaded, that he will not suffer you to quell the proud, fearless, and undaunted spirits of the Africans forever; for in his own time, he is able to plead our cause against you, and to pour out upon you the ten plagues of Egypt (Houchins 1988, 19; Richardson 1987, 39–40).

There are actually three kinds of violence exposed here. First is the struggle *against* oppression, exemplified in another encoded reference to the Turner revolt: "the proud, fearless, and undaunted spirits of the Africans." Second is the unjust violence of tyranny itself, which the slave owners are further compounding with the sin of hubris. This reveals the third violence: God's just vengeance. Stewart invokes the exodus story and the plagues visited upon the oppressors not merely to reminisce: as a prophet she is enacting the threat of judgment.

Now Stewart addresses Turner's revolt, with a remarkable biblical reference to the arrest of Jesus:

We will not come out against you with swords and staves, as against a thief; but we will tell you that our souls are fired with the same love of liberty and independence with which your souls are fired. We will tell you that too much of your blood flows in our veins, and too much of your color in our skins, for us not to possess your spirits (Houchins 1988, 19–20; Richardson 1987, 40).[23]

Stewart makes an allusion here to Matthew 26:55, when, at the moment of Jesus's arrest, he asks his captors, "Are ye come out as against a thief with swords and staves for to take me?" Stewart could not have been aware of the fact that Nat Turner explicitly compared himself to Jesus. A white journalist asked Turner if he would admit, given his impending execution, that his visions had been false. Turner simply replied, "Was not Christ crucified?" (Grant 1974, 59). Like Antigone, Turner appeals to a divine law beyond the arbitrary inhumanity of the racist state, and takes comfort in the fate he shares with Jesus: being condemned to death by an arrogant state.

Stewart's use of this most *cosmically* unjust arrest and the execution of Jesus achieves something distinct from Turner's self-defense, but not contradictory to it. She deliberately leaves the 'as' clause open: it is not clear who she is placing in the role analogous to Jesus. Remembering that her tone is consistently prophetic, not conciliatory, it seems unlikely that she intended the slave owners to be compared in any way to Christ.

At the very least, she implies that Blacks will not treat the slavocracy like thieves, though whites have behaved despicably like robbers. This ambiguity is extended further when she points to a unity of souls and blood created by the multiracial realities of America. With this, she can genuinely undercut the hypocrisy of the white Christians by postulating a *human* desire for freedom shared by Black and white.

Stewart will not leave this *human* vision at the abstract level: it is fiercely mediated by the social and historical realities of antebellum America:

> We will tell you, that it is our gold that clothes you in fine linen and purple, and causes you to eat sumptuously every day; and it is the blood of our fathers, and the tears of our brethren that have enriched your soils (Houchins 1988, 20; Richardson 1987, 40).[24]

Once again, Stewart has taken the biblical text beyond its original frame, binding the master and slave in a symbiotic relationship of injustice and inequity. The parable of the rich man and Lazarus the beggar, as related in Luke 16:19–31, is a simple role-reversal. The rich man "was clothed in purple and fine linen, and fared sumptuously every day" (16:19), while Lazarus is portrayed as a local beggar "laid at his gate," not as the servant or slave of the rich man. When Lazarus and the wealthy man die, their fortunes switch: Lazarus is in heaven, while the rich man is tormented in hell. What Stewart has done is inherently more political: she has said that wealth and poverty are linked systemically and inextricably, a fact which she gleans from the specific context of American racism. The poverty of the Black slaves and the wealth of white America are in a causal relationship. So it is hardly surprising that she follows this with the bold announcement:

AND WE CLAIM OUR RIGHTS (Houchins 1988, 20; Richardson 1987, 40, emphasis in original).

Stewart has demonstrated both the human and the historical need for freedom, but in this direct declaration—which she emphasizes—the inevitability of Black freedom and women's liberation is both disarmingly simple and historically embedded. We must realize that this statement put her in direct danger: it was against the law in much of the nation to suggest such an idea for Blacks, and it was unprecedented to declare it publicly for women.

It seems no accident to me that this most explicitly risk-taking passage, in which she exposes herself and the movement for freedom in which she participated, immediately precedes her cautionary admonition to her brothers in slavery:

> We will tell you that we are not afraid of them that kill the body, and after that can do no more; but we will tell you whom we do fear. We fear Him who is able, after He hath killed, to destroy both soul and body in hell forever. Then, my brethren, sheath your swords, and calm your angry passions. Stand still and know that the Lord he is God. Vengeance is his, and he will repay. It is a long lane that has no turn. America has risen to her meridian. When you begin to thrive, she will begin to fall (Houchins 1988, 20; Richardson 1987, 40).

Certainly it is possible to read this passage literally, as a request to Turner to cease and desist, and as a plea for religious quietism, waiting for God to do the work of liberation. And I believe this is the reading she wanted the ignorant to receive. But that would not be an accurate contextual meaning to draw from Stewart's writing, which demands active participation in liberation. The last line gives it away: "When you begin to thrive, she (slavocracy America) will begin to fall." On this "long lane that has no turn," the inevitability of Black freedom includes the inevitability of Black thriving; i.e., of Black self-development. And the content of that thriving, while it would certainly include Stewart's usual themes of education, morality, and religious piety, does not exclude—indeed, it actually seems to call for—the *overthrow* of white slavocracy.[25]

Once it is understood that Stewart is consistently encoding her statements, then it makes sense that while she *seems* to be telling her angry brothers to sheath their swords, she *simultaneously* invokes and extols two other incendiaries:

> God hath raised you up a Walker and a Garrison. Though Walker sleeps, yet he lives, and his name shall be had in everlasting remembrance (Houchins 1988, 20; Richardson 1987, 40).[26]

To those who supported slavery, these two men were considered as culpable as Turner, so by invoking them, Stewart takes a risk by association. But she endangers no one else—Garrison is the *only* living person she mentions by name, and his fame precluded anonymity. Her praise of

Walker indicates a more apocalyptic role for black masses than passivity, which would temper any literal reading of the "sheath your swords" admonition.

This paragraph concludes with a similar pair of intertwined "mixed" messages. First is her reading of Psalm 37:

> I, even I, who am but a child, inexperienced to many of you, am a living witness to testify unto you this day,[27] that I have seen the wicked in great power, spreading himself like a green bay tree, and lo, he passed away; yea, I diligently sought him, but he could not be found; and it is God alone that has inspired my heart to feel for Afric's woes. Then fret not yourselves because of the men who bring wicked devices to pass; for they shall be cut down as the grass, and wither as the green herb. Trust in the Lord, and do good; so shalt thou dwell in the land, and verily thou shalt be fed (Houchins 20; Richardson 1987, 40).

Stewart here summarizes much of Psalm 37, which I would characterize as a parent text to the Sermon on the Mount, but with the added bite of righteous vengeance in its tone. Like Stewart's own discourse, the psalm is not strictly opposed to violence; Stewart's audience would have known these verses too:

> The wicked plotteth against the just, and gnasheth upon him with his teeth.
>
> The Lord shall laugh at him: for he seeth that his day is coming.
>
> The wicked have drawn out the sword, and have bent their bow, to cast down the poor and needy, and to slay such as be of upright conversation.
>
> Their sword shall enter into their own heart, and their bows shall be broken (Psalm 37:12–15).

Stewart is making another oblique reference to Turner, since he did become the instrument by which the oppressor's swords were thrust into their own hearts. God does not work without agents who—consciously or unconsciously—enact his wishes. As she argues in her 1832 speech to the Afric-American Female Intelligence Society: "God has said that Ethiopia shall stretch forth her hands unto him. True, but God uses means to bring about his purposes" (Houchins 1988, 60; Richardson 1987, 53).

Stewart ends this densely woven paragraph by comparing two notable white Americans:

> Encourage the noble-hearted Garrison. Prove to the world that you are neither ourang-outangs, nor a species of mere animals, but that you possess the same powers of intellect as those of the proud-boasting Americans (Houchins 1988, 20–21; Richardson 1987, 40).

The reference to "ourang-outangs" is a very specific one: this line of speculation marked the nadir of Thomas Jefferson's racist "scientific" thought. "Jefferson's public ruminations about black intellectual inferiority and a possible sexual connection between Africans and orangutans outraged the free black community" (Egerton, 1997, 32; cf. Hinks 1997, 200–201, 206–209), and was scathingly excoriated by David Walker in his *Appeal:*

> I call upon the professing Christians, I call upon the philanthropist, I call upon the very tyrant himself, to show me a page of history, either sacred or profane, on which a verse can be found, which maintains, that the Egyptians heaped the *insupportable insult* upon the children of Israel, by telling them that they were not of the *human family*. Can the whites deny this charge? Have they not, after having reduced us to the deplorable condition of slaves under their feet, held us up as descending originally from the tribes of *Monkeys* or *Orang-Outangs?* . . . Has not Mr. Jefferson declared to the world, that we are inferior to the whites, both in the endowments of our bodies and of minds? It is indeed surprising that a man of such great learning, combined with such excellent natural parts, should speak so of a set of men in chains (Walker 1965a, 72, original emphases).[28]

Stewart's reference to Jefferson is a tightly telescoped version of Walker's, but she takes care to *highlight* the role of Black *intelligence*, while also making differentiations within the white community by contrasting Garrison to Jefferson. Denouncing Jefferson's racism in the immediate wake of Turner's uprising, which many whites pointed to as evidence of Black savagery, again assumes a different valence than doing so before. Stewart underlines this by impugning the "proud-boasting" nature of white racism, thereby deflating white self-assurance about their own intelligence, while calling on Blacks to defend themselves *intellectually* as well as in deed.[29]

BETWEEN TWO BROTHERS

Returning to the Hegelian notion of mutuality between men and women, it is salutary to note how Stewart recognizes that she is the *equal* of Walker and Turner, especially in the context of struggle. It is in making that recognition that she becomes increasingly feminist. Her later talks, from 1832–1833, show this tendency most explicitly, conveying a growing militancy and anger at those who would silence her because of her gender. But the seeds of equality were planted long before their harvest in the nature of her relation to Garrison, Walker, and Turner. While she subscribes to some of her era's conventional ideas about gender, her language toward these comrades is remarkably free of any heterosexist innuendo, gender hierarchy, or sexist assumptions concerning her "proper" role in relation to male leaders.

Dunayevskaya's comment that a brother, being equal, brings out the best in you, now takes on a new twist in relation to feminist thought. True mutuality between men and women is unlikely to occur within the structural inequities of the patriarchal family—a reality Hegel could not see or refused to see (Mills 1996, 63f). Instead, new relations between men and women have a better chance of occurring in the intertwined realms of activity and thought. In the case of Maria Stewart, when the dialectic of freedom was moving around, in, and through her, her equality with her "brothers" was about being equal to the formidable task of abolishing slavery.[30]

Stewart's religiosity also supports her in this equality, since the Second Great Awakening produced the unintended consequence of rendering the spiritual equality of all people into a cry for social equality. Stewart announces that from the moment of her conversion:

> I felt a strong desire . . . to devote the remainder of my days to piety and virtue, and now possess that spirit of independence, that, were I called upon, I would willingly sacrifice my life for the cause of God and my brethren (Houchins 1988, 4; Richardson 1987, 29).

As Richardson notes: "Resistance to oppression was, for Stewart, the highest form of obedience to God. . . . Religion and social justice are so closely allied in her analysis that, to her mind, one could not be properly served without a clear commitment to the other" (Richardson 1987, 9). Stewart's religiosity balances the immediate struggle with a larger vision of meaning in human existence. Stewart's embrace of religion graces her activity and thought with a "dual eschatological hope," which "contained both vertical and horizontal dimensions . . . freedom both within and beyond history. (She) did not believe that black Americans should wait patiently for God to satisfy their thirst for freedom and justice in heaven" (Young 1977, 50–51).[31] There is also the forward movement provided by her prophetic calling, which Richardson terms a spiritual imperative:

> the same imperative that had communicated itself to Denmark Vesey, Gabriel Prosser, and her contemporaries, David Walker and Nat Turner. By perceiving her mission as in that line of militant spiritual descent, she veered sharply from the prescribed sphere of women's religious activity. In that regard, her willingness to embrace armed struggle would put her at philosophic odds with her colleague and publisher, Garrison . . . in the early 1830s, in a real sense alone in unexplored territory, (she was) a woman placed by God—as she saw it—on an ethical and societal frontier (Richardson 1987, 25).

This alliance of religion and politics, of a woman finding her voice and exhorting the freedom struggle, contains an implicit philosophy of revolution. It is this that Raya Dunayevskaya recognized in Stewart when she quoted from this 1831 publication as a way of dramatically introducing the intertwining of the feminist and Black dimensions in American history (Dunayevskaya 1991, 79). She notes that in that same year, Nat Turner "held that the idea of freedom is present in every slave so tempestuously that 'the same idea prompted others' to rebel." But what Dunayevskaya singled out in Stewart's speech was her insight into the connection between women's labor and women's minds, where Stewart says, "How long shall the fair daughters of Africa be compelled to bury their minds and talents beneath a load of iron pots and kettles?" (Dunayevskaya 1991, 79; Dunayevskaya 1996, 262; Houchins 16; Richardson 1987, 38). Indeed, Stewart was a domestic worker, a poor woman speaking to others who were in poverty (Sterling 1984, 154; Houchins 1988, 24). Her philosophic vision comprehends life as a totality, which includes labor and thought, Black and white, female and male. Writing about Maria Stewart's invocation of Haiti's revolution, Loewenberg and Bogin comment that

> Humanism in Afro-American life is the counterpart of American humanism. The history of black women is part of a larger whole . . . *Black women did not acquire knowledge of pain and sorrow vicariously* . . . There was no hint of exclusiveness in the posture of black

women reformers. They stood squarely for all mankind . . . Freedom
was the ideal, before emancipation and after, in America and elsewhere
(Loewenberg and Bogin 1976, 35, emphasis added).

The comparison of Stewart and Antigone demonstrates how much
more dramatically and fluidly the dialectic moves when embodied in living history. Creon and Antigone destroy each other in a face-off of rigid
moral absolutes. Stewart avoids this rigidity by nuancing questions of violence, revenge, tyranny, and injustice. Unlike the pacifist antislavery advocates, Stewart reads the subtle differences between specific forms of
violence. In defiance of convention against women's public political participation, she not only speaks, but she assumes her own authority in relation to biblical texts.[32]

Prior to her unjust execution (which she thwarts by the self-defined
act of suicide), Antigone knows she is a failure for embracing death,
"what law of the heaven have I transgressed? What god can save me
now?" (Sophocles 1947, 150). Bound to tradition, Antigone is bound to
fatalism. Conversely, where she is bound to biblical religion, Stewart
seizes the text for a situation and purpose beyond its original intent,
whose only trajectory is the inevitability of freedom. Antigone seeks to
bury her brothers and thus join them in death, while Stewart grasps the
initiative to continue her comrades' work. While the sexism and racism
of our own time have kept Stewart's name from its deserved fame (which
raises the fatalistic question, does one *have* to be a martyr to be remembered in struggle?), Stewart's revolutionary role had effects well past her
public retirement in 1833.

Dunayevskaya often commented on how, while Hegel piously
wanted to valorize religion, the logic of his own dialectic led him to see
the philosophic absolutes transcending even religious consciousness. In
getting past the irreconcilable contradictions of ethical consciousness—
the ones which condemned Antigone—Maria Stewart's religious voice
carried past any limitations to ever-new, ever-complex human freedom.
Whether through the Bible, her politics, or both, Stewart caught the fact
that freedom is not automatic, but part of a struggle. What makes her
speak to our time is her actualization of that struggle, as a struggle for the
mind of humanity.

ACKNOWLEDGMENTS

Many people assisted me in the writing of this paper, but the greatest
thanks must go to my colleague Sue Houchins and the Marxist-humanist

philosopher, Raya Dunayevskaya. In an amazing bit of synchronicity, I was introduced to Maria Stewart's work through both Sue and Raya within days of each other in the summer of 1992. Others who have assisted greatly include Laurie Green, Michelle Gubbay, Lois Helmbold, Urszula Wislanka, Ron Brokmeyer, Olga Domanski, Lou Turner, John Alan, Benita Ramsey, Toni Clark, and the many students with whom I have read Stewart's work, at both Pomona College and San José State University.

NOTES

1. Stewart's first name is pronounced "Mariah."

2. To cite one recently rediscovered example of this, in 1850, the British Chartist and Hegelian philosopher, Helen Macfarlane, quoted this line from Antigone to support her decision to be a revolutionary: "even in England a few of us who belong to the 'better sort' . . . have repudiated all claim to be considered respectable, because for them the words Justice and Love are not mere empty sounds without meaning; because they say—like Antigone in Sophocles—the laws of God are not of today, nor of yesterday, they exist from all eternity" (Black 1997, 5).

3. Hegel, 492: "The opposition of the ethical powers to one another, and the process of the individualities setting up these powers in life and action, have reached their true end only in so far as both sides undergo the same destruction."

4. This is what Marx would develop in the 1844 Manuscripts: "The immediate, natural, necessary relationship of human being to human being is the relationship of man to woman." See Dunayevskaya 1996, 189–225.

5. The reference is to Fanon: "The native challenge to the colonial world is not a rational confrontation of points of view. It is not a treatise on the universal, but the untidy affirmation of an original idea propounded as an absolute"(Fanon 41).

6. Stewart supplies much of her own biographical information in the opening pages of "Religion and the Pure Principles of Morality." All references to Stewart's texts will be given from both editions of her work, edited by Sue Houchins and Marilyn Richardson, respectively.

7. The Hortons give a census figure of 1,875, which represented 3 percent of Boston's population (Horton and Horton 1979, 2).

8. Richardson speculates in this direction, 1987, 7. The new biography of Walker by Peter Hinks, definitive in its scope, compounds the speculation by placing Walker as a direct student of Denmark Vesey in South Carolina in the months leading up to Vesey's betrayed revolt; Hinks 22–62. See also Pen 1998.

9. See also Aptheker's introduction to Walker 1965a, 46, Hinks 116–172.

10. This sort of attack on black learning is a major mode of racism in America to the present day. Therefore, it is not surprising that Maria Stewart dedicates the balance of her life to teaching activities, a subject that I will not explore here. But her insistence on education and literacy should be read against this background, rather than being consigned to a politics of respectability, as it so often is. See Porter 1936 and Richardson 1987 for more details on this later phase of Stewart's life.

11. Speculation over the cause of Walker's death continues to the present day. Hinks feels that the evidence points to Walker's death being from natural causes, but he lists the historians who feel otherwise, 269–270.

12. See Richardson 1987, 7, 92–93, 123 n. 19 for details on the legal fraud committed against Stewart.

13. In some ways, the defeat of Turner's rebellion, even after such a fortuitous coincidence of skills, meant that the black slaves had to find some other means of overthrowing slavery. As Dunayevskaya points out, "it was after Nat Turner's hanging that the question to be answered was how to transcend the isolated slave revolts in order to end slavery, and the new form created was the Underground Railroad, of which the most famous conductor was Harriet Tubman" (Dunayevskaya 1996, 93).

14. Stewart makes a scathing critique of the "powerful force of prejudice," including an indictment of white women who will not act in solidarity with black women, in her first public speech in 1832. She explicitly compares the situation of blacks in the North to the slaves in the South and says "I consider our condition but little better than that" (Houchins 1988, 51–52, Richardson 1987, 45–46).

15. Lou Turner's biography of Nat Turner, p. 37.

16. Blacks initially represented 75 percent of the subscribers to the *Liberator*, and since it was published in Boston, it often addressed specific incidents and personages from Boston's black community (Litwack 1961, 236; Horton and Horton 1979, 82f). One solid piece of evidence that Stewart was a regular reader of the *Liberator* in the months prior to her becoming a writer for the paper can be found in the poem, "The Negro's Complaint," which is attached to the end of her Productions; it "appeared, in part and without attribution, in the 19 March 1831 issue of the *Liberator*" (Richardson 1987, 75–76; see also Houchins 1988, 83–84).

17. Richardson 1987, 17. Stewart was not alone in drawing on the American Revolution as a source of inspiration, especially in Boston: "In the petition of 1777, blacks pointed out the inconsistencies between the conditions of slavery and the principles of the American Revolution. This became a recurrent theme in nineteenth-century black protest. Boston blacks were acutely aware of the contributions and sacrifices made by members of their race in the fight for American

independence and were quick to remind Massachusetts authorities of the pride black Bostonians felt as patriotic Americans" (Horton and Horton 1979, 27–28).

18. Shanks 144; other key passages used by the Abolitionists from Jeremiah included 21:12 and 22:13.

19. I use the King James translation here, since it is the one Stewart would have read and heard. But the language of Bright's translation is much more immediate: "And so, this is what Yahweh has said: You have not obeyed me by proclaiming emancipation each to his brother, and each to his neighbor. So, believe me, I am going to proclaim your 'emancipation'—Yahweh's word—to the sword, to disease and starvation! And I will make you a sight to horrify all the kingdoms of the earth." (Bright 1965, 220; for discussion of the background to this incident, see 223–24).

20. This comes from a letter printed in the *Liberator*, July 14, 1832; it is not found in the Houchins edition of *Productions*. Likewise, the Houchins edition contains Stewart's complete *Meditations*, which are not given in Richardson 1987.

21. Bright translation, 21. See Cunliffe-Jones 23–27 for more on this tension in Jeremiah.

22. References include the French Revolution, the Polish revolution of 1830, and the Greek revolt against the Ottoman empire in 1829. Most significant, though, are the Haitian revolutions, which were well-known to American Blacks; the media cover-up and distortion of the events there were every bit as prevalent in the white mainstream of the nineteenth century as they are today.

23. Stewart had previously condemned white rapists in this essay–"thou hast caused the daughters of Africa to commit whoredoms and fornications; but upon thee be their curse"–so her reference to blood here is charged with a feminist insight (Houchins 1988, 18; Richardson 1987, 39).

24. Nat Turner was especially attracted to the Gospel of Luke; see Wilmore 65f.

25. Fanon's thoughts on violence are pertinent to much of this discussion: "if the last shall be first, this will only come to pass after a murderous and decisive struggle between the two protagonists" (Fanon 1968, 37).

26. Stewart also mentions Walker by name earlier in this essay (Houchins 1988, 5; Richardson 1987, 30), and by clear allusion in her February 1833 speech as "the man that has distinguished himself in these modern days by acting wholly in the defence of African rights and liberty . . . although he sleeps, his memory lives." (Houchins 1988, 64; Richardson 1987, 57). Garrison is mentioned explicitly in her farewell address (Houchins 1988, 74; Richardson 1987, 67), and by inference as "our noble advocate" in the February 1833 talk (Houchins 1988, 69; Richardson 1987, 61–62). In one of the most amazing biographic events in their

respective lives, Garrison and Stewart were reunited in 1879—only months before they both died—after a lapse of forty-six years (Richardson 1987, 80–81, 89–90).

27. This passage echoes Jeremiah's calling, Jeremiah 1:4–10.

28. See also Walker 1965a, 72–79. The reference to Jefferson's "excellent natural parts" seems to me to be the bitterest intentional irony on Walker's part.

29. Walker was also adamant that blacks needed to respond forthrightly to Jefferson in thought; he says that the job cannot be left to whites only (Walker 1965a, 77–78).

30. This is a paraphrase from Mary Daly's *Gyn/Ecology*: "there is no equality among unique Selves . . . what each asks of the other is that she be equal to the task at hand" (384).

31. Young is actually discussing Walker here, but the model precisely fits Stewart's theologizing.

32. In this she is not only prophetic, but anticipates contemporary liberation theologians, as did Nat Turner in his visionary, militant spirituality (Turner 1999).

REFERENCES

Adams, John. 1807. *Sketches of the History, Genius, Disposition, Accomplishments, Employments, Customs, Virtues, and Vices of the Fair Sex, in All Parts of the World. Interspersed with Many Singular and Entertaining Anecdotes*. Boston: Joseph Bumstead.

Andrews, William L., ed. 1986. *Sisters of the Spirit: Three Black Women's Autobiographies of the Nineteenth Century*. Bloomington: Indiana University Press.

Black, David. 1997. "Helen Macfarlane and the Dialectic of the Democratic Idea," *News and Letters* 42:4:5, 9 (May 1997).

Bormann, Ernest G., ed. 1971. *Forerunners of Black Power: The Rhetoric of Abolition*. Englewood Cliffs: Prentice-Hall.

Bright, John. 1965. *Jeremiah*. The Anchor Bible, volume 21. Garden City: Doubleday.

Cunliffe-Jones, H. 1966. *Jeremiah: God in History*. 2d ed.. London: SCM Press.

Daly, Mary. 1978. *Gyn/Ecology: The Meta Ethics of Radical Feminism*. Boston: Beacon Press.

Daniels, John. 1914. *In Freedom's Birthplace: A Study of the Boston Negroes*. New York: Negro Universities Press.

Dunayevskaya, Raya. 1977. "Talk to Women's Liberation Committee, January 4, 1977." unpublished talk.

———. 1991. *Rosa Luxemburg, Women's Liberation, and Marx's Philosophy of Revolution*. 2d ed. Urbana: University of Illinois Press.

———. 1996. *Women's Liberation and the Dialectics of Liberation: Reaching for the Future*. Detroit: Wayne State University Press.

Egerton, Douglas R. 1997. "The Obscure Hero." Review of *To Awaken My Afflicted Brethren: David Walker and the Problem of Antebellum Slave Resistance* by Peter Hinks, *The Nation*, May 26, 1997, 32–33.

Fanon, Frantz. 1968. *The Wretched of the Earth*. Trans. Constance Farrington. New York: Grove Press.

Giddings, Paula. 1984. *When and Where I Enter . . . The Impact of Black Women on Race and Sex in America*. New York: William Morrow and Company.

Gilkes, Cheryl Townsend. 1994. "The Politics of "Silence:" Dual-Sex Political Systems and Women's Traditions of Conflict in African-American Religion." In *African-American Christianity*, edited by Paul E. Johnson, 80–110. Berkeley: University of California Press.

Grant, Joanne, ed. 1974. *Black Protest: History, Documents, and Analyses, 1619 to the Present*. 2d ed. Greenwich: Fawcett.

Hegel, G. W. F. 1807 (1967). *The Phenomenology of Mind*. Trans. J. B. Baillie. New York: Harper and Row.

Hinks, Peter P. 1997. *"To Awaken My Afflicted Brethren": David Walker and the Problem of Antebellum Slave Resistance*. University Park: Pennsylvania State University Press.

Horton, James Oliver. 1993. *Free People of Color: Inside the African American Community*. Washington: Smithsonian Institution Press.

Horton, James Oliver and Lois E. Horton. 1979. *Black Bostonians: Family Life and Community Struggle in the Antebellum North*. New York: Holmes and Meier.

Houchins, Sue, ed. 1988. *Spiritual Narratives*. New York: Oxford University Press.

Kraditor, Aileen S. 1969. *Means and Ends in American Abolitionism: Garrison and His Critics on Strategy and Tactics, 1834–1850*. New York: Pantheon Books.

Litwack, Leon F. 1961. *North of Slavery: The Negro in the Free States, 1790–1860*. Chicago: University of Chicago Press.

Loewenberg, Bert James and Ruth Bogin, ed. 1976. *Black Women in Nineteenth-Century American Life: Their Words, Their Thoughts, Their Feelings*. University Park: Pennsylvania State University Press.

Lukács, György. 1977. *Young Hegel: Studies in the Relations between Dialectics and Economics*. Cambridge: MIT Press.

Matthew, Anjilvel V. 1970. *The Message of the Hebrew Prophets*. Bombay: Bharatiya Vidya Bhavan.

Mills, Patricia. 1996. "Hegel's Antigone." In *Feminist Interpretations of G. W. F. Hegel*, edited by Patricia Jagentowicz Mills, 59–88. University Park: Pennsylvania State University.

Min, Anselm Kyongsuk. 1996. "Liberation, the Other, and Hegel in Recent Pneumatologies," *Religious Studies Review* 22:1:28–33.

Nelson, Truman, ed. 1966. *Documents of Upheaval: Selections from William Lloyd Garrison's The Liberator, 1831–1865*. New York: Hill and Wang.

O'Connor, Lillian. 1954. *Pioneer Women Orators: Rhetoric in the Ante-Bellum Reform Movement*. New York: Columbia University Press.

Pease, Jane H. and William H. 1990. *They Who Would be Free: Blacks' Search for Freedom, 1830–1861*. Urbana: University of Illinois Press.

Pen, Jennifer. 1998. "David Walker's Radical Awakening: Review of *To Awaken My Afflicted Brethren: David Walker and the Problem of Antebellum Slave Resistance* by Peter Hinks," *News and Letters* 43:2:1, 8 (March 1998).

Porter, Dorothy B. 1936. "The Organized Educational Activities of Negro Literary Societies 1828–46," *Journal of Negro Education* 5:555–576.

Quarles, Benjamin. 1969. *Black Abolitionists*. New York: Oxford University Press.

Raboteau, Albert J. 1994. "African-Americans, Exodus, and the American Israel." In *African-American Christianity*, edited by Paul E. Johnson, 1–17. Berkeley: University of California Press.

———. 1997. "The Black Experience in American Evangelicalism: The Meaning of Slavery." In *African-American Religion: Interpretive Essays in History and Culture*, edited by Timothy E. Fulop and Albert J. Raboteau. New York: Routledge.

Reed, Harry A. 1993. "Maria Stewart." In *Black Women in America: An Historical Encyclopedia*, edited by Darlene Clark Hine, Vol. 2, 1113–1114. Brooklyn: Carlson Publishing.

Richardson, Marilyn. 1980. *Black Women and Religion: A Bibliography*. Boston: G. K. Hall.

———. 1987. *Maria W. Stewart: America's First Black Woman Political Writer: Essays and Speeches*. Bloomington: Indiana University Press.

Sernett, Milton C. 1975. *Black Religion and American Evangelicalism: White Protestants, Plantation Missions, and the Flowering of Negro Christianity, 1787–1865*. ATLA monograph series No. 7. Metuchen, NJ: Scarecrow Press.

———. 1985. *Afro-American Religious History: A Documentary Witness*. Durham: Duke University Press.

Shanks, Caroline L. 1931. "The Biblical Anti-Slavery Argument of the Decade 1830–1840," *Journal of Negro History* 16:132–157 (April 1931).

Sophocles. 1947 (442 BCE). *The Theban Plays*. Trans. E. F. Watling. New York: Penguin.

Steiner, George. 1996. *Antigones: How the Antigone Legend Has Endured in Western Literature, Art and Thought*. New Haven: Yale University Press.

Sterling, Dorothy. 1984. *We Are Your Sisters: Black Women in the Nineteenth Century*. New York: W. W. Norton and Company.

Stewart, Maria. 1987. Maria W. Stewart: *America's First Black Woman Political Writer: Essays and Speeches*. Ed. Marilyn Richardson. Bloomington: Indiana University Press.

———. 1988 (1835). *Productions of Mrs. Maria W. Stewart*. Boston: Published by Friends of Freedom and Virtue. In *Spiritual Narratives*, edited by Sue Houchins. New York: Oxford University Press.

Turner, Lou. 1999. "Nat Turner (1800–1831): Slave, Liberation Theologian, Slave Insurrectionist." In *Notable Black American Men*, edited by Jessie Carney Smith. 1137–1142. Detroit: Gale Publications.

Walker, David. 1965a (1829–30). *One Continual Cry: David Walker's Appeal to the Colored Citizens of the World*, with an essay on *Its Setting and Meaning* by Herbert Aptheker. New York: Marzani and Munsell, Humanities Press.

———. 1965b (1829–30). *David Walker's Appeal in Four Articles; Together with a Preamble to the Coloured Citizens of the World, but in Particular, and Very Expressly, to Those of the United States of America*. Ed. Charles M. Wiltse. New York: Hill and Wang.

Walker, Robbie Jean. 1992. *The Rhetoric of Struggle: Public Address by African American Women*. New York: Garland Publishing.

Wilmore, Gayraud S. 1986. *Black Religion and Black Radicalism: An Interpretation of the Religious History of Afro-American People*. 2d ed. Maryknoll, NY: Orbis Books.

Young, Henry J. 1977. *Major Black Religious Leaders: 1755–1940*. Nashville: Abingdon.

CHAPTER 23

January 16, 1997: Message from Maryam Rajavi, President-Elect of the Iranian Resistance

MARYAM RAJAVI

Before all else, allow me to express my profound gratitude to those responsible for arranging this international conference and my best wishes for its success. This conference is undoubtedly a constructive step towards raising the demands of women on an international level and realizing their rights.

I would very much have liked to be with you, to speak with you at close hand. I could have listened as you spoke of your experiences, and I could have spoken to you about the experiences of the Iranian people and Resistance in their confrontation with the woman-hating regime ruling Iran.

And so, let me begin by saluting you and all the women yearning for freedom who are struggling around the world for equality and liberation. And let me salute the enchained women of my homeland, Iran, and pay tribute to the tens of thousands of Iranian women who have been martyred or tortured in the struggle to bring freedom to their nation, held captive by the antihuman Khomeini regime.

Despite advances in many countries, particularly in the final decade of the twentieth century, towards eliminating gender discrimination, women everywhere still suffer the same pain and the same problems. Thankfully, after a century of struggle for freedom and equality, the refusal to recognize that these problems exist has, to some extent, been resolved.

As many women experts emphasize, the most crucial of women's common pains is their exclusion from political power and leadership. I believe that at least in the advanced and developing societies, this problem is at the root of most of women's suffering, deprivation, and difficulties. Some believe, or even preach, that participation in the political leadership should be the final stage of equality. This perception may be correct from certain angles. It is, however, important to understand that we have now arrived at a point at which we must courageously step forward to resolve this issue—which I consider the most basic, fundamental building block to equality. Why? Because without it, many of the other achievements of the women's movement will never become permanent or reliable.

Addressing the question of women in power and decision making, the platform of the Beijing conference emphasized that women's equal participation in decision making is not just a demand for simple justice or democracy, but may be viewed as essential if women are to count. In Iran, under the terrorist, religious dictatorship of the mullahs, women do not have even a minimal role in political power or leadership. They enjoy virtually no political or social rights, and the fundamentalists deny even their basic human identity.

Women are arrested and flogged and their dignity is attacked. Nine-year-old girls are forced into marriages, condoned by the mullahs' laws, with sixty- or seventy-year-old men. Desperately poor families sell their little girls. Women are not just denied access to top or key positions; women employed in clerical jobs, as teachers, workers, and thousands upon thousands of other positions, have been fired. To this tragedy must be added the suffering of several million widows, and other women and children who are homeless as a result of the unpatriotic war waged by this criminal regime.

Most importantly, there are the tens of thousands of women—elderly women, pregnant women, young girls—who were viciously tortured and sent before the firing squads, in some cases without even having been identified, solely for resisting against the mullahs' despotism. On the eve of their execution, young girls were raped in accordance with an official decree of the mullahs.

The head of this regime's judiciary—Mullah Yazdi—officially declared that "[a] woman does not have the right to leave her home without her husband's permission, not even to attend her father's funeral procession" (*Friday prayers*, 27 Nov. 1992).

Mullah Azeri-Qomi says, "The religious leader may, against the wishes of the father and girl herself, forcibly give her in marriage."

Mullah Saddoughi, Khomeini's representative in the central regions of Iran, once said in the Council of Guardians, "For us, it would be a shame, scandalous, if a woman were to become president or prime minister."

Worst of all, the mullahs attribute all of their misogyny and backward teachings to Islam, thereby taking advantage of the people's religious sentiments. Allow me, as a Muslim, Iranian woman, to declare that these murderers who suppress the people, especially the women, of Iran in the name of religion, and who export backwardness and terrorism, have no relationship whatsoever to Islam or Iranian culture. They are peddlers of religion. To advance their own shameful, inhuman objectives, they take advantage of the name of Islam.

Like all of the world's great religions, Islam is a religion of peace, liberty, and equality for all. It preaches love and mercy. Nevertheless, these criminals try to justify their antipathy to women, to the notion that human rights are universal, and to the principle that human rights are women's rights, under the pretext of "defending cultural values." For years, however, the Iranian public has watched as the mullahs officially declared their aversion to the culture, history, and values of Iran's people. In truth, the mullahs' crimes have one, and only one, objective: to preserve and prolong their hold of power.

I should add here that the heart of fundamentalism beats in Tehran, within the reactionary regime of the mullahs, where officials trample upon the rights of women and try to reverse the international trend, especially in Islamic countries, toward equality. The fundamentalists acted out their loathing against the principle of equality at the world conference on women in Beijing. In today's world, you cannot speak of the liberation and equality of women without talking about the abuse of women's rights by the fundamentalists. In this context, I would like to reiterate my call, before this conference and before the free-thinking women who have worked to make it happen, for a united front against fundamentalism.

Dear sisters, I wish to inform you that throughout these long years, happily, the people and Resistance of Iran, especially the women, have never submitted to the ruling fundamentalists. They have defended their dignity, their freedom, and their rights with all their might.

After a hundred years of activism in the social struggle, Iranian women suddenly found themselves under attack by the terrorist, religious dictatorship of the mullahs. They did not submit; indeed, they rose up, to actively take part in the political confrontation. They joined the

Resistance against backwardness and defended democratic freedoms. Today, they are giving voice to the cry of an enchained, oppressed, but proud and resistant nation.

Fifteen years later, these front-runners now fill key positions of leadership in the resistance against reactionaries. Women hold fifty-two percent of the seats in the Resistance's parliament-in-exile. The command staff of the National Liberation Army is essentially comprised of women, and the Leadership Council of the Mojahedin Organization, the most prominent of the Resistance, is comprised entirely of women. Women command and act as administrators at all levels. They command combat units, mechanical units, and technical units. They run political affairs and manage organizational affairs. Today, in our movement, divisions between "women's work" and "men's work" are obsolete.

How did we do it? Twelve years ago, our movement—locked in a life-or-death struggle with the mullahs' regime—realized that the progress of our freedom movement demanded that women also take on the most serious, crucial positions of responsibility. At that time, our women played an extensive role in the resistance against Khomeini, but in practice, we could not make our objective a reality.

We studied the matter at length and ultimately concluded that the principal problem was skepticism about women's abilities. This lack of faith was not limited to the men. The women of our movement, the very same women who were the source of this commendable heroism, did not believe that women could take on more responsibility. Our awareness of the problem led us to conclude that we must target this lack of faith.

Next, we determined that gradual change would never do the job. The real way to shatter this mentality was for women to participate in leadership. Thus began a process of internal changes in the Mojahedin, designed to make women believe in themselves. At the same time, the men had to overcome their hesitation about accepting these qualified women, who had fought shoulder to shoulder with them in all the arenas of the struggle for freedom. In this process, our women overcame their lack of faith. Not single, scattered stars, but a galaxy of liberated women took on key positions of leadership.

The most outstanding characteristics of these women are their sense of responsibility, willingness to learn, commitment to discipline, remarkable determination and, most importantly, selflessness and humanness. Obviously, they have had a very beneficial influence on the workplace.

We saw the first signs of success in a new interaction among the women. They knew that before anything else, they had to like the women around them. At work, and in authority, a sense of solidarity had to prevail. They had to accept each other as commanders.

Next, we saw another important change in our women. They did not stay within the confines of organizational or political circles. They penetrated an environment which, more than any other, seemed exclusively male and closed to women. The women of the Resistance conquered the military.

Of course, this was no simple task. Beyond all the inherent difficulties and mental reservations, when the time came for military tasks, it was assumed that this was a man's domain. To keep the women from starting off with comparisons of male and female capabilities, we initially organized separate units for them. Later on, when they had demonstrated some of their capabilities on the job and in command, we formed coed units, some of which were commanded by women. Gradually, we began to see signs, such as requests for transfers to units commanded by women, that the women were demonstrating superior skills in administrating and commanding the units under them.

You know well that in addition to all the difficulties mentioned above, one of the most problematic aspects is how to preserve a healthy moral atmosphere under such circumstances—an army of men and women. Many of the armies in the West have failed here. In other words, this is an impossible task without a revolution in ideas and opinions about women, whether among themselves or among men. Perhaps rather than mentioning many of the values that blossomed in this revolution in ideas, I should recall instead the role these women played in safeguarding a healthy relationship between the sexes. They made the creation of a male/female army, with proper, humane inter-relations and formidable military prowess, a possibility, to the surprise of many observers.

One of the most glorious results of our experience has been that the progress of women not only did not exclude men as a consequence, but in fact promoted their liberation and enhanced their capabilities. Obviously, it was no simple matter for the men to confront these changes head-on. It was hard to accept the new status of women and believe in their ability to accept responsibility. They had to struggle against the idea of male superiority. Fortunately, however, in the framework of a common Resistance by women and men for the freedom of their people and homeland, our men welcomed these changes, despite the hardships. They took pride in keeping pace on the path to equality. Why? Because in a world of discrimination, men are also captives, imprisoned by self-interest and the desire to dominate. Really, a man who denies the human dignity of those closest to him—his mother, sister, wife—has to first deny his own humanity. How can any individual in good conscience accept oppression? As we strove to eliminate gender discrimination, we saw a generation of men regain their humanity. In accepting the leadership of women, they demonstrated the utmost of liberation and freedom.

KEY POINTS FOR THE EQUALITY MOVEMENT

Please allow me to share with you the most important points learned during the Iranian Resistance's twelve-year experience. I have underscored the significance of these points on several occasions. They are:

1. If systems based on gender suppression are to be uprooted, then women must, before all else, prepare the grounds by engaging in political and social activism.
2. Along the same lines, women must take on the responsibilities of political and social leadership. In the movement for equality, at least fifty percent of the positions of responsibility must be occupied by women. Affirmative action for a period will compensate for the historical deprivation of women. To this end, it is imperative to have quotas promoting an ever greater role by women in responsible positions in society. The spirit and intention of such privileges, in any case, are to liberate and enhance the ability of men and women to take on responsibility, and to do away with exploitation and gender discrimination.
3. The liberation of men depends on the liberation of women, and the emancipation of women should result in the emancipation of men. Solutions that simply switch their places and reinforce the male/female conflict will not result in the liberation of women. Because of the inherent unity and humanity of women and men, solutions that promote genuinely humane interaction and true equality between women and men are absolutely realistic.
4. Although it is exactly what the backward misogynists do not want, this principle must be emphasized: Women's rights are human rights. These rights encompass all the individual and social freedoms cited in the Universal Declaration of Human Rights, according to which, women are the masters of their own bodies and feelings and have the right to control pregnancy.
5. The conflict between family, social, and political responsibilities is a common problem that confronts all women. We are con-

vinced that the right of women to freely choose, especially combatant women or activists in the equality movement, must be recognized. They must be allowed, whatever the circumstances, to determine their priorities with regard to political and social responsibilities.

In conclusion, I once again call for your support on behalf of a people and a Resistance fighting tooth and nail for democracy and equality in their homeland against a misogynistic, anti-human dictatorship. In particular, I urge you to support the Iranian women's struggle.

I deeply appreciate your sincere attention to the experiences of the Iranian Resistance. I hope that there will be more opportunities for us to exchange views and convey our experiences in order to advance our common goal for the equality and liberation of women.

CHAPTER 24

"You Have a Voice Now, Resistance Is Futile!"

SHASHWATI TALUKDAR

It has rightly been claimed that women and minorities have been under-represented in both mainstream and high-art film and television. It is said that "their stories" have remained unarticulated and their voices marginalized. Therefore, finding a form that will "tell their story" has been seen as a powerful corrective to this marginalization. I refer here to the personal documentary. A form that uses personal experience as its cornerstone. The personal documentary has been seen as a form that will subvert the narrative of oppression. Bringing personal experience to public discourse will perform a counter-hegemonic miracle.

Before we enthusiastically applaud the personal documentary as liberatory, it would behoove us to question its liberatory claims. There are two aspects to this exploration. First, the form of the personal documentary is an interesting site of performance for a particular kind of politics. Second, the personal documentary as a commodity has implications for how it is used.

THE PERSONAL DOCUMENTARY AS A TEXT

The personal documentary includes, as its basic elements, subject matter that is the personal experience of the maker. The film/video product usually has a first person voice-over or text; it uses records of the personal life of its subjects, like super-8 home movie footage or family photographs, and, finally, its imagery uses objects and events in a symbolic way, such that these objects or events function as expressions of the subject's/maker's subjective experience, or a recreation of the subject's history (e.g., Su Friedrich's *Sink or Swim* or Rea Tajiri's *History and Memory*).

These formal features of the personal documentary are the result of an unease with the Voice-of-God documentary and ethnography. The colonial gaze of documentaries like *The Song of Ceylon* or even *Nanook of the North* has been thought to be circumvented through the self-reflexivity of the personal documentary. Simultaneously, within feminism, the notion of the masculine-scopophilic gaze has been very important for the evolution of the personal documentary as a way for women and people of color to become subjects rather than objects. By telling their stories, women and minorities have been considered empowered to subvert the dominant structures of subjectivity, bringing to fruition the slogan, "The personal is political." In short, they presumably fulfill the promise of individual freedom through a liberal-humanist project.

I would argue that the personal documentary functions very much like its close relative, the religious confession. Like personal speech by victims of sexual abuse, the personal documentary is in danger of re-inscribing the very discourses it seeks to disrupt.

In his *History of Sexuality, Part I*, Michel Foucault outlines the role of the confessional in scientific practice and its importance in the enlightenment project of producing knowledge. The production of knowledge being the engine for regulating life, the confessional, for Foucault, is implicated in the processes of power. It is a potent method of producing knowledge at the sites where matrices of power intersect and make themselves visible.

Foucault further argues that the multiple uses that were made of confession made it possible for individuals to be penetrated by relations and mechanisms of power on a scale that was unprecedented. Central to his theory of power is the idea of knowledge. Western civilization has invented branches of knowledge, organized as science, to support a project of finding and stating the truth. When we put the personal documentary next to the project of power-knowledge, we see that the discourse being produced here is supposed to contribute to our knowledge of hidden and unspoken truths, of forces that influence, and in some way distort, the life being represented. The filmmaker's speaking out is thus a way to confront these forces and to counter them by taking control of who does the speaking. I would argue that this is not always the case. When a speech act takes place, it does so in a matrix of power relations, and speaking out may function as an act of capitulation rather than resistance.

When we examine the personal documentary, side by side with the confessional, certain discourses come into focus.

The personal documentary and the confessional are sites where an act of communication—a speech act—takes place. The action of "speaking out" in the confessional or the personal narrative is organized around designated listeners and speakers. It is assumed that, before the moment of speaking, the speaker was constrained and that the act of divulging this information is therefore a necessary remedy to the previously felt constraint. The information residing in the speaker is something that is uniquely the property of the speaker, the significance of this uniqueness lying in the fact that the information is usually personal in nature. The content of the personal narrative is the flesh and bones of subjectivity. The speaker will usually divulge incidents in his/her life—something only s/he happens to know: memories, pasts, and feelings. The personal documentary film could be called the confessional film.

Confession, as the method of religion and science, underwrites a certain pathology. This pathology then gets assigned to the speaker. Thus the speaker, while breaking the constraint of silence, makes her- or himself available to be assigned the role of patient, victim, sick individual, hysteric, or, in some way, outside the bounds of normality.

The interesting question to ask at this point is, "Who has the power?" Within Foucault's formulation of power, the nature of confession ensures that the power stays with the listener/audience, even though the speech comes from the speaker/maker.

THE VIEWING

Examining the institutional setting of the personal documentary makes some of these discourses more visible. The institutions in question are the film festival and the museum exhibition.

I will briefly examine the "call for entries" from a fairly prestigious venue, the Golden Gate Awards Competition in San Francisco. In the 1997 Golden Gate Awards Competition, a new category, the first-person documentary, was announced. First-person documentaries are described as, "Documentaries in which the director becomes in integral part of the topic through a strong autobiographical element."

A close reading of the category description allows certain elements of its liberal-humanist discourse to emerge. The first person narrative is deemed a document. What the filmmaker is about to show us is not fiction; it is based on empirical fact—facts that have been documented for the benefit of an unknowing (and unknown to the maker) spectator. This documentation concerns a topic in which the director is an integral part. The question to ask is, "What purpose does the maker's presence serve in the piece?" The presence of the director ensures a reflexivity that will allay any fear of participating in the scopophilic gaze of the filmmaker. Here the gaze of the camera is going to be turned on the filmmaker her- or himself. The audience may rest assured that the responsibility for any voyeurism is with the filmmaker, according to the argument that a gaze turned upon the gazer is no longer voyeurism, but self-exploration and introspection. In this equation, the innocence of the audience is assured. Spectators can imagine themselves as kind, liberal, and sympathetic to the "issues" of the maker.

The "integral" presence of the director ensures the integrity of the maker, as well as that of the audience. The lack of distance between the maker and the subject matter, while a corrective to the notion of "objec- tivity," precludes the possibility of abstract cognition or theorizing. The subject matter is something the director "experiences," not something s/he can "theorize about." Thus the director's participation in the "topic" implies authenticity. Empirical knowledge confers the authority of pri- mary, unmediated source material.

Who is the director within this construction? Judging from the Golden Gate committee's description, it is somebody who is part of the topic that is being documented. In the language of ethnography, the di- rector is the "native informant." Like a good native informant, s/he will bring forth information from the hermetic depths of his or her experi- ence. Because this information will be something only the maker has ac- cess to, we, the viewers, will be educated; as reflectors of the maker's "selfhood," we will be affirmed as knowing subjects.

The maker is someone who is like us ("us" being the liberal-human- ist subject) and also unlike us. This contradictory position of the maker provides two kinds of viewing. First, we can identify with her/his strug- gle to be a liberal-humanist subject. Second, since s/he is also unlike us, we can also regard the maker as "Other." Viewing becomes an occasion to assert, "Thank God, it's you and not me." Thus the maker's empirical evidence and inability to theorize that experience become an opportunity for us, the liberal viewer, to do the theorizing, and to understand our po- sitions via that of the maker. The maker as "Other" holds the mirror up for "our" understanding of ourselves.

To resist the power of the confessional mode of personal documen- tary, I made a video, *My Life as a Poster*, in 1995. The video was a care- ful reproduction of all the tropes of the personal documentary. It had a first person voice-over, which told the story of my sister, who was mur- dered by her husband, and the tragic consequences this incident had for the narrator, who is me, and for my family. There was one other important element in this story; it was false. Every word had been invented. I was merely replicating the genre.

In the video, a movie poster featured as a family-album as a gesture to the presence of super-8 home movie footage in personal documentaries. The narration includes words like "painful dislocation" and "fragmentation," staples in the vocabulary of the personal documentary. The fact that this was an invented story was an important part of the diegesis. I wasn't telling "my story," but merely parodying the demand that I tell my story. However, the knowledge of the story's falsity was superfluous in the universe where the video was functioning as a commodity.

After a series of screenings at festivals like Women in the Director's Chair, the Asian American Festivals, and the Margaret Mead Festival, it became quite clear that the fakeness of this autobiography was being read in different ways, or not at all. Sometimes quotation marks would appear around fake, as if even I, the maker, did not realize that the story was in actuality true. The *Catalogue* of the 1997 Whitney Museum of Art Biennial singles out the video's "complex relation to personal history," characterizing it as "about a family trying to escape painful memories of India by coming to America." These "narratives of violence [are] played out against formal traditional surfaces . . . Talukdar narrates a tragic story through a kind of animation theater, played out across the idealized surface of an Indian movie poster." These sentences are unironic in their use of the words "personal history." The falsity of the central narrative is not the subject of this analysis. The fake narrative is, in fact, taken literally. The curators of the show have no doubt that the tragic story is connected to the maker's personal history. Their description is predicated on the idea of "affirm[ing] the humanistic idea of storytelling." Here storytelling confirms a humanistic ideal because the story is personal history. Thus, "telling your story" confers authenticity on the narrator, who will lead us to the truth, getting to the truth being the ultimate ideal of a humanist-liberal discourse. Secondly, the use of the word "traditional" is significant here. It is being used in the context of "India," which is coupled with "painful memories" and "narratives of violence." The understanding of Indian society as traditional, and therefore violent and painful, are *a priori* to the viewing. Thus, the maker functions as a "good" native informant. Within the construction of the Whitney curators, the "good" native informant performs the function of a broker, peddling a traditional culture, ensuring that the customers' hands are clean. The video is merely a commodity to fill a niche. The niche is the need for confessional films.

Within the institutional setting of the festival and museum, the non-commercial film is a fetishized commodity that often functions as a conduit for colonial discourse. The institution, in defining how a work is to be seen, stakes out the parameters of an image economy, where makers and viewers, through the fetishized film product, can confirm and re-confirm the discourses predicated by the confessional film. It is important to note that many makers are complicitous in this exchange. They are willing to see their co-optation as political resistance.

In closing, I would like to reassert that even when disadvantaged groups are conferred a resistant voice, in practice, this may work as a reversal. Given the market economy of images, the complicity of makers and viewers in promoting a discourse that maintains the status quo is a position in need of examination and critique.

REFERENCES

Flaherty, Joseph. 1922. Nanook of the North. Motion picture. No city: Paramount Pictures.

Foucault, Michel. 1990. The History of Sexuality: An Introduction, Volume I. New York: Random House.

Friedrich, Su. 1990. Sink or Swim. Videorecording. New York: Women Make Movies.

Tajiri, Rea. 1991. History and Memory. Videorecording. New York: Akiko Productions (New York: Women Make Movies, distributor).

Whitney Museum. 1997. *Catalogue of the 1997 Whitney Museum of Art Biennial.*

Wright, Basil. 1934. The Song of Ceylon. Motion picture. No city: Denning-Cinema Contract Ltd.

PART IV

Where Are the Frontlines?

CHAPTER 25

Women's Activism in Rural Kosova

ELI

This is a story of a typical women's meeting held in an isolated area of Kosova during a time of great oppression of the people. Like other rural parts of Kosova, there are no roads, telephones, and no easy access to health care. In this meeting the women decided to do something about these problems. All names are changed.

BEFORE THE MEETING

Teuta, a women's activist from the village we are in today, has been visiting women regularly over the past year. She has gone along the muddy paths and across the mountain tracks from farm to farm. Amidst the cows, water buffaloes, chickens, and children, she has met with the women, many of whom she knows from teaching their kids. They welcome her with tiny cups of sweet Turkish coffee and, squatting in the yards, continue to build a fire or prepare the dinner as they share about their lives. Teuta makes sure everything is OK and supports the women. She asks them to come to a meeting soon.

We have to choose the times of our meetings carefully. If there is a wedding, we can't expect many women to come (although sometimes women have left the festivities to come to the meeting then returned back to the wedding afterwards). If it is a big holiday, such as Bayram or Easter, then women and girls will be busy preparing large amounts of food for the guests. If it is harvest time, they will be busy in the fields. So, to schedule today's meeting, Teuta has worked around the season and the different religious celebrations.

343

Women come to the meeting, urged on by women friends, by Teuta but also by their men folk, who, after our frequent chats with them in the tea shop, the bus, or in their meeting room, now understand the importance of women being able to better control their own lives and be at the forefront of change in their communities. The men have seen the results—the first libraries to be opened, a school built, girls now playing volleyball when before they stayed inside the farm walls, and rural women with their own magazine. The men think all these things are a great improvement and tell us so.

I meet a group of women in town as I wait for the rickety old bus to take us over the tracks into the villages nearer the mountains. I am surprised to see the women; usually they are reluctant to come into the town, as their distinctive traditional costume marks them and has somehow given them a reputation for primitiveness. It is traditional for the men to travel outside the farm, not the women. Nadije, one of the older women, urges me to come and look into her bag. It is full of sanitary napkins. "Oh, lass . . . see, we are trying them for ourselves since you showed us how they stick and are better than our old rags." We chuckle together. For the first time in years these women have come into town, and it is for themselves, not for some chores for their sons. This is change.

DURING THE MEETING

As we arrive in the village, young girls trickle down the hill towards the schoolhouse. And then the shepherd boys see the bus and run to get their mothers. We walk together to the meeting place with the kids weaving in and out of our small crowd and asking if there will be music. Very soon the cold, dull schoolroom brims over with eager women and girls. The married women edge themselves onto the rough wooden benches. Some of them stroke the benches familiarly even though they haven't been to school since they were engaged in marriage at the age of fifteen. Everyone greets everyone else, asking about their families and what has been happening since we last met. Depending on the village, there might be thirty women and girls or as many as 230.

I read their faces and can feel their mood. I look long into the eyes of one beautiful, soft face, which appears so sad. I ask her name. She hesitates, silent for minutes. "Hada," she says. And I tell her she is beautiful, that the colors of her embroidered skirt match her eyes. I see a tear.

What's new? The women fall into a discussion about their lives. There's a new bride in the village, but she's not here today; maybe she's visiting her cousin. It seems that many of the children have been ill, but the clinic in the city is too far away for the women to go. They ask about polio, remembering the cases we had last year. The women start to dream of solutions to the problem of how to get to the clinic. They decide that the clinic should be here in one of the villages. We devise a plan; the activists will bring together a new team, try to get the building and money, and negotiate in the capital city so that it will be run and staffed by the Kosovar medical charity.

But then I hear some murmurs; I'm wary that it might be negative gossip about Meriban. Since she allowed her daughter, Merite, to go and study medicine in the parallel University in Prishtina, she has been under attack from the other women. The women say that she is not a good mother and that her daughter will just be going after men. For weeks in meetings, I've been holding Meriban up as a heroine, trying to turn attitudes around. Then I catch the words and see Meriban smile—the women are saying that they envy her for having the courage to support her daughter. I ask the girls what they want to be when they grow up and many of them now say, "Doctors, like Merite."

The beauty with the embroidered skirt I first greeted still seems shaken. I go and hug her. She explains, "The thing is . . . I compared your words telling me I am beautiful with the words of my husband, who tells me I have the face of an animal. You asked me my name and it touched me, for since marriage I am only called wife-of-Gani. This is the first time in twelve years I have heard my own name."

After more talks and jokes, I find one of the girls has brought her tambourine. Women dance at weddings with all faces critically on them. At meetings we celebrate women's freedom, the fact that we have a space together where there are no demands to perform or do things for others; it is just a place to be ourselves. Two of the older women join the young girls and get the rhythm going; eventually, as the pace gets faster, we all join in singing. We have changed the words of a traditional song so that it celebrates girls going to school and studying to improve ourselves. The young girls don't want to stop the song, but there are children waiting back at home. All the women leave the room changed— they are uplifted. Meriban thanks me for what she calls "women's medicine."

AFTER THE MEETING

Our activists sit down and plan the next stages of the clinic project, and the final details for organizing the first girls' sports day in the region. We are all on a high and determined to get the clinic.

After some months of tough negotiating, raising money from the community, and getting a building, the clinic is formally opened. Since then it has been staffed by nurses who receive nothing for their labor. The clinic is always full.

UPDATE: OCTOBER 1998

Over one quarter of the people of Kosova have been forced out of their homes by the Serbian forces. Most of these homes and much of the land have now been destroyed, and areas around them have been mined. People want to go back, but they have little to go back to. No one feels safe.

The school where this meeting was held briefly became a place of torture. Women and children from one village were forced to go there and were held hostage by paramilitary forces for two days and nights without food or water or anywhere to defecate. Then they were released. Many men have been "arrested" and many are missing. A pattern has begun of this village's women being taken by the police and interrogated. We do not know really what happened during these interrogations. The doctor from our hospital was put in prison. Supplies of medicines had been confiscated—but now are returned. Other medical staff from this clinic have all been threatened by the police.

Women's meetings continue, but any gatherings are dangerous. Now we work with the trauma and grief of our community, trying to re-build again what was so brutally destroyed.

The international community is promising large amounts of money for Kosova. But it seems that little of it will be controlled by rural women's groups or by local groups at all. Locals, women in particular, are now being more excluded from decisions about their future than ever before. Unfortunately, it seems that many of the international organizations now in Kosova have no understanding of women's issues and are actually importing sexism and bad practices along with their aid and their well-paid international consultants. These problems have also been faced in many other parts of the world; anyone who has ever read a book on development knows, in advance, that they will occur.

Women in Kosova see that the international politicians and aid agencies seem unable to learn from their well-documented mistakes, and these mistakes are affecting our lives. Perhaps the time has finally come to dismantle the whole framework of what international politics and aid are about. Foreigners (mostly men) in high-paid, short-term positions as politicians, journalists, and aid workers should not be controlling the fate of people in places in which they have no long-term interest. Maybe many women around the world gradually chipping away the structures of this new imperialism might help it to fall. Until it is dismantled, Bosnia is doomed to be repeated. Not just in Kosova, but in other parts of the world.

CHAPTER 26

The Soldier and the State
Post-Liberation Women: The Case of Eritrea

SONDRA HALE

INTRODUCTION

An Eritrean woman fighter told me in 1994, "Of course the women fighters in the field were a model for the rest of society. We believed we could do anything that men can do—and in the long run we can change the whole society."[1] Such buoyant optimism was not the rule. Another woman fighter of the Eritrean People's Liberation Front (EPLF) remarked bitterly: "As for us, upon re-entering [civil] society, *we find that we are liberated but not free. In the field [the military struggle] we were not liberated, but [we were] free.*" My research question builds on these two viewpoints: Are the women fighters of the EPLF going to succeed as models of emancipated women within a liberated society? Or, are they simply symbols of a romantic era that has passed, metaphors for and icons of the struggle? We have certainly been led to believe (and I believe) that they were models during the struggle and that the struggle itself was a model for other progressive movements throughout the world. Just as post-apartheid South Africa is under considerable global scrutiny, those who know Eritrea's contemporary history are watching very carefully. The EPLF has an international reputation for enlightened class, gender, and race politics, forged in a long military (and strategic) struggle.

I am interested in the emancipatory possibilities for both socialism and feminism, their combinations, and the contradictions that inhere. For such an exploration it is especially instructive to examine the participation of women in social movements, one of the foci of this volume. In this essay, I concentrate only briefly on Eritrean women's participation in the liberation struggle, doing so in order to emphasize my primary concern, the obstacles they face in civilian life. I focus on the problems for women in this period of state-building, constitution-building, and the government's simultaneous attempt to maintain control and build democracy in peacetime. Nation-building has been made especially difficult in a one-party state, People's Front for Democracy and Justice (PFDJ, formerly EPLF), operating amidst the emergence of nine "nationalisms," which are mainly, but not exclusively, based on ethnic identities and are approximately divided along religious lines. Eritrea is approximately half Christian, half Muslim, borders a militant Islamist state—Sudan—and is dominated by the Highland Tigrinya-speaking Christians (de facto, if not de jure). These groups were unified in the later years of the war, but problems are emerging. The government is actively addressing the problem of Tigrinya and Christian dominance amidst such diversity; the newly-developed constitution (1996) should offer some protections for minorities and potentially oppressed groups. However, problems are immense and suspicions run high. This is the context of my topic.

We have many recent historical examples of the fact that often creating an *esprit de corps* and the context for mass mobilization is much easier during a military struggle. Within limits, it is even easier to build the kind of camaraderie that might look like egalitarianism. Life in bunkers often looks like democracy. But is it democracy and can it be maintained?

During the time of my research, Eritreans were at peace after thirty years of military struggle (1961–1991) for independence from Ethiopian rule.[2] Analyses of the effectiveness of EPLF in civilian life may prove revealing. My aim has been to analyze the situation for women "fighters" as civilians or quasi-civilians.

My primary research method was to collect the stories and testimonies of the women of the EPLF who had served at the front (or "in the field"). But because of the way that women experienced a "cultural re-entry," I wanted stories of civilian life as well as war life.

One of my general research interests is the cultural positioning of women in most liberation movements to serve the movement. I began to recognize that sometimes revolutionary men abandon women to a "traditional" culture, expecting women to maintain the culture or maintain the family, often as a symbol of resistance. The effect can be to freeze that culture. The second effect is to romanticize the role of women: as mothers, as mothers of liberation fighters, and as the "keepers of the hearth." Sometimes, women have even been romanticized as soldiers. Another related process of liberation fronts has been to expect women to represent the "morality" or central ethic of the movement. The Eritrean situation is an unusual combination of these. Unlike some post-liberation struggles, where women have had to struggle openly with male sexism and moralism in political and personal life, Eritrean women fighters are more or less being left on their own to cope with civilian life and mainstream society. As a result, mainstream society is imposing on women a high level of social morality and traditional values that the women fighters were not expected to observe in the field. I argue that little of what was addressed by the EPLF during the struggle was related to women's *private* lives. In civilian life, there is even less recognition of the special problems women encounter in private life. The effect of leaving women to experience the heavy hand of tradition in their private, civilian lives is to deny many of the social gains that EPLF women had experienced in the field.

I have been asking whether or not there are/were some inherent problems in these liberation movements and/or organizations that made the task of addressing and resolving women's issues so difficult at the end of the military struggle. Our task might be to explore the dynamics of these movements (1) in terms of the contradictions within the organizations; (2) in view of the *nature* and length of the military struggle and the role of women in that sphere; (3) with respect to the roles of women in non-military operations during the struggles; and (4) with consideration for the long- and short-term revolutionary strategies, especially the issue of the relationship of the movement to "traditional" or various spheres of vernacular culture.

Like many feminists who work within a revisionist Marxian framework (in my case, socialist feminism), I want to know not only if a particular movement has addressed gender (women's) interests, but just *what* these interests are and how they are defined. Are they seen as conflicting with either men's interests or the national interests? Do women have a greater tendency to consider issues such as health and nutrition, sanitation, child welfare, family security, and the like (sometimes referred to as "practical women's or gender interests"[3]) as "national issues," while men distinguish between "national" and "gender" interests? Has the emancipation of women been a process initiated by women on their own terms? Has the movement been nourished by any indigenous women's institutions? Has there been a need for an autonomous women's organization and what is its relationship to the mixed-gender "mass" organization?

It is in thinking about this last point that I have become especially interested in the relationships of the National Union of Eritrean Women (hereafter, NUEW, or the acronym HAMADE[4]) and the EPLF—during the struggle and in peacetime. Revolutionary movements throughout the world have considered women to be "helpmates," and the roles that women are encouraged to play in the struggle are often as seen as extensions of their domestic and or "traditional" roles. Likewise, women's organizations have often been used as a stable of supporters and as substitutes for men at certain points in the crisis. Or, women's issues have been defined in such a way as to trivialize them and keep them isolated, defining them only as "women's issues" as separate from the "broader issues," or conflated with "men's issues." Such diminishing of the importance of women's participation can have the effect of dulling or delaying the development of women's political consciousness—and men's, too—and often results in women's issues being forgotten when the struggle (e.g., a military conflict) or crisis, is over. It is here where the Eritrean case becomes salient.

The test will be whether or not the EPLF-inspired government can succeed in applying the gender, race, and class ideology, developed in the bunkers, to civilian rule. Women transformed themselves "in the field," developing/creating free association in marriage, free social relations, relaxed social customs and habits, revolutionized ideas about childbearing and rearing, realizing changes in the gender division of labor, land ownership, and greater political participation. If these could be held onto, I and others argued, then we might have a new model for human relations to guide us in the twenty-first century.

Yet, as a left feminist activist, I have been concerned for some time about how things seem to fall apart for women when the war is over. Why and how does this happen? Do we look at the contradictions within the revolutionary organizations themselves? Is the answer in the *nature* of the military struggle and the role of women in that sphere? Do we look to the relationship of the movement to religio-kin structures and various other spheres of culture? Maybe we should analyze the symbolism and metaphors of the revolution that did or did not serve women's agendas. Do these symbols have a transformed meaning after liberation?

THE ERITREAN LIBERATION MOVEMENT: THE EPLF AND THE NATIONAL UNION OF ERITREAN WOMEN (NEUW OR HAMADE)

Many observers have categorized Eritrea's struggle as a paragon of a democratic and effective movement. Why have observers been more hopeful about Eritrea than we have been about other struggles and what are the reasons for our reservations? Here are some of my preliminary arguments:

The Positive Features: For the purposes of this essay I have isolated over a dozen positive features that set Eritrea apart from many other liberation movements and that, taken as a group, have resulted in an exemplary movement.

First and foremost, Eritreans took advantage of a protracted military struggle (in this case, thirty years). Such span of time gave them time to re-envision the society, not only learning from the mistakes of the past, but correcting them in their own movement. I discuss the vision itself as a separate positive below.

Moreover, the length and intensity of the struggle gave an opportunity for, and in fact necessitated, the entry of women into the military struggle in various capacities. Entry into the struggle was referred to as "entering the field," which included not only the combat areas, but also the liberated areas that were not necessarily in the combat zones, but where people were serving the struggle in other ways.

The intensity of the war also necessitated women getting military training and serving in combat. In fact, all women fighters had to be available for combat at any time. One of the women I interviewed, an artist and art teacher, was called to the Front three times, once for an entire year. The EPLF estimated that some one-third of the combat force was comprised of women, and some 40 percent of people in the field. The statement that women made up 30 percent of the combat force is not sufficiently explanatory, however, because of the contradictory position of women serving in the military and in combat. In fact, women were trained separately and then incorporated into the general armed struggle, which raises the old question and historical tension between protections for women versus equal treatment.

Furthermore, women took part in *all* aspects of the struggle. Only at the very beginning of their entrance into the field were women given special consideration and protections, or positioned in military roles that were seen as extensions of their domestic labor or the "nature of women" (e.g., spies, nurses, teachers, child care workers).

In other words, contrary to the histories of most militaries, women were not expected to be "irregulars." That resulted in women getting full military benefits and in not being demobilized before men (i.e., cut loose from their military salaries and benefits), as we have seen in most military histories.

Furthermore, when women entered the military struggle, they were not thought of as "substitutes," as in the "Rosie the Riveter" case during World War II United States or in the Algerian struggle. At least some women were in the military struggle all along—and, ultimately, in all aspects of it. That is not to say that women were not used as "irregulars." Some of the most important people in the struggle were not even "in the field." Among these were the mainly older women, those beyond suspicion, who served as couriers and spies in the urban areas, especially in Asmara. I interviewed "Haregu" (Haregu Tesfu Menameno), who owned a hotel just outside of Asmara. She regaled me with stories of hiding EPLF fighters, storing their guns, distracting *derg* (Ethiopian regime) soldiers, passing messages, and the like.

Related to the above point, the EPLF is said by nearly everyone to have moved beyond the tokenism of viewing women as merely the supporting chorus. In the field women were not only 40 percent of the fighters and 30 percent of the combat force by the 1980s, they were over 80 percent of the dentists; some 30 percent of the transportation electricians; and 43 percent of the barefoot doctors. There were women commandants, political educators, and representatives on the Organizational Congress.[5]

Perhaps most significantly, when parts of the military movement had to move into the bunkers and/or related shelters, literally underground, women and men lived communally with little or no privacy. They shared in all of the domestic tasks and enjoyed a large measure of camaraderie. Such communes were practice for socialist communes in civilian life.

The *modus operandi* for disseminating the socialist, egalitarian ideas of the EPLF has been widely heralded as exemplary of political and social education "in the field." First of all, a number of children and young people who entered the field—either with their parents or on their own—were too young to serve in military positions. Although everyone over a certain age had some six months of military mixed with political training, the continuation of the education of the fighters and children of fighters was a primary goal of the EPLF. To achieve that goal, Revolutionary Schools were established all over the liberated areas. These schools were a combination of academic and socio-political education. They also served the populations in the liberated areas from which the EPLF was trying to recruit. A number of my interviewees, mainly teachers in the field, described forcing children to attend school or actively propagandizing among the local population to convince them to send their children to school. However, the education was not just for children. In a country where the literacy rate and knowledge about national and international politics were very low, adult education became (and still is) primary. Among these adults, women were an especially targeted population, as were girl children.

In addition to the Revolutionary Schools, designed for those who were too young to serve in military positions, adult education was carried out. Every small military unit (equivalent to a platoon) had a military leader and a political commissar. The latter was responsible for determining the important questions for the group to discuss. Among these commissars were a number of women. But not many. There were not many women military leaders, either, but this number was growing by the time the struggle ended.[6]

Another level of education was carried out clandestinely in the occupied areas. For example, the National Union of Eritrean Women was very active early in the struggle in recruiting and politically educating women about the struggle, meeting in small cells throughout the country. An EPLF fighter explained her work with the NUEW and the force and coercion they had to use to educate girls in the rural areas:

> When we were working in the field as teachers (most of us were in the rural areas), we were also helping each other through the National Union of Eritrean Women [HAMADE]. At that time, there was a great struggle with the rural people. Men who saw themselves in charge of the family did not want to send their girls and women to a meeting or seminar. But we were seen as teachers [i.e., not political]; they made no political connection. But when we taught them, we would insert the rights of women—in social studies, in science (I used to teach about health), their country, their environment, and about developed and undeveloped customs. There was a political struggle between us and those with undeveloped ideas. So we took young women and children (seven to fifteen years old) by force for the revolutionary school. We transferred all our ideas to them. They believed us and influenced their families. We also went house to house and introduced ourselves to their parents. When we met their mothers, we also talked with them about their rights and their future. This is how we communicated our ideas to the rest of society. We had two fights—with the enemy and with traditional culture. We will continue this way in the future until we succeed.

While education in the field and within occupied Eritrea and the rest of Ethiopia was important, international education was, also. The EPLF was very active in both giving and taking ideas to and from international socialist and feminist discourses throughout the 1970s and until the "strategic retreat" under the Derg. These ideas were important in the formation of the EPLF's ideology and strategy and significant in arousing some international support, until the 1980s when the Soviet-armed *dergue* (regime) became militarily stronger and more brutal. The EPLF called for a "strategic retreat." This involved moving the struggle completely underground and engaging in clandestine activities. The consequence was that the movement pulled inward and became more isolated within the international context.

Another important area of political and cultural education that the women (and men) I interviewed repeatedly stressed was the use of cultural shows to teach people about diverse cultures at the same time that the EPLF was trying to build a national culture. Forming cultural troupes and disseminating politics through agitprop was an effective organizing tool.

One cannot overlook the importance of having a *vision*. The advantage that the EPLF gave itself was the time and space to re-envision society, preparing for a time when the EPLF would be the state and EPLF ideology the guiding principles of that state. This meant, then, a "trial run"—virtually testing one's state apparatuses while in the field. Some of the concerns that are most directly important for women are detailed below:

1. Personal status laws were scrutinized and revised, giving equal rights in the marriage union and the right of divorce, and addressing child custody issues.

2. Also, first tested in the field was the "Policy of Land Redistribution Formulated by the EPLF" in 1982, which not only transformed the land system for the peasants, but enabled women to own land. This trial run and its legacy was perhaps the most impressive *economic* emancipatory statement by the EPLF; it was further developed after independence by the party in its civilian guise (i.e., the PFDJ). In a society where women had not owned land, this document was striking and revolutionary. It asserts: "The right of women to own land is fully recognized and protected." A 1994 article in the *Christian Science Monitor* highlights the successor law that gives women (whether married or not) equal rights with men to use residential and agricultural land (all land is owned by the government). NUEW President, Askalu Menkarios, is quoted as saying, however, that: "There is no simi-

lar campaign to promote equal rights in the workplace or to defend the hard-won gains made by my women fighters, who now find it extremely difficult to return home to villages where they are considered unmarriageable due to their self-assertiveness."[7]

3. Among other visionary areas for women in the National Democratic Programme of the EPLF was the special section on "Women's Rights." Among the statements are (a) the development of a national women's union; (b) freedom from domestic confinement; (c) the promulgation of equitable marriage and family laws; (d) equality to men in politics, economics, and social life; (e) equal pay for equal work and parental leave; (f) provision for child care and kindergartens; (g) a stipulation to protect women workers from harmful work; (h) leadership development; and (i) the eradication of prostitution.[8]

4. Among the most impressive *social* emancipatory documents, manuals, and events for women were the EPLF marriage laws and the various training seminars on love and marriage offered to both men and women in the field. In a struggle that lasted so long and in which new settlements and populations were established, it was to be expected that people would want to get married and raise children. Eventually, the EPLF had to develop policies for such unions that were not only compatible with military life, but part of the vision for a new society after the struggle. The long period in the field, under one authority, was seen as an opportunity to develop progressive marriage laws.

5. Like most liberation movements, the EPLF is not entirely open and tolerant on issues of sexuality. Interviewees and others timidly responded to my questions about sexual relations in the field, evading my queries about rumors that, at the beginning of the military struggle, people were executed for breaking sexual mores proscribed by the EPLF. However, it appears that this was exaggerated information; most of my interviewees claimed that people were not executed, but, as Worku Zerai, NUEW leader during the struggle, claimed, the punishment had been "severe."

However, after 1978, women had begun to enter the field in large numbers, forcing a reevaluation of the social/sexual rules. A male fighter, Kifloum Kidane, informed me that the EPLF rather quickly concluded that, human nature being human nature, such severe policies would not work. The decision-makers developed a policy whereby, if a man and a woman were about to embark on a relationship, the couple had to inform and petition the EPLF. In essence, they had to be given permission to have a relationship and were officially recognized as having such. Then, ironically, after proclaiming that they were having a relationship, they would frequently be stationed in two different locations.

Having suggested that I am critical of the sexuality and personal union/partnership policies of the EPLF, I should mention a 1980 EPLF seminar on marriage that reminds one of Aleksandra Kollantai's "winged eros."[9] Certainly, in perusing the content of the seminar, one cannot say that the EPLF failed to struggle with issues of sexuality, romance, and relationships. The contents of the seminar, if even remotely practiced, place the EPLF in the vanguard of progressive personal politics for the time. Every fighter with whom I conversed on these subjects mentioned either attending or hearing and reading about the seminar. That people were willing to engage these topics because it was a respected portion of EPLF ideology was a triumph in itself. A few even referred to their unions as "open" or "free."[10]

The importance of the existence of an effective national women's organization cannot be overlooked. There is little doubt that the NUEW has played a major role in forcing the issue of the emancipation of women to the forefront of the struggle. For all of the period of the struggle, the NUEW was an affiliate of the EPLF, one of its branches, so to speak. How much autonomy and/or independence there is and was is arguable. Women, through the NUEW, had considerable representation in the field, with the executive committee of the NUEW attending the Organizational Congress. In order to offset gender discrimination, or, as the EPLF put it, "positively discriminate for women," 80 percent of the Congressional seats were generally contested, with women being eligible for these, but additionally 20 percent were set aside for women.

Therefore, from its inception in 1979, the NUEW was an important part of the EPLF. In fact, central to the EPLF's founding was the institutionalization of the role of women in the liberation movement and a call for the establishment of a national union of women.

But a striking and perhaps telling act occurred in 1993. The NUEW, which claims to have over 100,000 members, declared itself independent from the EPLF, making it officially a nongovernmental organization

(NGO). During the national struggle, HAMADE had worked on recruitment, for the movement, on consciousness-raising in the villages of the liberated areas, and on international and national propaganda. Currently, in addition to recruitment, the program of the NUEW has involved fighting for and then protecting/enforcing women's land rights; carrying out literacy campaigns; developing cooperatives; representing women in the development of the new constitution, which will include playing a role in developing new marriage and family laws; leading the struggle to end female circumcision; gaining child care and parental leave; training women for leadership roles; campaigning for the eradication of polygamy and prostitution; promulgating labor laws as these relate to women; and working on various health issues.

With regard to the NUEW's independence from the EPLF, there was some disparity of opinions about just how "loosely affiliated" the NUEW is. Some of the staff of the NUEW informed me that most members are *not* EPLF members; whereas others that I interviewed insisted that the NUEW is still under the tight control of the EPLF, and that most of its members are also EPLF members. One EPLF dissident insisted that the NUEW has no autonomy.

Yet, if the recruitment of women into public political life is to be considered a significant index of liberation—as the NUEW believes by making it one of their aims—we might want to observe the figures in the recent election for the regional assemblies. For example, in the Gash-Barka election to elect a seventy-four-member assembly for three regional assemblies (the *zobas*, or districts, of Gash-Barka, Anseba, and Debub), 67 women competed out of 299 candidates; five women were elected in the "open" contest with men, while other women contested for the "special seats" reserved for women. To break it down, for Anseba where 288 candidates entered the election, nineteen women out of sixty-seven were elected. In Debub, seventy-nine people were elected, including twenty-three women; in the general election 318 people ran, including only four women. Thirty percent of the seats were reserved for women; and 110 women contested for these.[11] Judging from only one election several factors are clear—women are doing better in local level elections and are less successful at the general election level. It appears that women are willing to compete, even in the open contests with men, and that they are having some victories. But the gap is still significant. Since free elections are new, however, it is too soon to tell if women who hold elected seats will be able to translate these positions into real power.

SOME PROBLEMS

What does it mean to the men and women fighters to be reintegrated into civilian life in a society that gave hearty support to the EPLF-led movement? Because of the complexity of that society and its multiple voices (gender, class, religious, cultural, linguistic, and regional), the response might depend on who is talking. Although the EPLF had success in imposing one law during wartime, it is another matter to impose that same law on a highly heterogeneous society in peace-time. The extremely complicated application of EPLF law to the broader society is now taking place, and the responses are varied.

The Constitution: If the existence of special mention of *women* (and not only *gender)* in a constitution is an index of gender egalitarianism, then we might want to deconstruct the wording of that new Eritrean document. The new (1996) constitution was released to the public in mid-1996, after a long semipublic and public process, one that passed up the opportunity to devote a separate chapter to women and to experiment with a multiparty system.

Because of our experience in the United States of trying to secure separate and special protections for women (and other historically underrepresented and marginalized groups) in our constitution (e.g., the defeat of the Equal Rights Amendment), I was concerned about the possibilities that Eritreans might take this perfect opportunity to etch into the primary documentary guide to democracy the pronouncement of protections for women. With that primary question in mind and because I had noted that other drafts had not contained separate chapters on women, I interviewed three powerful women who had been part of the development of the constitution and in charge of public education. They informed me that there was little need for a separate chapter on women, that Eritrean women know that the EPLF has "served them well," that women "trust their government," and know that their government is "gender blind."[12]

Military and Civilian Strategies for Organizing: Everything hinges on whether or not the highly successful organizing strategies of the EPLF *in the field* could be translated to *civil society.* I asked the women fighters I interviewed about their problems in civil society some two years and four years after liberation, and then about the organizing strategies they are now using. One woman fighter complained:

> They [our families] were happy at first that we came back alive. But after a year it changed. We have very different ideas from the rest of so-

ciety. Women must stay at home and take care of their children, not go out and talk with men. We do not accept these traditional ideas of our parents, but it is difficult to change them. It is very hard for us because we were used to equality in the field.

Another fighter, who had spoken eloquently about how effective they had been in the field as organizers/teachers, seemed discouraged:

On the surface they [civil society] accept the [progressive] ideas, but underneath they do not accept equality for women. To change our parents, our society, we have to change their ideas. There is a struggle over the major differences between us. When we try to explain, they do not accept easily. When they saw that in practice we fought against the enemy, they could accept that. But they insist that we must [also] be married and bear children—and stay home and take care of our children.

And, then, like most of the women fighters I interviewed, she ended her statement hopefully: " . . . if we struggle more, we will succeed . . . Women need to be educated more to become like us—or more like us."

THE NATIONAL CURRICULUM

Is the National Curriculum being used as an active agent of change? The question leads me to another reservation, which emerged primarily from my interviews with women fighters who were training to be educators. Have the demobilized fighters placed too much reliance on education without totally evaluating the content and nature of that education? I have been analyzing the gender content of the developing National Curriculum. Although the gender images in the primary schools reflect a gender egalitarianism, such positive images of girls/women may need to be reinforced by more public education about the marginalization of girls and women. It became very clear to me from my interviews with officials at the Ministry of Education and from perusal of documents that the uncompromising and challenging Marxist-inspired and Freire-inspired, liberatory pedagogy [13] used in the Revolutionary Schools is being diluted and retreated from in the development of the National Curriculum. Women and oppressed classes are bound to suffer the consequences.

Idealistic attitudes toward education as a panacea prevail, without a critical evaluation of the *content* of that education and without considering just how educational curriculum and pedagogy can be considered as actives tools for change. But more troubling were the attitudes connected to "being educated" that I gleaned from my interviews with a number of women fighters. There was a tendency toward elitism (calling others "backward") by the more formally educated highland Christian Tigrinya-speaking group, with the potential for continuing discrimination against Muslims, half the population. There was an automatic assumption that a "traditional" culture was "backward." There was rarely any critical thinking involved in deeming a culture "traditional." There was also the tendency to attribute all "undesirable" customs to the rural areas, lowlands, and to Muslims, and to assume that educated people are mostly progressive and above and beyond oppressing others, including women.

But if education is a panacea, I argued to them, then Eritrea is in trouble, because social welfare issues, like education, are being neglected by the government in favor of economic development. My informants for this were often the same women and men who had expressed great confidence in education.

Related to the above elitist attitudes towards Lowland Muslims and "traditional culture" is the notion that EPLF fighters were somehow outside and above the culture. It is not too difficult to imagine how this attitude developed over thirty years of living in bunkers and in isolated, sealed-off areas. But the effect of "isolation" was psychological or mental instead of physical, as there was always a great amount of contact with the occupied areas and much movement of people. The EPLF had succeeded in developing a remarkable amount of political and cultural hegemony that resulted in an "us" and "them" mentality. Women fighters repeatedly used expressions such as, "*We* have to educate *them*." For all the attempts to break down class and race/ethnic/religious distinctions, the dichotomy between the "enlightened vanguard" and the unenlightened was distinct. Perhaps the peacetime establishment of mandatory national service, whereby urban youth have to work in rural areas, will be effective in breaking down some of the elitism.

Related to education and socialization is the breakdown of the fascinating combination in the field of the discipline of children (e.g., "Red Flowers") and the stress on freedom and challenging authority. Children of the fighters born and schooled in the field are now often looked upon in their civilian transition as "undisciplined." The fighters told me that their children were "free" in the field, and that in postliberation Asmara, they are noting behavioral changes in their children, especially the girls, who are now tending to defer to boys. Will the new national curriculum be able to offset this decline in liberatory childrearing? A national curriculum and a constitution that are not acting affirmatively toward women may not help.

Another potential problem may result from the strategy for dealing with the traditional religio-kinship structures. Few liberation organizations are so secularized as to aim at obliterating, through administrative assault or revolutionary legalism, the very social fabric on which the society was built. It will be instructive to observe how the Eritrean government, in a society that is nearly half Christian and half Muslim, will deal with aspects of *sharia* law and Islamic practices such as polygamy, as well as with many rigidly repressive Christian customs that run counter to EPLF ideology. Will it be possible for the government to convert aspects of religion into revolutionary tactics, that is, to use religion to bring some aspects of liberation—at least as transition? For example, with regard to Christian ideology and practice, I did not hear conversations about using some of the precepts of Christianity to build, for example, a "revolutionary theology." When Islam was discussed by Tigrinya-speaking Christians, there was often mention in some circles of fear of a "religious jihad." These negative comments were rarely offset by analyses of Islamic practices that are egalitarian. I never heard ideas about the creation of "Islamic feminism" or "Islamic Marxism" (e.g., the Iranian *Moujahadin*) discussed, for example.

The Existence of a National Women's Movement Tied to the Liberation Party: With regard to a national women's organization, it is too soon to tell how independent the NUEW will be and how innovative. There is the question of whether or not women and feminists can be more effective by infiltrating/permeating mass, gender-mixed organizations and undermining their sexism, or whether it is a necessity to be independent. Also, is the immediate postliberation period a time to launch a women's movement that may, for a time, be separate from the national movement?

How innovative has the NUEW been beyond literacy and cooperatives, and how egalitarian and regionally distributed is their work? Their work in getting the land ownership laws to serve women was admirable, as has been their work in the elections.

There is a question about what other women's organizations have been encouraged or allowed to exist by the government and/or the NUEW, and whether or not women's issues and movements become defined too narrowly, partially due to a "development mentality" that reduces everything to development, ergo, income-generating projects. Is there a need, in the Eritrean case, to develop a women's movement that emanates from, but radically transforms, indigenous structures, for example, women's popular culture and networks and their struggles as workers?

The NUEW itself, although staffed almost entirely of fighters, has become the establishment, another bureaucracy that is overburdened with work and yet selfish about sharing it with other agencies. Considering the beleaguered condition of the NUEW (where everything concerning women or gender is sent to them to handle), there is a need for other women's organizations and agencies—a division of labor is called for. Yet, the NUEW monopolizes women's issues, defining them in particular ways and possibly undermining or usurping all other organizations engaged in gender work. One such organization (BANA), designed to form cooperatives among demobilized women fighters, was undermined and had trouble surviving. The relationship between the Gender Unit of Mitias, the organization of demobilized fighters, and NUEW does not seem to be one of cooperation. There is little or no coordinating among these various gender or women's units connected with government departments, causing suspicion, competition for government resources, and the like. The girls'/women's section of the National Union of Eritrean Youth and Students was undermined by the NUEW and finally collapsed. The person I interviewed, who was, for a brief time, a staffer in the girls'/women's section, gave me a paper that the organization had published on women in Eritrea and asked that I not show it to anyone in the NUEW.[14] These are not positive signs, but they follow from the bureaucratization of the NUEW and other governmental and quasi-nongovernmental organizations. When the fighter—whether woman or man—begins to be viewed by the masses as just another bureaucrat, someone who can determine, with a nod of the head or stroke of the pen, a peasant or working-class person's future, then the *esprit de corps*, so carefully cultivated in the field, breaks down. People are no longer in the bunkers together, fighting and dying together. One of them is making a decision for the other. This is a massive dilemma in any revolutionary situation and on the day *after* the revolution.

Political Representation: With all of the egalitarianism of the field situation, there were still very few women in high ranking, decision-making positions, and the same is true of the postliberation period. The NUEYS (members of the NVEW), despite issuing caveats about only paying lip service to women holding equal power, claim that, "Prior to the Beijing Conference on Women's issues, [Eritrean] women made up 21 percent of representatives in the interim government. This far surpasses many industrialized countries, such as the United States. . . . "[15] Nonetheless, is 21 percent a satisfactory percentage? If, by design, there were half Muslims in the upper echelons of government, would it be impossible to have half women? There is a tension between claims to be "gender blind" and claims that affirmative action is needed. The 1997 elections discussed above offered hope that women may do well at a grassroots and regional level. Power at this level may be more significant than representation of women at a national level, that is, if the ideas about women's/gender issues can be built from the ground up.

Symbols and images, as we know, can be important in the development of a new nation. Women are often central to this national image construction, or subject-making, but in a negative sense. EPLF women fighters had begun the gender image-building in a positive way; they saw themselves, and were seen by others, as among the political and educated elites in the towns, as models of emancipated women. Women fighters as heroes form a familiar icon in postliberation Eritrea. But has that metaphor of woman warrior been transformed into concrete and ongoing liberatory conditions for women?

CONCLUSION

The movement of the EPLF is promising, even though it was initiated by men who only later saw a need for women to join. Women themselves were drawn into the struggle by forces related to them as women (e.g., destroyed homes and villages, tortured and murdered children, destruction of families, and their oppression as women in the society). That so many Eritrean women went into the field to escape oppressive conditions in the family and home—some actually fleeing—and were embraced by and found their liberation in the EPLF, speaks to the promise of the movement. Whether or not the bunker ideal can be maintained—or, more hopefully, enhanced—in civil society is the question.

The EPLF and Eritreans, in general, seemed to have learned a number of lessons from past liberation movements, and applied them. Moreover, it would seem consistent with the last thirty plus years that the EPLF would continue to work on personal, family, and sexuality issues—even within the framework of a very conservative society.

Repeated from my opening page, in summarizing the situation for women in Eritrea, one EPLF woman fighter, just demobilized and given the equivalent of five-hundred dollars to start a new life, delivered one of the strongest statements of my interviews: "As for us, upon re-entering [civil] society, we find that we are liberated but not free. In the field we were not liberated, but [we were] free."

What does it mean for a party like the EPLF and its civilian counterpart to travel the route from liberation front—an organization devoted to empowering the disenfranchised groups (women, peasants, Muslims, workers)—to a government assigned to control and manage these very groups? Elites who entered the struggle as "fighters" returned as elites. Peasants, with a few exceptions, returned as peasants.

As for women, we have an inconclusive portrait. If it is the case, as I was told, that many peasant, nomadic, and poorer women fighters are refusing to return to their indigenous towns and villages, opting instead to stay in the more liberal capital of Asmara, it leads one to argue that the EPLF's transformation of the individual was more successful than the transformation of the society. And what of the girl children of the revolution? What can we expect from them?

EPILOGUE

In 1998, Eritrea again went to war with Ethiopia, and that war continues as I write. It is still too soon to tell if the situation for women will be any different from the previous conflict. Or, will the people in power in the Eritrean government assess that the former egalitarianism of women in the field was not translatable to civilian life, take advantage of the new military crisis, and retreat from EPLF ideology?

The enemy is the same, but the government of that enemy (and its ethnic composition) has changed. Eritrea is shrouded in secrecy, so it is not possible to know if a comparable number of women were recruited into the new struggle or if going to war was one method for reducing the unemployment of men, so women will not be called up until they are needed. After experiencing what civilian life had to offer them, will the women fighters have the same enthusiasm for the late 1990's conflict? At this point in my research, the resurgence of militarism only raises more questions.

ACKNOWLEDGMENTS

The research for this essay, still in its initial stages, is based entirely on fieldwork in Asmara, Eritrea, the capital, and, except for data gleaned from interviews with members of the National Union of Eritrean Women (NUEW), in Asmara, suffers, therefore, from a lack of information about and observation of grassroots organizing by the NUEW in other areas of the country. Partially as a consequence of the above, I also rely heavily on more institutional and public forms of organizing, for example, organizing efforts of state parties and national organizations. Further, I have neglected the gender history and politics of the Eritrean Liberation Front (ELF), the first liberation movement begun in the early 1960s and now having the status of an opposition movement, and other parties. Nor have I told fully the story of women and the EPLF. It was not possible to do so in this brief essay.

This paper is based on two research trips to Asmara, Eritrea, 1994 and 1996. The materials were primarily collected through oral histories of women fighters and interviews with government officials and others; and on archival research in the United States and in Asmara government offices. I am indebted to the National Union of Eritrean Women, where I was affiliated, and I thank them for their materials. Among the NUEW staff I want to thank are the President Askalou Menkerios and the ex-Head of Research, Saba Issayas, Senait Lijam, Head of Education and Research, Yehdega Andehaimanot, in Research and Education/Library, Lydia Berhane (Library), and a number of other staffers. I relied on *Mosana* (variably entitled "The Voice of HAMADE"), the organ of the NUEW, for example, the Constitution (adopted at the Fourth and Transitional Congress in 1992), and the NUEW "Fact Sheet" (mimeographed, n.d., probably 1995 or 1996).

I am also indebted to the Department of Education, National Curriculum Division; to members of the Constitution Committee; to Mitias (organization of demobilized fighters); to the Asmara Teacher Training Institute; to Edna Yohannes, my primary Research Assistant in 1994 and part of 1996, to Selam Araya, my Research Assistant in 1996; to both Tigisti Mehreteab and Elsa Yacob who set up and translated some 1996 interviews; to Almaz (Alexa) Hale, my older daughter, who helped with the 1994 research; to Adrienne (Tsegoweini) Hale, my younger daughter, who helped with the 1996 research. Thanks also go to Kifloum Kidane, Aster Solomon, Giulia Berrera, Nancy Farwell, Eva Egensteiner, Dan Solomon Tsehaye, Dr. Asmarom Legesse, Laurie and Wayne Kessler, Sara Abraham, and "Mr. Joe," Aynalem Morcos, Ministry of Education.

Ideas for the paper are based on the thirty-six years that I have followed, first, the Eritrean Liberation Front (ELF), then the Eritrean People's Liberation Front (EPLF), beginning from my vantage point of Khartoum, Sudan, where I was doing research in the 1960s, and since liberation, the People's Front for Democracy and Justice (PFDJ). A number of my ideas emanate from a comparative approach to the study of gender politics. See for example, Sondra Hale, *Gender Politics in Sudan: Islamism, Socialism, and the State* (Boulder: Westview Press, 1996). This research was partially funded by the University of California, Los Angeles (UCLA) Centers for African Studies and the Study of Women. As for written sources, I have relied mainly on EPLF, NUEW, and other government and non-government documents. As for published sources, I gained a great deal from Amrit Wilson, *Women and the Eritrean Revolution: The Challenge Road* (Trenton: The Red Sea Press, 1991), especially the appendices.

NOTES

1. The term "fighter" was generally used for people struggling in any form as part of the EPLF, especially in the liberated areas; the phrase "in the field" refers both to areas already liberated and those being contested during the struggle.

2. Between the time of my fieldwork and the writing of this essay, Eritrea again went to war with Ethiopia. Fighting continues as I write. See epilogue.

3. Maxine Molyneaux, "Mobilization without Emancipation? Women's interests, the State, and Revolution in Nicaragua." *Feminist Studies* 11, no. 2 (1985): 54.

4. HAMADE is a Tigrinya acronym for Hagerawi (National) Maheber (Union) Dekenstio (Women) Ertrawian (Eritreans).

5. These are figures culled from a number of mainly journalist sources, for example, Lori Grinker, "'The Main Force': Women in Eritrea," *Ms.*, Vol. 2, No. 6 (1992), p. 47; and James C. McKinley, "Asmara Journal: In Peace, Warrior Women Rank Low," *New York Times International* (4 May 1996), p. 4; "Eritrea's Women Fighters Long for Equality of War," *The Guardian* (9 May 1996); and many others.

6. Some of the information on the political structure and activities of the fighter units I gleaned from interviews with about three dozen women fighters, but also with Solomon Tsehaye, Head of the Department of Culture at the time of the interview in 1994, Worku Zerai, part of the NUEW leadership during the struggle (interview in Asmara, 25 August 1996), a military judge, Letebrahan Kasai, who had been a military commander (interview 13 August 1996), with Abrehet Goytom, Head of Mitias Gender Unit, 12 August 1996 and with Asmarat Abraha (known as "Gwande" in the field), a famous woman fighter (interview in Asmara, 22 July 1996), who was said to have commanded an all-women unit for a short time (but who denied to me that there had ever been such a unit, interview in Asmara, 22 July 1996).

Unless otherwise indicated, all the following quotes from women fighters are from two group interviews I conducted with teachers/fighters who were taking an intensive English course at Asmara Teacher Training Institute (T.T.I.). The interviews were carried out 12 July and 15 July 1994, at T.T.I. I am indebted to my daughter, Alexa Almaz Hale, who was teaching them English, for setting up these interviews.

7. Don Connell, *Christian Science Monitor* (November 30, 1994), p. 10.

8. Although I eventually obtained access to original documents, I used the appendices in Wilson, ibid., especially appendixes 5, 6a, and 6B.

9. Wilson, ibid., Appendix 6b, pp. 194-197; reference to Kollantai is from Barbara Clements, *Bolshevik Feminist: The Life of Aleksandra Kollantai* (Bloomington: University of Indiana, 1979), especially Chapter 10, "Winged Eros," pp. 225–241.

10. By "sexuality," I am referring to heterosexuality. The EPLF, like most liberation movements in history, was closed-minded about homosexuality. In the face of rumors that, in the field, homosexuals were executed (information that absolutely cannot be confirmed), it was one of the topics fighters seemed very uncomfortable addressing.

11. "Big Voter Turnout Reported in Elections for Regional Assembly," *Eritrea Profile*, Vol. 3, No. 44 (11 January 1997), p. 1.

12. At the time of the interview (July, 1996), with three members of the Constitution Commission, a "final" draft was about to be released to the public for discussion and public education. The National Assembly had just approved the draft (July, 1996). The interview was with Zahra Jabir Omer, Tsega Gaim, and Mehret Iyoub. Most of the statements were from Mehret Iyoub.

13. Paulo Freire proposed that truly liberatory education requires teachers to be partners with students. They assist students in the emergence of consciousness and in speaking in their own active voices. *Pedagogy of the Oppressed* (New York: Seaview, 1971).

14. There is nothing especially startling about this document, except the bold competition with NUEW, plus the fact that the NUEW is mentioned only once and as only one organization serving women. It is also fairly hard-hitting on areas of women's health and what they refer to as "female genital mutilation." National Union of Eritrean Youth and Students, "Women in Eritrea" (Asmara: NUEYS, 1996, typescript). For more information on the NUEYS itself see another typescript document: National Union of Eritrean Youth and Students, "An Overview on NUEYS Background, Objectives, Organizational Information and Activities" (Asmara: NUEYS, 1996).

15. National Union of Eritrean Youth and Students, "Women in Eritrea," ibid., p. 2.

REFERENCES

Abraha, Asmarat. Personal interview. 22 July 1996.

"Big Voter Turnout Reported in Elections for Regional Assembly." 1997. *Eritrea Profile*. 3:44 (11 January 1997), 1.

Clements, Barbara. 1979. *Bolshevik Feminist: The Life of Aleksandra Kollantai*. Bloomington: University of Indiana.

Connell, Don. 1994. *Christian Science Monitor* (30 November 1994), 10.

Freire, Paulo. 1971. *Pedagogy of the Oppressed*. New York: Seaview.

Goytom, Abrehet. Personal interview. 12 August 1996.

Grinker, Lori. 1992. "The Main Force': Women in Eritrea." *Ms*. 2:6, 47.

Iyoub, Mehret, Zarah Jabir Omer and Tsega Gaim. Personal interview. July 1996.

Kasai, Letebrahan. Personal interview. 15 August 1996.

McKinley, James C. 1996. "Asmara Journal: In Peace, Warrior Woman Rank Low." *New York Times International* (4 May 1996), 4.

————. 1996. "Eritrea's Women Fighters Long for Equality of War." *The Guardian* (9 May 1996).

Molyneaux, Maxine. 1985. "Mobilization without Emancipation? Women's Interests, the State, and Revolution in Nicaragua." *Feminist Studies* 11:2, 54.

National Union of Eritean Youth and Students. 1996. "An Overview on NUEYS Background Objectives, Organizational Information and Activities." ts. Asmara: NUEYS 1996.

————. 1996. "Women in Enitea." ts. Asmara: NUEYS 1996.

Tsehaye, Solomon. Personal interview. 1994.

Wilson, Amrit. 1991. *Women and the Eritean Revolution: The Challenge Road*. Trenton: Red Sea Press.

Zerai, Worku. Personal interview. 25 August 1996.

CHAPTER 27

Beyond the Baton
How Women's Responses Are Changing Definitions of Police Violence

NANCY KEEFE RHODES

It is fitting that we spoke about police violence at the Frontline Feminisms Conference in Riverside, California in January 1997. The previous April, sheriff's deputies chased a truckload of Mexican nationals for miles and then beat those who weren't finally able to flee on foot—including a woman—as a news helicopter hovered above. Probably more people in the United States saw these now-notorious "Riverside beatings" than any other similar encounter between police and people since Los Angeles police beat Rodney King on 3 March 1991.

The Riverside beatings had a certain symmetry with the Rodney King case. With a somewhat different focus, I could have entitled this, "From Rodney King to Riverside: The Privately Transient and the Publicly Rootless." What could be more eternally transient than going down in history defined, as Rodney King was, as a 'motorist'? The Mexican "illegals" of the Riverside beatings—especially women and girls, who are jeopardized multiply by poverty, race, gender, and status—remind us that both "person" and "citizen" are tenuous categories.

Quite often when I have spoken in cities other than my own on police violence, I have begun by citing an example from that day's local newspaper. This has really not been very risky in the decade following Rodney King, when U.S. newspapers have covered police violence and community and legal response to it more than ever before. On 12 January 1997, just four days before the Frontline Feminisms Conference panel, Human Rights Watch (HRW) released a copy of their letter to U.S. Attorney General Janet Reno, along with a fourteen-page summary of concerns about abuses along the Mexican-U.S. border by Immigration and

Naturalization Service (INS) Border Patrol and other law enforcement. Following up on three previous reports, HRW documented further beatings, shootings, rape, and sexual harassment of women and girls.

The previous March, a border patrol office raped two Guatemalan women who were later assisted by the El Paso Border Rights Coalition. BRC is a project of American Friends Service Committee's Immigration Law Enforcement Monitoring Project (ILEMP), which reported to the 1995 UN Conference on Women in Beijing on 346 abuses—almost three-quarters committed by INS workers–suffered by immigrant women in Southern California, Arizona, and Texas from January 1993 to August 1995.

Human Rights Watch and the AFSC's ILEMP indicate there is widespread abuse by a particular segment of U.S. law enforcement dealing with foreign nationals. However, the garden-variety police violence toward U.S. citizens has also been easy to spot in most daily papers. By "garden-variety" I mean homegrown, pervasive throughout the nation (not just in cities, though that's another article). I also mean police violence of the classic sort, involving simply excessive force. Rodney King's beating was the classic scenario. We understand how to define "police brutality." Like some pornography, we know it when we see it. It just takes longer to see it when it happens to some people.

I want to address some aspects of how we think through what "police violence" actually is, how it affects our organizing in communities, and what it tells us about what we mean when we use the term "citizen." We think we know what "police brutality" is.

First, it's something that happens to men—but it can happen to women "too." The "classic scenario" also helps keep some kinds of police violence invisible and, to some extent, unintelligible as "violence to women." In particular, I want to address how the destruction of homes by police during commando-style drug searches damages women and their children who witness these raids, trauma that is sometimes on par with some refugee events.

I came to these issues from both organizing and research. When Rodney King was beaten in 1991, I was part of a community task force in Syracuse, New York, my home city. The task force was organizing community forums or "speak outs" on police behavior. Later, that task force successfully got city legislation passed establishing a "citizen review board" (CRB) to hear complaints of police misconduct. We believe the Syracuse CRB was the first such entity in the United States to include a provision for restitution based on the destruction of homes on grounds other than simple "search and seizure" violations. Before that another social worker and I had spent about two years meeting weekly with a women's support group in the county penitentiary. Nearly every week I heard about another home search from another woman, and not one of them had ever formally complained about having their homes trashed and their children terrified. Since then, I have interacted with many other communities throughout the country, both visiting them and, for about a year and a half, editing a national newsletter, *Policing by Consent*, about police accountability efforts. Across time and settings, the descriptions I heard came to have a certain consistency. How come everyone doesn't "know about" this kind of police violence? How come it was hard to get even a somewhat oblique provision for this kind of police violence into my city's local CRB law? What might this mean about how we construct categories like "citizen" and "rights"?

THE CLASSIC SCENARIO: MEN BEATING MEN

The Rodney King beating resonated profoundly with a large portion of the U.S. public. This was due, in part, to the video of King's beating being replayed so often by the media for its graphic and prolonged violence. But the Rodney King beating also just "fit." It embodied how we think about police violence with pervasively male features.

Traditionally, police brutality has been framed in terms of single individuals, usually male, who are defined immediately as "suspects," in physical combat, out in the street. I use the term "combat" on purpose. Military images have pervaded U.S. policing, ranging from the increasingly high-tech "war on drugs," to characterizations of police as "occupiers" dating from the 1960s, and earlier historical periods when the first police sought to protect portions of the community from escaped slaves in the South and the "dangerous classes" in Northern cities.

In the United States, the term "suspect" is racially coded, too. Who can forget the Willie Horton television ads from the 1988 Presidential campaign? And in the United States, combat between black and white men is historically sexually charged. Southern lynching, which lasted well into the twentieth century, was saturated with claims of "protecting white women's virtue." The New York City ballot initiative campaign on establishing a CRB in that city during the 1960s echoed this theme. Charging that "outside scrutiny"—notice how New York City residents were thus cast as intruders—would hamper police, the police union produced a poster depicting a white woman in a white coat, framed by a dark subway entrance, with the caption, "Would you want your officer to hesitate?"

Once use of force is recast as "abuse," communities then fight over whether these events are "aberrations" or "everyday experience."

In the classic scenario, such incidents occur primarily outside the home, either on the street or in police custody. Technically they are located "in public," though they may happen in isolated places such as alleys or parking lots, under cover of darkness, or within the protected, hence secret, context of "police business." Police aggressively discourage watching or documenting these incidents.

Suspects are depicted as lone, random, rootless marauders. In the past several years, the media has acknowledged that police abuse victims have families, due to the rise of mothers' activism in police cases—notably the killing of Jonny Gammage outside Pittsburgh (the Gammage family lives in Syracuse) and a number of New York City cases. Despite this shift, police form a contrasting community so stalwart that thousands commonly attend the "sea of blue" funerals of fallen comrades.

Let's stop for a minute and ask, as organizers, whether the Rodney King beating "helped." From my point of view: yes, no, and yes again.

WHAT THE RODNEY KING BEATING ACCOMPLISHED

When the King beating occurred, my community was beginning lengthy and sometimes polarized deliberation about establishing a citizen review board, as was New York City to the south of us (Syracuse is about three hundred-plus miles away from New York City). From the morning after the King beating, I monitored the *New York Times* for several years on a daily basis to track how that publication covered police violence. For at least the first year, an average of three articles daily reliably appeared on that case and on related police issues or history. This was an incredible gold mine for activists in a mid-sized, "upstate" community who wanted to educate our city councilors with a constant stream of newspaper clippings. Certainly the King beating raised awareness and provided an arena in which to educate both the public and policymakers about police violence as a social problem.

In at least three ways, the King beating also made organizing harder. Some of the most active and innovative organizing around police accountability in the United States has occurred in mid-sized cities during this past decade. But Syracuse and similar communities have had to wrestle constantly with whether we were "like" Los Angeles or New

York City. Often fairly defensive about living in a backwater, Syracusans seized on denying that such "big-city" evils could happen "here." Indeed, as the '90s have unfolded, such denial of violence in our own backyards has characterized most violent episodes.

Second, if "that" were "police brutality," then a whole range of other conduct was not. The King incident entrenched a narrow definition of police misconduct as men beating up other men. It kept other victims invisible, and it kept the range and extent of other misconduct invisible, too.

Third, the Rodney King beating sometimes made the issue of police violence harder to raise in some quarters. Our task force in Syracuse had been working a year and a half already in March 1991. To this day, diehard opponents still claim both the task force and the CRB were "knee-jerk reactions to Rodney King."

THE RAPE STIGMA ANALOGY

At best a mixed blessing to activists, the Rodney King beating reinforced denial and entrenched a narrow definition of police violence. It also provided opportunities to expand the identity of police violence victims and the definition of that violence itself.

About a month after the King beating, I read a column in my local morning paper that had been reprinted from the *Baltimore Sun*. The columnist claimed that as the second most underreported crime in the United States, police misconduct was outdone only by rape. I wrote to the columnist seeking to document that statistic further; I never got an answer. But I have found intriguing and compelling the parallels between the two types of violence. It is no coincidence that victims of both crimes often remain silent. Both crimes involve vastly unequal power relations. Victims of both crimes share similar stereotyping and discrediting. Victims of both crimes often wind up as "suspects" themselves.

"Suspects" are, by definition, stigmatized and discredited already. This has several consequences, including the following six.

First, "suspects" are already guilty. There is the classic line, "You must have been doing something. . . " Many police believe that administering "street justice" is part of their job; this is exacerbated in periods when police believe that the guilty are going to go free more often than not. "I was just doing my job" compares to "boys will be boys" in claiming the inevitable. Many police corruption cases in this decade contain an element of this. Both the New York State Police fingerprint scandal and Philadelphia's "Dirty 39th Precinct" scandal of trumped-up drug charges, included officers' beliefs that the justice system needed "help." I recall accounts of convicted officers claiming that they "only framed the guilty ones."

Second, a closely allied idea is that victims caused their own injury or death. "What was she doing there, at that hour? Dressed like that? By herself? Drinking that much?" And so on. Doubters recite a similar litany of insinuation about those injured by police, who are typically charged with resisting arrest. In the classic police scenario, assumed threat substitutes for assumed seduction to justify attackers behavior to the lay public (The claim that she posed a threat to the police is the cover story given by officers in the brutal murder of Tyisha Miller in Riverside California in March 1999. Eds.) Most rape is not really "about" seduction and desire. It is a staple of college campus date-rape prevention programs to point out that most women are raped in their own homes (or dorm rooms). Activists (and probably most police administrators and criminal justice professionals) know that most police misconduct occurs when police authority is challenged, not while police are interrupting violent crimes—where police perform remarkably well. As those concerned with reforming "hot pursuits" practices know, really egregious disobedience would be running away. Both the King and the Riverside beatings occurred after high-speed chases.

Third, "suspects" lie and seek revenge. Media corroboration (such as a videotape) of eyewitness accounts is vital because police aggressively play on the low credibility of suspects. A staple argument against independent review of police is that "vindictive" suspects would "flood" the system with "frivolous" complaints. Nationwide, "SLAPP" suits by police suing citizens for false reports have risen dramatically in the '90s.

Fourth, fear of retaliation. Because of greater power and credibility, assailants in both police violence and rape situations may be able to punish you for "telling." Victims are already discredited; they are not safe from retaliation if they were not safe from violence to begin with. The prospects of both legal and extra-legal harassment have the famous "chilling effect."

Fifth, the burden of change is on the victim. In his book, *Stigma*, Erving Goffman taught us that it is the job of the stigmatized to manage the discomfort of "normals" with their plight. Historically, this steered community response to rape. In 1979, the first federal antirape legislation established rape centers. These provided emergency aid, but the major remedy was "teaching" women how to avoid rape—not teaching men not to rape or punishing them if they did. Similarly, county human rights commissions and other such bodies put out brochures on "how to avoid conflict with police." Some give tips about "not upsetting" police, or advising young people to waive their rights regarding both searches and giving information. This contrasts sharply with a "know your rights" approach, which is often branded as "too confrontational." This situation mimics the personal dynamics in abusive relationships.

Sixth, like rape and lynching, a beating is a warning to others, and serves a social control function.

For many municipal policymakers and elected officials, these six points provided the first illumination. They could understand that public thinking and policies about rape had changed in the United States over the last twenty years or so, even when their own experience might not include either rape or run-ins with police.

THE POLITICS OF HOME: TRASHING APARTMENTS AND PRIVACY'S POWER

To a large extent, the organizing challenge in Syracuse's CRB campaign was a battle of definitions. From the first draft of the CRB law, the task force argued for as wide a definition as possible of "police misconduct," and opponents argued for the narrowest possible view.

Women's participation on the task force and in the neighborhood speak-outs accomplished a first critical distinction. Some women had dealt with police and courts during domestic violence crises, making way for "passive misconduct" as a category. "Passive misconduct" means withholding a response, failing to intervene, or, more concretely, standing by and watching, not bothering to get there very fast, not writing down the woman's complaint, the classic "take a walk around the block to cool off" in lieu of arrest. Accounts from those experiencing gay-bashing and harassment, mistreatment of people with disabilities, and, more recently, provocation by white racist gangs bolstered the need for this category: such persons had often waited for police help and found it just didn't arrive in time.

The birth of "passive misconduct" transformed the classic scenario into "active misconduct"—a species of police violence, not its entirety. This category emphasized the action's intrusiveness (including both force and verbal abuse), not its mere physicality.

This distinction opened the way for a third category addressing violence to one's surroundings—an "ecological" violence, if you will. Syracuse women did speak about the increasingly common practice of police trashing homes during drug searches. This was initially not intelligible to many public policymakers because "suspects" were typically assumed to be lone, rootless individuals.

Further, these searches took place in "private" spaces, but were most common in certain blighted, "high-crime" areas of the city inhabited by the poor and people of color, places where privacy's power itself had eroded. Almost always, these were rented apartments, and eviction often followed. Often the police targeted the woman maintaining a home for her association with a man—a son, grandson, brother, partner, even cousin or nephew—who "might be found there." Thus women became bystanders in their own homes and their ordeals became incidental and secondary.

The American Psychological Association defines trauma as "outside the range of normal human experience." This includes extreme and violent direct experience or witnessing brutality, death, war, forced migration, and natural disasters. "Destruction of one's home" is one such major traumatizing event.

Advocates from the two major agencies receiving such complaints in Syracuse reported they regularly got two to five calls per week about home trashing. They informally estimated that maybe 90 percent of these incidents involved small children witnessing the search.

For a five-year-old, say, or even an infant, the destruction of one's living space—especially by police as agents of adult, community authority—would be clinically traumatic.

Advocates said that children sometimes watched police "subdue" parents or other familiar adults, or were forcibly taken out of the room but could still hear the beatings. People accused police of shoving women with infants or toddlers in their arms into walls. There were descriptions of pets shot, entire sets of dishes systematically broken, holes punched in walls, plumbing ripped out, food dumped in piles on the floor.

Afterward, such children sometimes had nightmares and showed clingy behavior, sleeplessness, decreased trust in adults, sudden "immaturity," anger and anxiety, poor school performance, poor concentration, confusion, and ambivalence about police. Schools noticing these children might, at first, attribute problems to general poverty or ongoing family lifestyle, not to specific events involving police action. Many guidance counselors and social workers would readily understand the harm in watching one parent batter the other, yet they didn't see police behavior as "violence," because they think the police are "saving" the children.

Most people did not complete their formal complaints with these Syracuse agencies. And both agencies confirmed that they did not have a box to check on their in-take form for trauma to youngsters who were bystanders during such rampages, so they did not formally count these incidents. Instead, they saw such incidents in legalistic terms as "search and seizure" violations, although the New York State Division for Human Rights had, on rare occasions, successfully arranged compensation for residence repairs, medical treatment, and professional counseling for youngsters.

Children who have been in violent police home searches show the same symptoms as those suffering wartime and natural disaster traumas. For kids, these searches are in the same league as an earthquake or a flood coming to their neighborhood. Treatment for such children emphasizes healing the family collectively and keeping families intact. But many of the children who suffer from home search traumas are very likely to be taken out of their families by child protective services, the mental health system, or the justice system.

Such effects magnify in urban areas where searches occur more often and where people, although renters, may not be transient to their neighborhood itself. Extended families may suffer several such incidents. Syracuse has a history of community displacement and large-scale housing shifts dating from the 1960s "urban renewal" efforts. Such displacement shattered an historically vibrant and tightly knit black ward of the city within the past couple of generations.

In 1980, the United States had 10,000 women in prison. Today that figure has swelled sixteen times. According to the Legal Services for Prisoners with Children, in partnership with Justice Works Community in New York City, over two-thirds of women prisoners are there for simple drug possession or low-level drug violations, and eighty percent are mothers. According to the U.S. Justice Department, the recidivism rate nationwide among women is seventy-one percent.

In recent years we have witnessed warning events of police overrunning the vulnerable "private" realm, even before any prominent discussion of "home trashing" and its trauma began. In 1984, New York City police shot and killed Eleanor Bumpers while evicting her from her Bronx apartment. Behind less than one-hundred dollars in her rent, elderly, ill, and frightened, she had brandished a cake knife from across the room at six well-armed officers who crashed into her apartment. In her important essay on Bumpers in the *Alchemy of Race and Rights* (1991), Patricia Williams points out that the officers' successful defense in court centered on their actions being "entirely legal."

In 1993, police in Tyler, Texas shot and killed Annie Rae Dixon—another elderly bedridden black woman—during a drug raid on the wrong house. In 1996, the city of Boston settled a lawsuit for the death of Reverend Alcie Williams, an elderly black minister who was literally scared to death during another "wrong address" drug raid. More ominously, in 1993, a number of police officers in Gastonia, South Carolina were tried and convicted for a long-standing practice of using their shift breaks at work for systematically torturing homeless people for amusement.

Informal abuse of the homeless by police takes the erosion of privacy's boundaries to its logical end. Police trash homes during drug searches in the name of "defending the home" and "family values." Police and policymakers may not regard such dwellings as "homes" at all.

To unravel this, look at the source of privacy rights that make one's home one's "castle." We are more concrete than we think. Individual privacy rights spring from the original "real" property—land. A fairly select circle of "equals"—adult, white, male property-owners—monopolized voting and civic participation in colonial America and the early years of the United States.

These basic attributes still act as fixatives for citizenship and sturdy privacy rights. The vocabulary of civic participation reflects this with terms like "having a stake" and "stakeholders," which are throwbacks to literally staking out one's territory. In this context, citizen status myopically attaches to particular nations, generally one's own—as if other countries somehow didn't have "citizens." People become loose aggregates without these fixatives to anchor and distinguish them—to be managed in lots, corralled in their sectors, fenced out of "ours."

The Israeli policy of "collective punishment," when sealing or bulldozing the homes of Palestinian dissidents, has features in common with police home trashings in concentrated urban areas of the United States, as does the frequent invasion of private homes in the North of Ireland by both security forces and paramilitary units. Usually we focus on heightened law enforcement activity along borders as evidence of the growing militarization of police, but women and children are becoming the direct targets of a more guerrilla-like police warfare inside homes.

THE STRENGTH OF INDIVIDUAL RIGHTS AS A BASIS FOR U.S. POLICE ACTIVISM

At one remove from their basis in property rights, the theory and legal remedies associated with individual rights have historically driven progressive U.S. activist campaigns for police accountability. For a host of reasons, including the structure of the U.S. justice system itself, issues have been channeled in this direction, and argued in these terms.

Lay progressive activists want personhood, not property, to be the basis for human rights. This position provides a certain clarity. One needn't be good, or popular, or right, or wealthy—only human. Activists around issues of police violence, often guided by lawyers trained in the U.S. justice system, prefer the individual rights approach for the following three reasons.

By conviction. Many activists believe this approach values human life above property. We began organizing around home search traumas in Syracuse with blown-up color photographs of trashed apartments—not bloodied, weeping children. When inadvertently caught in the ecological violence of some home searches, children have developmental issues that simply weren't considered before. And when they are dismissed as mere "bystanders," the women maintaining these homes sustained immense "collateral damage."

By strategy. "Don't dilute the agenda," some activists sternly warned. Given an anticrime political climate and scarce resources, both community and legal activists will tend to triage issues as well as cases. Winning in court takes precedence over "secondary" needs, such as counseling for youngsters or fixing the broken kitchen door this winter instead of ten years down the road. What is most clearly arguable or likeliest to generate public outrage is not always the most critical in the long-term. For example, filing untruthful police reports as another category of misconduct just isn't very sexy. When we proposed this as a category for Syracuse's CRB, some veteran activists thought it was far afield from the "outright" brutality they were after. Yet Syracuse police fought opening these official written accounts most bitterly and vehemently.

By need. Some issues really are urgent. Here are five issues that concern women but which are otherwise sufficiently within the classic scenario that they don't need much "translation" for public action to be possible.

—Domestic violence in police families. Attached as a rider to the 1997 federal budget, Senator Frank Lautenberg's "domestic violence gun ban" forbids anyone ever convicted of misdemeanor domestic violence to possess a firearm, including police and military. Police resistance to this measure has been mighty and prolonged. But if the gun ban could expose the prevalence of intimate violence committed by police, doubters might believe that police could beat strangers from stigmatized groups.

—Sexual harassment of women police by male officers. Besides demonstrating a major form of male officers' resistance to women joining their ranks, this problem underscores key issues such as the "code of silence," the inadequacy of internal complaints procedures, and the fear of retaliation.

—Women and new police technologies. After rising abuse of pepper spray, sometimes resulting in death, activists have been seeking bans on pepper spray in some United States cities. With a sudden chivalry, male police have argued that women officers' safety depends on this and other questionable new weapons.

—Women inmates and sexual abuse. Most of the 116,000 women inmates in the U.S. are guarded by men, and complaints of sexual abuse have skyrocketed in recent years.

—Both lesbians and prostitutes suffer serious active and passive police misconduct.

Each of these issues addresses serious women's concerns and can be argued in terms of individual rights.

FROM ZONE TO COMMUNITY

It is self-defeating to insist that police brutality only be construed so that we oppose it in terms of the classic scenario. This polarizes all deliberation, creating the "false choices," which, E. J. Dionne argued in his 1992 book, *Why Americans Hate Politics*, is why fewer and fewer people risk participating than ever before. Earlier attention and action on less lurid police misconduct might prevent eruptions of the classic scenario. Aggressive police campaigns against accountability have emphasized maintaining this polarization so that even any slight questioning of police behavior is automatically assigned the extreme position of "cop bashing."

Further, we need to reclaim the term "citizen" as an international term, a public status that ensures equality in a reciprocal fashion among nations instead of a chauvinistic privilege used for denigrating foreign nationals. The increased attention on border abuses provides us with some hope; for instance, in an international context, police misbehavior is frequently labeled properly as "torture." Were this perspective to enter

U.S. discussion of police violence, we might seriously address proper treatment for those who have been traumatized, including those who have endured home searches.

REFERENCES

Dionne, E. J. 1992. *Why Americans Hate Politics*. New York: Touchstone.

Goffman, Erving. 1986. *Stigma: Notes on the Management of Spoiled Identity*. New York: Simon and Schuster.

Williams, Patricia. 1991. *Alchemy of Race and Rights: Diary of a Law Professor*. Cambridge: Harvard University Press.

CHAPTER 28

Black Women and Labor Unions in the South

From the 1970s to the 1990s

IDA LEACHMAN

My topic is the struggle of labor that Black women in particular—not excluding the men—are having in the Deep South. I live in Memphis, Tennessee. It is on the borderline with Mississippi. As vice president of the Furniture Division of the International Union of Electrical Workers (IUE), I service the southern region.[1] That takes in Texas, Oklahoma, Florida, Mississippi, Louisiana, Alabama, North Carolina, and South Carolina. I also serve as vice president of my local union, Local 282, which is an amalgamated local.[2] We have some fifteen different shops in our local from Jackson, Mississippi, to Nashville, Tennessee, in a four-hundred-mile territory.

The question I want to address is: Has the struggle changed since before the Civil Rights movement, and if so, how? Georgiana Williams writes about how it was in Mississippi back in the days of segregation. It has been a long time since then. Both of us have grandchildren. I even have one great-grandchild. I can remember when there were "colored" drinking fountains. They were filthy. On buses, we rode in the back; on trains, we had a special car right behind the engine and coal car, with all the smoke. There were no planes flying in those days. Now we can ride in the front of public transportation, if we can afford to buy the tickets.

In the 1960s, there were not too many Black women in workplaces at all in Memphis, other than in laundries and in homes doing domestic work. The Black women did the cooking, cleaning, tending to the babies and working in laundries. There were no Black women in skilled jobs. The 1964 Civil Rights Act allegedly outlawed discrimination based on race, sex, age, and national origin. But discrimination has not stopped. What has happened is that management has gotten slicker.

* * *

Back in the early 1960s, I went to apply for a sewing machine operator job at a sewing factory called Blue Goose that made men's work pants. When I applied for the position that was open, I was told that they only hired Blacks on the presses. I told the lady that I did not press— even at home. After the 1964 Civil Rights Act was passed, I applied again at the same plant. There were several white women also applying for jobs. Each woman was asked to state her experience, but as a Black woman I could not have worked in a sewing factory before. The plant manager went to the white ladies and asked them, "What job would you like?" One said, "Well, I'm a side seamer. And I stitch." Others replied that they did this and that. Finally, I was the last person, so he had to come to me. I was still asking myself, "What in the world can I say I have done?" As he got to me, I was looking at him. He had a shirt on with pockets. So I said, "Oh, I sew pockets. You know, like the one you got there." And he said, "That's exactly what we need, a pocket setter." I was hired that day.

I worked there until that plant closed down the sewing operation. Then I went into another sewing factory, which had been opened up by the plant manager and supervisor at Blue Goose. They asked me to come with them and I did. That was in 1969, after the 1968 Sanitation Workers Strike in Memphis, when Dr. King was assassinated. When I went to United Uniform, the workers were attempting to organize a union. I tell you, you have never heard such antiunion talk as what came from that employer. Those workers lost that union then, and we remained nonunion until 1977.

By 1977, Willie Rudd had become president of Local 282. Willie Rudd, who is now president of the Furniture Division as well as Local 282, is a Black man. His aim was to organize. In 1976–77, he organized the Memphis Furniture Company in Memphis.[3] There were about thirteen hundred workers, the majority of whom were Black women. That plant was opened back in the late 1800s and they built it on the plantation style. On any given morning, when they got ready to hire, the boss would come to the door. The people would have to stand outside, and he would come to the door and look over the crowd. He would simply say, "Hey you, boy," or "Hey you, girl." This went on until Willie Rudd organized that plant.

In 1977, Mr. Rudd also began to organize my shop. During the company's captive audience meetings—which workers were required to attend because they were held during working hours—management would ask the workers, who were both Black and white, to look around and see who was going to be over you. Willie Rudd is a Black man, and Local 282 is a majority Black union. Look around and see who is going to be taking your money. I asked, "What is wrong with who is leading this union? You have been taking our money all along. What's wrong if he wants to take it?" I took that company on during those captive audience meetings. Come election day, we won that election.

When we won the campaign, my co-workers said that they wanted me for their steward. "We have seen you in action when we didn't have a union," they said. "So we know that you will take up for us." I became steward. I attended organizing classes. And when there was an opening on the international staff for a Black woman organizer, I was there and I was prepared. From that time on, from 1978, I have been organizing, negotiating, arbitrating, and fighting.

* * *

Today, Blacks can pretty much go where we want and live where we want if we have the money. That's how we are kept under control now. We have a suburb near Memphis called Germantown. In Germantown, you don't see us Black people and even some other groups of people, because it is an elite suburb. At the other end of the spectrum is the area around the Army Defense Depot in Memphis, a military distribution center, which recently closed. Radioactive and other toxic warfare chemicals were dumped there for over fifty years. God only knows what is underground that is being fed back into the people through the water supply, causing high cancer rates and birth defects. Here these people stay, both Black and white, because they cannot afford to get out of there.[4]

There are so many people who work forty hours a week and yet qualify for food stamps because they work for minimum wage. The minimum wage has been raised from $4.25 to $5.15. Even at that, one can hardly make a living wage. Some people say that some is better than none. I don't know if that is true or not. How about a whole lot of abuse? No abuse is better than a whole lot; so, if I have got to be abused, I guess I would rather have a little bit. But abuse is abuse. Laurie Green's article discusses the labor movement. The labor movement in America is why we have the forty-hour week, public schools, and a lot of benefits that we now take for granted. Now they are attempting to do away with the forty-hour week and the eight-hour day.

I represent both Black and white workers, the majority being Black. In the South, employers believe that white people won't support a Black union. I do have some white people in our union that are just as mean as I am; but, for the most part, the employers are correct. This is why industry from the North moves to the South. In Tupelo, Mississippi, about one hundred miles from Memphis, there is a nest of manufacturers that have come from the North, because they were promised a union-free environment.

Beyond the Memphis city line, across the state border, is a little place called Olive Branch, Mississippi. They named the city that because they could extend that "Southern hospitality," the olive branch. We represent the Serta Mattress workers there in Memphis. Serta wanted to leave Memphis because of the tax breaks that other cities give manufacturers: If you come here, you can operate tax-free for ten years, we'll sell bonds to give you operating money, and we have cheap labor for you. Serta went to the Olive Branch Chamber of Commerce, and the Chamber told them that because Serta had union workers, it was not welcome in Olive Branch. That town was not going to sell land to Serta, nor were they willing to rent it to them. Serta could not go to Olive Branch because they had a union. So they went to Batesville, Mississippi, and right now they are operating between Memphis and Batesville. My local still represents Serta, the workers who are now in Batesville. Companies do not just get rid of a union that quickly.

As I said, employers have gotten slicker in their discrimination. Companies that move to the South from the North come for the antiunion climate. Even when we do succeed in winning a union election, they do everything they can to avoid signing a first contract by bargaining in bad faith. Management either has to agree to a contract, close the plant, or get the workers to decertify the union. They figure that if they don't agree to a contract, they can eventually convince the workers to decertify the union.

In Somerville, which is in Fayette County, Tennessee, east of Memphis, workers at Somerville Mills, Master Apparel, and Allison Corporation voted in Local 282. Somerville Mills and Master Apparel are headquartered in New York and Allison is in Livingston, New Jersey. Somerville is important in the history of the Civil Rights Movement. They had a tent city there in 1959–60, when Blacks started to register to vote and the sharecroppers were forced off the plantations.[5] Today, Local 282 is the only industrial union in Fayette County. Those workers at Somerville Mills made garments for Victoria's Secret, Fredricks of Hollywood, and Laura Ashley. Their products don't come cheap. In July 1988, Somerville Mills workers voted the union in—about three hundred women, mostly Black. From July 1, 1988, until today, Somerville Mills refused to negotiate a first contract. They tried to get a decertification petition passed by the workers twice, but they failed, mostly because of Marandy Wilkerson, the chief steward, and the kind of fighter she is. To get a decertification, you have to frighten or fool the employees. It's illegal for management to initiate a petition, but that only stops them if they get caught.

At Master Apparel in Somerville, the company also tried to decertify the union. And at Allison, after the first contract expired, they talked the chief steward into resigning and then passing a decertification petition. All these attempts to decertify the union were ruled illegal by the National Labor Relations Board except at Master Apparel, where another union election was held and the workers voted the union back in. Then in 1996, Somerville Mills and Master Apparel both closed their sewing operations.

In January 1996, Somerville Mills notified us that production was going to be closed down and moved to Mexico. After about April 1996, there was allegedly no production going on in the plant. They had shut down. Marandy Wilkerson, being the person that she is, kept an eye on the plant. Every day she would go by and see trucks coming in and going out with products. When we investigated it, we filed charges with the National Labor Relations Board. The Labor Board issued a complaint against the company, and the company's attorney agreed to meet with us. He told us that if we didn't believe that they were not doing any sewing production, we could come out and look for ourselves. We took him up on the offer of a tour.

When we got to the plant, they had cleaned everybody out. The workers had left so fast that someone's lunch was left on the table. Sewing machines were still hot. A computer in the shipping room was hooked up and ready to go. There was a pile of printouts on the desk. When Marandy walked over to look at them, the company attorney ran over and grabbed them and said "You can't look at these." I walked over to a trash can. Lo and behold, there were two computer printout pages in it. So I reached into the trash can and got them out. It showed how many orders they had and how many were due. The attorney told me, "Ida, you can't see that!" I told him, "Well, yes I can. It was in the trash." He told me again that I could not see those papers. I had them in my hand and I told him, "Now, John, don't snatch it from my hand." He replied again that he had to take it, and sure enough, the fool snatched it out of my hand. He even broke my finger nail. And I knocked the hell out of him!

These unfair labor practices aimed at getting rid of Local 282 in Somerville, Tennessee, are what we have to face in the labor movement—and not just as they affect Black workers. Back in the 1980s, our local union represented nearly three thousand workers from twenty-six different shops. As an amalgamated union, we represent food products, clothing, mattress and furniture, just everything. If you wanted a union, we were there, and we still are there for workers.

But the weakening of the National Labor Relations Board has hurt the whole labor movement. Labor laws have been changed since the Wagner Act first set up the Labor Board in 1935 and the board can only enforce the law. The Taft-Hartley Act in 1947 weakened the Wagner Act by allowing states to pass "right-to-work" laws preventing union shops. In another change, workers can be permanently replaced if they are on an economic strike or anything other than a strike against unfair labor practices. Employers hadn't bothered to use that decision until Reagan permanently replaced air traffic controllers during the PATCO strike that began in 1981.[6]

Since then, Congress has not fully funded the Labor Board, so the Board cannot enforce the law effectively. We have one case, Allison Corporation in Somerville, that has been held up in Washington for over three years. After the company instigated a decertification attempt, an administrative law judge ruled that what the company did was illegal, and they should recognize the union. The company appealed the decision to Washington, and, for three years now, those workers have gone without representation.

Let me show you in another way how slick companies have gotten today with discrimination. Down in Jackson, Mississippi, we had a furniture plant called Hood Furniture owned by Warren Hood, one of the most powerful men in Mississippi. Back in 1989, the IUE organized that plant and won it by one vote. It took almost two years to get certified, because the company filed objections to the election. Finally, the courts certified the union as the bargaining agent. Because we were in the Furniture Division, the IUE assigned Hood to Local 282. I was assigned to negotiate the contract and reorganize the workers. I had to go to court just to get the company to the bargaining table.

Once they got to the table, the attorney representing the company noticed when he walked in the room that he was going to have to deal with a Black woman. After three sessions, he saw that he was not going to intimidate me. He then called the union's district president, who is a white man, and told him if he got Ida Leachman out of there, he would agree to a contract. I told him that if my being there was going to hinder a contract, I would move out. And I did leave. But when I left, the one who went in was even more militant than me—Willie Rudd, president of the

Furniture Division and Local 282. I know that attorney was thinking, "God, I wish you would bring Ida Leachman back." The company declared that they would never deal with Willie Rudd and Local 282. Back in 1993, the company called IUE President William Bywater in Washington and they cut a deal. Hood Furniture told the union to take the shop out of Local 282 and give it back to the International—and they did it. They assigned it to IUE Local 797.

But let me tell you, these hundreds of angry folk, mostly Black women, carried the ball. Those workers said in 1993 that they were going to have Local 282 as their bargaining agent or they weren't going to have a union. Out of the four hundred workers, only fourteen signed check-off cards for payment of union dues to IUE Local 797. Since Mississippi is a "right-to-work" state, this meant that they had only fourteen dues paying members out of four hundred. These workers even went out and had T-shirts made which said, "Don't Blame Me, I Didn't Vote For It. Member of Local 282." When the contract was ready to expire in 1996, the workers again said that they were going to have Local 282 or no union. Because of the politics brewing in the International union, President Bywater said to Brother Rudd that Local 282 could take back Hood Furniture. Willie went back into Jackson, Mississippi, and pulled together a labor and civil rights coalition down there. On 20 September 1996, Hood Furniture signed a contract with Local 282.[7]

Within two weeks, the company announced its closing. They had gone on record as saying that before they dealt with Willie Rudd and Local 282 they would close, and that's exactly what they did. In early 1997, Hood sold the company to Strait Furniture Company, which refused to recognize the union. The National Labor Relations Board ruled that the company had inherited the bargaining unit. The law stipulates that if a company sells to another company that retains the majority of the workers in the bargaining unit, they must recognize the union. Strait still refused to negotiate. The case went to a hearing in mid–1998 and the administrative law judge issued a bench ruling requiring them to bargain with Local 282. Strait then appealed that decision to Washington, where it is stuck, like the Allison case. We cannot file grievances, collect union dues, or negotiate a contract. But we are continuing to help the workers in other ways. In February 1999, the plant manager, Jonn Cathcart, slapped a Black woman worker. Before this incident, he had been verbally assaulting workers by cursing and threatening physical violence. Local 282 is continuing to help the workers fight this abuse along with health and safety violations and other problems.[8]

Certain companies are determined not to deal with Black unions that are willing to defend all workers. Some were willing to close down or run to Mexico to avoid this kind of union. With NAFTA in place, corporate America is free to take our work to Mexico, Guatemala, Haiti, the Philippines, or China to get it done. The companies running to the South are willing to do anything to stay nonunion. Local governments are working with companies to control people. As long as workers are not unionized, they have no rights on the job about how much they earn, the conditions in which they work, and what kind of treatment they receive.

If they can keep people from organizing, it keeps power from the people. One worker has no power. But think what we could do if all workers would organize. Women, whether white, Black, Latino or Asian are really all in the same boat. We are less respected than anyone else.

When you talk to people, look them in the eye. After a while, you can get just about anything you want. I went into negotiations once with a company attorney from New Orleans. This attorney sat across from me at the bargaining table and tried to intimidate me. We went into a staring match. It went on and on, but he would not look off. I said to myself, "I will die and go to hell before I will be the first one to look off." Not a word was said. I would bat my eyes but never moved them from his face—not to the right and not to the left, just straight ahead. Finally, after two grueling hours, he finally dropped his head and he told me that he was ready to negotiate. The moral of this story is, ladies, do not let anyone intimidate you. Stand up for what's right, fight for yourself, and protect each other.

NOTES

1. The United Furniture Workers of America (UFWA), first organized in 1939, merged with the International Union of Electrical Workers (IUE) in 1986. The UFWA became the Furniture Division of the IUE.

2. Local 282 was incorporated in May 1943 as part of the United Furniture Workers-Congress of Industrial Organizations (UFW-CIO). In amalgamated locals, membership comes from multiple shops instead of one shop. The union, therefore, initiates organizing drives among workers in unorganized shops. For more on Local 282's history, see Deborah Brown Carter, "The Impact of the Civil Rights Movement on the Unionization of African-American Women: Local 282-Furniture Division-IUE, 1960–1988." In *Black Women in America*, edited by Kim Marie Vaz (Thousand Oaks, Calif.: Sage Publications, 1995), 96–109.

3. Memphis Furniture workers first won representation by Local 282 in February 1944, but lost it after a bitter eight-month strike in 1949. Local 282 again organized Memphis Furniture in 1955, but representation was lost for a second time in 1958. By drawing local and national political attention to the campaign, Rudd successfully reorganized Memphis Furniture in 1976–77 against enormous union-busting resources marshaled by the company to fight Local 282. See Deborah Brown Carter, *The Local Labor Union as a Social Movement Organization: Local 282, Furniture Division-IUE, 1943–1988* (Ph.D. diss., Vanderbilt University, 1988), 48, 100–101.

4. On the environmental justice struggle by Defense Depot of Memphis, Tennessee, Concerned Citizens Committee (DDMT-CCC), see Doris Bradshaw, "Black Memphis vs. Toxic Defense Depot," *News and Letters*, December 1996, 8; and Kenneth Bradshaw, "Uncovering Toxic Racism," *News and Letters*, December 1997, 8.

5. For an account of the sharecroppers' movement in Fayette County, see Robert Hamburger, *Our Portion of Hell: Fayette County, Tennessee, An Oral History of the Struggle for Civil Rights* (New York: Links Publishers, 1973).

6. The Supreme Court ruled in 1972 in NLRB v. International Van Lines that an employer may hire permanent replacements for economic strikers. For more on legal changes regarding replacement of strikers, see Betty W. Justice, *Unions, Workers and the Law* (Washington, D.C.: BNA Books, 1983), 145–146.

7. On the history of labor struggles at Hood, see also: Hood Furniture Workers, "Hood Furniture: Secret Contract Repudiated," *News and Letters*, December 1993, 3; and Michael Flug, "Seven-Year Fight Wins Hood Furniture Contract," *News and Letters*, October 1996, 1.

8. As of March 1999 the Strait case is still pending at the National Labor Relations Board in Washington. On Hood closing, see Michael Flug, "Hood Furniture Closing is Anti-Union Racism," *News and Letters*, November 1996, 3; and Hood Furniture Workers, "Leaving Hood with Fighting Legacy," *News and Letters*, December 1996, 3.

CHAPTER 29

From the Mississippi Delta to South Central Los Angeles

GEORGIANA WILLIAMS

I am going to write about my journey from Mississippi to South Central. Mississippi is not far from Memphis, and everything that Ida Leachman discussed, I lived. It makes me feel real good to know that some sisters and brothers are fighting to change the Deep South. It's past time for it to change. And it's going to take people like Ida, who stayed in the South, to make it change.

I didn't want change. I wanted to leave, so I got the hell out as fast as I could.

I am the daughter of a sharecropper, the sixth of thirteen children, born in the hills of Mississippi where the white man was the law. You did what you were told. We were told that we were free. I am here to tell you that we were *not free*. We lived in a shack and raised our own food. When it was a bad year and we could not raise a good crop, we only had brown gravy and bread to eat.

I still don't know how we would have survived had it not been for my grandmother, who would speak out. She was the granddaughter of the master of the plantation. She would say to Mr. Hawkins, "I want some food for my family." He would tell her, "Dora, we ain't gonna make no money this year." And she would answer back, "We didn't make any money last year either."

I remember he told everyone on the plantation not to send the children to school. "They don't need to learn how to read and write in order to work in the fields." He put a padlock on the schoolroom. When Big Mama finished her field, she got a friend to take her out to Mr. Hawkin's house. She went to the back door and knocked very gently. Teapot, the

395

housekeeper, answered. She knew my grandmother because she was on the plantation and down the road from where we were. Everyone called my Big Mama, Miss Vanney. She said, "Oh, Miss Vanney, what are you doing here?" And Big Mama replied, "I came to see Mr. Hawkins." Mr. Hawkins came to the back door and asked, "What you want, Dora?" And Big Mama told him, "I finished my crop and I want my children to go to school. And they are *not* going to work in anybody else's field." He paused and said, "Okay." The locks were removed from the school as long as the plantation existed, until the 1970s.

The slavery laws were just removed from the books recently, but then they created new laws that benefit the lawmakers. After the Civil Rights boycotts in the 1950s and 1960s, the law stated you would have to go to court to get permission to boycott or demonstrate, because in the 1960s, they refused to integrate and all the Blacks boycotted the town. That caused many businesses to close. A Greek man who had a cafe was the first one who took down the "colored" and "white" signs. He said, "I wasn't born here, and in my country we don't have this mess. I am not going to lose my cafe because of this." The Riverside Cafe is still there today.

Fighting for my son Damian wasn't a big thing, because my whole life has been a fight for survival. It is better and clearer when your boss is a bastard, because then you have no doubt who the enemy is. When he is nice and considerate, you think he is your friend, but the truth is that both the bastard and the nice boss want the same thing out of you—your labor, and as hard as you can.

At an early age, I made up my mind that I was not going to stay in those fields. I would not let any man hold me back. Women in the South, both Black and white, had no voice. We were taught to be submissive to all men. I couldn't curse out loud, but I would say to myself, "I'll be damned if I will do that!"

My grandmother is an example for all Black women. Had it not been for her, there's no telling what would have happened on that plantation. I am very thankful to be the granddaughter of a lady who had the courage to speak. She did not allow the things that went on in other families to happen to us. My great-great-aunt had no say over her own body. Her sister's husband had four children by her. This made the plantation owner very proud. The plantation owners were pleased when big men would breed women on their plantations. The big man could breed *any woman he wanted*, and there was nothing any woman could say. So you can see why I said I'd be damned if it would happen to me. I barely made it out of high school. I did well in nursing school. Then I got the hell out, at the age of twenty-one.

I didn't know I had moved to a greater hell until 12 May 1992, when my son Damian was arrested. I didn't know then what I know now, that all these years I was facing racism. I was too naïve to understand, because it was nothing like where I came from. Years of combustion and anger is the reason for 29 April 1992. The LA rebellion was against racism, police abuse, harassment, homelessness, poor schools, and no ability to get work. And some of it was against worthless politicians whose goals were to create wealth and power for themselves.

Years of mistreatment left South Central bitter about empty promises of making life better. People had been looking for that better life even long before the 1965 Watts Rebellion. Movement after movement, movement after movement, and nothing came out of it. Nothing ever came out of it—no jobs, no food, poor housing, and poor schools. Businesses in the community charged higher prices, and no monies were being put back into the communities. We were treated like thieves by the market owners every time we went into a place of business. They watched every step any of us made. By 29 April 1992, everyone was angry over the Rodney King verdict—but there is more that the media did not tell.

The media did not tell how, for years, the police had been all the time at Florence and Normandie, beating up on young Black men. They even beat my son Mark, then arrested him and arrested Kermit and Shawndell. So by the time of the Rodney King verdict, there were a lot of Black people in the community—and outside as well—who were already angry. They said: "We're not cavemen. They beat Rodney King, but they're not going to beat us anymore!"

The young Black men in the community were very angry about what had happened to people like Shawndell, to Mark, and to Kermit. They took bricks and bottles, and ran the cops' asses out of South Central. They said they were angry and would be angry until they received justice.

A group of mothers, sisters, and grandmothers have banded together to make sure that every time we know a Latino or a Black young man is going to court, the courtroom is filled with Latina and Black mothers. We will continue to fight for justice in the courtroom and for justice in the community. We monitor the justice system, keep a video camera and a 35mm camera with us, and as soon as we see the police, we start filming.

Let me tell you, cameras make a difference. We pack the courtrooms. We meet with lawyers. We protest. We write letters. We jam phone lines and FAX lines. We make ourselves known.

We supported Geronimo Pratt and welcomed him when he was released. We supported the efforts to keep Mumia Abu Jamal from going to the gas chamber. Geronimo and Mumia were railroaded by the criminal justice system.

I have and will continue to fight for all people for justice and dignity. A great inspiration to me was Charles Denby, a Black man from Alabama whose roots were similar to mine. I read his book, *Indignant Heart: A Black Worker's Journal,* and I laughed and I cried. The same thing that happened to Black people in the 1920s happened to me in the 1950s and 1960s—and is still happening in the 1990s.[1]

NOTES

1. Charles Denby, *Indignant Heart: A Black Worker's Journal.* Detroit: Wayne State University Press, 1989.

CHAPTER 30

"A Struggle of the Mind"

Black Working-Class Women's Organizing in Memphis and the Mississippi Delta, 1960s to 1990s

LAURIE BETH GREEN

As the 1990s began, African-American women catfish workers in the Mississippi Delta—in the same Sunflower County where Fannie Lou Hamer inspired other Black sharecroppers in the Civil Rights struggles of the 1960s—initiated a new phase in the labor movement by launching the most militant strike the Delta had seen in years (White 1997). Workers at the Delta Pride Catfish plant in Indianola had first won their battle for unionization in 1986, and gone on to organize nearly every catfish plant in the region. Most Delta Pride workers were single parents only recently off the welfare rolls. When the local all-white board of 178 catfish producers that owned Delta Pride responded by increasing harassment in the plant—even proposing to further limit bathroom "privileges" to lunchtime in an attempt to control and humiliate workers—these women voted to strike in 1990 and won. In the years since, however, the catfish industry, supported by local and state government, has bolstered efforts to eradicate unionism throughout the region and re-instill a fear of fighting back. Employers have even used new state workfare programs to create a second tier of low-wage workers threatened with losing benefits if they are fired. As Sarah White, a worker who has become a leader in the movement, observes, "[S]o many companies in the South today still practice that plantation mentality on workers. If you believe in the dream, you can overcome this, but it is a struggle of the mind" (White 1996, 4).

Whether the "plantation mentality" Sarah White and others are fighting refers to discriminatory and disrespectful treatment by their bosses–in the old cotton fields or the new catfish plants–or whether it refers to workers' internalized fears of fighting back, this dual-faceted concept reaches to the heart of struggles of race, class, and gender in the Delta region today. As companies searched for cheap nonunion labor in the 1980s and 1990s, many headed not across the border but to regions within the United States like the Mississippi Delta. In doing so, they discovered new resources in federal and state welfare and labor legislation, and old resources in the South's political, social, and economic climate. African-American working-class women became pivotal to all-out efforts by the state and by private employers to restructure labor in the 1990s. As many of these women began creatively organizing and fighting back, their concerns spilled beyond purely economic issues to questions of life and labor that involve race and gender as well as class. Most significantly, they engaged in "struggles of the mind" against the "plantation mentality."

These ongoing battles impelled my historical research into the unfinished and even unrecognized struggles of African-American working women during the Civil Rights movement. In the 1960s, Black working-class women's activism became a significant dimension of the Freedom Movement in both the rural and urban South, intrinsically linking together civil rights, labor, and feminist issues. As sharecroppers such as Fannie Lou Hamer and others became pivotal to the Freedom Movement in the rural South, women working in manufacturing and laundry sweatshops waged different but related battles. Such struggles made it clear that "freedom" went beyond questions of integration and equal opportunity—despite the fact that African-American women had been the most excluded group from nearly every industry in the South outside of laundries, domestic work, and agricultural labor (see Ida Leachman's essay in this collection). After plant doors opened to Black women, thousands helped organize unions to counter harassment, discrimination, and "slave wages" in sweatshop industries. In the same period, other African-American women initiated a welfare rights movement in Memphis. The unique and unfinished nature of this organizing in the 1960s has been newly appropriated today by a post-civil rights generation of women facing the limitations of the Civil Rights movement.

Such activism was rarely discussed in histories of the Civil Rights movement until recently, when several scholars (Flug 1990; Carter 1995; Greene 1996; Brown 1997; Green 1999) highlighted the significance of labor struggles initiated by Black women workers. This scholarship probes the multifaceted dimensions of this organizing, which linked together work and community, race and class, gender and labor, making all part of the larger vision of freedom. Feminist historians writing about African-American women's activism during the Freedom Movement, such as Kathryn Nasstrom (1993), have also critiqued previous works on the Civil Rights movement, which focused nearly exclusively on male leadership or on issues that claimed the largest news headlines in the 1960s, thus creating a gendered historical memory that erased many of the concerns dearest to women activists. In addition, activist-thinkers, like Sarah White, have begun to bring their own stories to larger audiences, not just for history's sake, but as a contribution to an urgently needed dialogue about future pathways (White 1996).[1]

In this essay, I build on such scholarship by discussing the critical consciousness that emerged among African-American women engaged in labor organizing in Memphis during the 1960s Freedom Movement, and its relation to ongoing struggles in the Mississippi Delta region in the 1990s.[2] Such an analysis can help us sort out powerful questions about the meaning and means to freedom that these movements have raised. I briefly explore how the new generation of Black women activists fighting in the Delta today has confronted the limitations and possibilities of earlier labor and Civil Rights struggles. As single mothers battling against both their employers and the state at the close of the twentieth century, they have refused to leave either race or class or gender at the level of the implicit, and by viewing the struggle as one of the mind—of consciousness—as well as of activism, they reveal much about the challenges that liberation movements face today.

In analyzing this critical consciousness, I have borrowed from feminist and radical philosophic categories, which I see as crucial to formulating a new feminist politics of race, class, and gender for the twenty-first century. First, I draw on feminist writings that reject relativist, depoliticized "diversity" concepts and insist on a multiculturalism that incorporates the history of power relations in capitalist societies into analyses of women's struggles at particular cultural and political junctures of race, nationality, class, gender, and sexuality. As Chandra Mohanty put it so aptly, we need a new "politics of location" based on the "historical, geographical, cultural, psychic, and imaginative boundaries" that give rise to political self-definition (1992, 74).

By analyzing Black working-class women's struggles with this "politics of location" in mind, we can draw out implications that extend beyond that specific "location" to larger questions about freedom and liberation. If feminists have debunked the abstract universals of Western thought, including those of the left, we are also badly in need of a new "concrete universal," in which the concrete, multilinear movements of "self-developing men and women" are continually, dialectically, deepening a broader philosophy of liberation (Dunayevskaya 1991, 180). African-American working-class women's movements in the Delta, by critiquing limitations within radical praxis and designating today's challenge as a "struggle of the mind," drew me to another feminist philosophic category—Raya Dunayevskaya's concept of "revolution-in-permanence," which I address more fully below. There is a "dual rhythm of revolution," she argues, which "demands not only the overthrow of the old, but the creation of the new" (1991, xxii–xxiv).

MEMPHIS, 1964–1968

> *We felt like we could say, 'We am a woman,' but*
> *we felt like we wanted justice. We wanted more*
> *than just the supervisor standing up over us*
> *treating you like you wasn't a human being.*
> —OTHA B. STRONG

In February, 1968, 1300 sanitation workers walked off their jobs in Memphis, Tennessee, in a strike that riveted the nation. The burgeoning protest marches drew Dr. Martin Luther King, Jr., to Memphis, culminating in his tragic assassination at the Lorraine Motel in April 1968. It took another quarter of a century for the National Civil Rights Museum to open at the Lorraine Motel and for scholars of the Civil Rights movement to begin discussing the sanitation workers' slogan, "I Am a Man," which declared their full inclusion in humanity.[3] Even so, few, other than the participants themselves, have recognized the grassroots community support movement that made possible that courageous assertion of humanity. That community movement was constituted largely of African-American women.

As I began to interview women participants—some of whom became well-known community leaders while others remained less well-known—I made two discoveries. First, the Sanitation Strike itself grew out of several years of activism in Memphis that spilled well beyond the bounds of what is usually called the Civil Rights movement and included intensifying struggles of Black working women and welfare rights activists. Second, 1968 had become a touchstone for later generations who were forced to address the questions: What happened after? What happens when a liberation movement, despite its depth, is incomplete? In this case they were addressing the aftermath of the 1960s Freedom Movement.[4]

Among my interviews of African American women activists, most remarkable to me were the stories from women who were in their twenties or thirties in the 1960s, with full-time jobs and responsibilities as mothers that kept them out of the sit-ins of the early 1960s. Indeed, many told me they did not really participate in the Civil Rights movement until the 1968 Sanitation Strike. However, they then described the impassioned confrontations they engaged in with the race, class, and gender relations of the Deep South as they sought to transform their workplaces in the mid-1960s.

Significantly, most of these fights took place after 1964, the year the Civil Rights Act was passed and the point at which so many Civil Rights histories end. Clearly, a second chapter of the movement began to unfold in Memphis after 1964, as the Black Freedom movement, as it was called, infused the nearly moribund labor movement in the city with a new energy.

The 1964 Civil Rights Act included Title VII, an Equal Employment Opportunity provision banning discrimination with regard to "race, color, religion, sex, or national origin." This legislation hardly pacified the movement that had engulfed Memphis since early 1960, when Black students across the South riveted national attention with their demands of "Freedom Now!" Instead, it inspired hundreds to flood the Equal Employment Opportunity Commission and the NAACP with complaints. At the same time, a new kind of movement among Black workers, especially women, had begun to coalesce by the mid-1960s. Among women in industries that had traditionally employed Blacks, such as laundries and small manufacturing plants, as well as those first entering workplaces from which they had previously been excluded, organizing increased early in the 1960s and surged after the Civil Rights Act. In 1965, this spirit of protest also took hold among the poorest of Memphis's African-Americans, as women welfare recipients living in public housing projects organized the city's first welfare rights movement, in coalition with similar efforts in cities around the country.

This organizing followed structural economic and demographic shifts after World War II, which had swelled the Black labor force in Memphis. Many furniture and garment manufacturers had moved South in search of nonunion, low-wage labor. At the same time, agricultural workers in the rural mid-South had migrated to Memphis, in part as a response to mechanization in the cotton fields and industrialization in Memphis. Beyond these structural changes, for Blacks, migration to the city held out an opportunity to escape the oppressiveness of social relations of race and class in rural Mississippi, Arkansas, and west Tennessee. Their rejection of Delta plantation culture did not end with migration, but inspired new forms of resistance during and after World War II. The 1960s Freedom Movement, powerful as it was, not only nationally but in Memphis itself, provided a still newer historic context, in which social aspirations transformed into liberatory visions. African-American working women not only responded to this new milieu, but helped create its very fabric.

For some women, the 1964 Civil Rights Act meant new job opportunities that had previously been closed—but even then, they had to use all their determination and ingenuity to get such jobs. Earline Whitehead (1995), for example, in the decade before the Civil Rights Act, moved from private day work to a five-and-dime store to small manufacturing plants. Working in the early 1960s at Memphis Steam Laundry, she participated in her first union drive. In 1965, she landed a job at Hunter Fan, where previously the only Black women employees out of a workforce of six hundred had cleaned the restrooms. Upon hearing that Hunter Fan wouldn't hire African-American women over thirty-two, Whitehead, then thirty-nine, suddenly became seven years younger. Ida Leachman, in her essay in this volume, tells a parallel story about her creativity in getting hired as a pocket setter at Blue Goose Uniform in 1965.

Whether women gained entry into plants previously closed to them or continued to work in jobs they had held before the Civil Rights Act, thousands plunged into their first experiences of union organizing during the 1960s. Others got jobs in plants that were already organized, but experiencing a new militancy among workers. Eddie Mae Garner (1997), for example, found herself leading impassioned wildcat strikes among Black workers at the Ivers and Pond piano manufacturing plant, which helped resuscitate the anemic Furniture Workers union. What had happened to galvanize these determined and even passionate efforts? In part, the explanation lies in how each perceived, in their workplaces, precisely the discriminatory, disrespectful, and even abusive "plantation mentality," which they associated with white bosses and landowners in the rural Delta. Nearly all were migrants from rural Mississippi, Arkansas, or west Tennessee, who had sought to leave that "plantation mentality" behind when they moved to Memphis.[5]

Sally Turner explained to me that women at Farber Brothers wanted a union because their boss shorted their pay at the end of the week. Black women worked in one area of this auto accessories manufacturing plant while the white women worked "up the hill." In explaining her passion for the union she said:

> [T]hat struggle was [that] we didn't have a water fountain. No water fountain in 1965. We had a bucket. One of them country buckets that I already done left in Mississippi. They goes out in this hardware store and buys a bucket and a dipper. A dipper! And brought it back there and had everybody dipping (Turner 1995).

This comment impressed me greatly. Like most participants in the organizing drives among African-American manufacturing and laundry workers in Memphis in the mid–1960s, Sally Turner had moved—if not raced—to Memphis from the rural Mississippi Delta when she came of age. Her memories of the Delta and the meaning they held for her clearly shaped her interpretations of experiences in the city. Historical memories thus helped structure a new political consciousness in a different historical and geographic context—or, as Mohanty puts it, a new "location" (1992). Still newer political expression emerged when hundreds of Black working-class women risked their livelihoods to participate in union organizing drives in Memphis in the mid-1960s.

Women I interviewed felt white bosses and public officials had treated them as something less than mature adult women. Hazel McGhee—who was out on strike with the laundry workers for seven months in 1967–68, returning just in time for her husband to walk out with the Sanitation Workers in February 1968—recalled that her employer, Metro Uniform, required horrendously long hours:

> They wanted to, I guess, drive you, that you hadn't worked enough. They talked to you . . . like you was their child. That was their mistake . . . You don't talk to adults like you're talking to a child. You address them in the proper way. And you ask them to do things, don't tell you—you got to do nothing. Because you don't have to (McGhee 1995).

Willie Pearl Butler, who temporarily stopped work to take care of a disabled child, became a founder of Memphis's welfare rights movement in 1965, because she had similar concerns about being driven and disrespected. Butler felt the whole welfare system "made you feel that you belong to them, that you was no longer human. They control your life" (Butler 1995). Ann Wilson Harper (1997), another important welfare rights activist, told me that one reason she became an activist was to protest the abusive attitude of a white woman social worker who opened her front door with a handkerchief and rudely pointed to each of her children demanding, "Who is his daddy?" Each woman had grown up in rural Mississippi or Tennessee and moved to Memphis hoping for different social relations than those they had known back home. Re-encountering the "plantation mentality" spurred each to fight back.

But why did their critiques of such attitudes become the basis of social activism in the 1960s? Sweatshop conditions had changed little from previous decades except that more Black women now encountered bosses and supervisors who harassed them about using the restroom, paid them low wages, shorted their pay, and kept them long hours in unventilated buildings. Indeed, these conditions continue today in the Delta, as Ida Leachman testifies in her essay. Similarly, conditions at the welfare office had changed little, except that by the mid-1960s, harassment revolved increasingly around issues of racialized single motherhood.

In the historic context of the Civil Rights movement, the differential shifted between fear and fighting from what it had been several years earlier. Alzada Clark (1996), a major figure in labor organizing among furniture workers, along with her late husband, LeRoy Clark, asserts that the Civil Rights Act and the Sanitation Strike helped break down barriers holding people back from organizing. "[T]he people had begun to feel like you just don't have to be afraid and began to understand many things that happened." Naomi Jones (1997), who helped organize the union at Hungerford Furniture in 1964, also felt the Civil Rights movement "took a lot of fear from people." She told women in her shop that "God will take care of us." Indeed, nearly every woman I interviewed recalled feeling that God would look out for them and had sanctioned their quest for equal respect and dignity. Jones explained that even their religious understandings had undergone change in the 1960s, as they increasingly identified with the liberatory theology exemplified by Dr. King and rejected familiar, conservative interpretations of the Bible.

These comments about shedding their fear and developing a liberatory perspective in the 1960s allow us to explore more deeply the change in consciousness among women who organized in the 1960s. Sally Turner commented on the lack of options she and others had felt growing up:

> I have heard people say: I'll just get up and get out of here in the nighttime. But in the meantime, it was like they was glued in and they was afraid to step out of it because they was thinking they didn't have anywhere else to turn to. Because when they leave Mr. Jones and went on

to Mr. Henry, it would be about the same way . . . And so you were just
kind of locked in (Turner 1995).

Turner's comments, especially her point about feeling "glued in" and
"afraid to step out of it" because the alternatives seemed all-too-familiar,
indicates the significance of what Sarah White today calls "a struggle of
the mind." Turner and other women constantly combatted a sense of fear
and inevitability in themselves and other workers that they identified with
the rural Delta and considered another facet of the "plantation mentality."

This concern extended to a broad terrain of gender, race, and class
relations. Sally Turner, for example, learned after her wedding, that her
husband had arranged a sharecrop deal. "I brought two suitcases in a
car," she said. "When I left [after hearing about this deal], I left with
them, walking." Not only did she insist then that her husband would need
to follow her to Memphis to maintain their marriage—which he did—but
she continues to feel pride that while he slipped away at night, she had
"left in the day" (Turner 1995). Turner encountered this same fear of demanding change during the struggle to unionize Farber Brothers during
the mid-1960s, a decade after she migrated to Memphis. Several women
feared joining the union because they might lose their jobs (Turner
1995). However, in the historic context of the 1960s, a majority voted for
the union because they believed change was possible. The Freedom
Movement offered a liberatory vision—a new social imaginary with both
sacred and secular roots—which made social transformation appear necessary, urgent, and possible.

Others also directly counterposed fear and being "glued in" to a
recognition that you have to fight to change things. As women in their
late twenties or thirties in the 1960s, each one had already taken stands as
individuals in an attempt to alter their lives, well before they got jobs in
factories and still worked as cooks, maids, or laundry workers. Although
labor historians have often bypassed African-American women's experiences as domestic workers, viewing them as personal service workers
constrained by loyalty to employers and isolation from other workers,
many women took actions that indicated long-standing anger at racial
servitude.[6] Hazel McGhee quit a day work job in the early 1960s when
her white female employer suggested she take off her shoes and scrub the
porch while spraying it with water (McGhee 1995). Willie Pearl Butler
quit her job as a maid when her male employer began demanding sexual
favors (Butler 1995).

Quitting, or getting oneself fired, it seems, should not be underesti-
mated as preludes to organizing. Many women, angered at how they

were treated by white employers, took significant personal risks even before they were able to organize with other workers. Nevertheless, in the
1960s, battling the plantation mentality took a form different from quitting or getting oneself fired. The Civil Rights movement, and the invigo-
rated labor organizing it catalyzed, provided a context in which women
could fight together, and even expect to win discernible changes.

In 1968, the sanitation workers' slogan, "I Am a Man," became a ral-
lying cry for a large proportion of the city's African-American working-
class population. The assertion of one's full humanity became the explicit
basis for a social movement that drew to its pickets, marches, and mass
meetings thousands of individuals, the majority of them women, who
had never marched before. By 1968, however, hundreds had already participated in union organizing drives, which had engaged this same oppositional consciousness about what it meant to be a human being. Many
women told me what the sanitation workers' slogan, "I Am a Man,"
meant to them. Their responses revealed the depth and multidimension-
ality of their thought in terms of race, class, and gender. Otha B. Strong[7]
was part of the 1968 hospital workers' organizing campaign, which resulted in their joining the same AFSCME Local 1733 representing the
sanitation workers. She commented on what it meant to her when "I Am
a Man" became the hospital workers' slogan a month after the Sanitation
Strike ended:

> Well, we felt like we could say, "We am a woman," but we felt like we
> wanted justice. We wanted more than just the supervisor standing up
> over us treating you like you wasn't a human being (Strong 1995).

"I Am a Man," far from excluding women, was reinterpreted by them in
relation to their own experiences. These experiences had given them concrete ideas about the new human relations they were fighting for as part
of the Freedom Movement.

Gender, as it intersected with race and class, became significant not
only in women's experience of discrimination and abuse but in their understanding of themselves. Hazel McGhee commented on what "I Am a
Man" meant to her, when her husband joined the Sanitation Strike, just
one month after her laundry workers strike had ended after seven gru-
elling months:

> If you can be a man, I can be a woman. If you're strong, I can be strong.
> Now that's the way I feel about it. . . . I said, "Oh, if I could stay out
> several months, I'm sure you can stay out." . . . I don't think I would

have liked it, after I had done been out seven months and two weeks, and he done went out and stayed a couple of days, that would make me feel like that he wasn't like the slogan, a man. But he really wanted to go and he stayed out. And I was very supportive of him (McGhee 1995).

McGhee's comments suggest to me—as did Sally Turner's when she recalled leaving Mississippi in the daytime—that she felt women could be strong in a way that paralleled men, but also in a way that inspired, supported, or even ultimately challenged men in fighting for their rights. For some women, joining the Freedom Movement or fighting for a union could also mean leaving men who tried to bar their participation.

The Sanitation Strike of 1968 manifested a new relation between Civil Rights and labor that represented a summation of several years, if not decades of individual and collective struggle, in which African-American working-class women had been crucial participants as both activists and thinkers. A new stage of labor activism, which was led by Black workers but included many whites, was energized by the Sanitation Strike. It persisted well into the 1970s, through the economic recession of 1974–75 and into the Reagan era. Black working women were crucial precisely because they pressed beyond given boundaries in the movement, seeking a fuller kind of freedom than that represented in any civil rights legislation of the 1960s and even in the most familiar discourse among movement leaders.[8]

WHAT HAPPENS AFTER? THE LEGACY OF SOJOURNER TRUTH

African-American working women's demands for dramatic changes in social relations, as they were articulated and acted upon during the 1960s, became the basis for a new moment in the dialectics of liberation in the post-civil rights era of the 1980s and 1990s. A series of conflicts erupted in Memphis and across the Mississippi Delta region, which highlighted the incompleteness of the Freedom Movement in the United States. Many participants critiqued the shortcomings of the movement by contrasting their concepts of freedom to the actual direction of the movement. "To me, the Freedom Movement was about equality," writes a woman now in her forties who joined the Civil Rights movement in Mississippi as a teenager and is now a service industry worker and labor activist in Memphis. "This was the struggle that I was in. It boils down to just being treated like an equal, being accepted for your mind, for yourself as a person, not being seen as a thing or a color." She continues, "It seems to me that the idea of freedom now is an entirely different version. The struggle has become one of materialistics, not human concerns or human rights" (Rolack 1995). Her concern that "equality" was made into a question of material gain instead of new human relations is shared by many participants.

While this worker's experience spans the decades of the Civil Rights movement and post-civil rights activism, some young Black women involved now in labor and other activism in the South have only the most general historical memories of the Freedom Movement. Many also feel cut off from struggles ongoing today outside of the South in other parts of the United States or internationally. "We lived in a closed-in little town that really wasn't knowledgeable about what was going on, like so many other areas in Mississippi that are closed," comments Sarah White. Most Delta Pride workers had no experience in unions and had only a faint recollection of the Civil Rights movement until they became labor activists in the 1980s. Nevertheless, White and many others believe it is up to her generation to continue the struggle the Sanitation Workers and Dr. Martin Luther King, Jr. undertook in 1968 (White 1996).

Raya Dunayevskaya's category of "revolution-in-permanence"—a term she draws from Marx—amplifies the historic and philosophic significance of these workers' concerns about "what happened after" the 1960s Freedom Movement. Dunayevskaya connects this category to social protest movements, which she saw challenging radical thought to alter its vision of revolutionary change. These reach from post-World War II movements within so-called "existing socialist" countries, such as Hungary, Poland, and Czechoslovakia (she considered them "state-capitalist"); to African liberation movements; to groups within radical movements in the West which pressed for more inclusive, multidimensional visions of liberation. Dunayevskaya pays especially close attention to the prescient challenges Black women posed to both nationalist and feminist movements (Dunayevskaya 1989, 213–266; 1991, 79–87).

To further probe the challenge of "revolution-in-permanence" and the question of "what happens after" revolution, Dunayevskaya examines Sojourner Truth's commentaries at the end of the Civil War, when Truth hoped to see slavery "root and branch destroyed," now that it had been legally abolished (Truth 1972, 569). When abolitionists and woman rights supporters clashed in 1867 over the Fourteenth Amendment, which assigned voting rights to Black men, but excluded women from the electorate, Truth disagreed with just about everyone. "I come from another field—the country of the slave," Truth (1972b, 569) announced at an equal rights convention—immediately distinguishing herself from white suffragists who viewed slavery as already resolved and opposed giving the vote to Black men if white women were not so empowered. Truth then critiqued the views of such great abolitionists as Frederick Douglass, who held that this was the "Negro's hour" and saw women's rights as secondary: "[I]f colored men get their rights, and not colored women theirs, you see the colored men will be masters over the women, and it will be just as bad as it was before," Truth declared (1972b, 569). "I am for keeping the thing going while things are stirring, because if we wait till it is still, it will take a great while to get it going again." Dunayevskaya seizes on Truth's term "shortminded" (Truth 1972a, 568)—articulated during an 1853 debate over women's rights—to show that her critique of Douglass and other abolitionists who believed women's rights could wait was a *philosophic* one: "[I]t was a new language—the language of thought—against those who would put any limitations to freedom" (Dunayevskaya 1991, 82).[9]

Truth's "language of thought" anticipated critiques expressed by many Black feminists in the late twentieth century who found concepts of liberation among both white feminists and Black male nationalists too constricting. It also reverberates with Marx's banner of "revolution-in-permanence" which, she argues, appropriates the Hegelian category of "negation of the negation" and transforms it into the "dual rhythm of revolution"—not just the overthrow of oppression but the creation of new human relations (Dunayevskaya 1991, xxii-xxiii). It is that "dual rhythm" she captures in the Truth story. It also creates a link of continuity and discontinuity between Black women's organizing in the 1960s in order to be treated "like a human being" and Sarah White and others' prescient critiques in the 1990s of the Freedom Movement's shortcomings and the "struggle of the mind" they must engage in today.[10]

FROM THE 1960s TO THE 1990s: CONTINUITY AND DISCONTINUITY

African-American working-class women's fighting in the Delta for new human relations both inside and outside of the plants in which they work have reconnected them to the battles of working women during the 1960s Freedom Movement. At the same time, however, their self-consciousness about needing to go beyond where the earlier movements left off marks them as a new post-Civil Rights generation facing new challenges. If women in the 1960s attempted to push beyond existing parameters of how "freedom" had been defined to ensure that their concerns about social relations and self-development would be included, then those fighting today have had to face the need for what Marx called "permanent revolution."

In part, these challenges have arisen because of the restructuring of both capital and the state since the mid-1970s. Delta Pride, for example, the multi-million dollar catfish processing corporation that built its plants atop Mississippi's old cotton fields, sought a docile, low-wage labor force in the early 1980s. The Black single mothers they hired continued to receive child support and food stamps even while working full time—in other words, the catfish industry was subsidized by the state of Mississippi. The restructuring of capital in the last two decades has involved not only globalization, but the intensification of labor within the borders of the United States. While high-tech mass industries relocated from inner cities to predominantly white working-class areas of the South and the Sun Belt, sweatshops in the garment, furniture, and service industries have multiplied in predominantly black and poor rural and urban areas. At the same time, the retrogressive politics of Reaganism, which have been extended by both the Republican right and the Clinton administration, have aligned enormous forces against workers who attempt to organize. During these same decades, Congress has helped undermine the National Labor Relations Board (see Ida Leachman's essay), reorganized the welfare state to bring it more in line with the needs of capital, and targeted health and safety protections.

Workers entering into these hell-holes of the 1980s and 1990s, such as the new catfish processing industry, have had to confront not only the material structures of both capital and the state, but the ideological ones as well. Sarah White, who began working at Delta Pride Catfish when it first opened in 1981, comments, "To some mothers, the job at Delta was putting the welfare lines behind them; to others it was a dream of finally having a decent job, a decent wage. But to the owners of Delta Pride, it was a way to make millions off of slave wages" (White 1996, 1). Her words incisively challenge current political ideology about getting women off of welfare so they can become "independent." For White, entering the catfish plants meant a new fight for independence of both body and mind against the old "plantation mentality." By the mid-1980s, these women had organized a militant labor movement characterized by tremendous passion, courage, and unity. As White writes, "The fight wasn't about wages in the beginning. It was about just being treated with respect and letting that next person know that you're a human being too. We learned that you didn't have to stand back and just take abuse. There's a route to change things" (White 1996, 2).

Why have the forces aligned against Black workers' organizing efforts been able to continue their repressive grip in a region of the United States which thirty-five years ago was the site of a militant Civil Rights movement? The answer lies not only in the restructuring of capital and the reactionary direction of labor legislation; it is embedded as well in internal contradictions in the labor and Black movements. For example, when workers at Somerville Mills organized to join the militant, Black-led Local 282-Furniture Division-IUE, of which Ida Leachman is vice president, the company tried to coerce them into voting for the International Ladies Garment Workers Union (ILGWU) instead.[11] The parent company for Somerville Mills had already learned at its other plants that the ILGWU didn't put up the kind of resistance that Local 282 did. Similarly, after workers at the Memphis franchise of Dobbs International, the airport catering company, won their year-long strike in 1994 to retain older Black women workers whom the company had tried to lay off, their local was reorganized by the Teamsters. The newly elected white male local leadership, along with the company, worked together to defuse worker militancy, replacing the old Black union representative with a new Black rep who tried to squash the militant in-plant leadership. At the same time, when striking Black Dobbs workers appealed to Civil Rights politicians in Memphis for assistance, they found many unwilling to even pay lip service to their efforts.

Many of the African-American women engaged in these struggles have become sharply critical of both union bureaucrats and Black politicians. "I've always been a fighter," writes one Dobbs worker. "But the 1980s was a cooling off period when people went to sleep because they thought they were there. This is the time when the Black politicians decided they were going for themselves" (Rolack 1995). Implicit in this critique of politicians is a concern over the many activists who believed that they had won the fight when they won integration or were hired into better jobs, and who then stopped fighting during the 1970s and the 1980s.

Other workers, such as Marandy Wilkerson, shop steward at Somerville Mills until the company ostensibly moved its sewing operations to Mexico in 1996 (see Leachman essay), worries that activists in the Freedom Movement and afterwards began to take "freedom" for granted. After the 1994 elections, which catapulted Newt Gingrich and the radical right into dominance, Wilkerson commented, "I don't think the Republicans ever stopped trying to take over. The problem is that we stopped . . . So all the time we stopped struggling and went about our business thinking things were resolved, they were waiting for an opportunity to turn things around . . . I've decided you're never a 'winner.' You're just a fighter. If you ever stop fighting, you lose." She continued, "Nothing is going to change until we get to the root of things. Dealing with things from the surface will never solve anything" (Wilkerson 1995). Wilkerson's comments locate the crisis facing Southern African-American women workers and others in the labor movement, not only in external forces like the Republican right (which has its own representatives in Somerville), but in the internal contradictions in social movements. Her concerns suggest the need to grapple with the legacy of Black working women's movements over the last three decades, especially their implications for revitalizing the labor and Black freedom movements on a more radical and inclusive basis, resistant to truncated and even oppressive solutions.

Sarah White's description of the battle today as "a struggle for the mind" challenges both scholars and activists to work out new historical retrospectives and theoretical outlooks. A new understanding of the "politics of location" and its relation to the concept of "revolution-in-permanence" can help in this endeavor. Whether it is the way Black women's multidimensional struggles in Memphis in the 1960s pointed to a fuller transformation of human relations than is generally recorded in histories of the Civil Rights movement; or whether it is the issues raised by women activists in the Deep South in the 1990s about the need to transcend shortcomings in the labor and Civil Rights movements, these questions demand serious rethinking about the relation between such struggles and broader visions of social change.

NOTES

1. In addition to the lecture and journal article cited here, Sarah White is also at work on a full-length autobiography, which details the origins and trajectory of the catfish workers' struggles in the Delta, as well as her own development as an activist and thinker.

2. The historical portion of this paper is drawn from my research for my work-in-progress, "Battling the Plantation Mentality: Consciousness, Culture and the Politics of Race, Class and Gender in Memphis, 1940-1968" (Ph.D. diss., University of Chicago, 1999).

3. On the Sanitation Strike, see Joan Turner Beifuss, *At the River I Stand: Memphis, The 1968 Strike, and Martin Luther King* (Brooklyn: Carlson Publishing, 1989); Gerald D. McKnight, *The Last Crusade: Martin Luther King, Jr., the FBI, and the Poor People's Campaign* (Boulder: Westview Press, 1998). Both are important studies, yet neither addresses the grassroots support movement made up mostly of African-American women, beyond following its male religious leadership.

4. So ubiquitous has this question become over the past three decades that it was raised at the Frontline Feminisms conference by women from a wide variety of international contexts.

5. Compare this to Georgiana Williams' piece in this collection.

6. In contrast to labor historians' bypassing of domestic workers, see Tera Hunter's excellent book, which concentrates largely on organizing by southern domestic workers: *To Joy My Freedom: Southern Black Women's Lives and Labors after the Civil War* (Cambridge: Harvard University Press, 1997).

7. Although Strong has remarried and officially taken a new family name since the 1960s, she continues to hold on to this name: Otha B. Strong!

8. Deborah Brown Carter also emphasizes that the Civil Rights movement galvanized a new stage of labor militancy among Black workers and that Black women had emerged at the forefront of such struggles at least by the 1970s. See "The Impact of the Civil Rights Movement on the Unionization of African-American Women: Local 282-Furniture Division-IUE, 1960-1988." In *Black Women in America*, edited by Kim Marie Vaz (Thousand Oaks, Calif.: Sage, 1995).

9. Truth's distinctive position regarding Negro and woman suffrage during debates over the Fourteenth and Fifteenth Amendments is analyzed in several new biographies, with Stetson and David's (1994, 163–200) explication of Truth's originality as a Black feminist coming closest to Dunayevskaya's view. Painter (1996) also asserts that "Truth stood for both Blacks and women without stating priorities" (229), but her emphasis is on debunking the image white suffragists such as Elizabeth Cady Stanton and Susan B. Anthony created, which aligned Truth with their views and counterposed her to other Black Abolitionists. Mabee and Newhouse (1993) downplay Truth's position by asserting that "Claims about Truth's role as a feminist have often been exaggerated" (182). None of these commentators discussed the philosophic significance of Truth's critiquing the limiting of the meaning of freedom after the Civil War had ended. Gloria Joseph (1990) emphasizes this point when she embraces Dunayevskaya's insistence that Truth represents "both 'revolutionary force' and 'revolutionary reason' " (38), reasserting her point that feminists need to learn " 'the language of thought, Black thought.' " Most recently, Sharpley-Whiting (1998), also drawing

from Dunayevskaya, has compared Truth's critique of "shortmindedness" to Frantz Fanon's philosophic insight into the "pitfalls of national consciousness," since "both recognized that liberatory processes had to be total and in permanence" (1998, 99).

10. Marx used the term "permanent revolution" in his famous 1843 essay, "On the Jewish Question" (Marx 1978a, 36), and his 1850 Address to the Communist League following the 1848 Revolutions in Europe (Marx, 1978b, 510–511). To Dunayevskaya, the term represents his unique understanding of the "dialectics of revolution," in which, even after revolution has been won, private property abolished, and communism established, there is still a need for what in 1844 he called "positive Humanism, beginning from itself" (Dunayevskaya 1996, 10).

11. The ILGWU has since merged with the Amalgamated Clothing and Textile Workers Union (ACTWU) to form UNITE. For more on the Somerville Mills struggle, see Leachman's essay in this volume.

REFERENCES

Beifuss, Joan Turner. 1989. *At the River I Stand: Memphis, The 1968 Strike, and Martin Luther King.* Brooklyn: Carlson Publishing.

Brown, Millicent Ellison. 1997. *Civil Rights Activism in Charleston, South Carolina, 1940–1970.* Ph.D. diss., Florida State University.

Butler, Willie Pearl. 1995. Interview with author, 19 August, Memphis. Tape recording. Behind the Veil Collection, Special Collections, Duke University, Durham, North Carolina.

Carter, Deborah Brown. 1995. "The Impact of the Civil Rights Movement on the Unionization of African-American Women: Local 282-Furniture Division-IUE, 1960-1988." In *Black Women in America*, edited by Kim Marie Vaz. Thousand Oaks, Calif.: Sage Publications. 96–109.

Clark, Alzada. 1996. Interview with author, 20 August, Memphis. Tape recording. In possession of author.

Dunayevskaya, Raya. 1989. *Philosophy and Revolution: From Hegel to Sartre, and from Marx to Mao.* New York: Columbia University Press. Third edition.

———. 1991. *Rosa Luxemburg, Women's Liberation and Marx's Philosophy of Revolution.* Urbana: University of Illinois Press. Second edition.

———. 1996. *Women's Liberation and the Dialectics of Revolution: Reaching for the Future.* Detroit: Wayne State University Press. Second edition.

Flug, Michael. 1990. "Organized Labor and the Civil Rights Movement of the 1960s: The Case of the Maryland Freedom Union," *Labor History* 31 (Summer): 322–346.

Garner, Eddie Mae. 1997. Interview by author, 22 July, Memphis. Tape recording. In possession of author.

Green, Laurie Beth. 1999. *Battling the Plantation Mentality: Consciousness, Culture and the Politics of Race, Class and Gender in Memphis, 1940–1968.* Ph.D. diss., University of Chicago.

Greene, Christina R. 1996. *"Our Separate Ways": Women and the Black Freedom Movement in Durham, North Carolina, 1940s–1970s.* Ph.D. diss., Duke University.

Harper, Ann Wilson. 1997. Interview by author, 22 July, Memphis. Tape recording. In possession of author.

Hunter, Tera. 1997. *To Joy My Freedom: Southern Black Women's Lives and Labors after the Civil War.* Cambridge: Harvard University Press.

Jones, Naomi. 1997. Interview by author, 18 July, Memphis. Tape recording. In possession of author.

Joseph, Gloria I. 1990. "Sojourner Truth: An Archetypal Black Feminist." In *Wild Women in the Whirlwind: Afro-American Culture and the Contemporary Literary Renaissance*, edited by Joanne M. Braxton and Andrè Nicola McLaughlin. New Brunswick: Rutgers University Press. 35–47.

Mabee, Carleton, with Susan Mabee Newhouse. 1993. *Sojourner Truth: Slave, Prophet, Legend.* New York: New York University Press.

Marx, Karl. 1978a. "On the Jewish Question." In *The Marx-Engels Reader*, edited by Robert C. Tucker. 2d ed. New York: W. W. Norton & Company. 26–52.

———. 1978b. "Address to the Central Committee of the Communist League." In *The Marx-Engels Reader*, edited by Robert C. Tucker. 2d ed. New York: W. W. Norton & Company. 510–511.

McGhee, Hazel. 1995. Interview by author, 11 August, Memphis. Tape recording. Behind the Veil Collection, Special Collections, Duke University, Durham, North Carolina.

McKnight, Gerald D. 1988. *The Last Crusade: Martin Luther King, Jr., the FBI, and the Poor People's Campaign.* Boulder: Westview Press.

Mohanty, Chandra Talpade. 1992. "Feminist Encounters: Locating the Politics of Experience." In *Destabilizing Theory: Contemporary Feminist Debates*, edited by Michelle Barrett and Anne Phillips. Palo Alto: Stanford University Press. 74–92.

Nasstrom, Kathryn L. 1993. *Women, the Civil Rights Movement, and The Politics of Historical Memory in Atlanta, 1946–1973.* Ph.D. diss., University of North Carolina at Chapel Hill.

Painter, Nell Irvin. 1996. *Sojourner Truth: A Life, A Symbol.* New York: W. W. Norton & Company.

Rolack, Annie R. 1995. Letter from Memphis to Michael Flug, Chicago, 12 February 1995. In possession of author.

Sharpley-Whiting, T. Denean. 1998. *Frantz Fanon: Conflicts and Feminisms.* Lanham, Maryland: Rowman & Littlefield Publishers.

Stetson, Erlene and Linda David. 1994. *Glorying in Tribulation: The Lifework of Sojourner Truth.* East Lansing: Michigan State University Press.

Strong, Otha B. 1995. Interview by author, 8 August, Memphis. Tape recording. Behind the Veil Collection, Special Collections, Duke University, Durham, North Carolina.

Truth, Sojourner. 1972a. Speech to Fourth National Woman's Rights Convention, New York City, 1853. In *Black Women in White America: A Documentary History*, edited by Gerda Lerner. New York: Vintage Books. 566–568.

————. 1972b. Speeches to Convention of the American Equal Rights Association, New York City, 1867. In *Black Women in White America: A Documentary History*, edited by Gerda Lerner. New York: Vintage Books. 568–572.

Turner, Sally. 1995. Interview by author, 17 August, Memphis. Tape recording. Behind the Veil Collection, Special Collections, Duke University, Durham, North Carolina.

White, Sarah. 1996. "Organizing the Mississippi Delta Catfish Industry: An Autobiographical Work-in-Progress." Unpublished paper presented at the North American Labor History Conference, Detroit, Mich., 17–19 October.

————. 1997. "Change in a Closed Little Town," *Southern Exposure*: 44–46.

Whitehead, Earline. 1995. Interview by author, 16 August, Memphis. Tape recording. Behind the Veil Collection, Special Collections, Duke University, Durham, North Carolina.

Wilkerson, Marandy. 1995. Interview by author, May, Somerville, Tennessee. Transcript in possession of author.

CHAPTER 31

A State of Work
Women, Politics, and Protest
on an Indian Tea Plantation

PIYA CHATTERJEE

Lines of Demarcation. Consider, for a moment, lines drawn on a map: a grid of connections and demarcations, separations and enclosures. The cartography they mark is a necessary and abstract illusion. The certain black lines camouflage other barbed tales and their subterranean rifts. The bureaucrats of the state, you see, are busy calligraphers: they etch a historical atlas of constraints and some possibilities. These signify the borders of visible power: Spaces of the Nation protected by perimeters of might. Bangladesh, Bhutan, Nepal—and China in the back—crouch on the edges of the entrances, the departures. India wears army greens and jogs on the borders of gardens, which offer its elysian teas. The estates are fenced in by bodies bent in work, the edged borders of wire are eclipsed by the vast span of emerald forest. These are the borderlines of flesh, they turn, they move, they sigh into the imagined freedom of the green glimpsed from the edges of a sweating eye.

FEBRUARY 1999

I have returned to these plantations in North Bengal after a long hiatus to rekindle friendships with some women workers who do most of the field-work—the plucking of leaf—in the tea plantations of North Eastern India. My absence is charted by borders of power and echoes of a nation, the United States, that is present now only in the geography of my imagination. It has been six long years since my initial foray into these strange bonsai gardens of tea, and my initial education about the regimes of feminized labor, which make possible its green and golden fruit. I now meet

twelve women regularly—they are *saheli* (friends) from those years before—and we have organized ourselves into a *mahila samity* (women's
organization) and are focusing our efforts on small-scale income-genera-
tion projects and primary education. In the future, we dream about being
registered as a legal society, buying land, and opening up a clinic.

Despite the detailed and grassroots knowledges about their struggles, and their endurance in these landscapes of work, I remain drawn to
the palpable and strange beauty of the small forest of bushes that they
have cultivated, and from which they pluck the tea leaf. Every morning
before heading into the plantation village, I take a long walk alone into
the plantation, leaving behind the noise of the town. In the distance, I
hear the rat-a-tat-tat of an Indian army division in-training. Eden, I think,
requires its weapons. But despite the distant gunfire, I enjoy this green
walk and mention it to Bhagirathi Mahato, a friend in the *mahila samity*.

"But, *didi*, (elder sister)," she smiles, "why would you want to walk
in the *bagan* (garden) and alone?" She is surprised both by my solitude
and by my enjoyment of that particular landscape.

"Because it is beautiful," I say. "I like hearing the birds and being
among the trees."

She looks at me aghast. I interpret her response though we don't exchange a word. I see her imagining my walk of leisure into the vast reaches
of a quiet plantation as an incomprehensible thing. My site of philosophical pleasure is her place of bodily toil.

She ruffles my hair with affection and exasperation. "Ah, *didi*, you
are crazy," she says.

FAMILY STATES

The tea plantations of North Bengal constitute the economic vertebrae of
a vast region of North Eastern India. Tea planting and its enclave economy undergirds the agri-industrial fortunes of postcolonial Assam and
West Bengal. The seeds of imperial and neocolonial capital were sown in
the nineteenth century by British entrepreneurs and their administrative
counterparts, the bureaucrats of the raj.[1] The colonial planter raj encom-
passed a theatre of political alliance, collusion, and contest, and its script
writes these narratives into a compelling present. Predicated on a coercive labor regime, which was fortified by punitive legislation and the
military force of a colonial state, British Indian tea plantations and their
companies turned quick and heady profits. Isolated from the center of
mercantile commerce—Calcutta—labor administration was left in the

hands of individual planters who, if necessary, called upon local magistrates to translate into wider action their terms of jurisprudence.[2] As a result of this isolation, lines of direct political control from the capital were stretched thin and the planter ruled his domain like an absolute feudal lord. Plantations were, thus, fiefdoms that were internally governed but also protected by the not inconsiderable might of the colonial state.

While the external juridical powers of state apparatus contained labor resistance and "unrest," it was the internal economy of control that created the terms of a governance that was individual, idiosyncratic, and plantation-specific. In a significant way, each plantation was its own *desh* (country) and the planter's rule charted the terms of an internal "state" through governance, which grafted together both English and Indian notions of landed power. Thus, a complex narrative of a state-in-a-State, so to speak, created the feudal and colonial links within the intricate chain of command through which the *burra sahib* (senior planter) disciplined his labor force.

When a postcolonial planter asserts that a manager is not just a manager, but a *mai-baap* (mother-father) to his "family" of workers, he invokes the pre-colonial justifications and ideologies of rule; of a fealty to be grafted with colonial, indeed British, ideas of landed power. Yet, embedded within this benevolent version of command is an understanding that he is also a *raja*, a king. "You have to understand that we are kings in plantation country," I am told by a scion of an Indian planting family in Calcutta, "this was the way it was. We are their *mai-baap*, we even enter their fights and disputes. This is a total way of life. When you go to the plantations you will understand."[3]

The postcolonial plantation "family" is a dominant organizing metaphor of resounding historical power. Plantation work, which, in the field of plucking, remains arduous and coercive, is masked through this overarching metaphor of kinship, drawn through the colonial period and grafted by the symbol and style of Indian *zamindari* (landowning) rule and the British raj. Labor is, within this dominant ideological arc, a service of kinship and fealty to a self-fashioned Lord. When that labor is, to a large extent, conducted by women, then the terms of governance—and the creation of both coercion and consent in its disciplines—is eminently patriarchal. Women create, then, the backbone of this "family" through the labor of their bodies: they are the ideal subjects in the realm of a planter-father.

Following these colonial themes, the postcolonial *burra sahib* sits astride a social pyramid whose terms of power are decidedly masculine.

By the end of the nineteenth century, his English counterpart commanded a work force that was increasingly feminized. Because local villagers were reluctant to work within the harsh regimes of wage-labor, future workers were brought in from what was deemed "labor catchement" zones in the Chotanagpur Plateau, in present day Bihar, Madhya Pradesh, and Orissa. Most of the recruits came from communities deemed as "tribal," within colonial administrative parlance but who now are defined as *adivasi* (lower-caste).[4] A systematized labor recruitment scheme tried to ensure a steady supply of labor though these efforts were often thwarted by "desertions." Because many runaways were men, labor immigration now focused on persuading "family" batches to migrate into North Eastern India.[5] As a result, women began to constitute a large portion of the labor force and were put to tasks viewed as kindred to their customary village labor: weeding, hoeing, planting—and most importantly—the plucking of tea leaf. Around their apparent proclivity to good plucking—characterized as "nimble"—emerged a fetishism of labor practice that remains powerful to this day. Women's fingers and essentialized ascriptions of delicacy, speed, and craft came to inform the circulation of tea in the domestic and international marketplace. Indeed, it is a feminization and fetishization of labor practice that is indelibly connected to the fetishism of tea as product and commodity.[6] Because of the colonial strategy to "stabilize" recalcitrant male workers, women's willingness to work within the "family" scheme, and the consequent fetishism and feminization of tea, women workers became an iconic force within the annals of tea planting and cultivation.

Yet, despite this prominence as workers, and as bodily symbol of the commodity itself, women constitute the bottom layer of the labor pyramid. Women's location in the nadir of power is a result of a complex mesh of cultural and political history, in which an idiosyncratic combination of feudal and paternal norms came to define a distinctly gendered domain of labor organization in field and factory, and influenced customary patriarchal norms within the plantation's villages and "labor lines."

The colonial planter *mai-baap*, like any feudal lord, bestowed favors and arbitrated conflicts in his emerging and hybrid villages of workers. The legitimacy of his rule in the planter raj was certainly a fragile business because the apparent mutuality of his relationships with his new "family" was woven tightly into the coercive apparatus of the larger state. He began to craft his rule from within, by brokering a mediated consent from a cadre of workers who had some earlier prominence in home villages, or were entrepreneurial enough to themselves seek new mantles of authority. This emerging elite of workers assisted in labor recruitment, surveillance, and often took on the tasks of labor overseers and supervisors in both field and factory.

Very rarely were any of these important brokers of "indirect rule" women. The "internal state" of command—of assistants, staff, overseers, watchmen, and recruiters—was, and continues to be, distinctly masculine. Though deeply cleaved by ethnic and racial politics, and internal class and status distinctions marked by class and caste divisions, this social organization of work is profoundly gendered. Women have very little mobility up the pathways of this rule and, as such, daily governance and disciplining of work is strikingly paternal.

Postcolonial transitions in the relationship between the external and regional state and the plantation fief have been considerable. The most obvious and dramatic change has included the formal departure of the colonial administration and the staggered dismantling of British company ownership. Labor unions, not permitted before independence, were legalized. However, postcolonial labor organizing still took place within a narrow and controlled ambit. Though political parties, like the CPI (Communist Party of India) and the congress, created local trade union chapters, alliances between local police forces and the plantocracy quite successfully regulated wider challenges to its rule in the plantation belt. Sporadic movements of armed resistance in the early 1950s, for instance, were quickly and forcefully quelled. Individual plantations continued to manage their internal affairs—through labor disciplines and control—in terms strikingly consonant to the British raj.

STATES OF DISTANCE

The powerful communist and socialist rhetoric of North Bengal's regional politics has not translated into linkages that challenge the "internal states" of plantation governance. A curious stasis, and distance, marks this political landscape despite a two decade-long pro-labor regional state apparatus. The state government, distant in its Calcutta center of South Bengal, enacts a paradox in an ossified labor movement that barely traverses the distance between local cities like Siliguri, Jalpaiguri, and *bagan* politics. The imagined frontier and its hinterlands are created by these cartographies of distance and power: south to north, paddy fields to jungles, "civilized" to "wild."

What could account for these lines of political demarcation and distance? One is the protection of an agri-industrial capital base that fills the coffers of a depleted foreign exchange exchequer. The Indian tea industry is one of the largest foreign exchange earners for the Indian economy. A communist state government, in this instance, meshes its own economic survival with the compulsions of a national domestic economy itself held within the boundaries of a global order in which tea—euphemistically known as green gold—is a most necessary asset. But equally important, and within the specificity of West Bengal's political history, is a cultural politics within which an ethnicized distance in leadership and cultural contact marks a definite line of separation between, not only workers and planters, but workers and their regional union leaders.

Most plantation communities are lower-caste and so-called "tribal" communities, immigrants brought in from the Chotanagpur Plateau. Regional party bosses are primarily Bengali, and policymaking for wide union action occurs in local towns and cities, far from specific plantation issues and demands. Conventions and conferences are held through the year, but rarely do these Bengali leaders come into their specific plantation constituencies. Some of the *netas* (leaders) who invited me to several party conventions offered stark commentaries about this lack of consistent contact: "Look, *memsahib*,"[7] said one leader, "we are *adivasis*, we are not *babus* (Bengali staff, though common and sometimes derogatory apellation for Bengali men), so why should they take notice? They come during elections and clap their hands when we dance and then we don't see them again." While the relationship between Bengali political bosses, activists, and plantation workers is a complex and multilayered story within the postcolonial period, the cultural separation—and continuous commentary from women and men in the plantations about this social distancing—is a significant mediation of the kind of formal political organizing that has emerged within the plantation belt.

Finally, there is the palpable and well-defined absence of women workers from the spaces, and places, of political leadership. Cultural distance in contemporary labor history is mapped not only by the entrenched politics of caste and ethnicity: its last lines of control and exclusion are gendered.

The summer heat is yet to blaze, and the time of peak harvest—when work will limit their time and energy to sit or wander with me—is some months away. As a result, some of the women who have befriended me have time to introduce me to friends in other villages. Bhagirathi has told me of a Nepali woman in Chamurchi, Bhutan who is considered an incarnation of the Goddess Durga. She holds her rituals of propitiation and healing every week and one morning, Munnu Kujoor, Anjali Mirdha, and I go to her house and modest temple.

There, sitting within a circle of women from the town who have come to receive the Goddess's blessings, I notice a woman who gestures that she would like to speak with me after the rituals are over. As we walk out with her, Munnu and Anjali fall back. She is Bengali, as I am, and asks me to come to her house for a cup of tea. She lives in the town and is a leader of the *mahila samity* (women's society) affiliated with the CPI-M (Communist Party of India-Marxist). I am enthusiastic, because I assume that she is involved with plantation women. I tell her a little about my research intentions, and she breaks into my now well-rehearsed introduction. "Tell me one thing," she says, "are most of the women workers *adivasi?*" I manage to mumble a suitable response and make my escape, aghast at the question.

This is someone who lives in the middle of tea country: was her question a sarcastic one? We don't meet for tea.

Munnu and Anjali catch up with me as we take the path back to the plantation and ask me what happened. When I tell them about what she had asked, they shrug and laugh: "Why are you surprised?" they exclaim, "We are nothing to them. Everyone talks big about our *unnati* (upliftment), but we know what they really think. Will you meet her? Why don't you go?"

PATRIARCHAL STATES

With the acceleration of communist organizing in the late 1960s, particularly in North Bengal, and the ascendence of the Communist Party of India (Marxist) (CPI-M) into the seat of Calcutta government, local union politics became more visible in the plantation belt. *Netas* (union leaders), culling their power base from within the plantation "labor lines," began to broker and challenge the management more openly. As a result, plantation "law and order" took on an explicitly double-runged structure. Ironically, many *netas* were men who emerged from the very lineages of brokers—created by the planters—to become the middle-men of "indirect rule." Over one hundred years, mantles of authority were inherited by generations of men who had established their power within the now-settled villages. Though it is important to emphasize that not all leaders can claim these lineages, it is striking that many *netas* in the plantation where I worked traced their lineages directly to prominent overseers created (as such) by British planters. Because of this historically mediated connection to the *sahibs* (planters), the local *neta* is an ambivalent figure: he can collude with or challenge the management, he can be Janus-faced.

While in no sense as equally powerful as the *sahibs*, the new "big man" of the plantation village is different from his *sirdar* ancestor in one crucial way. He can, through the state's political machinery, challenge the planter's sense of absolute control. As such, the planter's strategy involves a careful balancing act through which he placates leaders and simultaneously asserts his supremacy over them. In some cases, the balance is thrown away by *kachar* (tough) union leaders who will not compromise on certain demands. Such leaders, who braved police guns or shouted down a *sahib*, are remembered as legendary figures by wider plantation communities.

In the tea fields of the old plantation, which was my home for a while, some of these men are remembered in the landscape of the field itself, in the tea blocks (*chopols*) within which women work. The *bhagat* (faith-healer) takes me for an initial tour of the field and points out a large *kathal* (jackfruit) tree that sits in the center of a *chopol*. "That, *memsahib*," he tells me, "is for Ram Dhan. We call it the Ram Dhan *chopol*. He was a good man, *khachar* (tough), and was not scared to talk back to the *sahibs*. We conduct a *gaon puja* (village ritual) every year. I collect money and conduct it with the village close to it, where he came from."

On the plantation's official map, this square piece of land is merely a number. But a history of a kind that spills beyond the cartographies of managed space has re-inscribed it into another kind of memory and its rituals of remembrance.

At Sarah's Hope, the plantation I am most familiar with, widespread challenges are a thing of the past and ordinary workers remain considerably dependent on union leaders for new jobs, *bigha* (casual) labor, dispute arbitration, and the like. In the tasks they perform, they create a powerful level of sub-patronage, no more explicitly stated than in the following words of one leader: "I am like the manager here. People will come to me first and I will do *phesla* (adjudication). Like if someone is having problem getting a labor quarter, or casual work. The *sahib* has given me *jimma* (responsibility). Only if it is a really difficult case will I take it to the *sahib's* office. Everyone comes through me and in that way I run the *bagan*."

Perhaps this leader's words stretch excessively the boundaries of the *sahib's* power. However, it is a self-representation that offers a vivid commentary about sub-patronage and one particular leader's vision of power and agency.

Postcolonial "indirect rule" in the plantation is a definite paternal business: a trickle-down patriarchal diffusion, if you will. The planter's *hukum* (order), deployed by various overseers, creates the twin arches of men's power over women workers. Women's participation in plantation politics is constrained by the terms of feudal power inhered in customary norms of men's dominance in the villages, and simultaneously hooked into the compulsions of labor disciplines and *mai-baap* rule.

Not surprisingly, women's participation in union *mahila samities* is minimal. "*Didi*," notes Sabina, "we work as we do. You have seen it. Everything we do. Some of the union work is good, but I don't have the strength. If I have to go to someone's house late at night for some meeting, who will care for my children? And my husband will object. It is too much, and then how people will talk this-or-that, so that is why I don't go. I will support them. I will pay the dues, but I cannot do more."

A few women, usually married or allied to important *netas*, comprise the *mahila samity* of one union. Indeed, women's participation is viewed as problematic by men and women in the wider plantation communities, not only because of time spent away from household responsibilities, but because women's involvement with strange men in public spaces, sometimes at night, is seen as sexually suspect. This is a domain of activity which, unlike the necessary public labor of women, is explicitly sexualized. It is inscribed by customary *pan-jat* (community/caste) understandings of appropriate and "moral" behavior: a woman, even if married, might be labeled a *randi* (prostitute) and most women will not risk this ultimate loss of public *izzat* (honor).

This dominant perspective of many plantation women about what they call *pa(r)tty pa(r)tty kam* (party party work) has resulted in their exclusion from important policy decisions, not only at the local level, but within the wider politics of surrounding townships and state-level union meetings. The explanations and interpretations they offer through these brief commentaries suggest both the explicit and subtle power of a gendered ideology within which "private" norms of sexual propriety—and the constraints of women's doubled labor—mitigate against their participation in this other "public" and "organized" space of plantation politics.

However, this absence in policy-making, or daily union work, does not translate into women's inaction when union-organized political actions do occur. Within the most common form of direct action— the *gherao* (surrounding the manager)—women are often seen on the frontlines of encirclement. Indeed, both *sahibs* and *netas* comment on this pattern and both suggest strikingly similar, even laudatory reasons for this vanguard effect of women's participation in the *gherao*. The first is that women have more *himmat* (courage) than men, and when a *gherao* is announced, will openly participate. Secondly, union political strategy involves deploying cultural codes shared with managers. Physically touching a woman, or harming her in any way, can incur a greater wrath during the tense moments of open confrontation. A shared understanding of bodily *izzat* by men, keeps at bay (even temporarily), the potentially violent counter-strategies of political repression.

Though *netas* are themselves from a variety of different communities within the plantation's strikingly diverse and hybrid villages, they are also entrenched "big men" who arbitrate conflicts within their specific "labor lines." Many are prominent members of *jat panchayats* (community/caste village councils) and will facilitate disputes around sexual and domestic conflicts. Within the customary power structures of the village, the *neta* wears two hats. He garners authority because of his ability to broker deals with the manager, and within village politics, he is often a respected elder. *Panchayats*, village councils which are ubiquitous arenas of socio-political decision-making in rural India, are the most important sites of arbitration in the plantations. The *neta* will sit in his own community's *panchayat* and will also facilitate conflict between different caste/communities when necessary. Despite the diversity of *jats* (caste/communities) in the plantation, there is one common pattern discernible in *panchayat* operations: women, though often called to be present as witnesses in domestic and sexual conflicts, are not formally members of these village councils.

The *Cha Bagan Mahila Samity* (CBMS) (Tea Garden Women's Organization),[8] of which I am a member, is unusual because most of the women in it are from a community that is prominent as a "general caste"[9] (not as *adivasi*) in the plantation. However, they are most visible because they are powerful brokers within their own communities. Indeed, some of the women in the group have taken over the general operations of their *samaj* (society) and are outspoken leaders in matters of marriage negotiations and domestic conflict. However, when a conflict reaches wider (noncommunity) forums for adjudication, then their subordination (and their exceptional power) is transparent.

I am introduced to Sandhya, a woman whose suffering at the hands of her in-laws has been considerable, and am told the history of the conflict. She is from the community and because of this members of the MS (though not as representatives of the MS) defended her. Sandhya's husband was "mad" and unable to work, though he had a "permanent job." Though jobs are customarily inherited by children, Sandhya's brother-in-law wanted his sick brother's job and had moved the union to work for him. Due to her husband's illness, Sandhya was the only wage-earner in her family, severely mistreated by her in-laws, and socially unsupported because she was married in from another plantation and distant from her own family and kin. Because the conflict concerned a permanent job, it went immediately to the union who supported the in-laws. The women from her community, in her defense, bypassed the machinations of the *netas* and *panchayat* and went directly to the manager who decided the case in Sandhya's favor. A few evenings after this victory, Bhagirathi was called to explain to a larger *panchayat* (in which several powerful local leaders were prominent) why the women had taken such a step.

Bhagirathi, in relating the story, was both incensed and amused. "They called me in the evening, alone. I did not have time to gather the others together. But why should I be worried? I know we did the right thing. They were all sitting there, in the empty school house—in a circle. They were respectful, no one shouted or anything, but I was the only woman there. *Yeh to sharam ki bat he* (this is, after all, a matter of shame). But I tied my *sari*[10] tighter and told them that, in principle, the job was to go to Sandhya's family and that is what we fought for. That she and her children were being cheated and we would not tolerate this. They thought they could intimidate me, but they didn't. What we did was *safa* (clean) and if they have problems with it, well, it is their problem."

It is rare for women in other communities to protest like this, or to deploy such direct and confrontational strategies with the planter. The planter's power and personhood is created through distance—it is the *neta* who navigates that distance for the mass of workers. I have offered this example, however, to demonstrate how women are not merely victims of a system that contains doubled patriarchal inflections: of village politics in which they are excluded, and plantation disciplines in which they constitute the lowest tier of labor. Though their subordination is a constant and daily reality, they manage and negotiate the structures in powerful and creative ways.

A STATE OF WORK (OR: WOMEN CHALLENGE THE "NATION")

Consider the bodied movement against green space again. Imagine these movements like invisible ink writing subterranean tales of absence and corporeal presence. Consider the calligraphers of both state and revolution:

see their fingers, fair and plump, holding the pen. . . . Mark the different contours of this historical flesh. Trace your soft fingertips around the whorls of secret and silent spaces: the terrain is black and nippled flesh. The fingers are poised: leaf by leaf they turn the pages of Progress. The Nation sighs, through this soft tracing touch, the body of its own possibilities, its own round redemption.

Moniki *Mosi* (aunt) unfurls her umbrella, hitches it into her apron, and beings plucking the leaf with a deft twist of wrist. It is mid-morning, the sun is not so high, but she tells me that she likes the sturdy reminder of the umbrella against her body. The sun, she assures me, will soon be high. Bhagirathi and Anjali point to the edge of the *chopol* as a place I can sit. The *daffadar* (overseer) has given the *hukum* to begin and the twenty women, each of whom has taken a single row of bushes, begin to move through the field. The geography of their movement is linear as they move, tea bush by tea bush, from one end of the *chopol* to the other. Wiping the sweat from her forehead, Bhagirathi smiles. "*Didi* (sister)," she says, "the *daffadar* never puts another group of women opposite to us. You know why? Because a leopard could be hiding in the middle of the *chopol* and if it is trapped, it will attack us. This way, it can escape. But, I know of a few women who have still been mauled. This is how we have to work."

She is matter-of-fact. I am aghast. Later, on a stroll through the village, a one-eyed woman is pointed out to me. The Order of Women's Lines must consider the vicissitudes of the Wild, crouching in bewilderment in this strange lilliputian forest, staring with amber eyes at the threatening and approaching movement of the bushes.

I walk with Moniki Mosi's and Bhagirathi's *dol* (gang) from the field to factory for leaf weighment. The eleven o'clock siren for lunch has sounded. Bhagirathi grouses about the unions: "Look at the amount of *chandha* (dues) they take for 15 August (Indian Independence Day). The children get a sweet and we are lucky if we get a *luddu*. (A *luddu* is a large round sweet often sold in *dhabas* (tea stalls) and offered at wedding and rituals. It is also used, colloquially, to suggest that one is being "taken for a ride.") "I mean: isn't this day supposed to be about the *azad* (freedom) of the country? The *sarkar* (government) should be feeding us *garib* (poor) and instead we feed them."

In this important critique, Bhagirathi conflates the *sarkar* with the unions. I ask her if she knows where the union money goes. She shrugs: "Who knows? What can we do? *Yeh log to men aadmi he*" (these people are "main people"). Later in the evening, at her home, I learn that an open conflict with their union leader has been brewing. The *bata-bati* (exchange of words) occurred because her *dol* has been asking that the union arbitrate a case which involves a sister in their community. This sister's family has had to share residential quarters with another family and now demands new housing. The leader in question, according to the group, was not paying attention to their demands and after much inaction, had declared that the case had to go to the *sarkar*.

Infuriated, Bhagirathi comments: "I told the *neta*, *didi*, I told him—who is the *sarkar* to us? We want you to speak to the *sahib* and make him hear our *dukh* (sorrow). He has not done anything yet. Because of this, we are not putting our union *jhandha* (flag) in the *chowpatty* (crossroads in front of her home). In the past, the union *jhandha* (flag) has gone from here to the factory. This year, we will not allow this. In fact, we are thinking of doing another *jhandha* and having our own ceremony. But the *chokra* (young/unmarried) boys in the lines are telling us that we can't do this. The other union has already told us that they would do *bichar* (arbitration) and so now our *neta* has told us that he does not want to lose us."

As the story around this conflict emerges, it is clear that the grievances are multilayered. The sister with inadequate housing is now joined by another complaint: another woman's husband did not get the permanent bungalow service job that he was promised by the same *neta*. The *dol* (women's labor gang) is now refusing to pay the union bonus of ten rupees. After some negotiations with the erring *neta*, the dues are paid and the threat of secession (to another union) is negotiated away. On 15 August the Indian flag is carried from the *chowpatty* (open area/crossroads) to the factory as is the custom in this *gaon* (village) cluster.

There are several intersecting themes of community solidarity, collective organizing, and symbolic negotiations, that delineate the contours of this specific instance of women's protest. For one, Bhagirathi's *jat* (community/caste) are prominent in the plantation's factory line, and their husbands and fathers are men who have married and moved into the clan networks in the village: they are *ghar-jamais*, son-in-laws who live with their wives' families. These men, including their father-in-laws, have garnered some of the status jobs in the plantation: as *chowkidars* (watchmen), favored *barburjis* (bungalow cooks), and factory *sirdars*. Bhagirathi and her husband run a small, but successful store, which opens out onto the *chowpatty*. He, too, married into her family. The higher economic status of this *jat*, their self-construction as a *bara jat* (big community), and the place of women within a matrilocal kinship of the *jat*, as a tightly-knit and powerful group of multigenerational women, serve to make their conversations, and the threat of boycott, a serious one.

They are women who are not only fighting for other women within the *jat*, but also for men. What is at stake is not women's separate prestige—but a sense of prestige, which is linked collectively to their *samaj's* (society/community) status and *izzat*. They are also protecting their men. Yet it is precisely their collective gendered identity (as respected wives within a *bara jat*, superior community) and their reputation as tough women (who are often on the frontlines of labor action) that is at play. It is a contest that the rival union is keen to join, because they know women can be formidable allies.

However, the story of the quick denouement of the women's threats remains unclear. I am told, casually, that "it has been worked out." The young men's verbal disciplining of the women's threatened boycott of the flag procession suggests that there may have been a masculine veto, from within the clan itself, against such action. But this cannot be verified: the possibility of rupture sinks without a ripple.

It is a theatre of political action, which threatens to seize a very significant symbolic and ritual event within the plantation year: the celebration of Indian Independence Day. The *neta* faces public humiliation in front of the *sahibs* and rival leaders who will participate in flag hoistings near the workers' canteen behind the factory. The procession from the *chowpatty* (an open space) in front of Bhagirathi's store is a small but important journey that connects this vital compass of "lines" to the center of village life, the canteen field where flag hoisting will take place. A strategic takeover of that site by Bhagirathi and her *dol* (gang) is a symbolic act with repercussions well beyond a small *dol*-union skirmish. It will reach the ears of other workers in other villages, rival unions, and even the managers. If they decide to have their own ceremony, it will be tantamount to a mutiny. Though a failure in the sense of an outright challenge to union hegemony, what is important is the manner in which gender, *jat*, and status do mobilize one women's *dol* (gang) to discursive action with considerable effect.

Recall for a moment, Bhagirathi's critique and conflation of *sarkar* and union: "Look at the amount of *chandha* (dues) they take for 15 August (Indian Independence Day). The children get a sweet and we are lucky if we get a *luddu* (sweet). I mean: isn't this day supposed to be about the *azad* (freedom) of the country? The *sarkar* (government) should be feeding us *garib* (poor) and instead we feed them."

In her reflection of *azad* (national freedom), she gestures towards an understanding of the plantation as a state, its rule enabled by the union as *sarkar* (the *sahib* as *mai-baap* has exited stage left). Most significantly, in her triply conflated register of plantation/state/nation, Bhagirathi recognizes that these are politics that failed the unequal reciprocity, which set the terms of a symbolic economy of "obligation." The union-*sarkar* (union-government) has not done its duty. For a small moment, it becomes illegitimate. Not worthy of a flag, or a procession.

WALKING WITH ANJALI THROUGH THE FIELD

Another morning to join the *dol*. We walk through the *chopol*, cutting a weave through the lines of bushes. They need pruning, Anjali tells me; they are as high as our shoulders. We cut an angle across the rows of green. The walk to join the *dol* is a long one, and soon I sigh with tiredness.

Anjali laughs, "Ah, *didi*, you are too soft. If you had to walk this everyday, your body would be as hard as mine. Like wood, you would not break. What to do, we have to be that hard, in our selves. This is the *Kaliyug* (the Time of Kali, the Age of Destruction). This too will pass. Come, let us go quickly before it gets too hot."

I unfurl the umbrella. We continue to walk through the veridian swathe of this endless landscape, hands pushing away the reaching and snarled branches of the tamed trees, their wooded and brilliant illusion of order. In the distance, the women bend and move, bend and move.

NOTES

1. Amalendu Guha, "Colonisation of Assam: Second Phase 1840–1859," *Economic and Political Weekly* 25:3 (1986), 295.

2. For an excellent and thorough discussion of nineteenth-century legislation pertaining to labor control, see Ramkrishna Chattopadhyaya, "Social Perspective of Labor Legislation in India, 1859–1932. As Applied to Tea Plantations" (Calcutta, 1987).

3. Confidential and detailed interviews with Indian company owners and managers (the *sahibs* or planters) were conducted between June and August 1991 in Calcutta and North Bengal. Fieldwork continued through January 1993 and resumed in January 1999.

4. Many of the autochtonous communities from the Chotanagpur Plateau (who constitute the majority of workers in North Bengal) refer to themselves as *adivasis*, a term denoting "original inhabitant" status, though it too remains a problematic "catchall" term. The term encompasses a huge diversity of communities such as the Oraon, Munda, and the Gond. Within the plantation, "general"

caste communities will distinguish themselves sharply from *adivasis* and call themselves *sadan*. Others waging a protracted struggle for an autonomous subnational identity, refer to themselves as *Jharkhandis*, a claim of political territory and identity marking the Chotanagpur plateau, known historically as the Jharkhand. For detailed studies of the political history of these communities, and nomenclature, see K. S. Singh, *Tribal Movements in India*, Vol I (New Delhi: Manohar Publications, 1982) and Susan Devalle, *Discourses of Ethnicity: Culture and Protest in Jharkhand* (New Delhi: Sage Publications, 1992).

5. For rich comparative perspectives on a gendered policy of plantation labor recruitment, see Ann Stoler's *Capitalism and Confrontation in Sumatra's Plantation Belt, 1870–1979* (New Haven and London: Yale University Press, 1985); cf. Rhoda Reddock, "Freedom Denied: Indian Women and Indentureship in Trinidad and Tobago, 1845–1917," *Economic and Political Weekly* 20:43 (October 1985), WS-70.

6. I discuss in detail the historical lineaments of the fetishism of the commodity as inextricably connected to the feminization of labor in "Travels of Tea, Travels of Empire." In *A Time for Tea: Gender and Labor on an Indian Plantation*, (Duke University Press, forthcoming).

7. The term *memsahib* emerged through the colonial period, and used to describe the higher status of British women. In the postcolonial period, still a counterpart of a *sahib*, the *memsahib* signifies upper-caste/class woman. In the plantation, more specifically, she belongs to the higher reaches of the plantation management.

8. This women's organization—formed in August 1998—is a nonunion, nonparty, nongovernmental and non-company forum. It is organic, from within the community (I am the only noncommunity member) and is being formalized under the West Bengal Societies Act as I write. Focused on income generation projects with an aim to fund small literacy and health programs, its explicit intent is not to challenge the plantation status quo—or the power of the netas. The effects of these organized efforts, however, may be varied and unexpected. Within this specific example, however, I would like to emphasize that the case offered occurred before this *mahila samity* was created. The individuals here are not speaking as members of the *mahila samity*.

9. The relationship between the *adivasi* or "tribal" communities (often viewed as outside the caste system) and the communities who are "general caste," or who define themselves as *sadan*, is marked by complex rules of commensality, pollution, marriage practices, rituals etc. However, distinctions in social practice are difficult to ascertain, particularly in mutligenerational and close-knit communities. Indeed, social distinctions, which may be upheld in the old home countries, are now blurred, though they will appear in discursive expla-

nations of difference. Nepali workers view themselves as more "Hindu" than even the communities that define themselves as *sadan* and not *adivasi*. Yet, in moments of conflict or discussions about plantation history, a sense of class identity (we are poor; we are workers) is paramount.

10. The *sari* is worn by women across the subcontinent. Yards of cloth tied across the waist in pleats, it is a national dress that cuts across class, caste, and community.

REFERENCES

Behal, Rana P., and Prabhu Mohapatra. 1992. " 'Tea and Money versus Human Life': the Rise and Fall of the Indenture System in the Assam Tea Plantations 1840–1908." *Journal of Peasant Studies*, nos. 2-3 (1992): 142–171.

Bhadra, Mita. 1992. *Women Workers of Tea Plantations in India*. New Delhi: Heritage Publishers.

Bhowmik, Sharit. 1981. *Class Formation in the Plantation System*. New Delhi: People's Publishing House.

Breman, Jan. 1989. *Taming the Coolie Beast: Plantation Society and the Colonial Order in South East Asia*. Delhi: Oxford University Press.

Chakrabarty, S. 1988. *Working Class and the State: A Study of the Duars Plantation System*. Thesis submitted for the Ph.D. (Arts) Department of Political Science, Calcutta University.

Chatterjee, Partha. 1986. "The Colonial State and Peasant Resistance in Bengal 1920–1947." *Past and Present*, no. 110 (February 1986).

Chatterjee, Piya. 1995. " 'Secure this Excellent Class of Labor': Gender and Labor Recruitment for British Indian Tea Plantations." *Bulletin of Concerned Asian Scholars* 27:3:43–56.

———. *A Time for Tea: Gender and Labor on an Indian Tea Plantation*. Durham: Duke University Press (forthcoming).

Chattopadhyaya, Ramkrishna. 1987. *Social Perspective of Labour Legislation in India: 1859–1932. As Applied to Tea Plantations*. Ph.D. thesis, History. Calcutta University.

Craton, Michael. 1978. *Searching for the Invisible Man*. Cambridge: Harvard University Press.

Dasgupta, Ranajit. 1986. "From Peasants and Tribesmen to Plantation Workers: Colonial Capitalism, Reproduction of Labor Power and Proletarianisation in North East India, 1850–1947." *Economic and Political Weekly*, (January 1986).

Devalle, Susan. 1992. *Discourses of Ethnicity: Culture and Protest in Jharkhand*. New Delhi: Sage Publications.

Guha, Amalendu. 1986. "Colonisation of Assam: Second Phase 1840–1859." *Economic and Political Weekly*. 25:3, 295.

Jain, Shobhita. 1988. *Sexual Equality: Workers in an Asian Plantation System.* New Delhi: Sterling Publishers.

Kurian, Rachel. 1982. *Women Workers in the Sri Lankan Plantation Sector: A Historical and Contemporary Analyses.* Geneva: International Labour Office.

Morissey, Marietta. 1989. S*lave Women in the New World: Gender Stratification in the Caribbean.* Lawrence: University Press of Kansas.

Raman, Vasanthi. 1991. *Child Labour in the Tea Plantations of North Eastern India.* New Delhi: UNICEF and Ministry of Labour and Social Welfare.

Reddock, Rhoda. 1985. "Freedom Denied: Indian Women and Indentureship in Trinidad and Tobago, 1845–1917." *Economic and Political Weekly* 20:43 (October 1985), WS-70.

Sircar, Kalyan. 1986. "Labour and Management: First Twenty Years of Assam Company Ltd. (1839–1859)." *Economic and Political Weekly*, 21:22 (May 1986), M41.

Stoler, Ann. 1985. *Capitalism and Confrontation in Sumatra's Plantation Belt, 1870–1979.* New Haven and London: Yale University Press.

Xaxa, Virginius. 1985. "Tribal Migration to Plantation Estates in North Eastern India: Determinants and Consequences." *Demography India.* (Vol. XIV, No. 1, 1985), 70.

Contributors

Piya Chatterjee is a historical anthropologist of South Asia who teaches on gender and class issues. Her research interests include women in social movements, international "development," colonial history, and labor. Her book, *A Time for Tea: Gender and Labor on an Indian Plantation*, is forthcoming from Duke University Press. She is currently working with tea plantation women workers in North Bengal to set up a women's group focusing on income generating, primary education, and health issues. Because of her practical involvement with plantation communities, the relationship between academic theorizing, practice, and the issues of accountability they raise remain a consistent theme in her work.

Angela Y. Davis, professor in the History of Consciousness Department at the University of California, Santa Cruz, is known internationally for her ongoing work to combat all forms of oppression in the United States and abroad. Over the years she has been active as a student, teacher, writer, scholar, and activist/organizer. Professor Davis's long-standing commitment to prisoners' rights dates back to her involvement in the campaign to free the Soledad Brothers, which led to her own arrest and imprisonment. Today, she remains an advocate of prison abolition and has developed a powerful critique of racism in the criminal justice system. She is a member of the Advisory Board of the Prison Activist Resource Center, and currently is working on a comparative study of women's imprisonment in the United States, the Netherlands, and Cuba. She is the author of five books, including *Angela Davis: An Autobiography;*

Women, Race & Class; Women, Culture, and Politics; and *Blues Legacies and Black Feminism: Gertrud 'Ma' Rainey, Bessie Smith and Billie Holiday. The Angela Y. Davis Reader,* a collection of her writings that spans nearly three decades, is forthcoming from Blackwell Publishers.

Eli has been part of women's groups in the Balkans since the early '90s.

Benina Berger Gould, Ph.D. is an adjunct professor of Psychology at Saybrook Institute in San Francisco, a research associate at the University of California International and Area Studies, Center for Slavic and East European Studies, and in private practice in Berkeley, California. She received the Fielding Institute of Psychology Social Justice Award in 1987. From 1988–1990, she was a Carnegie Avoiding Nuclear War Fellow at the Center for Science and International Affairs at Harvard University's John F. Kennedy School of Government. She has co-edited two books, *Growing Up Scared? The Psychological Threat of Nuclear War on Children* and *The Global Family Therapist: Integrating the Personal, Professional, and Political.* She has published numerous articles and is presently working on a critical, oral history of the Berlin Wall Crisis in 1961.

Laurie Beth Green is a lecturer at the University of Chicago. Her dissertation, "Battling the Plantation Mentality: Consciousness, Culture and the Politics and Race, Class and Gender in Memphis, 1940–1968," grew out of many months of interviews with African-American activists in Civil Rights and labor organizing in Memphis, Tennessee. Laurie is a scholar and activist in feminist, race, and labor issues. Her previous research focused on African-American women in the Great Migration and the Garvey movements.

Sondra Hale, who has spent six years in the Middle East, North Africa, and the Horn, teaches Anthropology and Women's Studies at University of California, Los Angeles. She wrote *Gendered Politics in Sudan: Islamism, Socialism, and the State* and has written a number of articles on gender, Islam, Islamism and social movements. She is president of the Association of Middle Eastern Women's Studies and is a long-time activist.

Donna M. Hughes holds the Eleanor M. and Oscar M. Carlson Endowed Chair in Women's Studies and is the director of the Women's Studies program at the University of Rhode Island.

Fatima Ahmed Ibrahim has been fighting for the freedom of the people of Sudan for over forty years. She is a principal figure in the history of the Sudanese Women's Union, which was awarded the United

Nations Human Rights Prize in 1993. She is currently an active member of the governing council of the National Democratic Alliance (a coalition of banned Sudanese political parties in exile).

Vesna Kesic is the founder of the Women's Human Rights Group B.a.B.e. (Be active, Be emancipated) in Zagreb, Croatia. She has been the recipient of a grant from the Research and Writing Initiative of the Program on Global Security and Sustainability of the John D. and Catherine T. MacArthur Foundation, and she has done advanced research at the New School for Social Research.

Gwyn Kirk is a teacher, writer, and member of the Bay Area Okinawa Peace Network and the East Asian-U.S. Women's Network against U.S. Militarism. She has taught Women's Studies at several colleges and universities across the nation. She has also lived in squatted houses in London and worked as an organizer, researcher, urban planner, and community gardener. Her publications include *Women's Lives: Multicultural Perspectives* (Mayfield, 1998) (co-edited with Margo Okazawa-Rey) and *Greenham Women Everywhere* (South End Press, 1983) (co-authored with Alice Cook), as well as contributions to academic anthologies and activist publications, particularly focusing on eco-feminism and women's peace politics. She holds a Ph.D. in Political Sociology from the London School of Economics.

Ida Leachman is the vice-president of the Furniture Division of the International Union of Electrical Workers (I.U.E.) in the southern United States. She is also vice-president of her local union, Local 282. Leachman is a long-time activist in union organizing and civil rights issues.

Vinka Ljubimir now works as a psychologist and researcher in Croatia. She also works on projects to rebuild the destroyed villages near Dubrovnik and to support local refugees.

Irene Matthews teaches World Literature, Latin-American Literature, Writings by Women, Literary and Film Theory, and Postcolonial Theory at Northern Arizona University. Her major interests include Mexican and Brazilian women writers and their lives. She is also interested in translation, considering a good translation the closest thing to a true— artistic and critical—appreciation of a work of literature. She wishes more of her students could read the works she loves in the original language.

Kathryn McMahon teaches in the Women's Studies and International Studies programs at California State University, Long Beach. Her activism includes current work with the Coalition to Abolish Slavery and Trafficking. Her research includes a book in progress with the working title, *Women of the Southeast Asian Diaspora.*

Julie Mertus has worked extensively with women's human rights groups in Central and Eastern Europe, particularly in the former Yugoslavia, where she worked for two years during the war. Presently she is a professor of law at Ohio Northern University and a consultant for many NGOs on gender, human rights, and refugee issues. She was previously Counsel to Helsinki Watch, a MacArthur Foundation fellow, Fulbright fellow, and a Human Rights fellow at Harvard Law School. Ms. Mertus is the author of numerous general interest and academic articles for the *Nation*, the *New York Times*, the *Chicago Tribune*, and other presses. Her most recent publications include: *Kosovo: How Myths and Truths Started a War* (Berkeley and London: University of California Press, 1999), *The Suitcase: Refugee Voices from Bosnia and Croatia* (Berkeley and London: University of California Press, 1997) (co-editor), *Local Action/Global Change: Learning About the Human Rights of Women and Girls* (New York: UNIFEM and CWGL, 1999), "The Human Rights of Women in Central and Eastern Europe," *American University Journal of Gender and Law*, Vol. 6 (Spring 1998), 369.

Habiba Metikos is one of the preparers of the compilation, *The Suitcase*. Along with Rada Boric and with the support of Oxfam, she organized the group of refugee contributors and local women's organizations who decided how royalties from *The Suitcase* were spent. She counseled other women refugees at the Center for Women War Victims. After many complications, her family was reunited and now lives in Canada, where they are struggling to adjust to a new life.

Lepa Mladjenovic is a feminist activist in Belgrade, Serbia. She is the co-founder of Women in Black, the SOS Hotline for Women and Children Victims of Violence, and the Autonomous Women's Center Against Sexual Violence.

Zorica Mrsevic was born in Belgrade, Yugoslavia. She completed law school and obtained an MA in Law at the Law School University of Belgrade in 1986. She has worked as professor of law in the Second High School of Economy in Belgrade. Since 1979, she has been a researcher in the institute of Criminological and Sociological Research in Belgrade. Since 1992, she has taught Theory of Violence and Women's Human Rights in the Center for Women's Studies in Belgrade. In 1996–97, she was visiting professor at the University of Iowa College of Law, where she taught "Comparative Feminist Legal Theory." Since 1997, she has been a member of the executive board of the Yugoslav Lawyers Committee for Human Rights. In 1999, she was a visiting fellow in the Gender and Culture Department of the Central European University in Budapest, Hungary.

Isis Nusair, a Palestinian from Israel, is a graduate student in the Women's Studies Program at Clark University. She is currently working for Human Rights Watch.

Margo Okazawa-Rey is a professor of Social Work at San Francisco State University and a member of the Bay Area Okinawa Peace Network and the East Asia-U.S. Women's Network against U.S. Militarism. She works in university, public school, and community settings addressing issues of racism and their intersection with other forms of oppression through activist scholarship, education, and community organization. She is particularly interested in problems affecting peoples of color, especially women. Recent publications include *Women's Lives: Multicultural Perspectives* (Mayfield, 1998) (co-edited with Gwyn Kirk) and *Beyond Heroes and Holidays: Practical Guide to Anti-Racist, Multicultural Curriculum and Staff Development* (Washington, D.C.: Network of Educators on the Americas, 1998) (co-edited with Enid Lee and Deborah Menkart). She holds an Ed.D. from Harvard University Graduate School of Education.

Lucinda Joy Peach is Assistant Professor in the Department of Philosophy and Religion at American University. She teaches and publishes in areas at the intersection of law, ethics, gender, and religion, including legal philosophy, bio-ethics, feminist philosophy and jurisprudence, the role of religion in lawmaking, the effectiveness of women's rights as human rights in international law, gender ideology in law and religion, and feminist ethics in relation to war and violence. She is editor of the book *Women in Culture: An Anthology* (Blackwell, 1998).

Maryam Rajavi is the Iranian Resistance's President-elect. Born in 1953, Rajavi has a degree in metallurgical engineering. She joined the movement against the shah's dictatorship in the early 1970s. One of her sisters was executed under the shah's regime and another was murdered by the Khomeini regime while pregnant. After the shah's overthrow, Rajavi played a key role in the Mojahedin social section. She was elected joint leader of the Mojahedin organization in 1975 and became the secretary-general of the organization in 1989. From 1987 to 1993, she served as Deputy Commander-in-Chief of the National Liberation Army of Iran. In August 1993, the National Council of Resistance elected Mrs. Rajavi to the presidency for the transitional period following the mullahs' overthrow. She has subsequently resigned from her posts in the Mojahedin and the NLA.

Nancy Keefe Rhodes is a certified social worker and a chemical dependency therapist. She has spoken and written on police violence and human rights issues for the past decade. She is former editor of *Policing*

by Consent, A national newsletter on police accountability. She is a doc-
toral candidate in the social sciences, and has taught sociology in The
Maxwell School at Syracuse University.

Jennifer Rycenga writes on the intersection of politics, sexuality,
music, and religious experience. She has published articles in *Queering
the Pitch* and *Keeping the Score*, and is a regular contributor to *The Lesbian Review of Books*. She is an associate professor at San José State
University and a political activist and thinker in revolutionary causes.

Cathy Salser, a Los Angeles-based artist and founder of "A Window Between Worlds" (AWBW), has spent the last eight years working
with battered women and their children, offering art as a resource for
healing and empowerment. Cathy began this work in 1991 as a single
tour across the United States aimed at sharing art in a way that could
make a difference. Working with AWBW executive director Dolores
Sanico since 1992, Cathy has built upon the success of this initial tour.
AWBW has developed into a nonprofit organization dedicated to the use
of art as a means of ending domestic violence. During 1998 alone,
AWBW reached over 2,400 women and 2,800 children. For women and
children struggling to find the strength and vision to build violence-free
futures, art becomes a "window between the words."

Shadia el Sarraj was born in Gaza. Her family left Palestine, where
they used to live in Beir El Sabaa now known as Beir Sheva, in 1948.
Shadia, at the age of sixteen, was married. After her fourth child, Shadia
studied economics and graduated with a degree in 1986. In 1990, during
the intifada, she joined the Gaza Community Mental Health Programme
as a volunteer in the financial department, where she later became the NL
auditor and the Public Relations Officer. In 1993, she conducted a pilot
study on the psychological, economic, and social problems of women,
and wives of political prisoners and their families. Using the study's finding and with the help of the GCMPH staff, a proposal was developed and
the Women's Empowerment Project established. The project's main goal
is to improve the quality of the lives of women victims of violence, their
families, and their communities by strengthening means for local rehabilitation, education, and income-generating opportunities. Shadia is
also a board member of several national organizations.

Sorayya Shahri was born in the southwestern city of Khorramshahr
in Iran. While studying economics at Tehran University, Mrs. Shahri
began her political activities in 1979 with student associations supporting the Mojahedin. Subsequently, she was put in charge of organizing
Tehran teachers sympathizing with the Mojahedin. Following the begin-

ning of mass executions in Iran in June 1981, Shahri was in charge of logistics and supplies for Mojahedin bases. She joined the National Liberation of Iran after its birth in 1987 and served as a member of the General Command of the NLA for a number of years. Her husband was murdered by the governmental regime's terrorists in 1987. Shahri became a member of the National Council of Resistance in 1993 and is currently the chairwoman of NCR Committee on Finance and Procurement and coordinator of the offices of the Iranian Resistance's president-elect.

Jacqueline A. Siapno was born in Pangasinan, Philippines where she finished high school before immigrating to the United States. In the past ten years, she has worked closely with social movements in the Philippines, Indonesia, East Timor and, Aceh and has been called upon to speak about the contradictions in the politics of gender and nationalisms in these regions in international public fora. She held a postdoctoral fellowship at the Humanities Research Institute, University of California–Irvine, with the residential seminar on "Gender and Citizenship in Muslim Communities." She received her Ph.D. in South and Southeast Asian Studies from the University of California–Berkeley in 1997. Her passionate lifetime commitment is to the critical interconnectedness of the intellectual and the political and struggling for girls and women's access to education in Southeast Asia.

Saundra Sturdevant is a photographer and historian living in Three Rivers, California. She is a member of the Board of *Bulletin of Concerned Asian Scholars*. She and Brenda Stoltzfus co-authored *Let the Good Times Roll: Prostitution and the U.S. Military in Asia* (New York: The New Press, 1993).

Gila Svirsky was the director of Bat Shalom, an Israeli women's movement for peace. Before she became director of Bat Shalom, Svirsky was director in Israel of the New Israel Fund, a major funder of Israeli organizations that foster democracy, pluralism, and peace. She is also a board member and former chairperson of the B'Tselem human rights organization.

Shashwati Talukdar was born and raised in Dehra Dun, India. Presently she lives in New York City. She has produced several films and videos.

Marguerite R. Waller co-organized the conference "Frontline Feminisms: Women, War, and Resistance" at the University of California, Riverside, where she is professor of Women's Studies and English. She has published extensively on constructions of gender and sexuality in literature (Dante, Petrarch, Shakespeare) and visual culture (Italian cinema, virtual reality, U.S./Mexico border art), and became involved with women's groups in the former Yugoslavia while teaching women's studies and film as a Fulbright Lecturer in Hungary in 1993.

Georgiana Williams is a mother, nurse, activist, and thinker. Reacting against the framing of her son Damian, accused in the Reginald Denny beating, she co-organized the LA4+ Defense Committee. Williams helped launch the monitoring of courtrooms of Black and Latino mothers in the wake of the Los Angeles Rebellion.

Index